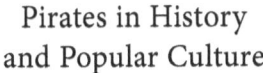

Pirates in History and Popular Culture

Edited by ANTONIO SANNA

McFarland & Company, Inc., Publishers
Jefferson, North Carolina

LIBRARY OF CONGRESS CATALOGUING-IN-PUBLICATION DATA

Names: Sanna, Antonio, 1978– editor of compilation.
Title: Pirates in history and popular culture / edited by Antonio Sanna.
Description: Jefferson, North Carolina : McFarland & Company, Inc., Publishers, 2018 | Includes bibliographical references and index.
Identifiers: LCCN 2018023796 | ISBN 9781476673776 (softcover : acid free paper) ∞
Subjects: LCSH: Pirates—History. | Pirates in popular culture.
Classification: LCC G535 .P56 2018 | DDC 809/.93352—dc23
LC record available at https://lccn.loc.gov/2018023796

BRITISH LIBRARY CATALOGUING DATA ARE AVAILABLE

ISBN (print) 978-1-4766-7377-6
ISBN (ebook) 978-1-4766-3309-1

© 2018 Antonio Sanna. All rights reserved

No part of this book may be reproduced or transmitted in any form or by any means, electronic or mechanical, including photocopying or recording, or by any information storage and retrieval system, without permission in writing from the publisher.

Front cover image © 2018/ands456/waewkid/iStock

Printed in the United States of America

McFarland & Company, Inc., Publishers
  Box 611, Jefferson, North Carolina 28640
  www.mcfarlandpub.com

To my school colleagues,
who have always encouraged and supported me,
and to my friends,
who have enjoyed and shared my jovial spirit.

Table of Contents

Introduction   1

Part I: Pirates in History

Historical and Fictional Pirates: A Review
    ANTONIO SANNA   7

Piratical Societies as the Blueprint for Social Utopia
    CLINT JONES   25

A Pirate Business Model
    CHRISTOPHER KETCHAM   37

Swashbuckling Sexuality: The Problem with Queer Pirates
    NICK MARSELLAS   50

"The Boy-Sublime": Sir Lionel Lindsay and Piracy
    JAYSON ALTHOFER *and* BRIAN MUSGROVE   61

Part II: Pirates in Literature

Sea-Wolves, Smugglers and Seascapes: Captain Cruel Coppinger and Criminality in Cornwall
    JOAN PASSEY   75

Piratical Identity, Antarctic Solitude and Stolen Treasure in *The Frozen Pirate*
    MINKE JONK   88

Pirates and Orphans in Literature: From Victorian Boys' Books to James Barrie's *Peter Pan*
    EURYDICE DA SILVA   98

Really Romantic? Pirates in Romantic Fiction
    RACHEAL HARRIS   109

"Yo-ho-ho and a bottle of rum": Representations of Drunkenness in Literary and Cinematic Narratives on Pirates
    ANTONIO SANNA   120

Part III: Pirates in Cinema and on TV

The Image of the Pirate in Adaptations of *The Adventures of Tintin*
    MICHAEL CHARLTON   133

Masculine Ideal/Cultural Treasure: Long John Silver in *Treasure Planet*
    SUE MATHESON   144

"What would the world be like without Captain Hook?": A Freudian Analysis of Our Love for (Anti-)Villains
    TIAGO A.M. SARMENTO   155

"Take what you can ...": Disney's Jack Sparrow and His Indebtedness to the Pirate Genre
    SUSANNE ZHANIAL   167

Civilization's Monsters: The Doomed Queer Anti-Imperialism of *Black Sails*
    JESSICA WALKER   178

Part IV: Pirates in Other Media

The Servant, the Sinner and the Savior: The Pirate in Early Nineteenth Century Italian Opera
    ALEXANDRA V. LEONZINI   187

The Humorous, Sarcastic Case of the Pastafarian Pirates
    JEFF PARISH   200

"Gay and brisk": Constructing a Pirate's Image for Children
    WILLIAM NEWTON   213

Being a Pirate: The Use and Purpose of a Piratical Setting in *Rum & Bones*
    NICHOLAS MOLL   225

Pirate as *Homo Ludens*: Analyzing the Humorous Outlaw at Play in *One Piece*
    ARTUR SKWERES   236

About the Contributors   247

Index   251

Introduction

Fascination with pirates, their looks and habits, as well as their nefarious actions that span the seas of the entire globe, is an established phenomenon in contemporary culture that has rarely ceased to capture public attention since the 17th century. Actual pirates have inspired the fictional works of hundreds of writers throughout the past three centuries and they have been represented in ballads, folklore, literature, film for cinema and television that generally glorify the pirates' daring and lack of scruples. Three hundred years after their most renown, ill-fated actions, pirates have thus become strongly established in the popular imagination. However, the most sordid and cruel aspects that characterize these historical figures have been dismissed in favor of a romanticized version, one that portrays the typical pirate as an antiheroic adventurer and noble outlaw. Such an interpretation is partly legitimized by the very root of the Greek term *peiran*, which means "to dare" (Alessandro Aresu, qtd. in Ambrosini and Bartolini 105). The fascination with pirates lies primarily in their disregard for societal rules and conventions, their continuous dynamism, and the constant dangers they face when measuring up against such forces as nature (especially storms and tropical forests) as much as against other human beings. Pirates are figures of cultural anarchy, of rebellion against the status quo.

Although a great many volumes have been dedicated to the history of these sea marauders, critical attention is lacking in terms of their relevance in popular culture and their presence in such media genres as literature, opera, cinema, television, merchandise, manga, and anime. Historical studies on piracy currently on the market include David Cordingly's *Under the Black Flag* (1995), Cruz Apestegui's *Pirates of the Caribbean* (2002), Angus Kostam's *Pirates: Terror on the High Seas* (2001), Nigel Cawthorne's *A History of Pirates* (2003), Peter Earle's *The Pirate Wars* (2003), Markus Rediker's *Villains of All Nations* (2004), and Colin Woodard's *The Republic of Pirates* (2007). These volumes offer a detailed analysis of the history of pirates around the world, but they do not examine subsequent representations in various media. Moreover, these studies do not offer a full roster of interdisciplinary interpretations from such fields as philosophy, gender and queer studies, and psychology. Minoritarian concerns, such as those relating to indigenous identities among pirates and same-sex attraction, have received fleeting—if any—critical attention. Homosexuality among pirates is a theme treated only by B.R. Burg in *Sodomy and the Pirate Tradition* (1995) and Hans Turley in *Rum, Sodomy and the Lush* (2001). Both volumes analyze the masculine identity and gender issues of historical pirates, but they do not apply such a study to contemporary representations of them in popular culture.

Book-length publications such as Robert Gardiner's *Cogs, Caravel and Galleons* (1992) and Angus Konstam's *The Pirate Ship 1660–1730* (2003) focus instead on the shape and use of the vessels used by historical pirates. Likewise, Robert C. Ritchie's *Captain Kidd and the War Against the Pirates* (1988), Richard Zack's *The Pirate Hunter* (2002), Diana and Michael Preston's *A Pirate of Exquisite Mind* (2004), and Dan Parry's *Blackbeard* (2006) are concerned with the history of single buccaneers and pirates. The latter studies do not provide readers with analyses of recent and contemporary representations. The only volume that dedicates part of its contents to contemporary representations of pirates is David Cordingly's *Life Among Pirates: The Romance and the Reality* (1995), although it presents only a single chapter on the representation of pirates in cinema. Furthermore, Cordingly's volume is not recent enough to include a study of contemporary cinematic productions and it excludes the representation of pirates in other media.

The essays included in this collection have been produced by scholars in diverse fields such as popular culture studies, literature, women's and gender studies, philosophy, and film and media studies. They illuminate a broad spectrum of perspectives on the figure of the pirate, examining both old and new representations as well as studying both global and local characterizations of the figure. The picture that emerges from the 20 essays constituting this collection is therefore variegated and will allow readers already familiar with the history of pirates to discover many aspects of the subject that have been previously ignored in those volumes that focus specifically on historical pirates. On the other hand, readers who are not familiar with the history of pirates will be able to access both a general outline and specific angles of interpretation, especially in those essays that examine the similarities and differences between real pirates and their fictional representations.

The following essays explore several facets of this popular character both in terms of historical and contemporary accounts. This volume is, in fact, divided into four sections that are dedicated to the representation of pirates in history, literature, cinema and television, and other media. The first section of the book focuses on the history of piracy. Contrary to the numerous volumes published in the past on the subject, the five essays constituting this section offer specific case studies that have been previously ignored (or only partially mentioned) by scholars. The methodologies adopted by the contributors differ significantly from each other, thus offering the reader a variegated and compelling picture of the real world of piracy. Three of the essays analyze the habits and customs of historical pirates by focusing on their progressivism, their democratic ideals, their business policies, and their utopian lifestyle.

The first essay, by Antonio Sanna, reconstructs the development of the figure of the pirate by tracing its origins in history and then identifying its multiple fictional incarnations in different media such as literature, cinema, and television. The essay thus works as an instructive and formative introduction to the subject covered by the book, especially for those readers who are not completely familiar with it. In the second essay, Clint Jones maintains the argument that it is the successful utopianism of golden age pirates that today permits such a mythology to overcome the moral ambiguity often associated with piratical behavior. Christopher Ketcham's essay examines how pirates were adept at goal setting, project management, risk management, and team building—skills that small and large enterprises require today. His essay therefore explores how the pirate business model may be adapted to serve contemporary business. The next essay of the section, by Nick Marsellas, explores a minority group present within the pirate community during the golden age, homosexual pirates, and considers the more violent aspect of such relationships. The last essay of part one, by Jayson Althofer and Brian Musgrove, examines the anachronistic pirate coven that was created by the Lindsay brothers in mid–20th-century Australia. This group was founded on an elitist-utopian vision of a world based on the Rabelaisian doctrine of "Do What You Will" and Nietzsche's "Beyond Good and Evil."

Part two of the book considers the literary representations of pirates. The five essays are arranged in relative chronological order, allowing readers to follow the development and evolution of the literary figure throughout the centuries. Joan Passey's essay dissects the relationship between folklore and regional/national identity, in order to explore the ways in which sea criminality derived from and played into the construction of 19th-century Cornish identity. Minke Jonk's essay then contends that the novel *The Frozen Pirate* (1887) both condemns and condones piracy, thus suggesting that piracy is acceptable under certain circumstances. Eurydice Da Silva's essay analyzes the figure of the orphan in Stevenson's *Treasure Island*, John Meade Falkner's *Moonfleet*, and J.M. Barrie's *Peter Pan*. Racheal Harris focuses on the romanticized figure of the pirate in 20th-century romance fiction, a genre often ignored by critics. Antonio Sanna's second essay, the last in the group, bridges over to the next section by highlighting the representations (namely the abuse) of rum in both literary and cinematic narratives on pirates. The essay first sums up the history of the popular beverage and then interrogates a wide variety of texts from the 18th century to the present.

Part three of the book analyzes the cinematic and televisual representations of piracy, fleshing out both popular productions and lesser-known films. Michael Charlton examines *The Adventures of Tintin*, a 1991 television adaptation of Belgian writer and artist Hergé's 1940s comic series, which has been subsequently adapted by Steven Spielberg in 2011. The essay assesses how the social and cultural moments of the two adaptations affected their particular perspectives on piracy. The second essay, by Sue Matheson, explores the many cinematic adaptations of Stevenson's *Treasure Island*, focusing on the differences in the reception and significance between Disney's 1950 and 2002 versions. Tiago A.M. Sarmento applies Sigmund Freud's reflections on the *unheimlich* and the Oedipal Complex to the development of anti-heroes and villains in the films *Hook* (1991) and *Pan* (2015). The subsequent essay, by Susanne Zhanial, compares the character of Jack Sparrow in the *Pirates of the Caribbean* saga to many of his predecessors in literature and cinema. Part three concludes with an essay by Jessica Walker that examines the queer relationships depicted in the television series *Black Sails*.

The fourth and final part focuses on the representation of pirates in other media, such as opera, religious creeds, Japanese anime, videogames, and park attractions. This group of discussions begins with Alexandra V. Leonzini's essay on the political and social conditions that shaped the portrayal of pirates and piracy in Italian opera of the early 19th century. The two subsequent essays, by Jeff Parish and William Newton, address the comical, sarcastic, and "lighter" traits of the pirate in the contemporary belief system known as "Pastafarianism," and the ludic manifestations of the character in children's culture (including toys, games, and "experiential" pirate-themed attractions). Nicholas Moll draws on theories of genre and gamification to consider the pirate figure as essential to the communication of gameplay in the board game *Rum & Bones*. The final essay of part four, by Artur Skweres, examines the themes and comedic aspects of *One Piece*, a monumental Japanese anime produced since 1997.

The variety and range of perspectives in these aforementioned essays reflect the editor's belief that a study of the full complexity of the pirate, as well as a timely reassessment of the critical importance of the figure, requires both an interdisciplinary perspective and the fusion of different intellectual approaches across genres. The essays in this volume demonstrate a collective awareness of the pirate as a fundamental archetype in contemporary culture. Therefore, welcome aboard, enjoy this journey, and keep an eye on sails on the horizon!

Works Cited

Ambrosini, Maurizio, and Camilla Bartolini. *Capitani, odissee, leviatani: La navigazione nel racconto cinematografico.* Pisa, IT: Felici, 2012.

PART I: PIRATES IN HISTORY

Historical and Fictional Pirates
A Review

ANTONIO SANNA

Summarizing the whole history of pirates could be problematic because of the extensive quantity of their illegal activities throughout the globe in the past. Similarly, introducing the reader to an analysis of all the fictional incarnations of the figure of the pirate could be equally difficult because of the enormous amount of representations of the sea marauders in popular culture and in media as different as literary narratives, films, TV programs, toys, manga and anime, theatrical and operatic plays, and table games. This essay will reconstruct the historical and fictional development of the figure of the pirate by examining the most notorious texts in which it appears and the critical works dedicated to it.

Piracy has existed since the ancient times. As soon as navigation and commerce were firmly established in the Mediterranean Sea, these outlaws preyed on Phoenician, Greek, and Roman vessels. Pirates from Cilicia (in modern-day Turkey) were vanquished by the Roman fleet and peace at sea was maintained until the fall of the Roman Empire. Piracy also flourished in the Northern seas, where Danes and Vikings practiced it throughout the Middle Ages. The Red Sea and the Persian Gulf were equally dangerous areas for the safe navigation of merchant vessels, whereas during the late sixteenth century, piracy flourished in Southwest England, South-West Wales and South-West Ireland. These were land-based pirates who depended on the goodwill of local landowners, merchants and officials (Earle 18–19). The most formidable fleet of pirate vessels, however, was the one that roamed the South China Sea; it amounted to about 40,000 men (Cordingly 5).

Testimonials relating to the actions of the pirates throughout the world have largely been extracted via colonial and naval correspondence. These documents reported the survivors' accounts trials logs, the captains' logbooks, as well as records of the archaeological excavations of the wrecked vessels. The most important period considered at length by historians is the so-called golden age of piracy, whose date is roughly between 1660 and 1730. During this period, piracy flourished along the Atlantic coasts of America and Africa as well as in the Indian Ocean, but its major activity was concentrated in the Caribbean Sea. The period was renowned for the multiple efforts on the part of the English, French, and Spanish governments to eradicate the actual threat represented by these villains. As Peter Earle has specified, "pirates were to be destroyed, not just as enemies of mankind but as enemies of capitalism and commercial expansion" (147).

A fundamental distinction is necessary regarding the nomenclature of pirates. Although piracy is generally considered to be any act of robbery and murder committed at sea, several distinctive variants have appeared since the sixteenth century. The different terms "corsair," "privateer," "buccaneer," and "pirate" have been often used interchangeably and have caused some confusion in the minds of non-experts. Nevertheless, these terms indicate different groups of sea marauders. Indeed, corsairs were the pirates of the Mediterranean Sea, the most famous being those of the Barbary coast, the Sallee rovers, the knights of Santo Stefano, and those of Malta (Cordingly 7; Partner 94). In the Mediterranean, two main "fronts" battled each other: Christians and Muslims alike assaulted enemy vessels and took prisoners to sell as slaves or use as rowers in the galleys. The corsairs' actions were therefore motivated primarily by religion (Earle 39–52) and they lasted until the seventeenth century when the combined efforts of the European nations eradicated them.

Privateers were the captains and crew of an armed vessel who were authorized by their monarch (through a document known as the "letter of marque") to attack and seize the ships of a hostile nation. French privateering was particularly active during the middle of the sixteenth century, whereas English privateers rose to prominence after the ascendancy of Elizabeth I in 1558. The latter were motivated by patriotic and religious reasons, and Elizabeth herself ignored the protests of the Spanish ambassadors, condoned the captains of privateers, and even knighted Francis Drake in 1580 (Cawthorne 31–43). Many privateers turned to piracy in the periods of peace between hostile nations, either because they were unemployed or because of the temptation to indulge in barbarous and illegal actions.

Buccaneers were initially runaway servants and slaves (especially from the French colonies) who lived and hunted on the islands of Hispaniola and Tortuga in the second half of the seventeenth century. The first buccaneers were hunters, gamblers, and sharpshooters (Cawthorne 52), whose name derived from the wood grate (*boucan* or *boucaner* in French) that they used to cure meat. Subsequently, they were joined by felons, political and religious refugees, and social outcasts until they formed a small confederation of excellent marketers who used mainly small single-mast vessels (Preston 74–77). During the second half of the seventeenth century the use of the term "buccaneer" extended to all adventurers who assaulted Spanish ships and settlements. The most notorious buccaneers were Jean-David Nau (also known as Francois l'Olonnais) who raided Nicaragua and occupied Maracaibo and Gibraltar; Laurent de Graaf, who attacked Veracruz and Cartagena (Cawthorne 62–76); and Henry Morgan, who plundered the towns of Portobello and Panama, was elected Admiral of the Brethren of the Coast, and came to command a fleet of forty ships. In 1674 King Charles II knighted Morgan, who then retired near his plantation in Jamaica until his death in 1679. Another famous adventurer and buccaneer was William Dampier, who was also a hydrographer and naturalist. Dampier meticulously recorded his experiences and published them in several best-selling books at the beginning of the eighteenth century. He was the first man to voyage around the world three times, the first Briton to visit Australia and to describe Aborigines, and also the person who gave to the English language words such as *avocado*, *barbecue* and *sub-species*. Dampier's works were discussed at the Royal Society and they inspired Daniel Defoe, Jonathan Swift, and Charles Darwin (Preston 449–53).

Pirates is a term that comprises all those outlaws practicing robbery, assault, and murder on the high seas who cannot be included in the previous categories. Apart from the privateers who were out of work during the periods of peace between hostile nations and were forced to turn to piracy to survive, pirates usually were former mariners or sailors, professional seafarers in their twenties with sea-burnt complexions and rope-roughened hands (Cordingly 21–27). Many were also mutineers and criminals. According to Nigel Cawthorne, a pirate "would wear a sweatband or kerchief tied around his forehead to keep sweat out of his eyes. Over it, he would wear a tricorn hat, if he had one. His face would be blackened with the powder from his musket or the ship's great guns. He would certainly be unwashed. If he had been at sea for any length of time, his teeth would have dropped out and he would be unlikely to possess a full set of eyes, ears, hands and feet" (120). Pirates were armed to the teeth (pun intended); they usually handled boarding axes, pikes, muskets and blunderbusses, and their belts were heavy with two pistols, knives, and a cutlass. Moreover, as Cordingly has noted, "many of the men cultivated a macho image which was expressed in hard drinking, coarse language, threatening behaviour, and casual cruelty" (113).

Many critical studies have focused on the democratic and egalitarian aspect of the pirate community, which elected (and could depose) the captains and the quartermasters with a one-man/one-vote system and held a council of war for decisions about the vessel's route. There were no class distinctions aboard a pirate vessel, where surnames where replaced with *noms de guerre*, or nicknames (Earle 110). Life was certainly easier on pirate ships than aboard a merchant or Royal Navy vessel. The piratical naval code also established the division of food and booty, the rules to be respected aboard the ship, the punishments for those who transgressed them, and the compensations to be given for loss of limbs and body parts. On this last note, the loss of the right arm meant being paid 600 pieces of eight, the Spanish silver coin "which was the nearest thing to a world currency," or six slaves; for an eye or a finger, 100 pieces of eight or a slave might be paid out accordingly (Earle 115; Cawthorne 55). The worst crimes among pirates were cowardice in the moment of battle and desertion, which were punished by death or marooning (that is, being cast ashore on a rock or deserted island). Failure to keep arms in good condition was also considered to be a grave and punishable offense (Earle 173).

Pirates preyed on both passing vessels and coastal towns and villages. The practice of attacking and plundering settlements has diminished since the sixteenth century, as the expeditions of such privateers as Francis Drake against Spanish treasure ports, galleons, and mule caravans carrying gold from Peru testify. Winters were usually spent in the Caribbean, but piratical routes during the golden age included also the Atlantic coasts of North America and Africa as well as the Persian Gulf, the Indian Ocean, and Madagascar. In order to overcome large or well-armed vessels, many pirates joined forces and formed small squadrons of vessels. The assaults on passing ships were usually quick and sometimes brutal: first of all, the pirate vessel "showed its colors," an expression indicating the hoisting of the pirate's respective flag. The popular image of the black flag with a skull and crossbones as the "official" insignia of all pirates has been refuted by many historians. As Cordingly argues, "in the great age of piracy in the early eighteenth century a variety of images appear on pirate flags, including bleeding hearts, blazing balls, hourglasses, spears, cutlasses, and whole skeletons" (139). Red flags signaling the murderous intentions of the pirate crew were used as much as black flags. Besides, some pirates, such as Bartholomew Roberts, personalized their flags. The original name of the flags used by pirates was "Old Rogers" (the nickname for the devil), which later became "Jolly Roger" (Cordingly 142). The name "Jolly Roger" seems also to be derived from the French *joli rouge* (pretty red), the red flag flown by early privateers (Cawthorne 160).

After showing their colors, the villain swiftly attempts to overcome their victims and demand immediate surrender. In the majority of cases, the besieged surrendered without a fight. Otherwise, the pirate vessel opened fire on them in a practice called "the broadside," which consisted of the simultaneous firing of all the guns on a side of the ship at an average distance of 1,000 yards. They would then board the vessel, butchering many of its crewmembers and taking the rest of them captive. Even more violent were the fights between pirates and the Royal Navy officers who pursued the outlaws. Legendary is the battle between Lieutenant Maynard and Captain Edward Teach (also known as "Blackbeard"), which occurred at Ocracoke Island in North Carolina in 1718. This skirmish led to the notorious pirate's death and his crew's ultimate surrender. During the violent hand-to-hand combat between the crews of the two ships, immortalized by Jean Leon Gerome Ferris' famous 1920 painting *The Capture of the Pirate Blackbeard, 1718*, Blackbeard fought savagely and was wounded twenty-five times before falling on the deck. According to a report of the event, "the sea was tinctur'd with blood around the vessel" (qtd. in Cawthorne 204). During the return voyage Blackbeard's head was displayed as a trophy below the bowsprit of Maynard's sloop and the prisoners were then tried and executed.

After the ransacking of the ship, pirate captains would decide whether to spare the life of the remaining crewmembers or to kill them all, usually by burning or sinking the ship. The latter case was justified with the expression "dead men tell no tales." Not many first-hand accounts have remained from victims of these assaults, a predictable scenario. Sometimes the crew of the boarded ship were tortured to confess the secret location of gold or other valuables; the plunder of the vessel also included taking food, water, part of the ship's own structure, and any miscellaneous contents of the cargo deemed worthy of appropriation.

In between expeditions, pirates "careened" their vessels, usually once every three months in remote locations, although the most famous hiding places for the pirates included Port Royal, New Providence, the entire island of Madagascar, and the coast of present-day Mexico. Careening was a necessary action dictated by the need to clean and repair the ships' bottoms, which were regularly attacked by teredo worms and were congested with barnacles and weeds, both of which slowed the vessels down considerably. The essential characteristics of pirate vessels in fact included the need to be fast, seaworthy (that is, face the storms at sea without likelihood of structural breakdown), and well armed (Konstam 4–7). In between battles, life aboard pirate ships could be either rough or pleasant. Some pirate captains such as William Kidd, Ned Lowe, and Blackbeard, were sadistic towards their own crews and maintained strict discipline aboard their vessels.[1] However, life on board was not necessarily unpleasant: pirates had several pets (including monkeys and parrots, hence their depictions with these animals in popular culture). They also entertained each other with gaming, singing, dancing, and music. Another form of entertainment was conducting fake trials, both for fun and to be a kind of rehearsal for the future trials that awaited many of them.

Unless they retired once they garnered a substantial sum of money and their captains wrote them a letter that relieved them of any further involvement with piracy, those who were captured alive were tried by local colonial governors or brought back to England to face the court of the Admiralty. They were not allowed any legal representation and only a small number were absolved of the charges; these tended to be the few who managed to convince the jury that they had been forced to join the outlaws. As was the case with public executions during the Elizabethan age, great crowds gathered to witness the procession and hanging of pirates, whose bodies were then caged and displayed at the entrance of Caribbean ports or on the Execution Dock on the northern bank of the Thames in order for passing ships to be duly warned. The corpses were sometimes coated with tar to ensure a longer and more durable display (Cordingly 263).

By the beginning of the eighteenth century, piracy had become a major problem for trade, hindering the economic development of the West Indies and the British colonies on the Atlantic coast. A major decision on the part of King George I to eradicate such illegal activities through the use of three warships in the Caribbean, the appointment of a governor to the Bahamas, and the issuance of a proclamation assuring His Majesty's Pardon to offenders led to the end of the golden age of piracy. The offer of pardons was accepted by hundreds of pirates, but it was also rejected soon afterwards by many of them, who then resumed their illegal activities. The offer of substantial rewards for the capture of pirates, the use of naval patrols in the most affected areas, and the mass hanging of the criminals (hung in tens and twenties at a time) were other effective deterrents adopted at the time. Pirates were radically exterminated, their numbers dramatically dropping from a peak of 2,000 in 1720 to 1,000 in 1723 and about 200 in 1726 (Cordingly 236). By 1726, the most notorious pirates of the age had either been killed in combat or executed, including Calico Jack, Captain Vane, Captain Finn, Bartholomew Roberts (who took over 400 ships in a two-year career) and the aforementioned Blackbeard.

Nevertheless, piracy has experienced a resurgence in popularity in more recent times. Indeed, at the beginning of the nineteenth century, many privateers turned to piracy after the Napoleonic Wars, the War of 1812, and the Latin American wars of liberation (Cawthorne 223–26). Attacks, especially on American vessels, occurred for about ten years until Congress commissioned a special West India Squadron that was equipped with steam-driven ships. These vessels helped to extinguish piracy in the Atlantic by 1835 (Earle x). In the Mediterranean, European pirates were exterminated at the end of the 1820s and Algerian piracy was terminated by the French by 1830 (Cawthorne 9). The latest manifestation of piratical activities has occurred in Southeast Asia and Somalia, where these groups still constitute a real threat to local and international shipping routes. There are several videos on YouTube detailing the actual attacks by these pirates as well as the counter-measures against them. According to the International Maritime Bureau, an increase in the number of attacks was witnessed in the first decade of the twenty-first century as well as the early 2010s in Somalia, the Gulf of Aden, Malaysia, and the Strait of Malacca. Plundering the ships' cargoes, hijacking, kidnapping, and ransom requests are still occurring nowadays. Piracy has been favored off the coast of Somalia due to the African nation's total economic collapse in 1991, the absence of rule of law, a lack of infrastructure and governance, and stunning internal violence (British Broadcasting Corporation). In Somalia, pirate networks have flourished thanks to coercion and bribery and have won support from clan elders and militia leaders. Nevertheless, poverty, political instability, and a lack of central governance are among the probable causes for piracy in Southeast Asia as well.

Pirates have inspired literary artists since the sixteenth century, although initially they were depicted only in marginal roles, as is the case in William Shakespeare's *Hamlet* (1601) and *Pericles, Prince of Tyre* (1608). In both cases, their actions save the lives of one of the protagonists. However, pirates became protagonists only after the publication of several historical accounts and pamphlets during the second half of the seventeenth century. Among these, the most successful were John Esquemelin's *The Buccaneers and Marooners of America*, published in Dutch in 1678 and immediately translated in several languages, and Captain Charles Johnson's *A General History of the Robberies & Murders of the Most Notorious Pirates* (1724). The former recounts the historical circumstances leading to the advent of the buccaneers, their habits, and the inhumane tortures of their prisoners. It also includes many descriptions of the geography of the Caribbean. Johnson's volume, in contrast, draws on contemporary London newspapers and trial records to offer an accurate and entertaining account of many past and contemporary pirates and their crimes. *A General History* initially identifies the causes for the abundance of pirates in the Caribbean: the presence of many uninhabited islands furnishing both provisions and shelter; the great commerce in those seas by French, Spaniards, Dutch, and English ships; and the facility to elude detection among those "many inlets, lagoons and harbours" (8). Johnson then provides readers with an account of the legislative and military measures taken by English monarchs against the pirates' atrocious crimes as well as the local governors' proclamations against such "Enemies of Mankind" (54), whose names and expeditions are listed in detail along with some geographical details about Central and South American countries.

The pirates examined by Johnson include Henry Avery (famous for capturing the largest ship belonging to the Great Mogul in the Arabian Sea, an expedition that inspired the play *The Successful Pirate* [1713] by the homonymous Charles Johnson), Mary Read and Anne Bonny (who were cross-dressed members of the crew of the notorious Calico Jack), but also less famous names such as Edward England, Richard Worley, and John Gow. Johnson portrays both the point of view of the Royal Navy and that of the villains. His descriptions of the trials and deaths of "those miserable wretches, who may serve as a sad example of the little effect mercy has upon men once abandoned to an evil pursuit of life" (17) are very precise. Although the book tends to romanticize the villainous figures, Johnson is unequivocal in condemning their "deprived tempers" (113), the rivalry between old pirates and newcomers (319), and their criminal actions, arguing that "like their patron, the Devil, [these inhumane wretches] must make mischief their sport, cruelty their delight, and damning of souls their constant employment" (306).

A General History has proven extremely influential over all subsequent fictional representations of pirates, and authors such as Walter Scott, Edgar Allan Poe, and Robert Louis Stevenson acknowledged their debt to this volume. Since 1932, the authorship of *A General History* has been questioned by some critics, who attributed it to Daniel Defoe, especially because the latter contributed to the representation of pirates in the novels *Robinson Crusoe* (1919) and *Captain Singleton* (1720). In the former, the eponymous character is attacked by a Turkish rover of Sallee near the Canary Islands and is taken prisoner. Crusoe becomes the miserable slave of the rover's captain for two years until he escapes while fishing at sea. In contrast, *Captain Singleton* is the story of a boy kidnapped by gypsies, sold as a slave, and then forced to work for the captain of a Portuguese ship. After an attempt at mutiny, Singleton is marooned on Madagascar with a group of mariners. They head for the African coast and decide to cross the continent towards the Atlantic Ocean. The young boy is elected captain of the desperate group and after they safely reach England, they acquire a vessel and use the Atlantic as their home base. Defoe never lingers on the subsequent barbaric actions of the pirates and, most importantly, he redeems the title character through his repentance and final abandonment of the wretched profession. The same occurs in Defoe's *The King of Pirates* (1720), a romanticized first-person account about the piratic life of Captain Avery which focuses on the pirate's capture of prizes and his many changes of ships and crew. The text does not concentrate on his sadistic actions, but rather presents them as civilized and courageous.

During the rest of the eighteenth century, the figure of the pirate was again confined to minor appearances in literature. Jonathan Swift briefly mentions pirates in his 1726 masterpiece *Gulliver's Travels* when he narrates how the protagonist's third voyage is interrupted by two pirate vessels. The Dutch captain of one vessel is unnecessarily cruel towards his prisoners, threatening them with execution without any justified reason. He finally sets Gulliver adrift. Pirates appear briefly in Ann Radcliffe's *The Mysteries of*

Udolpho (1794), but their frightening actions are minor when compared to those of the *banditti* (the Italian term for outlaws), who are recurring villains in Radcliffe's oeuvre and characteristic of the Gothic period.

The figure of the pirate reclaims its importance in the literature of the first decades of the nineteenth century, especially after the successful publication of the narrative poem *The Corsair* (1814) by Lord Byron, and of Walter Scott's *The Pirate* (1822). The former praises the life of Captain Conrad, a sea adventurer who is forced into abstinence in order to conquer his prizes. He is a fierce and chivalrous character who has chosen a wicked life after being betrayed by his fellow men. A faithful woman awaits him ashore during his expeditions, but after he is captured by the Turks, she dies from grief. Byron praises the heroism of the character and his regret for the piratical lifestyle. Scott's novel, which was actually inspired by the life of John Gow, similarly revolves around a remorseful captain who is shipwrecked on the Shetland Islands, where he falls in love with the daughter of the local landowner and decides to abandon his wretched life. Captain Cleveland is finally forced to fight against a group of his former comrades because they want him to join them again. Scott's novels offers splendid descriptions of the wild and picturesque landscape of the islands, makes abundant references to real pirates, and frequently inserts the legends based on Nordic mythology within the narrative. Simultaneously, *The Pirate* represents with precision many of the villains' practices, from the application of their code and their reunions for the general councils to the rivalry between the members of the crew.

The nineteenth century then witnessed the publication of many texts on the figure of the pirate. It is difficult to offer a fully comprehensive list, but some literary works can be pointed out. James Fenimore Cooper's *The Red Rover* (1827), for example, is set in eighteenth-century Newport and realistically conveys the habits and spirit of a colony's inhabitants and the life on board a vessel, although much of the narrative is driven by conversations between the characters and on lengthy explanations rather than on the actions of the pirates themselves. These individuals appear mainly as honorable villains whose atrocities are barely mentioned. *The Pirate* (1836) by British novelist and Royal Navy officer Frederick Marryat introduces the reader to the technical language of navigation and to a complete description of the pirates' cruelty. The story focuses on the rivalry between Captain Cain and Francisco, a boy who refuses to take part in the atrocities enacted by the reckless pirate crew he has been forced to join after the death of his mother. Marryat guides the reader inside the vessels and on the high seas, directing their gaze over the characters while leaving the reader to formulate judgments about their actions. Although the narrator expresses some admiration for the pirate vessel *Avenger*, its craftsmanship, the discipline observed on board, and some sympathy for its mild-eyed, scarred Captain Cain, the subsequent description of the massacres committed by the pirates and of their final suspenseful trial condemns the villains' malevolent actions.

Edgar Allan Poe's short story "The Gold Bug" (1853) focuses on the character of Mr. William Legrant, who lives on Sullivan's Island and finds the treasure of Captain Kidd by associating the drawing of a bug on a thin parchment with a skull (the emblem of pirates), and then decodes the complex cipher indicating the location of the buried chest. His doctor, the narrator of the story, actually doubts Legrant's sanity until the two of them come into possession of an incredible fortune. *Coral Island: A Tale of the Pacific Ocean* (1858) and *The Pirate City: An Algerine Tale* (1874) by Scottish writer Robert Michael Ballantyne are adventure novels for boys. The protagonist of the former, Ralph Rover, embarks on a mission to the South Seas and is shipwrecked on an Edenic island whose splendid flora and fauna are a continuous source of wonder for him. After many months, a pirate schooner reaches the island and the protagonist is captured by the godless villains, who scare him with their looks and their terrible language. The first-person narrator is, however, more critical of the habits and especially the cannibalism of the indigenous peoples of the Pacific Islands than of the pirates' practices. *The Pirate City* follows the adventures of a merchant and his two sons after they are kidnapped and enslaved by Algerian pirates. They stay in bondage until Algiers is attacked by a fleet of English and Dutch vessels in 1816 in an episode known as "the bombardment of Algiers." The tale, which exemplifies the ethos of nineteenth-century imperialism and the Victorian notion of manliness, is historically accurate and portrays the differences between Christians, Israelites, and Muslims while depicting the exotic setting of Algiers as a lawless city in a constant state of war.

Among the nineteenth-century tales about pirates, the most original are *Fanny Campbell, The Female Pirate Captain* (1844) by Maturin Murray Ballou and *The Frozen Pirate* (1887) by William Clarke Russell. *Fanny Campbell* narrates the life of an educated and fascinating woman who commands a mutiny in order to free her beloved from a prison in Cuba. The eponymous character cross-dresses as a man and assumes the title of Captain Channing. She is loved by her crew and portrayed as constantly prepared and on guard, cunning, kind, and reasonable. Furthermore, the narrative is set against the backdrop of the American Revolution and the protagonist thus represents a patriot fighting heroically for the independence of the colonies against British oppression. *The Frozen Pirate* recounts the story of a shipwrecked sailor on a desolated island of ice, where he finds a schooner that has been trapped in a ravine for eighty-four years. The protagonist accidentally unfreezes an unrepentant member of the piratical crew who tells him several stories of past butcheries. The book was the first text ever to consider the theory of criogenesis. The descriptions of the sailor's dead companions and of the Antarctic landscape are nuanced and at times, even disturbing.

It was Robert Lewis Stevenson's *Treasure Island* (1883) and James Matthew Barrie's story of Peter Pan (first created as part of a 1902 novel which was converted into a theatrical play in 1904) that finally established the images of the pirate now deeply rooted in the popular imagination. He is typically a vicious double-crosser and one-legged seaman with a parrot on his shoulder. He also emerges as an elegant, distinct, and severe character who is bent on revenge. As Cordingly argues, "Long John Silver ... is better known than any of the real pirates of history and, together with Captain Hook, has come to represent many people's image of a pirate" (16). *Treasure Island* also inaugurated the traditional depiction of pirates burying their treasure—a practice that in reality was infrequent, such as with Captain Kidd, who buried his treasure in order to bargain his negotiations with Governor Bellomont. In Barrie's play and in *Peter and Wendy*, the 1912 novelization of it, the pirates constitute a real threat to the children, who come to realize the difference between a make-believe land and reality after they are hunted down by Hook, a multifaceted character who is haunted by the fear of the crocodile that relentlessly pursues him and finally kills him.

William Hodgson's *The Ghost Pirates* (1909) is the second English text from the first half of the twentieth century that treats the figure of the pirate. The novel focuses on a haunted ship and exemplifies the Freudian uncanny and Tzvetan Todorov's concept of the fantastic, which comprises the structural basis of Gothic tales. Hodgson's work was followed by Italian-English novelist Rafael Sabatini's novels *The Sea Hawk* (1915), *Captain Blood* (1922), and *The Black Swan* (1932), stories about passionate and charismatic characters who have been misjudged by their communities and become corsairs and pirates. They nevertheless believe in honor, seek redemption, and save damsels in distress. Sabatini's writing style is clear, his prose engaging and rich. The stories, adapted into a series of popular films during the 1930s and 1940s (and also more recently, stage plays) are filled with sword fighting, thrilling plot-twists, and irony. They also quote from historical documents. Contemporary to Sabatini's works and equally popular were Emilio Salgari's three cycles of novels, published between 1883 and 1915, on the corsairs, the Bermuda pirates, and the passionate and exotic pirate prince Sandokan. Characteristic of Salgari's novels (whose most famous titles include *The Black Corsair* and *The Tigers of Mompracem*) are the numerous historical, geographical, and botanical digressions, a vibrant writing style, and the identification of the author with all the characters (including animals). The narratives are set in India and the Malaysian Sea, where the novels' protagonists face the dangers both of the marine environment and of the tangled jungles that are populated by wild beasts.

Other books dedicated to the figure of the pirate that merit mention are Howard Pyle's *Book of Pirates*, a collection of seven short stories published posthumously in 1921 which set historical buccaneers and pirates in scenarios involving revenge, stolen and buried treasures, and tavern fights; John Steinbeck's *Cup of Gold* (1929), a historical novel about the life of Henry Morgan; and Richard Hughes' *A High Wind in Jamaica* (1929), a concentrated narrative that portrays controversial subjects such as sexual abuse, betrayal, and violence. The story is set in the nineteenth century and follows four children that leave a plantation in Jamaica and are kidnapped by pirates. Hughes' novel is proficient in depicting the perspective of the children (who could be interpreted as either culpable or innocent) and in reconstructing the process of recollection of traumatic memories. Other notable works of the periods were Arthur Conan Doyle's *The Dealings of Captain Sharkey* (1925), a collection of maritime short stories about a pirate captain whose barbarity horrifies his own crew, and Daphne Du Maurier's *Frenchmen's Creek* (1941), a romantic novel set in late seventeenth-century Cornwall that recreates the love between a woman bored with high society and an educated, brooding, as well as charming French pirate. Du Maurier's novel reflects upon the limited role and assertiveness of women in society at the time.

In the last thirty years, the market has been saturated by numerous books for children presenting pirates as heroic adventurers, such as the Norwegian series on Captain Sabertooth (begun in the 1990s), David M. McPhile's *Edward and the Pirates* (1997), Douglas Wilson's *Blackthorne Winter* (2003), and Melinda Long's *How I Became a Pirate* (2003). Books on pirates include both popular and less successful titles, such as the romances *The Pirate Next Door* (2003) by Jennifer Ashley and *To Catch a Pirate* (2007) by Jade Parker. There are also young adult novels *Isle of Swords* (2007) and its sequel *Isle of Fire* (2008) by Wayne Thomas Batson, and Emily Skrutskie's *The Abyss Surrounds Us* (2016). The fantasy novel *Pirate Freedom* (2007) is by Gene Wolfe. Jeffrey S. William's *Pirate Spirit* (2007) offers a novelization of Anne Bonney's life. Series of books on pirates include Gideon Defoe's *The Pirates!* (2004–12), L.A. Meyer's *Bloody Jack* (2002–14), Justin Somper's six *Vampirates* novels (2005–11), Tanith Lee's *The Piratica Series* (2004–07), and Tim Severin's *The Adventures of Hector Lynch* (2007–09).

Prominent among the novels on pirates published during the last few decades are Tim Power's *On Stranger Tides* (1987) and *Pirate Latitudes* (2009) by Michael Crichton, the best-selling author of *Sphere* (1987) and *Jurassic Park* (1990). The compelling narrative of *On Stranger Tides* makes abundant use of supernatural thematics (including voodoo, magic, resuscitation spells, and zombie crews) while narrating the search for the Fountain of Youth. Power mingles historical characters such as Blackbeard with the fictional events depicting the seawolves as ruthlessly addicted to violence and obscene language. The novel's vivid depiction of piratical life is accompanied by a particular attention to sensory details (the metallic smell of magic, for example) and to historical events (including the death of Blackbeard). Crichton's *Pirate Latitudes* is the story of an educated privateer who is charged with assembling and commanding a multiethnic crew to assault a Spanish treasure ship at bay in a fortified Caribbean cove. Crichton's volume relays a realistic portrayal of seventeenth-century Port Royal as a nest of cutthroats and diseases. Although the narrative is affected by its lack of revisions (it was published posthumously) and some of the characters are rather stereotypical and flat, the pirates' verbiage faithfully reproduces the language of the times. The story thus flows with a convincing momentum towards the climactic finale.

The popularization of the figure of the pirate in the twentieth century occurred mainly through depictions in cinema. Pirates have infiltrated all genres of cinema and television: they appear in science fiction (*Space Riders, Alien: Resurrection, Star Wars* and many *Star Trek* series), adventure films (*The Goonies*) and fantasy (*The Lord of the Rings, Game of Thrones*), but also comedies (*Abbott and Costello Meet Captain Kidd, The Jewel of the Nile*), superhero films (*Guardians of the Galaxy*), and even adult films (the erotic thriller *Pirates*). Furthermore, cinematic narratives that present pirate characters, such as *The Sea Hawk* (1940), *Captain Kidd* (1945), *The Buccaneer* (1958), and *Elizabeth: The Golden Age* (2007), can be categorized as historical films because of their (relative) adherence to historical fact and their reflection on contemporary events through the depiction of the past, as Jonathan Stubbs argues (79). Among these, several films that are dedicated to the figure of Blackbeard remain notable, including *Anne of the Indies* (1951), in which he is portrayed as a jovial but conscientious man; *Blackbeard The Pirate* (1952), which characterizes him as a foul but also cunning man; *Blackbeard: Terror at Sea* (2006), and the TV mini-series *Blackbeard* (2006), both of which are faithful to the historical narratives on the legendary marauder. The popularity and ubiquity of this figure may lie in his sheer uniqueness; as Captain Johnson indicates, his name came from "that large quantity of hair which, like a frightful meteor, covered his whole face and frightened America more than any comet that has appeared there a long time" (60).

The first film about pirates was *The Black Pirate* (1926), a two-tone Technicolor production that presented the breed as greedy, traitorous, desperate men who brutally assault a vessel, unceremoniously rob its passengers, and then hide their booty in a submarine cave. The film introduced on the silver screen the Jolly Roger (the skull and crossbones flag) and the practice of walking the plank (a practice that has actually been documented only rarely in pirate attacks after 1822). Black and white films produced in the two subsequent decades include *Captain Blood* (1935), the story of a physician unjustly condemned to be sold into slavery in Port Royal who redeems his position; *The Buccaneer* (1938), which is based on the life of French privateer and pirate Jean Lafoitte and represents the events of the 1812 battle of New Orleans; *The Sea Hawk* (1940), set in the sixteenth century and focusing on the rivalry between Elizabethan England and the Spain of Philip II; and *The Black Swan* (1942), a production characterized by the use of sumptuous costumes which captures the romance between a reformed pirate and a governor's daughter, as well as the subsequent appointment of Henry Morgan as Jamaica's governor.

On the one hand, these films set the precedents for future productions on pirates: exotic settings with grey cliffs, palms, an impenetrable jungle, and crystalline baby-blue seas are their typical settings along with maritime villages and forts armed with guns. The most recurrent thematic issues are the blossoming of romance between the male protagonist and a captured woman, and the choreographed duels between the hero and his antagonist(s) on the deck and up on the mast. The acrobatic duels express a "realism without blood" (Ambrosini and Bartolini 115) very different from the brutal reality of bloody death that transpired during assaults on a vessel. Between the 1920s and 1950s, Hollywood cinema thus established a connection between the body of the pirate and stardom through the choice of a series of actors that included Douglas Fairbanks, Tyrone Power, Errol Flynn, and Burt Lancaster (Ambrosini and Bartolini 106). As Cordingly has pointed out, "as far as Hollywood was concerned, pirates provided an opportunity for buccaneering heroes to rescue beautiful women from picturesque villains in exotic locations" (201).

On the other hand, films about pirates produced between the 1920s and the 1950s are largely inaccurate: they present a cast of white characters that certainly fails to reflect the actual presence of many non-whites aboard pirate ships. The deficiency is particularly stark in regard to black men who were freed from the slave commerce of the age. Furthermore, these films generally portray both pirates and their vessels' decks and quarters as relatively clean and orderly. This is certainly a distortion of reality intended to appeal to the audience's middle-class tastes. Pirate ships were actually damp and dark places, the crew's quarters being cramped, reeking of rotten meat (the main staple of a pirate's diet), and swarming with rats, cockroaches, and maggots. Pirate ships were therefore nests for disease, especially scurvy, malaria, yellow fever, and dysentery, and given their appetites for experimentation, a number of venereal diseases (Preston 200; Cawthorne 149–51). The first Hollywood productions sanitize the harsh life of pirates on board, men who were perpetually searching for fresh water and provision, facing perilous storms and the threat of starvation as well as suffering mentally during the long voyages between one destination and another. The three-masted vessels themselves represented in these and future films occupy large and impressive sets, but are again quite inaccurate, since historical pirates usually sailed aboard smaller vessels such as sloops, schooners, and brigantines (manned by less than twenty crew). They also used canoes and pirogues, among other small crafts (Konstam 3). After capturing a larger vessel, pirates usually stripped it of ornaments and decorations, subsequently loading it with guns. Raising over the maritime ladder by capturing larger and larger vessels was an operation that was, however, completed only by Bartlomew Roberts and Blackbeard.

In the subsequent decades, the cinematic pirate has appeared in humorous and light-hearted narratives as well. Films such as *The Crimson Pirate* (1952), *Abbott and Costello Meet Captain Kidd* (1952), *Il Corsaro Nero* (*Blackie, the Pirate*, 1971), *Yellowbeard* (1983), and two musicals (*The Pirate Movie* and *The Pirates of Penzance*, both from 1982) are indeed deliberately comical. These productions capitalize on the ludic aspects of the pirates' fights against royal officers or among pirates themselves. They exaggerate the choreographed movements with hilarious, parodic intent. Exotic locations, the search for a treasure, and revenge for past wrongs are instrumental themes in the performances. Any serious material might be juxtaposed with gags and absurd situations intended to present pirates as clownish and static characters. Similarly, those films on pirates that are set in the future use a light-hearted tone. This is the case in *The Ice Pirates* (1983), a compendium of quotations from previous science fiction films, and the animated adaptation of Stevenson's story, entitled *Treasure Planet* (2002).

From the 1970s forward, films on pirates have also focused on the gory aspects of the villains' attacks and have begun to use underwater frames for a more realistic depiction of their maritime adventures. The 1976 Italian production of *Il Corsaro Nero* (an adaptation of Emilio Salgari's story), for example, begins with a frame of the victims' corpses hung on the Spanish vessels' masts and insists on highlighting the cruelty of the Spanish actions against the indigenous population. The historical aspects of such a figure are also detailed in more recent cinematic productions; one example is Roman Polanski's *Pirates* (1986), an adventure comedy about the fights of a group of English pirates against Spanish forts and galleons for the possession of the Aztec golden throne. This light-hearted, even pleasant film establishes a marked contrast between the dissolute life of the seawolves (signified by their historically accurate, worn-out costumes) and the formality and elegance of their Spanish counterparts.

Another tendency of the films produced after the 1970s is to set the story in more recent or contemporary times, which thus offers a modern version of pirates. *Nate and Hayes* (1983), for instance, sets the narrative in the late nineteenth century and portrays the unscrupulous actions of a group of pirates and the boarding of an enemy vessel that reproduces with accuracy the actions of seventeenth- and eighteenth-century pirates. This approach occurs as well in the Swedish film *Håkon Håkonsen* (*Shipwrecked*, 1990), whose story focuses on the nineteenth-century shipwreck of a young mariner on a deserted island where a group of pirates has hidden their treasure. The Russian film *Pirates of the 20th Century* (1979), the horror flick *The Island* (1980) adapted from Peter Benchley's novel, and the comedy *Six Days, Seven Nights* (1998) are all set in contemporary times. Whether they are armed with Victorian rifles or modern machine guns, the pirates in these films are generally faithful to the historical record. Their boardings of passing ships are characterized by as much violence as the historical plundering that occurred centuries earlier. The attacks are cruel and sadistic, and therefore all the more realistic and touching for contemporary spectators, who can identify easily with the victims.

Popular literary narratives on pirates such as *Treasure Island* and *Peter Pan* have generated a good number of film adaptations. The adaptations of Stevenson's story include two silent films and more than fifteen works among cinematic and televised films—both live action and animated—that have been produced in the United States, Russia, Australia, Chile, Japan, and the United Kingdom. These include the black and white 1934 adaptation, the 1950 film by Disney, the 1990 adaptation with Charlton Heston, the 1996 version with the Muppets, and two TV mini-series produced in 2012 and 2015 respectively. These films, which also generated sequels such as *Long John Silver* (1954) and *Return to Treasure Island* (1996), differ from each other primarily for their use of special effects. Updated in accordance with the decade of their production, they also emphasize different aspects of the original story: the 2012 version, for example, is the only film to report the financial misadventures of the protagonist's mother.

Similarly, J.M. Barrie's story of Peter Pan was first adapted into a silent film in 1924, but it was immortalized by Disney's 1953 adaptation. Among the subsequent versions of the narrative, those that stand out are Steven Spielberg's 1991 *Hook*, which is the case because it functions as a sequel to the original story, set many decades after the protagonist has grown old and has forgotten about Neverland and his powers. Another is P.J. Hogan's 2003 version, whose special effects really transform Neverland into a magical place, and whose weather is influenced by Peter's states of mind. The most recent film about the boy who never grows old is *Pan* (2015), which presents the intriguing prequel story of the young protagonist's abandonment by his mother, his kidnapping by a flying pirate vessel from the orphanage, his first encounter with James Hook, and his role as a prophesied Messianic liberator of the indigenous tribes from the oppression of the pirates. Whilst *Treasure Island* films depict pirates as villains addicted to alcohol and motivated by greed and evil intentions, in the Peter Pan films pirates are rather clumsy and amusing. The famous Captain Hook is an elegant, mutilated Ahab seeking revenge against his own version of Moby Dick. Some of the films depict him as cruel or even murderous toward his own crewmembers, but the attention is never focused on the brutality of the actions he actually commits.

Pirate women are a rare phenomenon in cinematic films, a reflection of the reality of the seventeenth and eighteenth centuries, when they were deemed unfit for the physical demands of the work on the decks. Superstitious ideas were maintained about their unlucky presence on board. The only two documented cases of female pirates during the golden age concern Mary Read and Anne Bonny, whereas previous lists included the names of the Scandinavian Alwida in the fifth century CE, the Irishwoman Grace O'Malley in the second half of the sixteenth century, and the Chinese pirate leader Mrs. Cheng at the beginning of the nineteenth century (Cordingly 89–97). Many ships' codes of conduct included edicts against bringing a woman or a boy aboard, largely because women were considered to be distractions and a cause for quarreling among the members of the crew. Furthermore, white women were rarely taken as prisoners; accounts corroborate the sexual violence they were subjected to or, in the majority of cases, the respect with which they were treated (Cawthorne 23–25; Burg 118). Women of color were instead more prevalent victims of abuse and rape, after which they were sold into slavery (Earle 172). Nevertheless, few cinematic films portray women as captains of their vessels, hard-working and courageous characters who demonstrate loyalty to their crews. Cinematic women pirates are also expert fencers and as agile, cunning, and decisive in their action as their male counterparts, whose lives they may even save in a clear inversion of traditional gender roles. This is the case in *Anne of the Indies* (1951) and the box office failure *Cutthroat Island* (1996), whose female protagonists are bold captains who face battles courageously and apparently do not experience any pain from their wounds, much like a number of their male predecessors.

Over the past fifteen years, the most popular films about pirates have been those in the *Pirates of the Caribbean* franchise (2003–17). The five films, which are all listed among the top-50 highest-grossing productions of all time, are characterized by an extreme attention to historical details (such as costumes, décor, and settings) and by narratives filled with action, romance, and plot twists. Piratical practices such as the observance of the code and the marooning of prisoners are depicted with accuracy in these five films, which have elicited the appreciation of fans worldwide, thanks also to their blend of humor, action, realistic special effects, and the talent of the actresses and actors (among whom Johnny Depp excels in the role of Captain Jack Sparrow). Original and almost exclusive to the saga is the use of the supernatural through the appearance of zombie villains, sirens, the mythological Kraken, a heathen goddess, and the journey to the afterlife.

Representations of pirates in literature and cinema have also been accompanied by their inclusion in miscellaneous genres like opera, videogames, comics, toys, board games, park exhibits (for instance, the Pirates of the Caribbean attraction at Disneyland), performances (the hourly battles at the Treasure Island Hotel in Las Vegas), manga, and anime (among Japanese anime, such shows as *Captain Harlock* [1978], *Queen Emeraldas* [1978–79], *Sol Bianca* [1990–91], *One Piece* [1997–], *Mars Daybreak* [2004] and *Bodacious Space Pirates* [2012]). On television, the successful serial *Black Sails* (2014–17), which is based on a narrative that immediately precedes the fictional facts narrated in Stevenson's *Treasure Island* as well as the historical events of the golden age of piracy, has now reached its fourth and final season. The dreaded sea marauders that caused havoc in the past centuries and could be construed as the equivalent of modern terrorists have often been converted into romanticized, noble, and misunderstood figures. Considering the amount of fictional texts that (have been and) are being dedicated to the figure of the pirate, it is therefore legitimate to affirm that, in spite of their evil actions committed on the high seas since the seventeenth century, pirates are resilient figures in popular culture that continue to capture the imagination and affection of the contemporary public.

Note

1. Blackbeard's ferocity has been recently questioned in Arne Bialuskewski's re-reading of the historiographical sources on the legendary pirate. See Bialuskewski, 39–54.

Works Cited

Ambrosini, Maurizio, and Camilla Bartolini. *Capitani, odissee, leviatani: La navigazione nel racconto cinematografico*. Pisa, IT: Felici, 2012.
Bialuskewski, Arne. "Blackbeard: The Creation of a Legend." *Topic: The Washington & Jefferson College Review* 58 (2012): 39–54.
British Broadcasting Corporation. "Country Profile: Somalia." http://news.bbc.co.uk/2/hi/africa/country_profiles/1072592.stm. Accessed on 04/30/2017.
Burg, B.R. *Sodomy and the Pirate Tradition: English Sea Rovers in the Seventeenth-Century Caribbean*. New York: New York University Press, 1995.
Cawthorne, Nigel. *A History of Pirates: Blood and Thunder on the High Seas*. Toronto: Arcturus, 2003.
Cordingly, David. *Life Among the Pirates: The Romance and the Reality*. London: Abacus, 2004.
Earle, Peter. *The Pirate Wars*. London: Methuen, 2004.
International Maritime Bureau. "Live Piracy & Armed Robbery Report 2017." https://www.icc-ccs.org/index.php/piracy-reporting-centre/live-piracy-report. Accessed on 04/30/2017.
Johnson, Charles. *A General History of the Robberies & Murders of the Most Notorious Pirates*. London: Conway Maritime Press, 2002.
Konstam, Angus. *The Pirate Ship 1660–1730*. Oxford: Osprey, 2003.
Partner, Peter. *Corsari e crociati: Volti e avventure del Mediterraneo*. Cristiana Mennella (trans.). Torino, IT: Einaudi, 2003.
Preston, Diana, and Michael. *A Pirate of Exquisite Mind: The Life of William Dampier: Explorer, Naturalist and Buccaneer*. London: Corgi Books, 2005.
Stubbs, Jonathan. *Historical Film: A Critical Introduction*. New York: Bloomsbury, 2013.

Piratical Societies as the Blueprint for Social Utopia

CLINT JONES

Few archetypal figures in history have been able to create an enduring mythology that permeates multiple cultures and, in spite of the numerous known negatives associated with it, manage to be portrayed and accepted as desirable. Certain legends surrounding the piratical lifestyle have so permeated cultural mythologies that even though there is no known basis for the belief they persist—walking the plank being the most obvious example, followed closely by buried treasure and certain popular pirate expressions, like the use of the "arrgh, matey!"[1] But as Angus Konstam notes, "pirates have become almost mythical beings, and like any myth there is always a grain of truth behind the creation" (7). Contrary to the romantic versions of piracy most well-known in popular culture, many pirates were pressed into service under threat of death while many others willingly allied themselves with the rogues plundering the seven seas for a plethora of reasons—poverty, sadistic Navy captains, political ambition, adventure, and other reasons lost to time. Nevertheless, some pirates were blood-thirsty scalawags drawn to the life because it afforded them the opportunity to operate outside established law, that is, outside of preconceived notions of civility, citizenship, identity politics, and widespread jurisdictions designed to maintain order according to the rigid elitism of the day.

Historically speaking, piracy is quite likely the second oldest profession, and if it is not, it is certainly in the top five. Piracy, as a lifestyle, has long appealed to people from all cultures who are looking to get rich quick, who cannot live within the constraints of society, who suffer from disproportionate socio-economic inequality, or who are just drawn to the adventure of it. And, generally speaking, there is no good reason to assume that throughout history piracy has not had a certain allure to it borne out by the fact that outlaws have always been able to generate public support, especially among the lower classes of society, even as their actions antagonize the very public that is cheering them on. That rapport is on stark display in the relationship golden age pirates have with subsequent generations via cultural interpretations of them. Diverging from their outlaw counterparts throughout history, golden age pirates were operating in ways that were unlike their predecessors in certain aspects and, more importantly, were undertaking their outlaw ways in an age already beset by utopian dreaming.

In the early years of the sixteenth century Sir Thomas More wrote a sensational little treatise that would shape a literary genre, a cultural discourse, and a method of political critique for generations to come. His *Utopia* spawned imitations, sparked imaginations, and framed the way whole peoples would conceive of possibilities in both the Old and New World. In fact, actual utopian social experiments began to pop up across Europe and the New World for centuries afterward right to the present day. Many of these attempts were short-lived and no doubt many have been lost to history, but others thrived for a time and some were quite successful. Pirates, on the other hand, are not often thought of as utopians, though when we think of pirates in the mythological sense it is golden age pirates that our minds identify—pirates who lived during the age of utopianism and who operated within the limits of some utopian constructs. This essay will argue that piracy, as it has come down to us from its golden age, has managed to endear itself to generation after generation because, despite everything negative that could be said about pirates, they were successful utopians—and utopians are always hopeful figures even if they are tragically flawed.

To better answer the question of what makes a successful utopian, given that no utopia has managed to stay afloat for long outside fictional accounts, it is clear that fiction must be separated from fact to build a framework through which we can evaluate the motivations of persons who became pirates. By examining the content of a pirate's life, paying close attention both to how it has been portrayed in popular culture and to the actual realities of pirates' lifestyles that led so many to opt into piracy, it is possible to understand why people undertook the risks and hardships associated with piracy in order to have a shot at a better, and certainly more utopian, life. However, it is first necessary to demarcate the limits of such an inquiry with respect to what constitutes a utopian account of a better life. This is especially true with respect to piracy because it is fraught with danger and pirates rarely made it to retirement. The first concern, why piracy would appeal to anyone with even a shred of moral decency, can best be answered by William James.

Weighing the risks of living a life as a pirate against the rewards it seems fair to assert that, given the options facing most people who opted into life under the Jolly Roger, the rewards had to be substantial. In addition to the normal hazards of life at sea faced by all seafaring folks—whether on a merchantman, a naval vessel, or a pirate ship—including scurvy, extremes of weather, diseases, squalid living conditions, and poor-quality food rations, pirates had additional hardships. Pirate vessels were often overcrowded to ensure enough people were available to wage battle and, if necessary, sail captured ships to market; but, because the ships typically used by pirates needed to be small, fast, and easy to conceal, many pirates slept on the decks in fair weather and cramped miserably below decks in foul weather. Pirates, especially pirates with a reputation, had to be careful where they made their ports-of-call, and this could mean long times at sea, not venturing home, and living with the constant fear of capture. Being captured meant, in most cases, execution, and becoming the spectacle of a public execution when possible, leaving many pirates with the desperate choice of how to die rather than the choice between living or dying; this ever-present concern for death was only exacerbated by the dangerous work of capturing prizes. Faced with all that, what could entice someone to throw off the yoke of civilization and become a pirate? Obviously, there were many reasons pushing people into the decision, but the rewards had to have been worth the risk to make the choice a "live option," as William James might say (3).

James argues that for a choice to be a genuine choice it must meet three criteria: it must be live, it must be forced, and it must be momentous. A live choice has an emotional element to it: there must be something that attracts the chooser to the option. For a choice to be forced it must be disjunctive, that is, an either/or decision, where choosing one option eliminates the possibility of the other. Finally, the decision must be momentous, which means, for James, that the choice is quite literally life altering if not exactly life and death—though for someone considering piracy seriously the decision was clearly life and death (9–22). Undoubtedly, for many pirates, the decision to become a pirate had to have been a genuine choice and when making such a decision the rewards, and even the possible rewards, had to be considered somewhat greater than the guaranteed hardships, the additional hazards, and the possibility of an inglorious death. Increased freedom would have been just as big a draw as the potential increase in wealth and the freebooting, free-wheeling, lifestyle of rum, women, gambling, and tropical weather most of the time, had to weigh heavy on the scales of conscience all things considered.

When considered as a genuine choice piracy looks pretty good for the average-person-cum-pirate. Given that life for most people was destined to be impoverished, and even those that could get ahead could still look forward to a life toiling for the crown under the watchful eye of the church, the freedom of piracy—or, rather, the fanciful and romantic ideas that overshadowed the realities—must have looked rather enticing. This is especially true if the subject in question is passingly competent at life at sea—which in the age of sail would have been quite a few people. So, if the choice is between poverty and hardship on the one hand and poverty, hardship, and the opportunity to become wealthy, on the other, it is easy to see which choice is more desirable. Similarly, if the choice is between laboring away for church or crown on the one hand or, on the other, the chance to live democratically or, at least, exercise some autonomy, then, again, the choice seems clear. Framed with James's genuine choice pragmatism the choice to become a pirate seems like an easy one for people in the right, or even nearly right, circumstances. As a result, golden age pirates are distinct from their predecessors and successors in one pivotal way: rather than operating merely as common rogues out for a quick buck as, for instance, the pirates crucified by a young Julius Caesar were, or, as mere violent opportunists preying on innocents for the sake of preying on innocents as some modern day Islamic pirates have been accused of doing, golden age pirates were operating in a completely different world than those actors with whom they were entangled.

Golden age pirates work well as proxies for consumers of popular culture because they operate not only as *antagonists* to the modern state, but as *alternatives* to the modern state. The piratical lifestyle is one characterized by freedom and it is unsurprising that, as a result, a pirate's life would appeal to anyone feeling the burdens and constraints of modern society. This is especially important because the choice to become a pirate was radically different than the choice to be a thief or charlatan swindler; rather, opting into piracy was a declaration against all of human society, a clear sign that an individual had decided to abandon it and was consequently cast as a villain of all nations. Becoming a pirate meant becoming a literal outlaw, that is, to live outside the laws of society, and far from the "yo-ho-ho and a bottle of rum" that characterizes popular culture depictions of pirates. The reality is that many people turning to piracy were desperate, disillusioned, men (and women) facing unfair and unforgiving conditions—of course, some were just downright wicked individuals looking to bring chaos into the world, but those were few by comparison to the number of pirates operating in the golden age (Konstam 8). Equally true is the fact that close association with pirates likely affected an individual's behavior—violence breeds violence—which is why pirates are often represented as a dastardly lot by those who fell into their clutches. However, non-violence is a recent utopian concept and violence, even the savagery of the most notorious pirates, ought not automatically disqualify golden age piracy from utopian consideration.

Utopian visions are often the expression of a cultural hope for a better future and, because pirates were successful at ushering in a better social reality for themselves, they operate culturally as a benchmark for utopian dreaming. The standards of utopian societies are notoriously difficult to pin down because, quite literally, what constitutes a utopian vision, be it a blueprint for an attempt at building one in the present, or, just a theoretical ideal, can vary widely from person to person. For instance, the "city in speech" that Socrates proposes in the *Republic* is an ideal place which Socrates says could not exist in the real world (Plato, *Republic*, 369c). This, of course, does little to dissuade Plato from attempting to institute the utopian ideal in Syracuse when given the opportunity. Likewise, the utopian hopes of pirates would have varied from pirate to pirate, vessel to vessel, and pirate cove to pirate community. Nevertheless, certain practicable ideals associated with utopia were present in pirate's lives.

Utopias are misunderstood as being places of perfection that are totalizing when, in fact, they are often community level spaces, existing in opposition to the established order of the day, with many aspects that can sully their utopian reputation upon reflection. Thomas More's *Utopia* engages in warfare and slavery, both of which would have seemed perfectly natural to the late Medieval and early Renaissance mind, but which, today, are clear failures. Certainly, Aristotle, whose philosophy dominated much of the intellectual output of the late Medieval period, allows for slavery and argues that its existence is the result of certain individuals having been born for it.[2] Utopias vary in size, both in terms of their geographic make up and their populations as well as how the social order will be organized. Utopias exist in all socio-political theories and the anarchist politics of golden age pirates certainly fit into a utopian narrative.

The anarchist is an oft maligned figure in socio-political discourse because what has been associated with anarchism is riotous behavior, wanton destruction, and disorderly chaos. However, in addition to being misleading, this association is thoroughly modern, having crept into political discourse as such during the social upheavals and Cultural Revolutions of the early and mid-twentieth century in spite of having been given a thoroughgoing examination by philosophers like Emma Goldman and Rosa Luxemburg. However, if anarchy is taken at face value it literally means "without government" and pirates of the golden age were more than happy to operate outside the bounds of governance. This does not mean that they did not have their own style of cooperative government, especially while at sea, where seamen could vote to depose their chosen captain if he was not bringing in the plunder, happened to be unnecessarily stern, or had any number of undesirable qualities—undesirable to his fellow pirates. Pirates maintained insurance for the wounded, had greater equality in divvying up booty, and acted far more democratically than their landlubber counterparts.[3] Pirates managed to capture the essence of utopian movements and utopian ideals even if it is difficult to nail down exactly what constitutes a pirate utopia. Moreover, the difficulty of dealing with utopian pirates is intensified because their brand of utopia is much more akin to anarchism than it is to the peaceful hippie commune most people are likely to associate with utopian communities today.

Yet, it is important not to overstate the utopian elements in piratical life and this is even more important with respect to how the utopian underpinnings of piracy might have appeared to the run-of-the-mill landlubber—not to mention pop culture consumers today. David Cordingly, for example, refers to the pirates' penchant for democracy as an "admirable tradition" even while cautioning that such traditions are incompatible with the romanticized versions of pirates that exist in popular culture from Douglas Fairbanks early cinematic portrayals to Johnny Depp's Jack Sparrow (6). The enduring romantic version of piracy is challenged by Cordingly, who cites a young sailor, Philip Ashton, captured by pirates in 1722. Ashton describes his captors as, "a vile crew of miscreants, to whom it was a sport to do mischief, where prodigious drinking, monstrous cursing and swearing, hideous blasphemies and open defiance of Heaven and contempt of Hell itself was the constant employment" (qtd. in Cordingly 6). Obviously, such a condemnation would have sounded appalling to eighteenth-century ears, but he could be describing anything from a suburban high school to a dive bar today and, given the stranglehold both the state and the church had on individuals at the time, it is not much of a leap to understand how such a lifestyle could motivate opportunistic thinking.

We could argue that golden age pirates were not only utopians, but successful utopians, and this is demonstrated by an analysis of both life aboard a pirate vessel, focusing on the socio-political standards for living at sea among pirates, specifically the infamous Pirates Code, and a closer look at the mythos surrounding Libertalia (also called Libertatia). These two examples encapsulate the anarcho-utopianism of golden age pirates at the level of individual vessel and pirate commune and, thus, bookend all discussions about piratical utopianism. Despite the prevalence of Letters of Marque and the fact that many captains, especially established captains, carried those Letters as cover and often legitimately operated as privateers—a legal, if rightly frowned upon, enterprise—it is important to emphasize again that pirates operated nation-lessly and their lack of a nationality meant that their own communities and havens could be structured in ways that best suited their lifestyle without regard for how the rest of the world understood their lifestyle or reacted to it. Because of the near constant warring between European powers, and the ever-present animosity that existed even during times of peace, piracy was a big business for good reason. But even the hardiest seadogs needed a place to spend their loot, and having settlements that were willing to turn a blind eye to much of the pirate lifestyle was critical to the mythology of the golden age. Obviously pirate havens and sanctuary cities made life for pirates a bit easier and this is certainly so where these locales operated on land with the same morally ambiguous code of ethics as their seafaring counterparts.

English held Port Royal and French owned Tortuga are exemplary of the types of places pirates would retreat to and, as a result, have remained in the public imagination not only because of their affiliation with pirates, but because of their own reputations. These were places where, according to Admiral Edward Vernon, pirates could find people willing to support them, merchants willing to buy and sell their booty and pirates continually found favors and encouragement among the population (qtd. in Rediker 29). These places were common throughout the West Indies and are typical of the average pirate-friendly port or pirate stronghold throughout the age from the east coast of America to Bermuda to the northern coast of South America. But life aboard the ships was different because there were no civilians and no government officials that needed avoiding, bribing or cajoling to accommodate a pirate lifestyle.

Life aboard a pirate ship was regulated and managed by a code that was well known among pirates. Many pirates had codes that were specific to them, and codes could vary widely from ship to ship, but every pirate was beholden to the code even though there was a lawlessness to it. That is, living by the code was on par with an honor system and enforcement of the code was a communal responsibility. Most pirate codes are lost to history because they were not written down, or not written down in their entirety, are being safeguarded in Davy Jones's Locker, or were fabricated by authors to beef up sales, but that they existed is not in question. The most famous and complete surviving set of these guidelines belongs to one of history's most infamous pirates: Bartholomew Roberts. Robert's code contains eleven statutes to be followed by the crew and, again, accounting for certain personal idiosyncrasies, captures what would have been of concern to any pirates about to embark on adventures upon the high seas. Most interesting, in terms of the anarcho-utopianism of pirates, are the rules emphasizing equality and the common good, especially behaviors that might endanger the operation or another pirate's life. For instance, the first provision of Robert's code states, "every man shall have an equal vote in affairs of moment. He shall have an equal title to the fresh provisions and strong liquors at any time seized, and shall use them at pleasure unless a scarcity makes it necessary for the common good that a retrenchment may be voted" (qtd. in Konstam 234). Obviously, equality among the pirates was important at least in affairs of the moment, returning to port, chasing a prize, what to do with captives, etc.—that is, any time other than battle or other times of urgency when the captain would have the ultimate say. But it is hard to ignore the egalitarian equality of one man–one vote that would have found a home nowhere else at the time other than a pirate ship.

Additionally, Robert's code discusses how disputes will be settled (never aboard ship), how booty will be distributed (including, like Henry Morgan's code, an acknowledgment of insurance for injured parties), and punishments for failing in one's duty (death or marooning for deserting one's duties during battle and death for smuggling a woman aboard ship in disguise). Obviously, the latter would have been amended on the ship of Calico Jack Rackham who was known to cavort with the golden age's most famous female pirates, Anne Bonney and Mary Read. Robert's code also details the responsibilities each pirate had to keep his arms in fighting shape, restrictions on gambling at sea, and a curfew of sorts requiring the lights to be put out at eight o'clock (Konstam 234). Though Robert's code is specific to him, and Morgan's code is specific to his Panama campaign, Konstam confirms that even small pirate crews were known to draft similar tenets and live by them (234). Given the prevalence of the pirate code and the way the codes were crafted to ensure democratic privileges, equality, and promote the safety, success, and well-being of the crew, it is reasonable to view each pirate craft as a floating anarcho-utopian community.

Certainly, life at sea must occasionally be abandoned and it makes sense that, as utopian minded individuals, pirates would create a similar community on land. A place that would parallel the principles by which pirates lived as sea so a pirate utopia needed to be more than just a friendly stronghold managed by a European governor keen on using the pirates to his, or his country's, advantage. Whether or not such a place ever existed, accounts of such a place do exist. Libertalia, located on the northwestern coast of Madagascar, has existed in the public imagination as a pirate utopia since its existence was first popularized by Daniel Defoe, writing as Captain Charles Johnson, in *A General History of the Pyrates*.[4] Libertalia, Johnson tells us, was founded by one Captain Misson who may have been as fanciful as the community he was supposed to have founded. Misson was aided by his friend, spiritual adviser, and fellow sailor-turned-pirate, former priest named Caraccioli and his fellow pirate Captain Thomas Tew. According to Defoe, Misson's life is exactly the kind of story one would expect of someone destined to found a utopia for pirates.

Misson was born in Provence to an aristocratic house, an ancient family with a plentiful fortune, that also, however, produced numerous offspring. Misson, though a gentleman, had little hope of gaining anything other than that which he could carve out for himself with his sword.[5] After his education was complete at sixteen, his father wanted to secure for him a place among the Musqueteers. However, this did not occur because Misson, "was of a roving temper, and much affected with the accounts he had read in books of travels, he chose the sea as a life," which abounded with more variety, and would afford him opportunities to satisfy his curiosity about the world (Defoe 383). During his travels he visited Rome, met the disaffected priest Caraccioli, and the two became fast friends with Caraccioli ultimately agreeing to join Misson at sea. The two men would become expert mariners and, while Misson was busy endearing himself to the captain and crew, Caraccioli was busy using his down time to spread his own gospel amongst his shipmates.

Caraccioli, we are told, regularly criticized the church for its failings and governments for their excesses and both institutions for their abuses. His sermonizing earned him a small following of proselytes among the crew, Misson among them, who by now was a thoroughgoing deist. Caraccioli had more in mind than just turning the hearts and minds of his crewmates and regularly sounded them out on the possibility of taking possession of the ship. Caraccioli never had to resort to mutiny to gain the ship because a better opportunity presented itself in the form of a cannon ball. The *Victoire*, the ship Misson and Caraccioli were aboard, came into violent contact with the ship *Winchelsea* which, firing a blast into the *Victoire*, managed in one fell swoop to kill the captain, the second captain, and the three lieutenants, leaving the ship with hardly any command structure (Defoe 390). Rather than allow the Master to strike their colors, Misson took command and fought the *Winchelsea* in a running battle until the pursuit was ended when the *Winchelsea* inexplicably exploded and sank (Defoe 390).[6]

Here the utopian element of Misson's and Caraccioli's worldview comes out in one clear statement. After the battle, Caraccioli addresses Misson as captain and tells him the crew supports this—no doubt influenced by Caraccioli's soundings. Misson accepts the position and tells the crew, "that a great number of them had resolved with him upon a life of liberty, and had done him the honor to create him chief: that he designed to force no man, and be guilty of that injustice he blamed in others; therefore, if any were averse to the following his fortune, which he promised should be the same to all, he desired they would declare themselves, and would set them ashore" (Defoe 391). The crew cheers this change in their fortune and votes were cast to choose officers after which the newly elected leaders went to determine their course—none choosing to be put ashore. The boatswain then asks under which colors shall they sail and offers black as the most terrifying, but Caraccioli dissents by saying: "they were no pyrates, but men who were resolved to assert that liberty which God and nature gave them, and own no subjection to any, farther than was for the common good of all" (Defoe 392). After delivering a rousing speech about the obligations owed to a righteous leader and the burden to throw off the yoke of a careless or oppressive ruler he adds to great cheers:

such men are we, and, if the world, as experience may convince us it will, makes war upon us, the Law of Nature empowers us not only to be on the defensive, but also on the offensive part. As we then do not proceed upon the same ground with pyrates, who are men of dissolute lives and no principles, let us scorn to take their colors: Ours is a brave, a just, an innocent, and a noble cause; the cause of liberty. I therefore advise a white ensign, with Liberty painted on the fly, and if you like the motto, *A Deo a Libertate*, for God and Liberty, as an emblem of our uprightness and resolution [Defoe 392].

From this moment the die is cast for the only outcome that could follow, a utopian community. Though Misson and Caraccioli operated as pirates they also liberated slaves, empowered those men to become freeman whom were to be treated as having been created by the same omnipotent being and endowed with equal reason (Defoe 414). His treatment of slaves as equals was reflected in the diverse mix of persons inhabiting the settlement where men from all over Europe and Africa were represented. The freed slaves, and presumably any pirate who joined the Libertalians, were taught French by the other inhabitants and all the members of the community contributed to this learning so as to keep the classes small (Defoe 427). Libertalia had no use of money as everything was held in common—a sentiment reflected in Robert's first statute. In short order the inhabitants of Libertalia managed to build a dock, several fortifications armed with cannon taken from prizes, secured pasturage for 300 head of stock gotten in trade with natives, and had cleared, sown, and enclosed a good parcel of ground for agricultural purposes (Defoe 429). Life in Libertalia thrived and was, by all accounts, seemingly blessed for time.

The utopian settlement met its end, unfortunately, when natives, in two great bodies of men, attacked the settlement for reasons unknown. Because the attack had been unprovoked the men living there were unprepared for the assault and their numbers were greatly reduced by the fact that Captain Tew and others were at sea seeking prizes. The men, according to Misson, fought as best as they could against overwhelming odds, but it was in vain. Caraccioli was killed in the fight and those that managed to escape the wholesale slaughter were forced into hiding until Captain Tew returned. Upon his return, learning what happened, the two captains decided to leave, Tew for America and Misson for Europe, their utopian hopes dashed. But it turned out that fortune was not done with Captain Misson and while the captains were sailing toward their destinations, their paths not yet fully diverged, they were overtaken with a storm and Captain Misson's sloop was sunk within a musket shot of Captain Tew (Defoe 438).

The story of Libertalia is apocryphal in the ways that utopian narratives often are regardless of whether the community actually existed. That Defoe may have conjured the whole thing to sell his book is not out of the question, but the use of a utopian device such as Libertalia fits the time period quite well. The late seventeenth and early eighteenth centuries were beset by the discussions of liberty sparked by John Locke and inspired by the strange, the mysterious, and the fanciful that was the New World, a world where anything was possible and many others sought out space to build utopian communities. Pirates were able to outpace their contemporaries in the formulation and implementation of functional utopian societal norms, however, and the savage touch of liberty was brought to life by Defoe.

Political upheavals, social change, and scientific discoveries at the same time were making cities the focal point of the Enlightenment. As more and more people came to believe that polite society, commerce, and liberty were the benchmarks of the future, it is no wonder that the world emerging from the Enlightenment could not find a place for the utopianism of pirates. Nevertheless, the democratically minded pirate, with an eye toward egalitarianism and personal freedom, somehow managed to define an entire age without participating in its norms and expectations. It is for this reason that the pirate as utopian continues to attract and hold people's imaginations.

Given the socio-political discourse of the Enlightenment, both on land and at sea, piracy in the seventeenth and eighteenth centuries was radically different than piracy before that time or afterwards because the golden age pirate was, in spite of everything else, a working rough draft of the utopianism that also characterized the age. Though piracy continued after the golden age ended, and continues up to this day, piracy has never managed to recapture the spirit of life-as-alternative to the established order that demarcated for so many people what was simultaneously romantic about the pirate's life, the YoHoHo aspect, and the hardscrabble reality of it that most people could not bring themselves to embrace. The distinction is made perfectly clear, in the language of the day, when Woodes Rogers, governor of the Bahama islands, staged the hanging of eight pirates in 1718 for "Mutiny, Felony, Piracy" (Rediker 11). Each of the pirates in turn made defiant speeches "crying up a Pyrate's Life to be the only Life for a Man of any Spirit" (Rediker 11). What spirit were they referencing, one might wonder, but the answer is a utopian one.

NOTES

1. There is only one instance where there is evidence of someone being made to walk the plank which was a punishment otherwise popularized in popular cultural depictions. Burying treasure was something that pirates did, but most pirates did not hoard their booty choosing instead to spend their ill-gotten gains on liquor, women, and gambling. The vernacular of pirates was as diverse as the countries the pirates originated in and there is no doubt that a certain pirate vocabulary would have developed it would have likely mirrored the naval lingo most pirates were used to, so there is every reason to believe that pirates used the expression "shiver me timbers" which is a reference to cannon shot shaking or breaking the masts of a ship. However, some phrases, like "arrgh, matey," were likely popularized in the same ways that walking the plank was centuries later.

2. Aristotle argues that enslaving fellow Greeks may fall outside the parameters of defensible slavery, but nevertheless argues that some people are just born with a slave's soul. Aristotle would have been well known to Thomas More, though More's approach to slavery in utopia differs considerable from Aristotle's, the institution of slavery is still a feature of his utopian narrative.

3. Henry Morgan laid out a thorough payment plan for the wounded according to what injury was suffered during battle before he sacked Panama. He also stipulated that no man was permitted to take anything for himself during the battle as all booty would be held in common until it could be divvied up after the campaign. His code not only established what injured pirates could expect as recompense for injuries, but how the remaining loot would be divided based on services rendered and feats of bravery performed during battle. For a more complete analysis of Morgan's code see Konstam, 233.

4. The story of Captain Misson is the first chapter in the second volume of Defoe's work which contains many pirates that are less well-known today. Misson, however, establishes the pirate community, according to Defoe, with the help of the historically real Captain Tew. However, the known facts about Tew do not line up with Defoe's story, which has led many to call into question the truth of Defoe's narrative. Nevertheless, Defoe's having gotten the facts and details wrong, to say nothing of his own embellishments, do not necessarily render the existence of Libertatia fictional. However, researchers and archaeologists have discovered no verifiable trace of the community, which lends credence to the historical position that Defoe crafted the place in his own imagination.

5. Defoe claims to be relating the history of Misson from an autobiographical French manuscript written by Misson. The loss of the manuscript, or its nonexistence, has helped establish the fictional nature of Defoe's account.

6. Defoe will go on to assert that this information had never been known before until the French manuscript found its way into his hands. Again, this lends credence to the theory that this is all made up.

WORKS CITED

Aristotle. "Politics." *The Complete Works of Aristotle*. Jonathan Barnes (ed.). B. Jowett (trans.). Princeton: Princeton University Press, 1984, 1986–2129.
Cordingly, David. "Introduction." Angus Konstam, *Pirates: Predators of the Seas*. New York: Skyhorse Publishing, 2011, 6.
Defoe, Daniel. *A General History of the Pyrates*. Manuel Schonhorn (ed.). Mineola, NY: Dover Publications, 1999.
James, William. *The Will to Believe, Human Immortality, and Other Essays in Popular Philosophy*. Mineola, NY: Dover Publications, 1960.
Konstam, Angus. *Pirates: Predators of the High Seas*. New York: Skyhorse Publishing, 2011.
More, Thomas. *Utopia*. 3rd ed. George Logan (ed.). Robert Adams (trans.). Cambridge: Cambridge University Press, 2016.
Plato. "Republic." *Plato: The Complete Works*. John Cooper (ed.). C.D.C. Reeve (trans.). Indianapolis: Hackett, 1997, 971–1223.
Rediker, Marcus. *Villains of All Nations*. London: Verso, 2004.

A Pirate Business Model

CHRISTOPHER KETCHAM

Golden-age pirates operated a form of business organization that deserves to be examined to learn lessons about conducting business today. Pirates were adept at goal setting, project management, risk management, and team building. They believed in equal pay for all. Governance was through a democratic process that very few businesses today deploy. Executives (captains) were hired, could be sacked and replaced during the voyage by vote of the crew for dereliction of duty, poor performance, or cowardice (Rogozinski 175).[1] A ship's quartermaster was entrusted not only with profit distribution, but also with making sure, through proper accounting, that the profits were calculated fairly and distributed equally (Rogozinski 177).[2] Personnel (sailors) were equal participants, equal shareholders of, and equal beneficiaries of the wealth obtained through piracy, with the exception of boy sailors who got half shares (Rogozinski 169).[3] Even the captain, who usually was the owner of the ship, received only one extra share for his services (not votes) and more shares in the form of negotiated rents for the use of and depreciation of the vessel (asset) used to conduct pirate business. A hundred or more years before the first workers compensation or social security programs were created in Europe, pirates developed programs for accidental benefits for the loss of limb and life.[4] The conditions of existence during the golden age of piracy proved to be instrumental in producing the egalitarian business system that pirates developed and adopted.

First, this was the beginning of an era of burgeoning sea trade particularly by the colonial powers. At the end of the sixteenth century and the beginning of the seventeenth century European colonial powers engaged in a robust sea trade with their colonies and Asia. Sea lanes between Europe and the Caribbean and around the Horn of Africa to the Indian Ocean were filled with ships carrying valuable cargo in both directions (Rogozinski ix).[5] However, European powers remained wary of, and were often outright hostile to, each other. Britain, France, and Spain had historically divisive relationships.[6] Britain even gave commissions to private vessels called privateers to raid other nation's colonies and rob and sink opposing country ships on the high seas.[7] European navies patrolled the sea lanes, looking for privateers and pirates.

Second, the colonial powers needed sailors to man the large numbers of ships that were required to satisfy consumer needs in Europe. They turned to impressment and other means of acquiring necessary personnel, many of whom had not before been to sea. However, the life of a common sailor, whether on a merchant ship or the navy, was difficult and the pay low. The British navy (as did some merchants) impressed many of its sailors and subjected them to harsh discipline and long tours of duty (Woodard 36). While promises of welfare and assistance to returning British naval sailors was made, little governmental help was ever provided. Cruel merchant and naval captains and officers savagely beat sailors, and few if any of the profits of merchant vessels were allocated to common sailors. Governance, whether at the country, colony, or ship level of organization was autocratic and near absolute. Common sailors had little say in what happened to them while in the service of the navy or merchant vessels. As a result, there were many sailors who defected or abandoned ships at ports of call or after pirates captured their merchant ships on the high seas. On shore, sailors had few skills they could apply to earn a living. Many of these disaffected sailors turned to piracy.[8]

However, the golden age of pirates was short-lived. Jan Rogonzinski compiled information on the pirates off the coast of Madagascar and the pirate republic of Saint Mary's island between 1680 and 1720. Colin Woodard chronicled pirates in the Caribbean between 1715 and 1725 (Rogozinski viii; Woodard 1). The so-called golden age of pirates lasted only thirty years before naval forces captured or sunk pirate ships that had operated with impunity in pirate-friendly ports in the Caribbean and in the Indian Ocean. What undid the golden age of piracy and their liberal form of government was not greed, as many would assume, but two related reasons. First, unlike the privateers who were authorized to plunder ships bearing flags other than their own, golden age pirates were opportunistic, pursuing any flagged vessel that served their purposes. The British, particularly, who had vigorously dispatched privateers over the years, found themselves stung by the pirates, many of whom they had brought up in the system of privateering, and who began disrupting British commerce.[9] Second, so many sailors from captured vessels acquiesced without a fight and joined the pirates that the colonial powers began to worry that the pirate democratic ideal might spread to the mainland and even the colonies. As Woodard affirms, "dissatisfaction was so great aboard merchant vessels that typically when the pirates captured one, a portion of its crew enthusiastically joined their ranks" (Woodard 3). According to Rogozinski, "it was their success at self-rule that made the Saint Mary's marauders so dangerous to the English government" (Rogozinski xvi). In other words, democratic thinking, if it had spread to the land, might actually cause unrest in the monarchically ruled world. Their fears were not unfounded. Both the Americans and French revolted against monarchical rule at the end of the eighteenth century.

Not only did pirates develop a new form of self-governance, but they also became very wealthy through the business model they created which gave individuals incentive to take calculated risks. For example, Rogozinski recorded, in (approximate) today's dollars, what specific ships captains and their crews took as booty. Examples include: Captain John Taylor and crew ($400 million); Captain Condent and crew ($350 million); Henry Every and crew ($200 million); and John Bowen and crew ($100 million) (x). Each crewman on Captain Tailors ship earned net approximately 1.8 million in today's dollars. For Captain Condent's ship, each crewman earned net approximately 1.0 million in today's dollars. During the period of the golden age of piracy a $500 annual annuity was quite adequate for a person to be called middle-class.[10]

One reason pirates were successful therefore was that they were good project managers. All members of the crew were part of the project team that determined the objectives, the risks, the costs, and how the project (the voyage) would be implemented (conducted). In fact, the pirate project model has many of the same features that are considered best practices for project management today. Included in these best practices is the idea that people can work together to solve problems rather than having solutions dictated from higher authority. The pirates' distributed authority among the whole crew made the vessel and its voyage a single project. Few businesses today operate their ongoing enterprise as a project.

However, the golden age of piracy occurred before the industrial revolution. Most land-based entrepreneurs during this time were small family businesses. There was no mass production and goods were hand-made and sourced locally. Even merchant fleets were relatively small, often under the ownership and control of one or two investors. Most businesses, therefore, were family owned and operated. Any laborers they hired were minimally paid for their efforts, and almost never given a share of profits.[11] The owner ruled; the servant or worker obeyed. In the Americas, slavery took this one step further and that was to make slaves chattel property, nothing more than a tangible business asset like a cow that only deserved to be fed and sheltered for as long as that slave was productive. While the industrial revolution ushered in the era of large business and mass production, business organizational structure and management has not changed much from the hierarchical form that was present at the time of the pirate.

The utilitarian ideal of the general business model we see today, for example, puts the investor at the top, the principal beneficiary of the greater good for the greater number. As Milton Friedman argues, the agents of the business have only one mission and that is to maximize the wealth of shareholders. While managers must obey rules and regulations, anything else that *can* be done that will help maximize the wealth of shareholders *must* be done. Employees today are no longer slaves or indentured servants, but are still considered "human resources" (assets) whose direct responsibility is to maximize shareholder wealth. Organizational management structures under this model are fundamentally autocratic. One need only to look at the typical organizational chart to see the levels of power that flow down from the top officers, who themselves report to a board of directors elected by the shareholders. While there are variations, including matrix management, power and control generally remains in the hands of executives. Non-management employees, with few exceptions, have little say how the organization is run. Under this business structure there has always been a pay gap between workers and management. In other words, in addition to a hierarchical governance structure, a hierarchical pay structure assesses different values to different persons based upon the tasks they are assigned or the title they are given. There is no question that employee conditions in today's organizations are superior to that of the navies and merchant ships during the golden age of piracy. Even so, we should ascertain through further study, which employees in today's organizations would prefer, and would perform better in a pirate form of governance and pay structure to that of the more autocratic regimes in general practice today.

The pirate organizational structure required job differentiation much like today's businesses. At the management level, there was a captain and the quartermaster, who was responsible for tallying and distributing wealth derived from the theft of money and precious metals or the sale of pirated merchandise (Rogozinski 177–79). Sailors and crew all had different tasks associated with crew welfare (cooks and surgeons), navigation, sails, ropes, rigging, ship maintenance, weapons operation, storage management, etc. However, each was guaranteed equal profits regardless of rank, station, or duties performed. In other words, everyone was an equal shareholder in the enterprise undertaken by the vessel. The idea of the sailor as investor is different from the typical stock transaction. In the stock transaction, the investor pays a sum of money, at the going market rate or in a private equity transaction, for a specific share of the company. The pirate, on the other hand, invested his/her *person* in the enterprise, foregoing salary for an opportunity to share in the profits after the expenses of the voyage were taken out. Quite often the captain had seized the vessel of the voyage and thus had made no monetary investment to acquire the asset that would be necessary to fulfill the voyage's objectives. Therefore, in piracy, there was (with few exceptions) not the sunk cost associated with acquiring assets necessary for the conduct of the business enterprise. If the ship sank or a better ship was seized, it replaced the old one without any significant transfer of wealth for the pirate. However, this represented significant loss for the seized merchant ship owners, who, since the late 1600s, had been able to secure insurance from Lloyds against piracy or perils of the high seas.

It is difficult to compare today's business model with piracy because the pirate did not acquire the asset necessary to conduct business. Pirates stole the ship they needed to ply their trade. Therefore, the pirate obtained their income producing assets without financial investment. The owner of the vessel seized by the pirate lost his/her investment, but this loss could be hedged through the purchase of insurance. The insurer, of course, lost but then passed along the losses to the merchants in the form of higher premiums. The pirate had no hedge against seizure or sinking other than to find another suitable vessel to seize. Loss of life or loss of freedom was a critical risk of piracy. So was loss of stolen goods through sinking or capture by authorities.

Equal shareholding in piracy also meant that everyone had one vote. The vessel itself, while the captain generally owned it, was an asset through which the entire crew conducted its enterprise. The crew was assessed equally, shares for the rental of the vessel, and the depreciation due to wear and tear of the vessel, payable to the captain. Costs of the voyage were also deducted through the usual accounting practices of paying expenses from revenue first and then allocating the profits when all expenses are paid. However, ownership of the asset of piracy did not mean that the captain received any additional voting power. Therefore, each member of the crew received one share and one vote regardless of station, rank, or job duty.

Like any investor in the marketplace today, individual pirates assessed individual opportunities for joining one pirate venture or another. Because pirates were not employees, but independent contractors-cum-investors, they had the opportunity to assess captains and other crews based upon their performance in the pirate trade. Piracy was high risk but also high reward enterprise. The pirate as investor did not invest money, per se, but the use of the investor's personal services on board the ship with a considerable risk of loss of life or limb. As with any investor today, some individuals had greater risk tolerances and would sign on to riskier adventures that promised greater rewards. Others would choose less risky ventures where the captain was known to be opportunistic, but also cautious. As there was considerable risk to life and limb, the ship, through its articles, assessed each investor's share of the profits for welfare for grievous injuries that an individual sailor might receive. This benefit was created long before there were disability benefit programs, or the no-fault workers compensation programs that were enacted, beginning at the turn of the twentieth century. Therefore, the investors on any pirate voyage had some insurance (hedge) against the loss or diminution of the asset required for the voyage—themselves.

Pirates, of course, could return from a voyage empty handed or worse, be captured by government authorities that likely meant confiscation of wealth, execution, or long-term incarceration. However, pirate crews could become wealthy after one voyage. Because individual pirates were equal investors in the venture, the incentive to work was high. Equal rewards also mean equal risks. Death, incarceration, and injury were real risks individual sailors took. However, there was a built-in partial hedge to investor risk and that was the lump sum disability plan. Unfortunately, since pirates operated outside the law, there were no guarantees that the plan would be available to individuals should the ship be sunk or the vessel and its crew be captured by naval authorities.

While the egalitarian nature of golden-age pirate organizational management was a factor in pirate success, each voyage was treated as a separate project that required individual planning and an effective project plan. Because every voyage of the pirate ship was a new venture, after the voyage, individual sailors were free to join other pirate ventures or leave the industry of piracy to enjoy their wealth. We could argue that individual pirates controlled their own destinies, except when captured by the authorities. Piracy was a criminal enterprise, but it was no Cosa Nostra or Mafia. There was no hereditary or family structure that controlled the enterprise. While pirates often cooperated with each other and coordinated some ventures together, each voyage of each vessel was a discrete and non-contiguous project. Piracy was organized crime but did not operate like hierarchical crime families. They operated more like Jesse James' gang that robbed banks and distributed the profits more-or-less equally among the gang members.

We could therefore affirm easily that pirates practiced good project management according to today's standards. The contemporary Six Sigma® best practices approach, specifically, DMADV or Define, Measure, Analyze, Design, and Verify, can be used to exemplify the pirate project approach.[12]

> Define: first, the prospective pirate team (crew) assembled to consider opportunities to pirate. Intelligence gleaned from locals, other pirates, or corrupt officials provided potential targets.
> Measure: each pirate target was risk assessed in these ways. First, its individual capabilities for flight or defense. Next, whether it had naval or another escort, or was traveling in a convoy. Third, whether its cargo was worth the effort considering the risk of loss of life, limb, or ship in its acquisition.
> Analyze: the entire pirate crew would determine which targets were too risky to run down and those with cargoes that were not worth the effort. Some crews had

larger risk appetites than others, but, in the end, the crew chose targets that were optimal for their risk tolerance level.

Design: the pirate voyage was then planned according to regular ship provisioning, including required arms, to subdue the target vessel. Next, rules of the ship were codified into ships articles that the individual sailors voted on.[13]

This included the objective or target vessel(s) of the project, allocation of profits, and a list of infractions and the punishments that could be inflicted for their violation. Other rules included the right of the crew after discussion and voting to change the objective or conditions of the voyage as well as the rights of the crew to fire and replace officers or other crewmembers.

Verify: Before setting sail, confirm that the actual conditions match those that were anticipated in the planning phase. If changes need to be made, return to an appropriate earlier step in the planning process. This step is also necessary if during the voyage conditions change.

Though the pirates did not have the benefit of a best practices regime like Six Sigma®, they did use many of the same practices. For example, within contemporary best practices of project management, votes are taken at regular intervals to affirm that the team agrees with decisions that are to be made. Pirates used similar processes both during the planning phase and after the voyage began. Captain Charles Johnson lists many examples of situations on pirate ships where votes needed to be taken:

> When the pyrates [of Captain England's crew] came out to sea, they put it to a vote what Voyage to take and the Majority carrying it for the *East-Indies*, they shaped their course accordingly" [Johnson *Location* 1452, emphasis in original].
>
> "The Captain's [Captain Vane] Behaviour was obligated to stand the Test of a Vote and a Resolution passed against his Honour and Dignity, branding him with the name of Coward, deposing him of the Command, and turning him out of the Company" [Johnson *Location* 1827, emphasis in original].
>
> "Noting a provision from Captain Roberts' ships articles: 'Every Man has a Vote in Affairs of Moment, has equal Title to the fresh Provisions, or strong Liquors, at any Time seized, and use of them at pleasure, unless a Scarcity make it necessary, for the good of all, to vote a Retrenchment'" [Johnson *Location* 2645, emphasis in original].
>
> "Captain Mission called a vote on the possible route of the journey they would take next. He used the opportunity to explain both the benefits and the arguments against. He asked for the individual opinions of the crew. They eventually voted the route that the captain favored" [Johnson *Location* 4495].
>
> "Captain John Bowen and his crew captured a ship they saw to be superior to their own and voted to burn their ship and take over the captured ship as their pirate vessel" [Johnson *Location* 6033].

As with any project, things change even after good up-front goal setting and planning have been conducted. Intelligence on target ships could be wrong, storms could arise, naval vessels could be encountered, or a potentially more lucrative quarry could be spotted or discovered at ports of call. Each change in the project plan of any significance required the positive majority vote of the crew.[14] Unique to this form of governance, any member of the crew could propose changes to the charter or the objective of the voyage during the voyage, but any changes required a majority vote. In many of today's "democratic" republics, while the minority party can propose changes, only the majority party can authorize the beginning of the bill process or debate. In the world of the pirates, all were members of the majority because there were no parties. Certainly, there were factions and cliques, but the one-sailor-one-vote rule maintained order without giving certain members of the crew superior powers over any other. Like other democratic bodies, pirates created their own codes of conduct, the methods of investigation and adjudication, and the punishment for their violation.

The pirate business model was different from the business model today in one important aspect. The pirate seized the asset for the performance of work; today's entrepreneur must invest owned assets and/or borrow assets to secure the fundamental assets required to operate the enterprise. What the piracy business suggests is that there can be another way of looking at business that involves engaging individual workers (sailors) as equal investors in the enterprise. The accounting is still the same, operating costs, including the cost of debt and rents for the required asset are expended first and taken from revenue. Pirates, however, lived and worked in what we might call a company town, the ship. While pirates received no salary for ships work, they were fed and given shelter (expenses). In modern-day business, salaries are used to provide individual basic needs. The pirate business model gave all participants the right to participate in project planning and receive an equal share of the profits. Both are important aspects of the pirate business because they involved democratic process, entrepreneurial risk and reward, *and* modern-day project best practices:

> Democratic: all members of the pirate/project team are equal.
>
> Best Practices: everyone on the pirate/project team is equally invested in its design, creation, performance, and result.
>
> Best Practices: the pirate/project charter's (the ship's articles) outcome or goal is something everyone has agreed to and signed off on, and for which everyone on the pirate/project team benefits (or not) equally.
>
> Entrepreneurial: only if the pirate/project team's revenue exceeds expenses will the individual members of the team profit.
>
> Best Practices: through the ship's articles (project charter), those who are derelict in their duties or performance or otherwise undermine the efforts of the crew (team) can be punished either through disciplinary measures or loss of profit.
>
> Democratic: The entire crew voted on performance assessment and punishment. Today, punishment and reward is determined, generally, by management alone.
>
> Best Practices: changes in the project plan (the ship's articles) are also debated and voted upon by majority voting.
>
> Best Practices: pirate/project team members sign on to the documents of the proj-

ect charter and its plan (the ship's articles) they have agreed to and are held to the standards of conduct they developed. Those who do not sign the project charter (the ship's articles) do not become part of the team.

This governance and performance reward structure is not for everyone or every organization. Pirates were, on average, a very youthful bunch with unusually high risk-tolerances (Rogozinski 160). Members of such an egalitarian project team in a more modern organization will need to have higher risk-tolerance levels than those who require a fixed salary. As a society, we have become accustomed scheduling salary levels through skills and responsibility assessments. What the pirate version of the project model suggests is that while everyone has different tasks and responsibilities, the collective team effort towards meeting the objective is what matters and what will be rewarded. The combination of equal participation in project development and project reward means that conflicts of interests between individuals that arise from power, responsibility, and pay differentials are reduced. This pirate/project model is not Marxist. The project asset investors and invested team members are rewarded (or not) in pure capitalist fashion. However, rather than impose an autocratic top-down process of management and control, these are equally distributed among members of the project team. Everyone is invested, and everyone agrees to work under team-agreed conditions for a common reward at the end of the project.

The question of what is a project is an issue for any organization. A project may be related to a new product or an annual plan for ongoing operations. Creating a pirate form of project management would take careful planning, and the right participants. Most likely persons will not be living in a company compound where room, board, and other costs can be expended. As in any project, there will be the planning and development period where little or no revenues will be earned. Compensation models that represent but are not "salaries" could be developed. For example, during the planning and development period, the project team members could be paid an advance that is expended against future profits. Many of today's new-hire salesperson compensation programs have either a form of non-assessable subsidy, or a loan against commissions that is payable according to a schedule when the salesperson begins to earn commissions. There is considerable risk of loss to the organization and the salesperson if the salesperson does not perform, just as there will be to a subsidized pirate/project organization should the project's goals not meet expectations. Organizations could also require project participants to assume debt for the difference between what they have been advanced and the results of the project, which would provide some insurance (hedge) against organizational loss, subject to problems of personal bankruptcy, loan delinquency, and cost of collection from individual project debtors. Organizations would also need to assess rents against capital assets used by the project, subject to negotiation with the project team. The cost of rent assessment against future profits could incentivize the project team to be conservative with what assets it will need to meet the goals of the project.

When project participants are invested in the project, the question then becomes whether team members will assume responsibility in ways that regular employees do not. If a traditional project underperforms, a salaried employee has only the job to lose. This may result in months or longer periods of unemployment, but there is minimal to no other investment risk that the traditional project team member takes. On the other hand, if a project underperforms, the team member in a pirate/project environment not only can suffer the risk of unemployment, but also may have to reimburse the organization for that which has been advanced by the company. Therefore, the assessment of psychological and risk-tolerance suitability of each potential project team member will likely be critical to the success of the project.

A pirate/project business model is at best an ideal now because there are few contemporary case studies and data for similar models. Law firm partnerships are a reasonably close model for the partners, but associates in the firm have little say in the governance of the business. The pirate also needed to be risk tolerant. It will be important to determine what psychological and risk-tolerant profiles would best serve the pirate/project organization in contemporary society. We can also ascertain from project management consultants like Six Sigma® the benefits of best practices project planning as compared with other approaches. The combination of hiring the right entrepreneurial risk-tolerant team members and deploying known successful project planning and governance models should give us a baseline probability-of-success curve and standard deviation that will help organizations assess whether the pirate/project model would work for one or more projects in their organization. If, for example, the organization deploys an appropriate project management process, results can be compared with other organizations that have done the same. The larger the pool of data becomes, the more credible the probability of success curve will become. Independent variables such as weather, interest rates, consumer preference changes, commodities and transportation cost, and recessions can be considered for each individual pirate/project that is being assessed for deployment.

Pirates volunteered for the job, and chose the democratic mode of governance over more autocratic forms of governance (military, absolute master captain, slavery) for their business venture. Peter Leeson notes that researchers have "applied the logic of rational choice decision-making in the context of organized outlaws" (1050). While we may be able to make the same rational choice decision-making claims about pirates, pirates business practices are still criminal. Leeson cautions about the business model: "pirates were clearly organized criminals and yet were not primarily in the business of providing services to anyone other than their members" (1051). Pirates were owners and beneficiaries of their business, had no "customers," and produced no product or services for other than themselves. They had no external customers even though they cooperated with other pirate organizations towards a common goal. This is one major difference between the pirate organization and the modern lawful organization.

What the golden age pirates have shown us is that successful business models do not have to be governed through hierarchical management structures. Pirates used a compensation structure that rewarded success through profit sharing. While pirates became wealthy from their business model, we do not have answers for how a pirate business model today might influence contemporary problems of slack, productivity, quality, profitability, and the satisfaction of employees and shareholders."[15] Case study and data analysis will be necessary to gain further knowledge about the efficacy of a pirate business in today's culture and economy. Many would-be pirates walked on the ship having been abused by captains, whether naval or merchant. They had been subject to strict autocratic, even cruel rule, and given salaries and benefits subject to the whims of navies or merchant ship owners who, as Milton Friedman required, maximize owner and sovereign wealth at the expense of the working sailor.

Risk tolerance is a fundamental question for those who want to consider a pirate-like organization. Sailors in pirate-era merchant ships were not treated well by their employers, but not all became pirates. We must have a better understanding of what kind of person is an appropriate candidate to work in a contemporary pirate business model organization.[16] This includes not only the capacity to take reasonable risks, but also the wherewithal to see rewards in the future beyond the weekly paycheck and even the annual bonus. We must be cautious to jump to the conclusion that those who would make good entrepreneurs are good candidates to become a member of a pirate-like organization. If the person's inclination is to "sail one's own ship," the necessary skills of working as a team may be lacking. Another concern is, how much the person could lose if the pirate project fails. In many cases, pirates who jumped from merchant ship or the navy had little to lose because their prior employers often did not pay them a wage that they could save for leaner times.

We know that the pirate model worked for the pirates of the golden age. They became wealthy, and sailors from merchant and military ships often jumped ship to become pirates. However, risks of death, injury, and incarceration were high as well as the rewards. The sailors who became pirates were not trained specially to take risks. For the most part, pirates came from humble backgrounds, and had little education, even though many were skilled at their jobs. A contemporary pirate business model will not entail the same physical or incarceration risk as the pirates during the golden age. However, today if a contemporary pirate venture enterprise should fail, individuals have more wealth to lose than the sailors who became pirates. While this may be the case, thousands of people become entrepreneurs every day today, and many will fail. The difference between the pirate business model and the general entrepreneurial business model of today then is not "risk," per se, it is in how governance, risk, and reward are distributed. The pirates became wealthy because they shared equally in governance, risk, and reward. The pirate/project business model deserves to be tested today to see whether equality in governance, risk, and reward can increase productivity, profitability, and other performance measures of contemporary organizations.

Notes

1. Rogozinski could find no evidence of the crew replacing the captain. One reason he speculated was that voyages were short. However, he did record that Captain John Coxon resigned in Panama City after being accused of cowardice.

2. The quartermaster, like the captain, was hired and given an extra share for his services, also because his was a fiduciary responsibility that the entire crew counted on.

3. Peter Leeson explains the split of the profits: "the captain draws four or five men's portions for the use of the ship, perhaps even more, and two portions for himself. The rest of the men share uniformly, and the boys get half a man's share" (1070).

4. Lesson details one such employee welfare program: "they would be compensated as follows: for the loss of a right arm, 600 pieces of eight or six slaves; for a left arm 500 pieces of eight or five slaves. The loss of a right leg also brought 500 pieces of eight or five slaves in compensation; a left leg 400 or four slaves; an eye, 100 or one slave, and the same award was made for the loss of a finger" (1070).

5. Rogozinski records especially rich convoys in the Indian Ocean from Portugal, and the East-India companies from England, France, and the Netherlands (5). Colin Woodard affirms that in the Caribbean, "they occupied British outposts in the Leeward Islands, threatened to invade Bermuda, and repeatedly blockaded South Carolina" (4).

6. For example, the War of Spanish Succession, 1702–1712. Woodward also says that in 1702, "[a]n English battle fleet trapped twelve French ships of the line and most of the Spanish navy ... destroying or capturing all of them" (53). Simmering feuds in Europe led France, England, and Austria to align against an ambitious Spain in the War of the Quadruple Alliance at the end of the golden age of pirates in 1718–1720.

7. As Woodward explains, "some mistake Sir Francis Drake and Sir Henry Morgan for pirates, but they were, in fact, privateers, and undertook their depredations with the full support of their sovereigns, Queen Elizabeth and King Charles II" (2).

8. Peter Leeson notes that pirates were a diverse bunch, coming from most European countries, as escaped slaves, from America. Others were African and East and West Indian (1054).

9. Rogozinski discusses the nature and purpose of privateering in depth here (71–73).

10. Contrast this with today's CEO-Employee compensation differential. Captain John Taylor on the ship *Cassandra* ($280.M haul) probably would have made $2.0 million and each of his 280-plus sailors (Rogozinski 272, Note 56) (estimate, ship *Cassandra*) $1.0 million after ship and voyage expenses. Today's CEO (captain) would demand on average to be paid 300 times more than the employees (sailors). Using today's formula, Captain John Taylor would make $142 million and each of his 280 sailors $475,000 significantly decreasing the incentive for the team to perform (Hodgson 7).

11. Woodard says that not only were employees not paid well, the general conditions of the time included poverty, poor nutrition, and high incidents of uncompensated work-

related accidents. However, some merchants and shopkeepers did thrive in the port cities (33).

12. For more information on the basic process and certification program, consult the Six Sigma website at https://www.6sigma.us/six-sigma.php. Accessed on 07/16/2017.

13. Ships articles were nothing new, but pirates turned these articles into constitution-like documents that all agreed to. Even if a sailor did not agree with a provision but signed the articles, the sailor would be bound to all provisions.

14. "Each man swore a solemn oath to obey the rules, usually with his hand on the bible" (Rogozinski 167).

15. Slack: the difference in time between the planned path and the actual path in a project. Where they are the same, there is no slack. If the actual path is less, there was redundancy in the planned path. If the actual path is more, either the planned path was not properly determined or intervening factors require reconsideration of the planned path.

16. One important issue returns to Friedman. That is, how do we continue to maximize shareholder wealth when profits are shared equally among pirate/project team members? Non-dividend paying stocks rely upon the market to set the price of stock. If the company has better results because of pirate/project activities and successes, the shareholders will be rewarded. For dividend-paying companies, dividends can be expended to the project by formula, with provision for sharing in the profits of individual projects according to a set formula. In this scenario, dividends can be increased (or decreased). Actual accounting of expenses, revenues, and profits will take some thought to encourage entrepreneurship, informed risk taking, and to pay for companywide operating costs that are indirect assets used in the pirate/project, e.g., payroll processing, legal, basic IT services.

WORKS CITED

Friedman, Milton. "The Social Responsibility of Business Is to Increase Its Profits." *Corporate Ethics and Corporate Governance*. Zimmerli, Walther, Markus Holzinger, and Klaus Richter (eds.). New York: Springer, 2007, 173–78.

Hodgson, Paul. "Top Ceos Make More Than 300 Times the Average Worker." *Fortune* (2015). http://fortune.com/2015/06/22/ceo-vs-worker-pay/ Accessed on 04/01/2017.

Johnson, Captain Charles. *The Real Pirates of the Caribbean*. Kindle Edition: e-artnow, 2017.

Leeson, Peter. "An-*arrgh*-chy: The Law and Economics of Pirate Organization." *Journal of Political Economy* 115.6 (2007): 1049–94.

Rogozinski, Jan. *Honor Among Thieves*. Mechanicsburg, PA: Stackpole Books, 2000.

Woodard, Colin. *The Republic of Pirates*. Boston: Mariner, 2007.

Swashbuckling Sexuality
The Problem with Queer Pirates
Nick Marsellas

> "Well, then, I confess, it is my intention to commandeer one of these ships, pick up a crew in Tortuga, rape, pillage, plunder and otherwise pilfer my weasely black guts out."[1]
> —Captain Jack Sparrow [*Pirates of the Caribbean*, 2003]

The figure of the foppish pirate in queer pirate studies has been given undue leeway, with many imagining they know the nature of this character because of the media in which he appears. We often choose to dismiss or minimize violence committed by these characters, preferring instead to believe in a heroic, chivalrous piratical subject. We might write uncritically of the sexual freedom on pirate ships without considering how power structures on ships give freedom to some but not others. Throughout (and perhaps because of) queer pirate studies, pirates exemplify the lawlessness of radical queer anti-statism. Whether that radical queer anti-statism manifests as moral or immoral is a question that highlights deeper trends in queer studies more broadly, making the pirate an ideal figure for the investigation of scholars' deeper concerns about humanity's relationship to sexuality.

Nearly every article on the topic of queer piracy begins by mentioning Johnny Depp's performance of Captain Jack Sparrow in the *Pirates of the Caribbean* series (2003–17). Critics point to Sparrow's failure as a leader, heavy makeup, preference for negotiation over aggression, and energetic gesticulation (among other traits) as sites of queer performance that are immediately accessible to their readers.[2] Given Amber Heard's recent accusations of Depp's abuse during their relationship, it seems fitting to use Depp again to introduce this essay. Depp cites Barry Burg's seminal text *Sodomy and the*

Pirate Tradition for his performance—a text that most critical work on queer piracy cites as well (Binelli). Burg situates the pirate's relation to sexuality as one of liberation through sexual anarchy on the high seas. Burg's theoretical investments can be traced to an earlier scholarly tradition based upon the work of Christopher Hill, in which the pirate is analogous to (or even the same figure as) the radical revolutionary proletariat. In Hill's "Radical Pirates," he argues, "the survival of some radical [religiously tolerant, democratic, communist] ideas among the pirates whom Defoe describes is not impossible: it is, indeed, likely" (174). The scholarly opinion on queer pirates partly situates a pirate's sexuality as one more piece of his radicalism and liberation from the state. Pirates are consistently positioned as economic revolutionaries and their queerness as one more facet of that revolution.

This essay traces the intellectual heritage of "queer pirate studies" in order to understand the particular celebratory rhetoric with which scholars address pirates' queerness, and to suggest a need to balance this celebration with an acknowledgment of rape as another common feature of pirate sexuality. While imagining pirates as less beholden to the state's sexual norms can be quite useful for queer theory, it is also important to acknowledge the dangers of this kind of sexual lawlessness. The state's sexual norms and laws may be less easily brought to bear on the pirate ship, but scholars must be cautious not to elide the (often sexual) violence that happens at sea. Desubjectification (in the case of pirates, but also generally) allows for freer consensual sex, but it also allows for the rape of those with less power. Queer theory's distrust of the state, coupled with an anarchist bent within piracy studies, leads scholars to overlook these negative aspects of pirates' sexual lawlessness in favor of a laudatory application of the pirate as a queer radical figure.

Many scholars who examine historical gender and sexuality have struggled with terminology for gender and sexual concepts that the English language has only recently begun to name. Barry Burg chooses not to use the term "homosexuality" in his title because of a host of "scientific meanderings and sundry psychological nuances associated in modern usage with homosexuality," though he utilizes the term "homosexual activity" much to the same effect (xi, 2). Throughout this essay, the term "queer" is used as a marker of gender and/or sexual difference from what cis-heteronormative systems regard as normal.[3] While queerness is often defined by negation, identified through its resistance to oppressive systems, the term could also be understood to encompass certain circumstances not of resistance but of the absence of coercive cis-heteronormativity. Thus, piracy is not queer because it is in opposition to cis-heteronormative conventions on land (piracy's antinormative strategy, if it could be said to have any, seems to be "ignore" rather than "resist"). Piracy is queer because of the diminished presence of the cis-heteronormative state on pirate ships. Queerness, by this definition, is the ground of experience, before the imposition of various cultural mandates regarding sex or gender.

This essay uses the term "queer" for a number of reasons. First, though men attracted to men are over-represented in much of the field's scholarship, there is theoretical and topical coherence between studies of gender and sexual practices within queer pirate studies that is difficult to name without the term. Secondly, "queer" aligns more closely to non-identitarian conceptions of gender and sexual difference, whereas the popular "LGBT" signifies more static concepts of fixed identities based upon that difference. Also, "queer" does not necessitate knowledge of specific sexual practices or gender identification to act as a label. Thus, a situation, a space, a time, a fictional character, etc., may be understood as queer. Finally, an understanding of queerness as ontologically anterior to "normative" sex or gender implies that queerness can be found whenever cis-heteronormative systems have not exerted force on individuals; the term does not need to have been coined prior to a subject's existence as such, as with the debate regarding the use of "homosexual" for the description of individuals who lived before the nineteenth century. For these reasons, the term "queer" will be used to describe both the field of queer pirate studies and its historical subjects, except in quoting or summarizing the terminology of other scholars.

C.R. Pennell gives us a genealogy of pirate studies that organizes the field into three clusters: economics, ideology, and feminist criticism, with queer pirate studies (though not formally named) falling under ideology (8). In the introduction to *Bandits of the Sea: A Pirate Reader*, Pennell notes the ties between Burg's *Sodomy and the Pirate Tradition* and the ideological work of Marcus Rediker and Christopher Hill. This alignment indicates the important connections between queer pirate studies (with Burg as the subfield's founder), and scholars who see pirates as analogous to political revolutionaries. Throughout this "ideological" strain of pirate studies, the primary conflict is between the government and the individual. Examples like the anarchist pirate colony of Libertatia or Samuel Bellamy's famous speech against the piracy of government give leftist scholars plenty of source material to supply their analogies. This marriage of piracy and anti-statist sentiment lends itself to queer piracy scholars, who are particularly interested in how anti-statist communities manifest queerness. However, anti-statism is only one aspect of a queer world making project, and scholars cannot ignore the protections against sexual violence that the state affords in certain circumstances.

Burg situates pirate morality within seventeenth-century tolerance for homosexual practices in England, though he remarks on the added freedom from state sanctions that can be found at the farther edges of the empire. Burg claims that the West Indies were teeming with homosexual practices for a variety of factors, including the absence of "legal prohibitions, condemnation by organized religion, [and] the dominance of heterosexual institutions" (69). This coincides with queer scholarship's assertions that the ubiquity of heterosexuality is purely a result of ideological institutions. Without the heteronormative state's imposition on the pirate community, Burg argues, nearly all individuals were queer.

Pirate studies' assumptions about the pirate ship as a petri dish for political experimentation are best reflected in Burg's opening remarks in his chapter in *Bandits at Sea*, though these assumptions about the impenetrability of the ship can also be found throughout his earlier work: "the coterminal limits of the physical and psychological boundaries of the ship, when combined with its impermeability or insulation from outside influences, created an environment for the seventeenth-century mariner that has been characterized as a total institution" (211). Burg goes on to suggest that the total institution aboard the pirate ship resulted in a historically egalitarian homoerotic community. The foundations of queer pirate studies—the complex relationship to historical knowability, the presumption of egalitarian relationships, the interest in a community estranged from larger society—all find their origin in Burg's work.

After Burg's *Sodomy and the Pirate Tradition*, the second major text for queer pirate studies is Hans Turley's *Rum, Sodomy, and the Lash*. This book distances itself from what it sees as Burg's historical speculation and focuses on the "piratical subject"—an amalgam of *representations* of pirates, both those deemed historical and fictional, who operated during the golden age of sail. Turley reduces Burg's project to having "uncovered a few sodomy records in maritime archives" (45) whereas Burg himself characterizes his work as "very different than that undertaken by historians," calling it "interdisciplinary sociology" or "speculative social science" (xl–xli). Regardless of this distinction, Turley argues against a historical recovery project, claiming the impossibility of separating "the 'real' pirate who preyed on legitimate traders from the romanticized version accepted as the 'reality' in the twentieth century" (36). Turley sets up a strong dichotomy between his own project and his characterization of Burg's. He is indeed cautious not to make assertions about "real" pirates, whereas Burg has been met with skepticism for his conviction that homosexual acts "were the only form of sexual expression engaged in by members of the buccaneer community" (xxxix). Turley disavows claims of certainty around pirate sexual practices: "I shall not make claims that the pirate was a sodomite and that pirate ships were rife with buggery," a response to Burg (6). This disavowal of claims to historical certainty appears also in the work of Isabel Karremann, who affirms: "we cannot know what this reality actually was like, since all we have to go by are textual representations."

Nevertheless, this caution with historical claims does not extend to the popular cultural critique of queer pirates. A popular 2013 blog post (counting nearly 1,000,000 views) from *Cracked.com* includes less measured statements: "in 1645, the French government of Tortuga decided to import thousands of prostitutes to try to neutralize the rampant homosexuality, because this was the type of response that governments had to things. Not that it's likely to have made a great deal of difference, though—pirates in a matelotage shared everything, including wives" (Reidy). The Starz show *Black Sails* (2014–17) also foregrounds queer characters in its telling of the golden age of piracy, though with more nuance than the above-mentioned comedy/edutainment website.[4]

While a little historical speculation is not unwarranted, scholars often find affinity in Turley's analysis of the piratical subject. Turley acknowledges that most of the information we have on pirates was either created to appeal to literary audiences or to maneuver those convicted of piracy through the court systems with as little recourse as possible. For this reason, Turley is instead most interested in how the piratical subject can help scholars understand the culture in which it was created. The preponderance of queer pirate scholars finding the piratical figure more compelling suggests that there is less investment in a historical recovery project than in exploring the pirate as a site of imagination. Indeed, queer theory has largely set aside questions of who had sex with whom, as this type of speculation is inevitably met with skepticism. The onus of providing evidence is never on the dominant group—historical figures are assumed straight and can only be proven otherwise with unquestionable evidence. Modern queer pirate scholars evade this evidence problem by evoking the distinction between historical and cultural analysis initiated by Turley, often finding it more theoretically useful to assert the queerness of a representation than that of an individual.[5] However, this particular alignment with representational analysis perpetuates the unfortunate trend of eliding violence on the high seas.

The representational queerness of pirates can be fraught because theorization can lose some of the historical situatedness of a pirate's sexuality. Studying the piratical subject can lead to particular blind spots based upon scholars' own conception of that piratical subject. The popular image of the foppish pirate, combined with queer theory's desire for recuperative statelessness/lawlessness, can lead to undertheorization of the pitfalls of lawlessness, namely the forced reliance on the goodwill of those with power over others. This often manifests as a lack of attention to rape within pirate narratives, particularly the implications that rape has on queer utopian thinking. How does inclusion of rape affect the way that piracy has functioned as a site of exploration for queer ideas? Is the pirate still a useful queer theoretical tool if we acknowledge that the sexuality of the piratical subject includes rape? Queer theory need not turn away from theorizing state-sponsored violence, but it must also take into account physical violence in its search for egalitarian statelessness.

Within the context of queer theory, or queer politics more broadly, desubjectification is often viewed as the solution to state-sponsored violence. Tracing a lineage of thought through Louis Althusser and Judith Butler, subjecthood is the specter of queer theory—indicating the state's unwanted hand in the lives of those under its jurisdiction. A helpful counterbalance to this particular understanding of subjecthood can be found in the Black Atlantic theoretical tradition.[6] In Black studies more generally, there is growing interest in the distinct inscription of Black bodies as non-subjects through the history of the slave trade.[7] Particularly important for the study of pirates' "escape" from their interpellation by the state is a corollary experience of states not enforcing their jurisdiction, and thus protection, over people within the institution of slavery. A queer theory methodology often foregrounds the ideological violence a state enacts on its citizens, whereas a Black Atlantic methodology reminds us of the violence committed by individuals who benefit from the state's refusal to claim slaves as their citizens. To escape cis-heteronormative systems, queer theory speculates, is to escape the cis-heteronormative state itself. Queer theory favors individual liberty, thus privileging desubjectification and escape from the state's interference. This makes piracy a particularly fruitful site of inquiry for queer theory. Where does the state have less power than on the pirate ship, among the villains of all nations?

While queer theory might align with the egalitarian lawlessness of "radical piracy," a Black Atlantic methodology reminds us of the myriad of violent actors who do not disappear at sea, even (and especially) in situations where the state is not "subjectifying" individuals. The connections between desubjectification and physical violence are made particularly clear by Hortense Spillers:

> Those African persons in "Middle Passage" were literally suspended in the "oceanic," ... removed from the indigenous land and culture, and not-yet "American" either, these captive persons, without names that their captors would recognize, were in movement across the Atlantic, but they were also nowhere at all [72].

The statelessness of those African persons meant that there were no protections in place against violence committed against them. Recalling this Black Atlantic understanding of individuals not recognized by the state helps us to sober the more liberatory understanding of life at sea, though these two experiences can operate in tandem both theoretically and historically. In the case of pirate studies, the implementation of this methodology would complicate Christopher Hill's heroic radical archetype through the recognition of the subject's liberatory rhetoric and simultaneous violent subjugation of others.

One might ask Hill, can a pirate be both a Marxist hero and a violent rapist? What value is there in that sort of hero?

It is not only the physicality of the rape committed by pirates that must be acknowledged, but simultaneously the rhetorical camaraderie of the piratical subject and lighthearted invocations of rape. The phrase "rape and pillage" has a certain whimsy, bearing connotations of groups of people just as likely to show up in cartoons as in history books. Although David Mitchell's succinct skewering of "rape and pillage" is framed around Vikings, we can see the portability of the criticism, as the phrase is commonly used within the context of pirates as well:

> I don't quite understand why it is that "pillage" should take the curse off "rape," because it does, doesn't it? "The Vikings raped and pillaged their way through the North" sounds a lot merrier than "A gang of Norwegian sailors are suspected of a series of rapes in the Sunderland area." Add "pillage" to "rape," and suddenly it has a certain air of knockabout fun [Mitchell].

Mitchell suspects that the reason "rape and pillage" is treated with such levity, despite the seriousness of the crimes, is that it happened long ago. The phrase is generally connected to historical destruction, with more emotionally charged terms being favored for contemporary large-scale violence. It appears that "rape and pillage" has been used so frequently to describe historical characters who have otherwise been made innocent that the term now bears more connotations to children's stories than to the acts it describes. Regardless of this mitigation of the phrase's severity, pirates are still strongly connected to "rape and pillage" in the public's mind. If the piratical subject is an amalgam of culture's understanding of the pirate, we must understand rape as within the bounds of the piratical subject's sexual practices if for no other reason than pirates' proximity to the "rape" of "rape and pillage."

There are, however, staunch linguistic prescriptivists that insist that the phrase implies an older definition or "rape" as theft, not sexual violence (Hard-Beat). They suggest that the phrase "the pirates raped and pillaged throughout the island" bears no overlap to "the pirates raped throughout the island." According to the *Oxford English Dictionary*, rape's asexual definition, "the seizure of property by violent means" (early 14c), does appear before the more familiar definition:

> Originally and chiefly: the act or crime, committed by a man, of forcing a woman to have sexual intercourse with him against her will, esp. by means of threats or violence. In later use more generally: the act of forced, non-consenting, or illegal sexual intercourse with another person; sexual violation or assault (early 15c) [Rape, n.3].[8]

However, the asexual definition has largely fallen out of use—"Now *rare* (chiefly *arch.* and *literary*)"—with assumptions of the word's asexual use as metaphorical to sexual violence (Rape, n.3). The OED includes reference to the phrase "rape and pillage" but makes no distinction either for or against an asexual reading. The phrase's contemporary association with piracy, coupled with the predominance of the sexual definition of "rape," means that sexual violence is still a part of how the public imagines the raping and pillaging piratical subject, regardless to what degree that association is acknowledged.

The sexual welfare of subordinates aboard pirate vessels is of no particular concern to Barry Burg, whose historical/sociological conjecture assumes consent for nearly all of his subjects. "A number of commanders had youths for their exclusive use ... and although there is no way of knowing how carefully pirate Captain John Quelch looked after his Negro boy, the price the lad brought at auction in Boston after his master was captured, some £20, indicated he was in good condition" (Burg 122). Although we are not given the particulars of the boy's status, whether he was free aboard the ship, we might assume that his subsequent sale is evidence enough of his compromised position within the hierarchy of the ship, a position Burg instead suggests was privileged because of the high price at which he was sold. This position, where consent is coerced if present at all, provides a challenge for queer theorists who might wish to use the pirate ship as queer anti-statist institution.

Additionally, Burg is eager to separate homosexuality from pedophilia, though his apparent embarrassment at pedophilic pirates gives little justice to the cabin boys: "the most visible characteristic of pirate pedophiles is that in every case those men with a preference for boys were not integrated members of their crews [e.g., cooks, captains, surgeons]" (124). Attempting to invoke a "no true Scotsman" argument, Burg suggests that shipboard pirate culture was not pedophilic or abusive because pedophilic and abusive pirates were not a part of shipboard culture. It might make more sense to see this trend as exemplary of the complexity of a sexual culture without legal institutions. Burg admits that his speculative project is quite limited by the dearth of written accounts of pirate sexuality, though his celebratory project seems undeterred by the fact that many of the scant cases he uses to support claims of widespread homosexual practices are taken from court cases where sodomy is combined with rape (xlv). One can imagine that the challenge of finding evidence of consensual sodomy in court records is more difficult than finding records where an aggrieved party has sought legal recourse for rape. However, Burg bypasses the important distinction between his historical evidence of sodomitical rape and the claims that he makes about the open secret of pervasively homosexual pirate ships. Symptomatic of queer theory's search for utopian models, Burg is unable to reconcile his claims of the freedom from cis-heteronormativity with the coexisting reality of the rape (without recourse) of powerless pirates at sea.

Turley chooses to sidestep questions of consent altogether—focusing instead on piracy's literary homoeroticism and not engaging historical cases of rape committed by pirates, sometimes against other pirates. When Turley does mention consent, he does so flippantly: "on a continuum of homosocial behavior, violence and voyeurism are more acceptable to readers (and authors) than explicit suggestions of homoeroticism. Besides, pirates are too 'masculine' to indulge in consensual sodomy" (6). This would not be a particularly troublesome quote on its own—Turley could have argued that the piratical subject exhibits a negative, violent sort of homoeroticism in these instances. However, Turley quickly loses the raped subject in his desire to illuminate "the homoeroticism inherent in transgressive homosocial worlds" (4–5). Turley describes the violent forced prostitution and group rape of Blackbeard's wife as a homoerotic exchange, with little acknowledgment of the wife's subjectivity.[9] Likewise, throughout his book there is no consideration given to consent and whether or not homoerotic scenes are meant to carry consent.

Perhaps even more utopian than Burg's construction of shipboard life, Turley situates the pirate's homoeroticism within egalitarian community practices. In his analysis of Defoe's *Captain Singleton*, Turley evaluates the morality of pirates, separating "the 'good' pirates" from "the 'bad' ones, such as Blackbeard, Avery, and Low, pirates who are determined by their violence and their criminality, rather than by the 'ideals' of a government" (107). Turley then focuses almost exclusively on the homoerotics of these "good" pirates, without acknowledging the larger claims made earlier about inherent homoeroticism of all pirates, including the "bad" pirates he briefly mentions. This turn towards positive egalitarian queerness is symptomatic of the field, reluctant to engage the more politically tumultuous topic of violence in supposedly egalitarian communities. Turley spends a significant amount of time positioning his work in relation to Marcus Rediker and Christopher Hill, though not contradicting their claims of piracy's connection to egalitarianism. Queer pirate studies inherits these challenging implications of Turley's argument: piracy cannot simultaneously be egalitarian, inherently homoerotic, and devoid of consensual sodomy.

Queer piracy scholars would do well to mitigate the egalitarianism of Rediker and Hill and better understand the power imbalances still at play in pirates' sexual lawlessness. Turley shows us that the piratical figure is teeming with homoerotic implications (and with a little more digging we know that rape figures into that homoeroticism). "Egalitarianism" implies a certain camaraderie and reciprocity that, while often present, is not fundamental to relations between pirates. "Sexual lawlessness," however, bears none of the same assumptions. It is up to readers to place value judgments on the lawlessness aboard pirate ships. This understanding of pirates forces queer scholars to acknowledge the implications of an anti-statist platform—the absence of recourse for rape in lawless societies.[10]

This line of thinking leads us to the inevitable entanglement of queerness and egalitarianism. Is queerness always positive? Is there any capacity for queer violence? This essay suggests that queer experiences could be considered even more layered and multivalent than they have been in the past. Sex is not inherently violent, and queer sex is certainly not inherently violent, but it is worth considering whether violence prevents sex from being queer. Understanding the theoretical ground already established, the (a/im)morality of the pirate ship looks to be an excellent site for that exploration.

Notes

1. The script for this movie says that the line is "raid," not "rape," but Depp's pronunciation with a glottal stop (reɪʔ), coupled with the word's proximity to "pillage," suggests that Sparrow's intentions go beyond the movie's PG-13 rating.
2. Claire Jowitt, Isabel Karremann, Kathryn R. King, Martin Fradley, and Heike Steinhoff all reference Depp's queer performance, either as introduction or as explicit object of study.
3. The term "cis-heteronormativity" indicates the privileging of cisgender and heterosexual experiences at the expense of transgender and non-heterosexual (gay, bi, pan) experiences. The term indicates the stigmatizing prescriptive nature of systems that attempt to ascribe a "normal" gender or sexual identity/experience.
4. *Black Sails* (2014–17) is an interesting site to reexamine Turley's claims about the piratical subject because the show seems to be giving thought not just to Stevensonian representations of pirates but to less canonical pirate tales as well.
5. Jowitt, Karremann, King, and Fradley all make this move.
6. See Paul Gilroy's *The Black Atlantic*.
7. For more on this trend, see Alexander Weheliye's *Habeas Viscus*.
8. It is a telling linguistic peek into our society that the rape of a person is metaphorically referential to the violation of property, not that the rape of property is metaphorically referential to the violation of a person.
9. For more on authors using women as conduits for homosocial erotics, see Eve Kosofsky Sedgwick's *Between Men*.
10. Of course, it is true that in our current system there is still little recourse for rape victims.

Works Cited

Binelli, Mark. "Johnny Depp: The Last Buccaneer." *Rolling Stone*. November 12, 2012. rollingstone.com/movies/news/johnny-depp-the-last-buccaneer-20121112. Accessed on 09/13/2017.
Burg, Barry. "The Buccaneer Community." *Bandits at Sea: A Pirates Reader*. C.R. Pennell (ed.). New York: New York University Press, 2001, 211–43.
_____. *Sodomy and the Pirate Tradition: English Sea Rovers in the Seventeenth Century Caribbean*. 1984. New York: New York University Press, 1995.
Fradley, Martin. "Why Doesn't Your Compass Work? *Pirates of the Caribbean*, Fantasy Blockbusters, and Contemporary Queer Theory." *The Handbook of Gender, Sex, and Media*. Karen Ross (ed.). Hoboken: Wiley-Blackwell, 2012, 294–312.
Hard-Beat. "Rape, Pillage and Plunder." *WordReference*. December 7, 2015. https://forum.wordreference.com/threads/rape-pillage-and-plunder.3108212/. Accessed on 09/13/2017.
Jowitt, Claire. "'Parrots and Pieces of Eight': Recent Trends in Pirate Studies." *Literature Compass* 1.1 (2003): 1–23.
Karremann, Isabel. "'The Sea Will Make a Man of Him?' Hypervirility, Effeminacy, and the

Figure of the Queer Pirate in the Popular Imagination from the Early Eighteenth-Century to Hollywood." *Gender Forum: An Internet Journal for Gender Studies* 32.1 (2011). genderforum.org/wpcontent/uploads/2017/02/HistoricalMasculinities_Complete.pdf. Accessed on 09/13/2017.

King, Kathryn R. "Introduction: Hans Turley, Queer Studies, and the Open-Hatched Eighteenth Century." *The Eighteenth Century* 53.3 (2012): 265–72.

Mitchell, David. "The Phrase 'Rape and Pillage.'" *David Mitchell's Soapbox. YouTube*, November 20, 2009. youtube.com/watch?v=uJqEKYbhLU&index=56&list=PLC16EE381C0C5F09F. Accessed on 09/13/2017.

Pennell, C.R. *Bandits at Sea: A Pirates Reader*. New York: New York University Press, 2001.

_____. "Introduction: Brought to Book: Reading About Pirates." *Bandits at Sea: A Pirates Reader*. C.R. Pennell (ed.). New York: New York University Press, 3–24.

Pirates of the Caribbean: The Curse of the Black Pearl. Directed by Gore Verbinski. Walt Disney Pictures, 2003.

"Rape, n.3." *OED Online*. Oxford University Press, June 2017. Accessed on 09/13/2017.

Reidy, David, and Paige Turner. "5 Ways Pirates Were Way More Modern Than You Realize." *Cracked*. May 30, 2013. cracked.com/article_20448_5-ways-pirates-were-way-more-modern-than-you-realize.html. Accessed on 09/13/2017.

Spillers, Hortense. "Mama's Baby, Papa's Maybe: An American Grammar Book." *Diacritics* 17.2 (1987): 65–81.

Steinhoff, Heike. "'Yo-Ho, A Pirate's Life for Me': Queer Positionalities, Heteronormativity, and Piracy in *Pirates of the Caribbean*: A Queer Reading." *COPAS: Current Objectives of Postgraduate American Studies* 8.1 (2007), copas.uni-regensburg.de/article/view/99. Accessed on 09/13/2017.

Turley, Hans. *Rum, Sodomy, and the Lash: Piracy, Sexuality, and Masculine Identity*. New York: New York University Press, 1999.

"The Boy-Sublime"
Sir Lionel Lindsay and Piracy

JAYSON ALTHOFER *and* BRIAN MUSGROVE

This essay takes an Australian case study to argue that the deeply anchored trope of piracy can be readily appropriated to romanticize and mediate a reactionary political vision. The essay examines the complex interweaving of a political vision and the cult of piracy in the work of the Australian artist, writer, and critic Sir Lionel Lindsay. It threads together a consideration of Lindsay's life, politics, and Rabelaisian-Nietzschean aesthetic, then considers the way in which all these strands were hauled around the rhetorical figure of piracy. Consequently, the essay reads Lindsay's piratical fantasy life, pirate poems, related visual art, and a key prose work to trace the evolution of an increasingly reactionary politics.

The discourse termed "piracy"—with its familiar signs, images, themes, and narratives—is a rich, multivalent cultural lode that can be raided in many ways for a variety of ideological ends. As Martin Parker's review-article "Pirates and the Uses of History" usefully and succinctly points out, the reading spectrum of piracy veers from the view of the pirate life as shipboard democracy or collectivism to the equally resonant proposition that "the Jolly Roger was a brand which signalled to the market" (197)—a threatening art of making the deal that any capitalist enterprise would immediately understand. In Lindsay's case, the virile pirate and his life-world became the ciphers of an authoritarian ethos. It was a compelling cultural-political fantasy, in which piracy was read as representing both the character of a colonialist pseudo-aristocracy and the instrumentality of Capital.

By the late 1890s, Lionel Lindsay was at a switch-point in his aesthetic and political thinking. Born in 1874, Lindsay belonged to the first international generation of boys captivated by Stevenson's *Treasure Island* and piracy figured large in his developing world-view. As fin-de-siècle Australia moved towards Federation—the amalgamation of six separate colonies into full, formal nationhood in 1901—Lindsay fretted that the fledgling country would be swamped by the rising tide of socialism. The aspirant nation was a conflicted space, with the nascent but swelling trade union movement and other left factions colliding, often violently, with the interests of Capital and the business class that was essentially entrusted to frame the new nation's Constitution. To kidnap Walter Benjamin's terms, Lindsay came to see this as a "state of emergency" which might become "not the exception but the rule" (248). Lindsay found his reactionary response to this cultural emergency in the cult of the pirate.

In Lindsay's political aesthetic, the artist—as much as the politician— would serve as creator and promoter of national identity and values. The artist would be a spiritual guide, a pilot steering the nation through the turbulent waters of degraded modernity: a modernity blighted by mass culture, political upheaval, communist ideas, disrespect for tradition, and his great *bête noir*—the much-despised "Modern Art" itself. His political vision hinged on aesthetic mediation. In response to the apparent chaos and crisis induced by modernity, the true artist would restore the "natural order of things" by mediating ruling-class, capitalist values to the public through the excitements and iconography of piracy.

As Benjamin critically discerned, any "efforts to render politics aesthetic culminate in one thing: war" (234). For Lionel Lindsay that "war" was a classwar, exemplifying Benjamin's further point that "war only can set a goal for mass movements ... while respecting the property system" (234). Lindsay was nothing if not a defender of class privilege and property systems, and piracy provided the key metaphor for his vision of a culture ruled by exceptional individuals who simultaneously scorned "the mob" yet enlisted it into the cause of preserving property rights and social hierarchy.

At this moment in his career Lindsay was a struggling artist, living in rented rooms, attics, and makeshift "studios" that were nothing more than hovels. He subsisted by providing illustrations and copy for metropolitan magazines and periodicals like *Tocsin*, *The Hawk* (re-named *The Hawklet*) and *Free Lance*. However, his relationship to the market was deeply troubled. He referred to his commercial work as a "scurvy living" and borrowing a scatological vocabulary—part Rabelais, part pirate—he defamed his dependency on hack-work as tantamount to "eating the turd of the world" and turning out shit art to satisfy the cravings and craven tastes of a "filthy" and "futile" coprophilic public (Lindsay *Comedy* 76; *Discobolus* MS). Like a latter-day pirate, he could curse and raid the market when he was short of cash, and even sometimes influence its currents. Then, when his material needs were satisfied, he could withdraw to a monastic, Rabelaisian life of pleasure and indulge himself in the practice of "Fine Art."

Having moved from his pious, provincial home to Melbourne in 1893, Lindsay was still passing through a phase of dandyish self-fashioning. Those years were dominated by the cult of Aestheticism and Lindsay's library was the standard, period check-list of Aesthetic-Decadence: a flirtation with Flaubert, Baudelaire's *Fleurs du Mal*, Huysmans' *A Rebours*, Swinburne, Wilde, and Beardsley's *Yellow Book* crew. But as his biographer Joanna Mendelssohn observed, when the "nature of the charges against Oscar Wilde" became obvious, the "self-consciously heterosexual" Lindsay disavowed this disreputable interest and turned to piracy (70). The effete, retiring Aesthete-Decadent—sensuously surrendering to what Lindsay called an "eternal *nostalgia* for BEAUTY"—was displaced by a more robust but equally nostalgic role model (Mendelssohn 70).

For a short period jobs dried up in Melbourne so Lindsay took steerage to Sydney, the Harbor City, and immediately found it more rough-and-tumble and to his liking: "the romantic foreshores rising picturesquely from the blue water, dominated by the tall masts of sailing ships. Bluejackets and marines, larrikins and sailormen from 'Missisip to Clyde,' gave colour and character to the streets" (Lindsay *Comedy* 92). Sydney was the country's premier cosmopolitan entrepôt. It was a thriving metropolis, where ferryboats and the watery arteries of "Free Trade made living cheap" and abundant (93)—an experience that helped to consolidate Lindsay's mental linkage of piracy and Capital. And pirates were everywhere. Besides those he encountered in "my constant reading" of Petronius, Boccaccio, and Shakespeare (58), they featured in the Australian press, popular literature, and on the musical-hall stage. The pirate king of the Pacific—William "Bully" Hayes—was outstanding, appearing in sensationalist newspapers, magazines, a melodrama, and Rolf Boldrewood's novel *The Modern Buccaneer* (1894). The bulk of Boldrewood's novel was pirated from a manuscript about Bully Hayes by Louis Becke, another popular South-Seas storyteller, who published historical novels in collaboration with Walter Jeffery, such as *The Mutineer* (1898)—a version of the mutiny on the *Bounty* of 1789. The co-authors shared colorful pasts: Becke had been arrested, though acquitted, on piracy charges; Jeffery logged for mutiny. The latter became Lindsay's employer, drinking buddy, and close friend.

"I think no one knew Walter Jeffery, the managing editor of the *Evening News*, so well as I did. We were intimate friends for twenty-one years," Lindsay recalled in the 1940s. He romanticized Jeffery's maritime exploits: "run away to sea in boyhood ... rising to mate, was seven years at sea, and on his last voyage from India" was accused of mutiny for "taking the side of the crew" against the negligent, "mean captain" who had allowed eight men to die of scurvy on his watch. "We don't seem today," Lindsay lamented, "to have any clean-cut individualists like Walter Jeffery" (*Comedy* 221–26). In piratical figures like Jeffery, Lindsay discovered a combative male identity that affirmed an adversarial, Nietzschean view of the world.

Lindsay also became aware that the leading-lights of a maritime literary aristocracy—Robert Louis Stevenson and Joseph Conrad—had visited Australian ports. From there, he took temporary lodgings in dockside hotels, craving the company of *real* men who had plied the sea-lanes: sailors, he wrote, "seem ever the manliest sort of men" because "the great sea had washed from them the dross and complexity of the life of towns" (*Comedy* 94). This was a germ of Lindsay's depiction of piracy as pre-modern pastoral fantasy. He frequented the area of Sydney known as The Rocks: the archetypal, seedy harbor-side precinct of working-class slums, flophouses, prostitution, street gangs, and sailors' bars that served cocktails like "Blow-me-skull-off"—a heady brew of rum, wine, cayenne pepper, and opium. On one memorable night, Lindsay and a friend joined a "man-of-war's-man" with "two of his shipmates and a little marine" and "set out to do the town. I slept that night on the billiard table of the Ocean Wave hotel," Lindsay proudly remembered (*Comedy* 94). This was the young artist authenticating himself as a man of the world—a man who had earned his sea-dog stripes by dissipated association.

Lindsay's cultural politics became a farrago of poorly digested Nietzsche, a monocular right-wing understanding of Rabelais—*Gargantua* read with an eye-patch on—and piracy. He mixed his obsession with the image of the romantic, golden-age pirate with simplistic notions of a life lived "beyond good and evil" and the Rabelaisian doctrine "Do What You Will," to create a persona for the artist as above and unanswerable to humanist morality, civil law, and proletarian democracy. And as he formulated his cultural politics in the late 1890s, it was no coincidence that Lindsay began to produce paintings, drawings, woodcuts, etchings, and poems of pirates and the pirate life. "I was at this time immersed in Esquemeling's *Pirates and Buccaneers of America*, and painting watercolours of these picturesque ruffians," Lindsay recalled of a moment in 1897 when a bohemian socialist editor and friend dropped anchor in his studio. "Pirates? What had pirates done for humanity?" the visitor asked. They were nothing more than scoundrels, criminals, and murderers. Why waste time ennobling them, the caller continued, "when the poor were groaning under the heel of the bloated capitalist?" "I find pirates a damn' sight more paintable than your *proletaire*," Lindsay replied. "The pirate is a figure of Romance," beyond the petty moralism and "pretty academic socialism" that mentally afflicts the utopian leftist "improvers of mankind" (*Comedy* 79). Any farrago of ideas is inevitably a contradictory mess, so in Lindsay's mind by 1897 the figure of the pirate had come to represent both pseudo-aristocratic individualism—outside Nietzsche's "herd mentality"—and an exemplary actor in his celebration of middle-class, free-market capitalism: "Do What You Will" but by all means profit and prosper.

Lindsay moved-on to write pirate poems, jejune but often deftly metered and rhymed. These pirate stanzas showboat almost every stereotype or cliché imaginable: galleons full of doubloons plying the Spanish Main, Barbary Coast, or Caribbee; dashing, high-spirited young buccaneers; old sea dogs puffing their corn-cob pipes over tankards of ale and toddies of rum in smoky taverns, reminiscing about the glories and grandeur of yore. Nevertheless, the poems had a serious point. Collectively, they evoked a pre-modern world, exclusively masculine, where everyone knew his place in the order of things, ruled by an implicit code administered by the sea-borne aristocracy—the likes of Henry Morgan and William Kidd. The mere invocation of these symbolic names suggested that Lindsay was both imaginative re-creator and custodian of the values of a golden age ruled by exceptional men.

Pirates were regularly depicted as "princes" in Lindsay's literary art. His poem "In the Pages of Romance" bemoaned the historical loss of a class of free-booters which once enjoyed "the franchise of the sea" but in democratic modernity was "doomed to dull equality":

> Princes from the world's inconstancy,
> Wisdom and ignorance
> My buccaneers still sail with me
> In pages of Romance.

In his "Ballad of Buccaneering" Lindsay went further, representing the pirate as heroic reminder of greater days when "the world was full of colour and our blood was all ablaze"; when "pirates were the princes of Days That Used to Be." "For Today Is with Us," another pirate poem, asked "Who shall take strict account of Yesterday?"—the glittering epoch that "was—but nevermore." Loss was a familiar refrain in these poems: the loss of sense in modernity, the loss of immobile class structure and order, and the lost ethos of the remarkable, inspired outsider—pirate and artist alike.

Lindsay's pirate poems were exercises in pastoral nostalgia. This was a yearning for an idyllic countryside and its bucolic values, "natural" down-to-earth eternal verities, and the unchanging class structures that some versions of pastoral often entail. Lindsay transposed that reactionary version of pastoral onto the idealized ship-board community of good mates and jolly aquatic squires; drinking, smoking pipes, reminiscing about the good old days of "Morgan and Roberts, Kid and Vane, / England and Avery" who "shall never more attain" franchises of the high seas which were their birthright ("In the Pages of Romance"). In "At the Sign of The Three Pipes," piracy provided a reassuring fantasy and trans-historical consolation, as pirates of old and present-day down-at-heel artists met in an imagined garret to lift themselves above modernity's "common strife" in "deed, word, and thought":

> But we in our windy garret
> Cry hail to the boys of chance
> Who'll bring us a coloured parrot
> For the sake of our Great Romance.

Lindsay's prints from the same period visually celebrated the mate-ship of sea-faring—the trio depicted in the wood engraving "Pirates in Port" (1899) is probably the best known. But two of his etchings openly suggest the fusion of pirate and artist. "The Reader" or "Man Reading" (1896) shows a seated pirate, smoking and lost in the pages of a book. "The Smoker" (1898)—alternatively titled "Waiting Pirate" or "In the Tavern Himself"—pictures a lone pirate, again smoking with a tankard of ale on his table as he looks out the tavern window. Remove the signature hats, and these two images could easily be read as portraits of early eighteenth-century writers or gentlemen sages, absorbed in deep contemplation: the pirate as Enlightenment Man.

By the time he was knighted in 1941, for services to Australian arts, letters, and intellectual life, Lindsay had long left behind the bohemian garret and achieved respectability, eminence, and artistic recognition. He became "Sir Lionel" at the instigation of his close friend and confidante, Australia's Prime Minister Sir Robert Menzies, accepting the award from an honors system already archaic and out of step in a modernizing Australia. Sir Lionel finally belonged to an elite club—knights of the British Empire—though in his younger days he had always been fond of clubs of another kind. Commonly, these clubs were bohemian, exclusive, para-aristocratic, and aggressively male to the point of misogyny. Indeed, Joanna Mendelssohn detected an "all-pervasive unconscious hostility to women" in the Lindsay brothers' correspondence (xi). In the late 1890s, Lindsay was a founding member of bohemian fraternities, clearly modeled on eighteenth-century English gentlemen's clubs: the Ishmael Club and "a pleasantly disreputable club called the Prehistoric Order of Cannibals"—comprised of "young men involved in art" but essentially dedicated to drunken carousing (Mendelssohn 63).

The most exclusive of all was a three-man pirate cenacle, convened by the brothers Lionel and fellow artist Norman Lindsay in 1898, with Ray Parkinson, a journalist friend, who "too had been captivated by the pirate cult and accepted with delight" (Hetherington 31). They entertained themselves with Lionel's "gay and bawdy ditties" and collectively resolved to write a pirate novel in the shadow of *Treasure Island*—a literary enterprise shipwrecked by fantasy, game-playing, and excesses of Jamaica rum (27, 32). They had discovered pistols and cutlasses, remnants of a theatrical performance, then decked-out an inner–Melbourne "one-roomed brick shanty" and "hung a drawing of a Skull and Crossbones over the fireplace, and rolled in two or three barrels to heighten the pirate atmosphere…. The place looked every inch a pirates' lair" (31). With preposterous solemnity, the three grown-men dressed in bandannas and pirate garb, and on one occasion drove-off a group of back-alley thugs, brandishing their guns and swords (32; cf. N. Lindsay *My Mask* 148–49). They composed pirate ballads and ersatz sea-shanties— or "chanties," as they so elegantly dubbed them. Some of these chanties survived in the pages of *Norman Lindsay's Book: No II* (1915), including "Paddy Doyle," "Reuben Ranzo," and the dismal "Storm Along":

> Old Stormy he was a good old man,
> *To me way hay; storm along, John,*
> Old Stormy he was a good old man,
> *Come along, get along. Storm along, John* [52; cf. McCrae 117].

Not only is the punctuation quite wrong for a sailor's work song—listen to a folklorist like Ewan MacColl sing and phrase the genuine article—but the very thought of the Lindsay brothers raising a main-sail or hauling on a bow-line is almost more than the human mind can accommodate. But things worsened. The three intending, urban pirates swore an oath, literally signed in their own blood:

> Wherein We the undersigned builders and navigators of the *Royal Fortune* do hereby swear and solemnly affirm to navigate the aforesaid ship through all adverse winds, through fair weather and foul, through doldrums and tornado, until we have reached that harbsour of a Greate Success. As witness our hands and the blood of our hearts this 10th day of February in the year of our grace 1898 [L. Lindsay et al.].

It is difficult to nominate a better example of bathos, but this was absurdly "for real" and the blood-oath actually exists. As John Hetherington noted, the document is "in the La Trobe Library, Melbourne. The blood has rusted and faded but the signatures are still legible" (32).

All this might seem risible, except for the fact that when he died in 1961 Sir Lionel Lindsay was regarded as a "national treasure." His prints had been commissioned and exhibited internationally, and the *New York Times* carried an obituary naming him "one of Australia's leading artists"—as if Lindsay's exemplary life fused the aesthetic and political characters of a nation. He was a known connoisseur and controversialist—the latter principally because of his xenophobic, anti–Modernist letters to newspaper editors. This aspect of his career culminated in the irrationalist *Addled Art* (1942)—an anti–Modernist, anti-democratic, anti–Semitic conspiracy-theory tract. It was an intellectually addled volume in itself, described by one art historian as showing "the same hatred of democracy" as "leading fascist theorists" (Smith 216).

Lindsay and his siblings—particularly brothers Norman and Daryl— had been regarded by the Australian public and the nation's conservative political class not only as artists, writers, and critics but also pundits, tastemakers, and cultural gatekeepers for the first half of the twentieth century. His brother Daryl was also knighted, taking the title Sir Daryl in recognition of his directorship of the National Gallery of Victoria, and the Lindsay brothers enjoyed the friendship and company of some of the country's most influential politicians, judges, and captains of industry. There was the arch-conservative, anglophile Prime Minister Menzies, who praised Lindsay as a "whimsical" savant and master of "divine and disorderly" conversation ("Speech"); the transport magnate and frontier capitalist William Bolton; Sir Frederick Jordan, Chief Justice of the state of New South Wales and later its Lieutenant Governor, and the wealthy wool-broker Sir James McGregor.

In 1938, McGregor was the dedicatee of Lindsay's last, late pirate poem— "True Gold"—in which the wool merchant McGregor was transformed into the mythological Jason, seeker and keeper of the Golden Fleece. McGregor was revered for his connoisseurship, accumulation of worldly treasure, and bonhomie. "True Gold" harked back to Lindsay's earlier pirate verse and celebrated the revival of youthful spirits: "Ah! that draught! In my old blood / Youth again is springing" (*Discobolus and other Verse* 51–52). The poem links into a pattern of imagery in his pirate poems; patterning that articulates his idea of "the Boy-Sublime." In "Romance Redivivus," he rhapsodized:

> full-hearted ... the days
> When, on the tides of open chance,
> We, with the late-hour'd fire ablaze
> Watched the torn banners of Romance.

The Boy-Sublime encompassed the wild "blasphemy of gallant days," the necessary restoration of animal spirits and the compensatory fantasy of the buccaneering life—which happened to be identical to the processes of contemporary Capital:

> The Princes of our hearts were then
> No coloured covered books for boys,
> But black-souled scoundrels—proper men—
> Raw flesh and no poor painted toys;
> For, pictured to our waiting eyes,
> Grand brutes in silk and filigree
> We saw, in Esquemelling, rise
> Out of a dead forgotten sea.

The Boy-Sublime articulated Lindsay's devotion to the violent cult of socio-economic Vitalism. In contrast to an attenuated modernity, the Boy-Sublime followed a curve of return to the "Dear colourful days of a faded age, / Weapons and ways uncouth," and what Lindsay termed "the Great Desire" and "the grand Commune" of adventuring men ("At the Sign of the Three Pipes"). His aversion to modernity was cued by notions of cultural devolution, race decay, and the dissipation of manhood in an age that was atrophied and neurasthenic:

> But now that the world has lost its hold
> On the pageantry of Time,
> And only romance is a thing of gold
> In the heart of the Boy-Sublime ["Romance Redivivus"].

Poems of spiritual re-birth, such as "Romance Redivivus" and "True Gold," were also paeans to the jolly fellowship of men like McGregor. They were alchemical entrepreneurs, bold mercantile capitalists, and pretenders to blue-blood—Australia's contemporary "bunyip aristocracy" (Doyle 95).

The bunyip was a fabled Australian river monster, renowned for its guile and cunning. Coined in Sydney, in 1853, the term "bunyip aristocracy" satirized duplicitous, dissembling politicians, public officials, and businessmen who had a monstrous appetite for wealth, privilege, and power, and wanted to replicate the English class system in colonial Australia. Lindsay was at home in their company, and they sought his because his aesthetic-political outlook was not only germane to theirs but also a conduit for conducting their ruling-class posture into the public sphere: it was "our little group," "Bob' Menzies wrote to Lionel (Letter to Lindsay 1943). This blue-blooded clique hailed Lindsay as a champion of individualism, aesthetic order, tradition, and reactionary anti-socialism—a world-view formulated from Lindsay's piracy obsession and his fetish of the pirate as a Rabelaisian hero, whose ship was a sea-going Abbey of Thélème.

The Lindsay brothers hero-worshipped Rabelais and his books were fetish-objects. "A shilling volume of Rabelais went everywhere in his pocket," Hetherington wrote of Norman Lindsay, "like a priest's prayer book" (23). In the 1890s, Lionel Lindsay fantasized his bohemian household as "a little Thélème," conducting morning rituals (*Comedy* 51). At breakfast, this involved "a daily reading of Rabelais ... upon a text selected by me from the Rabelaisian lesson for the day" (43)—*Gargantua* press-ganged as a *Book of Common Prayer*. For Lindsay, in the pages of Rabelais there was no Bakhtinian dialogic imagination or heteroglossia; there was only one possible reading. He saw something in the pirate life that approximated Rabelais' Thélème: "All their life was regulated not by laws, statutes, or rules, but according to their free will and pleasure. They rose from bed when they pleased, and drank, ate, worked, and slept when the fancy seized them ... nobody compelled them ... to do anything.... In their rules there was only one clause: DO WHAT YOU WILL" (Rabelais 159). Thélèmites, in Geoffrey Ashe's summation, "tend to believe in privilege and selection. They seldom extend their ideas to mankind at large. But while their philosophy is not for all, it is not solitary either. Their minds run on exclusive clubs, on coteries and enclosures" (21). And for Lindsay, the Rabelaisian carnivalesque was not an interlude in which the world of authority was turned on its head but, rather, an on-going carnival where a reckless lumpen-aristocracy caroused to its heart's content and dreamed of a conservative, political restoration—a will to power. As Christopher Kendrick argued, Thélème was "an aristocratic utopia ... motivated by class prejudice" (97).

Fantasies of golden age piracy inspired Lindsay to imagine the establishment of a radical-right type of Thélème in Australia in the mid–twentieth century. In Marcus Rediker's terms, Lindsay hailed "the carnivalesque quality of pirate occasions—the eating, the drinking, fiddling, dancing, and merriment," but to a very different end than Rediker theorized (71). Piratic camaraderie, shipboard government, and "the grand Commune" of pirates comprised an elitist-utopian dream of contemporary Australia based on Thélème's "Do What You Will" and Nietzsche's "Beyond Good and Evil." As Lindsay wrote, "A new aristocracy of intelligence and ability is needed for there can be no civilization without some sort of aristocracy which the mob will not abide" (Letter to Smith 1943).

So far, then, this essay has charted how Lindsay confidently hooked up his personal pirate obsession with an authoritarian-aristocratic outlook in his social associations, poetry, and visual art. But the further decisive link he made of piracy, cultural authoritarianism, and market Capital was in an extensive prose work. Lindsay's most significant contribution to a politicized pirate literature was, undoubtedly, "The Story of the Abrolhos"—concerning the wreck of the Dutch ship *Batavia*—published in the popular Australian magazine *The Lone Hand* in 1909. Ironically, Lindsay's re-telling of the story was pirated from the Dutch-Australian writer William Siebenhaar's earlier account, which had translated "the authentic account published at Amsterdam in 1647" ("Story of the Abrolhos" 5; see Siebenhaar "Abrolhos Tragedy"). Siebenhaar denounced Lindsay's theft as the "slang of a modern author," overly pre-occupied with "the part played in the story by the pirates" ("Story of the Abrolhos" 5).

The "Abrolhos" story was a classic "voyage into disaster" narrative. The *Batavia*, sent-off from the Netherlands by the Dutch East India Company in 1628, was a well-provisioned immigrant ship, carrying potential colonist families and a hull of gold and silver for trade in the Spice Islands or wherever it set ashore. In 1629, the *Batavia* was wrecked on a reef off the western coast of continental Australia, and the human remnants of the wreck made their way to the unforgiving Abrolhos islands landfall. The tale of the *Batavia* was a gift for any sensationalist story-teller: an upright maritime enterprise flocked by storms, a ship blown off-course, a mutiny, the struggle to shore, isolation, then murder and the butchery of innocents—including women and children—and grim survival. The *Batavia*'s lawful captain, Pelsaert, recovered a longboat, undertaking an epic voyage, three thousand miles to the Indies then organizing a small rescue fleet. The murderous mutineers were over-powered and brought to justice: broken on the wheel and strangled on gallows.

Lindsay's version of the *Batavia* tragedy had all the drama, color, and gore of the actual history, and was vividly illustrated by his brother Norman. But Lindsay introduced another discursive thread into the narrative, absent from other accounts of the *Batavia*'s fateful journey. Lindsay's "Story of the Abrolhos" made the decisive connection of piracy and emergent maritime capitalism. For Lindsay, the sea-going Dutch Republic represented a high-water mark in the teleological current of capitalist civilization:

> The early part of seventeenth century was the Dutch Renaissance, when their art and commerce reached an importance never since regained.... Dutch merchantmen sailed upon every sea, ransacking the most unfamiliar places for their peculiar treasures. Their energy was indomitable ... ships so richly laden that it was quite in the natural order of things for the Dutch Government to fit out a larger fleet for the further encouragement of enterprise [358].

In Lindsay's revisionist history of the *Batavia* wreck, rampant "ransacking" was elided into respectable "enterprise," and the distinction between licensed trader, privateer, and pirate sunk without trace: "Piracy, to the congenitally sinister and lawless, has always made imaginative appeal, and in the seventeenth century, when there was no policing of the sea, every sailor afloat was a potential buccaneer" (359). As Marx observed of this dynamic phase of early-modern capitalism, "revolutions are not made by laws" (915)—and for once Lindsay would have agreed with the man he called "that disastrous Jew" (Letter to Smith 1934).

Those crucial passages in "The Story of the Abrolhos," effortlessly fusing the figures of the pirate and capitalist, returned Lindsay to *Treasure Island*. In Stevenson's novel, Jim Hawkins, hidden in the famous Apple Barrel, overhears Long John Silver's disquisition on piracy and respectability. Little Jim is surprised to discover that pirates are actually upwardly-mobile "gentlemen of fortune," as Silver imagines himself elevated to high public office: "in Parlyment, and riding in my coach," beyond the reach of "these sea-lawyers in the cabin a-coming home, unlooked for, like the devil at prayers"—the pirate as governor and law-maker, no less (Stevenson 62–64). Likewise, Lindsay's hale, virile Anglo-Saxon pirates had hearts of oak, as solid as the timbers from which their galleons were fashioned. Sometimes they were the loyal yeomen of the Capital ship, but more often its admirals. They were self-made, self-fashioned aristocrats: "gentlemen of fortune," just like the members of the Australian ruling class with whom Lindsay consorted. Indeed, they were the great helmsmen of capitalism's destiny. And that was precisely where Lindsay's life-long piracy narrative was intended to operate: to mediate the idea that rapacious Capital was actually the expression of a kind of historical romance. The men of Capital, his friends, with their decisive, swashbuckling actions, their glamorous treasure hunting, camaraderie, codes of conduct, and devil-may-care attitude to the pitiful common law of little men were to be admired—after all, was not that why "the mob" was captivated by pirates? As his brother Norman reckoned, "Where else is one to find a protagonist antipodal to man the herding animal?" (*My Mask* 148). Pirates, *argumentum ad captandum*.

Especially since the important work of Marcus Rediker, piracy has often been read through the alternative paradigm of ship-board democracy or anarchist collectivism. In this reading, the pirate becomes a revolutionary hero, plundering Capital's coffers and redistributing the booty to "the people," from whom it was stolen in the first place. This line is so pervasive that even a political activist like Tariq Ali borrowed the literary trope of piracy as genuine democracy to underpin his arguments in *Pirates of the Caribbean: Axis of Hope* (2006). Ali's polemic regarding the socialist or Marxist significance of Evo Morales, Hugo Chavez, and the great ancestor Fidel Castro was configured around the image that the trio "determined to rescue the stranded ship *Utopia*, to initiate more egalitarian, redistributive policies and to involve the poor in the political life of their countries" (25). But, as Martin Parker observed, this dangerously romanticized "guerrilla pirate ... an enemy of mercantile capitalism and the imperial state, and a social bandit who is supported by most common people" is not the only story available from the cultural lode of piracy (196).

Like any deeply embedded cultural iconography, piracy and pirates can be troped, or turned, to a variety of ideological ends. As other essays in this collection legitimately contend, the piracy trope can be read and deployed in the service of arguments that range from democratic socialism, anarchist collectivism, through feminism and queer theory, regional and ethnic identity-making, to the vicarious thrills of cinema and video-gaming. As Jim Hawkins found out at the sign of the Spy-glass, "I thought I knew what a buccaneer was like"—a reminder that the pirate is never a singular thing (Stevenson 46). From *Treasure Island* at least—if not before—the image of the pirate as liminal figure can be appropriated or problematized. When pirates are critically caught and eventually brought into the cultural dock, it is not entirely their fault. Their advocates and accusers reconstruct their lives and images, and argue endlessly for their decency or deviance. And Sir Lionel Lindsay's reactionary pirate obsession was a parochial, but provocative, example of how the discourse on piracy as "ship-board democracy" can be confounded or run aground and set on a very different political course.

AUTHOR'S NOTE

All of the pirate poems by Lionel Lindsay quoted here were written c. 1897–1898, published in *The Outpost: An Australian National Newspaper* (Melbourne) in 1900, and reprinted in Lindsay, *Ballad* n.p.

WORKS CITED

Ali, Tariq. *Pirates of the Caribbean: Axis of Hope*. London: Verso, 2006.
Ashe, Geoffrey. *Do What You Will: A History of Anti-Morality*. London: W.H. Allen, 1974.
Bakhtin, Mikhail. *Rabelais and His World*. Hélène Iswolsky (trans.). Bloomington: Indiana University Press, 1984.
Benjamin, Walter. *Illuminations*. Hannah Arendt (ed.), Harry Zohn (trans.). London: Fontana, 1992.
Doyle, Helen. "Bunyip Aristocracy." *The Oxford Companion to Australian History*. Graeme Davison et al. (eds.). Melbourne: Oxford University Press, 1998, 95.
Hetherington, John. *Norman Lindsay: The Embattled Olympian*. Melbourne: Oxford University Press, 1973.
Kendrick, Christopher. *Utopia, Carnival, and Commonwealth in Renaissance England*. Toronto: University of Toronto Press, 2004.
Lindsay, Lionel. *A Ballad of Buccaneering: An Appreciation of the Circumstances Which Influenced the Production of Sir Lionel Lindsay's First Six Etchings, Accompanied by Six of the Artist's Poems from the Same Period*. Robert C. Littlewood (comp.). Melbourne: Jester, 1980.
_____. *Comedy of Life: An Autobiography by Sir Lionel Lindsay 1874–1961*. Sydney: Angus and Robertson, 1967.
_____. *Discobolus and Other Verse*. Melbourne: F.W. Cheshire, 1959.
_____. *Discobolus, Manuscript Drafts: Verse: Juvenilia, 1897–1901; Senilia, 1938_____*. MS. Toowoomba Regional Art Gallery. Lionel Lindsay Gallery and Library Collection MS 2.2a.
_____. Letter to Sydney Ure Smith. 21 Mar. 1934. MS. State Library of New South Wales MLMSS 31.
_____. Letter to Sydney Ure Smith. 15 Apr. 1943. MS. State Library of New South Wales MLMSS 31.
_____. "The Story of the Abrolhos." Norman Lindsay (illus.). *The Lone Hand* (Sydney) 1 Aug. 1909, 357–67.
Lindsay, Lionel, et al. Pirate Oath Signed in Blood by Lionel Lindsay, Norman Lindsay and Ray Parkinson. Feb. 10, 1898. MS. State Library of Victoria MS 9104/3458.
Lindsay, Norman. *My Mask: For What Little I Know of the Man Behind It*. Sydney: Angus and Robertson, 1970.
_____. *Norman Lindsay's Book: No. II*. Sydney: N.S.W. Bookstall, 1915.
Marx, Karl. *Capital: A Critique of Political Economy*. Vol. 1. Ben Fowkes (trans.). Harmondsworth: Penguin/New Left Review, 1990.
McCrae, Hugh. *Story-Book Only*. Sydney: Angus and Robertson, 1948.
Mendelssohn, Joanna. *Lionel Lindsay: An Artist and His Family*. London: Chatto and Windus, 1988.
Menzies, Robert. Letter to Lionel Lindsay. October 13, 1943. MS. State Library of Victoria MS 9104/1601–1602.
_____. "Speech by the Rt. Hon. R.G. Menzies, C.H., Q.C., M.P., at the Opening of the Lionel Lindsay Art Gallery and Library—Toowoomba, April 4, 1959." TS. State Library of Victoria MS 9104/3167–69.
New York Times. "Sir Lionel Lindsay, Australian Artist." May 23, 1961, 39.
Parker, Martin. "Pirates and the Uses of History." Review of *Life Under the Jolly Roger: Reflections on Golden Age Piracy*, by Gabriel Kuhn, and *The Invisible Hook: The Hidden Economics of Pirates*, by Peter T. Leeson. *ephemera: theory & politics in organization* 10.2 (2010): 194–98. http://www.ephemerajournal.org/contribution/pirates-and-uses-history. Accessed on 06/06/2017.
Rabelais, François. *The Histories of Gargantua and Pantagruel*. J.M. Cohen (trans.). Harmondsworth: Penguin, 1955.
Rediker, Marcus. *Villains of All Nations: Atlantic Pirates in the Golden Age*. Boston: Beacon Press, 2004.
Siebenhaar, W. "The Abrolhos Tragedy. Stirring Times in the Seventeenth Century. Australia's First White Residents. The Batavia Castaways. How They Fought and Suffered. One

Hundred and Twenty-Five Massacred." *The Western Mail* (Perth) December 10, 1897, 3–10 http://trove.nla.gov.au/newspaper/article/33147481. Accessed on 10/13/2012.

_____. "The Story of the Abrolhos." Letter to the editor. *The West Australian* (Perth) November 25, 1909, 5. http://trove.nla.gov.au/newspaper/article/26243226. Accessed on 10/13/2012.

Smith, Bernard. "The Fascist Mentality in Australian Art and Criticism." *The Communist Review* (June 1946), 182–84; (July 1946), 215–17.

Stevenson, Robert Louis. *Treasure Island*. Peter Hunt (ed.). Oxford: Oxford University Press, 2011.

PART II: PIRATES IN LITERATURE

Sea-Wolves, Smugglers and Seascapes
Captain Cruel Coppinger and Criminality in Cornwall

JOAN PASSEY

Cornwall, a county lying at the extreme south west of England, surrounded on three sides by water, has a unique relationship with its sea. Historically, Cornwall has been represented as having a higher concentration of maritime disasters—specifically wrecks against its coast. This is explained in various ways throughout history, attributed alternately to the amount of traffic around the coast, the unpredictable waters, the rocks lying just beneath the surface along many parts of the coast, and occasionally, to the savage character of the Cornish themselves. There is a long history of the Cornish people being described in barbaric, criminal, and monstrous terms. Cornwall featured heavily in Gothic fiction throughout the nineteenth century, from Bram Stoker's *The Jewel of the Seven Stars* (1903) to Thomas Hardy's *A Pair of Blue Eyes* (1873) to Arthur Conan Doyle's "The Adventures of the Devil's Foot" (1910). Many noted Victorian celebrities visited the area and documented its barren landscape, uncivilized populace, and air of mysticism, primitivism, and magic, including Alfred, Lord Tennyson, Vernon Lee, and George Eliot. Periodicals, novels, poems, and short stories abound with narratives taking Cornwall's dangerous coasts and violent seas as inspiration. Cornwall, jutting out into the Atlantic, is the last slither of land until the unwary seaman hits the Americas, and such a vast swathe of ocean was a terrifying concept for many. Literature, periodicals, and legends across the long nineteenth century cemented the position of the Land's End as seemingly the end of the world itself—or at least, the end of the known world.

Cornwall's unique geographical position, as well as its unique culture, history, politics, language, traditions, and folklore, have rendered it different from the rest of England. While a county of the nation, Cornwall has historically seen itself as a distinct nation, rather than a region, and this has been defined and defended in different ways across the centuries. The Cornish are known in the popular imagination in different periods as being a rebellious, defensive people, and are often understood as foreign or other. Part of this "otherness" is deeply entwined with Cornwall's long maritime history. Cornwall has access to the world, and the world has access to Cornwall, in a different way than may be understood in other parts of the country, especially the relatively land-locked hub of London. Cornwall's international trade dates to antiquity due to its significant ore deposits and a history and reputation of advanced mining technologies. Legend states that the tin trader Joseph of Arimathea brought the child Christ to Cornwall on a quest for the finest tin. Other legends state that Cornwall and the Scilly Isles are the Cassiteride islands visited by the Phoenicians, as documented by Herodotus, and further embroiling the Cornish into an ancient history of piracy. Cornwall's exposure, as well as its rich minerality, made it an attractive locale for traders, and Cornwall has frequently and scornfully been viewed as more "globalized" than other parts of England. But this significant trade and maritime traffic in the area, combined with the rugged coastline, frequently provided opportunities for criminality. Despite its mineral riches and advanced industry, Cornwall has, at many points throughout history, been an incredibly deprived and poverty-stricken area. Famine, economic deprecation, and starvation were frequently accompanied by acts of violent desperation. More than that, the image of the Cornish as savages—violent animals, subhuman, even inhuman—was supported by legends of pillaging, wrecking, theft, smuggling, and piracy along the Cornish coast (Pearce; Appleby 202).

This essay explores the legends of the Cornish as purveyors of maritime criminality and their significance in the popular cultural imagination, especially in the nineteenth century, as a means of ascertaining the perception of this othered populace, and justifications for their continued marginalization. It explores the accusations of criminality cast towards the Cornish people and questions their legitimacy, and their basis in and perpetuation through popular legend and literature. Specifically, this essay will focus on the legend of Captain Cruel Coppinger, smuggler, pirate, and wrecker, as a case study demonstrating the circulation of myths of Cornish criminality—especially wrecking—in Gothic fiction and antiquarian accounts.

Wrecking is defined in different ways throughout its many iterations in history. For some, wrecking simply refers to the practice of foraging cargo from wrecks. For others, the words "wrecking" and "wreckers" have different, more active, and more sinister connotations, describing the act, and the people who commit the act, of intentionally trying to lure wrecks onto shore. One way in which to attempt this was to hold a lantern while riding a horse or ass along the cliffs on a stormy or foggy night. The poor conditions combined with the light bobbing away in the distance created the impression of the ship on the horizon, and thus the illusion that only safe, open, navigable waters lay ahead. This method is sensationalized in Sabine Baring-Gould's novel *In the Roar of the Sea* (1891), which provides a fictionalized account of the folk anti-hero Captain Cruel Coppinger, one of the most famed wreckers, smugglers, and pirates in South West legend.

There was significant debate throughout the eighteenth and nineteenth centuries as to whether intentional wrecking ever actually happened in Cornwall, or whether the legends are a product and consequence of the continued representation of the Cornish as barbarians. Sabine Baring-Gould, according to a 1908 article in *The Observer*, claims that "Cornwall has produced fewer rascals 'than almost any other county,' but then he expressly excludes wrecking and smuggling from the category of rascality. That is rather like making perjury a crime except when committed in the witness box" (4). The Reverend Hawker suggests that intentional wrecking occurred, though many of his fabulous accounts are to be doubted, as the second section of this essay will demonstrate. Robert Hunt was of the opinion that intentional wrecking was a historical practice, frowned upon by Victorian Cornishmen. These various debates encapsulate issues of authenticity, storytelling, and morality, as well as the more general interaction between fact and fiction, folklore and novelizations, that preoccupy Victorian thought. More specifically, these debates attempt to consider and account for disparities in the representation of the Cornish, and the role that fictionalization and imagination plays in the reception of a populace of regional peoples.

One author who contributed significantly to the reworking of Cornwall in the Victorian imagination was the Reverend Robert Stephen Hawker, a poet, writer, folklorist, clergyman, antiquarian, and eccentric. Throughout his career, Hawker confronted the dreadful reality of wrecking on the Cornish and North Devonshire coast, and his own garden became a burial ground for anonymous wreck victims. Hawker's writings on Cornwall, the Cornish people, and Cornish tragedy have ingratiated themselves into the popular imagination and popular fiction of the period, and Simon Trezise states Hawker as an influence on Walter White, Cyrus Redding, Wilkie Collins, Sabine Baring-Gould, and even Alfred, Lord Tennyson (56–58).

One of Hawker's greatest contributions to Cornish culture is the folk anti-hero Captain Cruel Coppinger, a legendary smuggler, wrecker, and pirate. Hawker's Coppinger is presumably based upon Daniel Herbert Coppinger of Hartland parish church, for whom there exists a marriage license signed in 1793 (Trezise 57–58). In 1802 there are records declaring his bankruptcy, but there is little other information pertaining to his life or fate. A letter from Hawker to his brother-in-law in 1866 asks "[d]o you remember bold Coppinger the Marsland Pirate? He died 87 years ago. I am collecting material for his life for *All the Year Round*. If you know any anecdotes of him or Dinah his wife will you let me know" (Trezise 57–58). Hawker writes to his brother-in-law again, asking "hadn't you an Aunt called Coppinger?," with his eventual recollection (or reinvention) of the events of Coppinger published in *All the Year Round* in December 1866.

In Hawker's 1866 tale Coppinger arrives on the north coast of Cornwall in a "terrific hurricane," while watchers for the wreck peered from the shore—"daring gleaners of the harvest of the sea" (537). Then, "[a]s suddenly as if a phantom ship had loomed in the distance, a strange vessel of foreign rig was discovered in fierce struggle with the waves," associating the foreign with the monstrous, the fearful, and the spectral (537). The wrecks against the tide, the shipmen terrified, but there is one "of herculean height and mould," who sheds his garments and throws himself overboard, swimming through the tumultuous waves (537). "With stalwart arm and powerful chest" he "rode manfully from billow to billow, until, with a bound, he stood at last upright upon the sand, a fine stately semblance of one of the old Vikings of the northern seas" Coppinger's strength and build renders him not only unnatural, but a figure of the ancient past re-emerging into the present day, significantly via the sea as vessel or communion of that past. Coppinger connotes the ancientness of Hercules and the Vikings, and in doing so serves as a figure of invasion and plunder, his foreignness and imperial muscularity fixing him as a figure of reverse colonization (537). The sea serves as a passage not just through space, but through time.

Coppinger then steals a cloak, a horse, and a girl called Dinah before the very eyes of the wreck watchers, thieving from the famous thieves. He speaks some "foreign language," and announces himself specifically as "Coppinger, a Dane" (537). Coppinger the Dane runs rampant through Cornwall, forcing Dinah to marrying him, claiming her father's farm, terrifying the local people, and quickly establishing a crew of smugglers and pirates. He claims the landscape as his territory, as the smuggling paths become "Coppinger's tracks" and he stores his wears in "Coppinger's Caves" (538). Coppinger essentially colonizes North Cornwall, and is continually associated with both the sea and the foreign, as he appeared before his lawyer with "dollars, ducats, dubloons and pistoles, guineas—the coinage of every foreign country with a seaboard" (538). Throughout, Hawker's focus is on the violence of Coppinger as a result of his otherness, with contact with that otherness resulting from global trade and maritime movement.

A later interpretation by Sabine Baring-Gould instead focuses on a romantic vision of Coppinger. Sabine Baring-Gould was a Devonshire antiquarian, collector of Cornish ballads and curiosities, as well as an Anglican priest and influential novelist, though he is most famous for writing the hymn "Onward, Christian Soldiers." Baring-Gould found similarity between himself and Hawker, both being eclectic scholars, priests, lovers of Cornwall, and writers of Gothic fiction. Baring-Gould found expression for his interest in Hawker through penning the biography *The Vicar of Morwenstow, being a life of Robert Stephen Hawker*, published in 1876. However, the work came under criticism by later biographers. C.E. Byles in a preface to a new edition of Hawker's life and letters in 1906 says that Baring-Gould's "literary debts are accorded very scanty acknowledgment," that the writer disregarded the wishes of the state and Mrs. Hawker, and borrowed largely from Hawker's published works without referencing his source (x). Byles takes particular umbrage with Baring-Gould's retelling of Hawker's tale of Coppinger in the biography, stating and it is "with some abbreviation, an almost word-for-word transcript from Hawker's 'Footprints,' with-out any inverted commas, or change of type, a footnote at the end of several pages being the only indication of borrowing. Readers unacquainted with 'Footprints' might reasonably suppose that Baring-Gould has told the story in his own words" (Byles, x). Yet the retelling in *The Vicar of Morwenstow* is not Baring-Gould's only retelling of Captain Coppinger, as he becomes the antihero of the later Gothic novel, *In the Roar of the Sea* (1891). In Baring-Gould's novel Coppinger comes ashore, and his reign of terror is only interrupted when he falls in love with the beautiful orphan Judith Trevisa. Judith fights to preserve her virtue, avoid Coppinger, and protect her twin brother, and Coppinger is tortured by his love for her. The novel describes the unique relationship the Cornish had with "The Roar of the Sea" and with wrecking in particular, as well as other aspects of Cornish particularism and criminality. The novel is littered with sensational scenes, from Coppinger dashing a puppy against a cliff to his eventual end, burning to death in his own cottage.

An early review of *In the Roar of the Sea* identifies Baring-Gould's imaginative invocation of Coppinger as one that situates Hawker's folk hero firmly in the Gothic tradition. George Saintsbury, reviewing for *The Academy* on June 25, 1892, states that

> [a]n "ugly" critic (if critics could ever be ugly) might, indeed, suggest that the hero of *In the Roar of the Sea*, "Cruel," or "Captain Coppinger," is only Mr. Rochester transformed from an inland squire to a Cornish smuggler, and made a little more robustious still. But Judith Trevisa is not much like Jane Eyre, and Oliver Menaida, the fortunate rival of Mr. Rochester—we mean Captain Coppinger—is a tall man of his hands and deserves his victory [610].

Sainstbury says that the novel contains "sensations without end" and that "[i]t seems curmudgeonly to quarrel with such a bountiful allowance of provender; and yet we are bound to say that Mr. Baring-Gould seems to us to have failed again, as he has constantly failed since *Mehalah* (where he succeeded), in adding one to the population of the novel world which lives and will live" (610). Perhaps Baring-Gould attempted to imbue his novel with the endurance of folklore by feeding from and into that tradition, and while *In the Roar of the Sea* was not reviewed as favorably as *Mehalah*, it still divided critics. A review in *The Speaker: The Liberal Review* from the 21st May 1892 states that "*In the Roar of the Sea* is without doubt one of the best novels that Mr. Baring-Gould has yet given us," and that this is, in part, a result of his "wild and romantic scenes" and "his strange, poetical melancholy," lending to the sense that "[i]t hardly seems to him that he has met [his characters] in a book, but rather that he has lived among them on the coast of Cornwall in the beginning of the present century" (629). It is Baring-Gould's invocation of folklore and his detailed, antiquarian approach to the curiosities of Cornwall that lead this reviewer to favor his work, a reviewer who admits that Cruel Coppinger is "a strong character, of a kind that inevitably wears a slouched hat and rides a black mare" (629).

Baring-Gould's synthesis of distinctly Gothic imagery with a folkloric antihero simultaneously embeds the Gothic into a longer tradition while breathing life into folklore for a contemporary, popular audience. This very much follows the pattern of the representation of pirates and piracy throughout the Victorian period. Their representation was semi-mythological, though vindicated with very real tales of horrors from around the world's coasts. Pirates were simultaneously a barbaric threat, and a sensationalized legend, providing fuel for penny dreadfuls, urban legends, and chap books throughout the period. Captain Coppinger, his ambiguity, his terse history, and his continued representation as real and unreal, are emblematic of the construction of the almost inhuman, barbarous, mythical pirate in the Victorian period.

The heritage of Cruel Coppinger is distinctly more ambiguous in Baring-Gould's novel than in Hawker's initial invocation:

> as I have said, I know nothing. I do not know whence he comes. Some say he is a Dane, some that he is an Irishman. I cannot tell, I know nothing, but I think his intonation is Irish, and I have heard that there is a family of that name in Ireland. But this is all guesswork. One thing I do know, he speaks French like a native. Then, as to his character, I believe him to be a man of ungovernable temper, who, when his blood is roused will stick at nothing. I think him a man of very few scruples. But he has done liberal things—he is open-handed, that all say. A hard liver, and with a rough tongue, and yet with some of the polish of a gentleman; a man with the passions of a devil, but not without in him some sparks of divine light. That is what I think him to be. And if you ask me further, whether I think him a man calculated to make you happy—I say decidedly that he is not. Rarely before in his life had Mr. Menaida [Uncle Zachie] spoken with such decision [157].

The irony here lays in Zachie not speaking with much decision at all, excepting his final conclusion.

Coppinger is portrayed as a shifting, amorphous, folkloric figure who adapts to the demands of the period, text, or locale. Baring-Gould here is addressing the dynamic, fluid nature of the folk hero and his numerous incarnations within his own rewriting. The reference to the Irish expresses an anxiety surrounding Celts in the Victorian period, as the Irish are so frequently represented as a migrating population who are "subaltern subjects, problematized, criminalized, suffering from various forms of discrimination" (Peach). The issues surrounding the Irish are issues surrounding "integration and assimilation," concerns familiar to the Cornish, who in this period are emigrating outwards, and are becoming an invaded people, rejecting assimilation with the English. The reference to the "gentleman" suggests the breakdown of class boundaries as a result of increased topographical and social mobility in the nineteenth century, a mobility emblematized by the newly accessible county. Coppinger is no longer purely Danish, alluding to the long and contested history between the Cornish and Danes (and thus suggesting ancientness, isolation, and conflict), but has become a generalized or homogenized "foreigner." This suggests a dissolution of identity in a globalized landscape, and a blanket fear of the generically "other" regardless of origin. Baring-Gould is capitalizing on the fluidity of the folkloric to adapt Hawker's early nineteenth-century Coppinger for a late nineteenth-century audience, as the ambiguous barbarousness of the smuggler becomes a vessel for contemporary anxieties.

Despite this nebulous national identity, unlike Hawker's Coppinger, Baring-Gould's is given a Christian name—Curll. While the name could be a play on "Cruel," the name given by Hawker, it could also be a literary reference to eighteenth-century English bookseller and publisher Edmund Curll (1675–1747). In the mid–eighteenth century Curll's name became synonymous with literary piracy, forgery, and unscrupulous publication and publicity. Curll, through repeated attacks by and on Alexander Pope, became associated with mercenary behavior, pornography, and obscenity. Sabine Baring-Gould as a bibliophile, historian, and antiquarian was doubtless familiar with Pope's relationship with Curll, and in using the name could be associating literary piracy with piracy on the high seas. Edmund Curll was born in the West Country, and there is a possibility that Sabine Baring-Gould is embedding his narrative in a longer West Country literary tradition to emphasize the scandalous, barbarous nature of Coppinger, while also alluding to the famed literary forgeries of Hawker, and the frequent accusations of theft and forgery cast upon his own person by supporters of Hawker. By aligning literary with maritime piracy, Baring-Gould is associating the fluidity of literature with the fluidity of the sea, while relating the moral ambiguity and uncertainties surrounding both practices—specifically emphasized within his novel as an ethical debate on the wrecking practices of a deprived population.

A further distinction between Hawker's Coppinger and Baring-Gould's is the nature of their endings. Hawker's Coppinger disappears off on his phantom ship of "foreign rig," never to be seen again. Margaret Ann Courtney's 1886 folkloric collection argues that Coppinger died, old, destitute, weak, and alone (100). The end of Baring-Gould's Coppinger is a highly-dramatized culmination befitting a novel of "sensations without end." While the supernatural edge of Hawker's Coppinger is heightened by his mysterious exit, denying the eternal folkloric hero human mortality, and suggesting his endurance through storytelling, Baring-Gould's Coppinger dies in the midst of a spectacle entrenched in literary history by burning to death in his own home, the significantly named Othello cottage:

> on the down, nestled against a wall that had once enclosed a garden, but was now ruinous, stood a cottage. It was built of wreck-timber, thatched with heather and bracken, and with stones laid on the thatching, which was bound with ropes, as protection against the wind. A quaint, small house, with little windows under the low eaves; one story high, the window-frames painted white; the glass frosted with salt blown from the sea, so that it was impossible to look through the small panes, and discover what was within. The door had a gable over it, and the centre of the gable was occupied by a figure-head of Othello. The Moor of Venice was black and well battered by storm, so that the paint was washed and bitten off him [21].

The allusion to Othello forewarns the reader of tragedy to come. With Coppinger cast as the foreign, swarthy, war mongering, seafaring Moor, and Judith as the doomed, waifish Desdemona. By referencing Othello, Baring-Gould is alluding to tragedy, revenge, obsessive desire, lust, gore, conflict, the threat of the foreigner, the threat of the dissolution of identity, the dissolution of the institution of marriage, and to maritime life.

Upon being reunited with Desdemona, Othello states that "[i]f after every tempest come such calms, / May the winds blow till they have wakened death, / And let the laboring bark climb hills of seas / Olympus-high, and duck again as low / As hell's from heaven!" (II.ix 170–175). In *In the Roar of the Sea*, however, the Moor of Venice is not calmed by the tempest, but "black and well battered by storm," suggesting the tragic irony of Othello's fate and foreshadowing Coppinger's fire-blackened body. The cottage itself serves the function of a Gothic container, the same as a ship, mansion, or castle; a claustrophobic, enclosed, imprisoning, dangerous space, drawn alike to a ship with the wrecked timber, a transformative product of disaster, aligned closer with the sea than land, much like Coppinger himself. This is an example of Sabine Baring-Gould lending Coppinger a concrete corporeality beyond the supernatural spectrality suggested by Hawker. Hawker labors to emphasize the phantom nature of the ship to emphasize its transgressive, liminal qualities, yet Baring-Gould renders Coppinger a flesh and blood man with a ship and house of timbers, making Coppinger's barbaric, savage behavior not the actions of a supernatural monster, but the actions of a man. This acts as a criticism of romanticization as a means of dislocating the barbarian from his culture of production, and thus obscuring the horrific reality of marginalized populaces.

While critics like Cryle and Trezise complain that Baring-Gould stole the figure of Coppinger from Hawker, it becomes apparent that Hawker's Coppinger was clearly inspired by a significantly longer, older literary and folkloric tradition in Cornwall enriched by anxieties surrounding the sea, seafaring, wrecking, and piracy. This line of causation rejects a single authoritative version of Coppinger, and instead identifies Coppinger as a fluid product of communal exchange, much like the image of the pirate more generally in popular culture.

The most pertinent example of an older tradition, with the most parallels to motifs of the tale of Coppinger, is the Cornish legend of the death ship, documented by Robert Hunt in *Popular Romances of the West of England* in 1865, and William Bottrell in *Traditions and Hearthside Stories of West Cornwall*, vol. 2 in 1873. Hunt's version describes a man "so monstrously wicked that even the pirates would no longer endure him," so that, instead of arriving in Cornwall on his own ship, he is thrown off a different pirate ship in irons and left to scramble to the shore (137). Like Coppinger, however, he "lived by a system of wrecking, pursued with unheard-of cruelties and cunning" (138). The ultimate horror of the pirate of the death ship is not his life, though Hunt's correspondent says his doings are "too frightful to tell," but his death— though, "one can't say he died; because he was taken off bodily" (138). This version of the end of Coppinger combines elements of the origins of Hawker's story and Courtney's retelling (that of Coppinger dying old and destitute), and elements of Hawker's later rewriting (that of Coppinger disappearing aboard his phantom ship).

Looking out to sea the local inhabitants see "a black, heavy, square-rigged ship, with all her sails set, coming in against wind and tide, and not a hand to be seen on board. The sky became black as night around the ship, and as she came under the cliff—and she came so close that the top of the masts could scarcely be perceived—the darkness resolved itself into a lurid storm-cloud" (361). The ship appears to be coming for the pirate, dying in agony in his cottage. The parson tries to expel the devil from the room, but

> all this time the room appeared as if filled with the sea, with the waves surging violently to and fro, and one could hear the breakers roaring, as if standing on the edge of the cliff in a storm. At last there was a fearful crash of thunder, and a blaze of the intensest lightning. The house appeared on fire, and the ground shook, as if with an earthquake. All rushed in terror from the house, leaving the dying man to his fate [139].

The house appearing on fire lends itself to Sabine Baring-Gould's ultimate conclusion for Curll Coppinger. The storm serves to simultaneously illuminate and obscure, a necessary process for the generation of gothic terror, as the lightning provides brief illumination and the sea drowns out noise, creating a space in which the senses are compromised and overwhelmed, and a distance between perception and reality that enables the perpetuation of superstition. The liminal space between fact and fiction is represented by Hunt's black phantom ship, sailing over land to claim the soul of the pirate in the midst of a fearful storm. This is an exaggeration of the wreck breaching the space between land and sea, and thus threatening the borders and boundaries of a people struggling to maintain their delineated sense of self amidst a dilution of identity generated by globalization and deindustrialization. The local people, terrified by this ultimate, spectral threat, build the dead man a hasty coffin, only for a black pig to inexplicably join their funeral procession, and the coffin to be burnt by lightning and whisked away in a "whirlwind" (363).

The image of the wicked being denied rest is graphically rendered, and the storm and whirlwind endure in Hawker's retelling 1866 of the ballad of Coppinger:

> Will you hear of the bold, brave Coppinger?
> How he came of a foreign kind?
> He was brought to us by the salt-water,
> He'll be carried away by the wind
> For thus old wives croon and sing,
> And so the proverbs say,
> That whatsoever the wild waves bring
> The winds will bear away [*Footprints* 165].

Hunt's collection also includes "The Spectre Ship of Porthcurno." While featuring a death ship, the servants aboard of "foreign and forbidding aspect" only come to land when one of them dies and requires burial (160). The local people agree to do so, only for the living servant and ship to disappear. Significant similarities to the previous death ship narrative include the fact that the strange pirate is a foreigner, "[n]o crew was ever seen," and that the apparition always appeared "when the storm was loudest" (161). The continual absence of crew aboard the phantom ship responds to contemporary anxieties surrounding the devaluing of labor and craft, and the disconnect of humanity from advancing maritime technologies. The image of the seafaring foreigner continually asserts the fear of reverse colonization, and reference to the storm suggests the severity of life on the Cornish coast, and the very real horrors caused by storms at sea.

Instead of black pigs, however, the Porthcurno pirate's grave is accompanied by dogs. The horror associated with dogs and the corpses of sailors near the Land's End could be associated with the myth of Pistil or Pistol Meadow, and the 1721 wreck of the Royal Anne Galley. Wilkie Collins references this legend, whereby stray dogs descend upon the washed-up corpses of the victims of the wreck, and so horrified were the locals who witnessed such carnage that no one has kept a dog as a pet at the Lizard Point since (105). Thus, the traditional association between the dogs of hell is infused with local color, as the ownership of dogs is directly associated with monstrous eating, dehumanization, and washed up bodies.

William Bottrell's later death ship includes "a dark strange man ... put ashore by a pirate ship" who goes on to practice active wrecking (247). As the wicked man lays on his death bed, "the chamber seemed—by the sound—to be filled with the sea splashing around the bed; waves were heard as if surging and breaking against the house, though it was a good bit inland" (248). The local people hear a hollow voice call "'[t]he hour is come but the man is not come,'" "as if coming from the sea" (248). Again, a storm sends a phantom ship inland to claim the soul of the wicked man, and a black pig and a lightning storm accompany his funeral, though Bottrell makes sure to emphasize that "nothing of the coffin but its handles and a few nails" remained, "for it had been set on fire, and all else consumed, by the lightning," again evocative of Curll's end in flame at his cottage (249). Bottrell's footnote states that "[i]t does not appear what business the black pig had in the funeral procession; such is the way, however, in which the story is always told" (249). The folkloric black pig as warning of death recurs in Irish mythology, suggesting a shared Celtic oral heritage, and again associating Coppinger with Irishness.

Both Bottrell and Hunt's tales are laden with Gothic imagery—the phantom ship, wicked foreign pirates, wrecking, storms and tempests, lightning strikes, the devil taking the form of the fly, death, funerals, and exorcisms, though the horror of each is dependent on the transgression of the sea into the death chamber, and the ship across land. The physical laws of nature are violated, land becomes sea, and the phantom ship mounts the coastline as a horrific inflection of the wrecks the pirate caused. This reflects a state of liminality rooted in nineteenth-century anxieties surrounding the delineation and protection of national and regional borders and boundaries, and ultimately the liminal status of the Cornish as simultaneously English and not-English, of the land and of the sea, as technologically advanced as the marine technology of modernity while as haunted, ancient and superstitious as the image of the phantom ship. Vitally, in both narratives, the sea communicates with the local people, transmitting or broadcasting a warning, given sentient voice, and cementing a unique relationship between the Cornish and the sea. The phantom ship is the embodiment of the sea as simultaneously a natural and supernatural force, suggesting the complex relationship between the seascape and coastal people. The sea is a functional surface used for fishing, trade, and travel, yet it is also unpredictable, tumultuous, and dangerous, embodying the practical necessities of modernity and the haunting terror of ancient superstition.

The legend of Captain Cruel Coppinger takes another form in the legend of the pirate of Tregeseal. The two tales differ only in name, and feature a dastardly, foreign pirate-wrecker coming to the coast of Cornwall on a "mystery vessel" and pursuing "a life of monstrous crime" (Norris 34). Other versions involve the pirate of Tregeseal being left on the coast by his own companions, bound up in irons (Burton 147). In many versions, the legend even culminates in the same way as the legend of The Wrecker and the Death Ship, where he dies during a thunderstorm and the superstitious locals are forced to perform a hasty funeral (Vulliamy 24).

The fiction and folklore of Coppinger is blurred into the reality of the man even further by 1909 in an article entitled "Cornish Wrecking" in *The English Illustrated Magazine*, which tries to illuminate the reality of wrecking practices and free the Cornish from libel (489–92). Despite the author having an acute awareness of, and their entire argument depending upon, the myths and legends surrounding wrecking, and how these fictional accounts feed into further fictionalizations and become absorbed into the popular understanding of the county, it is without a hint of irony they refer to the figure of Captain Coppinger as a real-life man. The author quotes the saying "save a stranger from the sea / And he'll turn your enemy," a phrase they say "owes its origin to the Cruel Coppinger referred to by Mr. Lock Szyima, a man who was rescued from a wreck, and who, in the years that followed, led a life of crime and bloodshed, and treated those to whom he owned his life and all who had befriended him with the most pitiless cruelty. Therefore, the base ingratitude of Coppinger passed into a byword" (491). Despite continuously criticizing the warping of Cornish history into barbarous shapes, the author perpetuates the myth of Coppinger, even using Coppinger as justification for the county's unwelcoming ways. Through a vehicle of an article claiming legitimacy and fighting for authenticity, the folkloric Coppinger is further cemented into Cornish culture, continually blurring the line between the reality of Cornwall and its myths and legends.

The survival, adaptation, and circulation of the figure of Cruel Coppinger, and the image of the shipwreck, through folklore and gothic fiction throughout the nineteenth century, and into the twentieth, is emblematic of the popularity of Cornish myth and legend in the nineteenth century, the barbarous positioning of Cornwall in the popular imagination in the period, and how gothic fiction absorbs older tales to reflect contemporary concerns. It is a symptom of concerns surrounding the maritime and the role of the maritime in the construction of national, regional, and global identity in the period, and the way the sea can be both bountiful and dangerous.

WORKS CITED

Appleby, John C. *Women and English Piracy, 1640–1720: Partners and Victims of Crime.* Suffolk: Boydell & Brewer, 2015.
Baring-Gould, Sabine. *In the Roar of the Sea.* London: Methuen & Co, 1892.
Bottrell, William. *Traditions and Hearthside Stories of West Cornwall.* Penzance: Beare and Son, 1873.
Burton, Samuel Holroyd. *The Coasts of Cornwall.* London: Werner Laurie, 1955.
Collins, Wilkie. *Rambles Beyond Railways: Or, Notes on Cornwall Taken Afoot.* London: R. Bentley, 1865.
"Cornish Wrecking." *The English Illustrated Magazine,* August 1909, 489–92.
Courtney, Margaret Ann. *Cornish Feasts and Folk-Lore.* Penzance: Beare and Son, 1890.
"Fiction." *Speaker: The Liberal Review,* May 21, 1892, 629.
Hawker, Robert Stephen. "Cruel Coppinger." *All the Year Round,* December 15, 1886, 537–40.
Hawker, R.S. *The Life and Letters of R.S. Hawker.* C.E. Byles (ed.). London: The Bodley Head, 1906.
Hunt, Robert. *Popular Romances of the West of England, or, The Drolls, Traditions, and Superstitions of Old Cornwall.* London: John Camden Hotten, 1865.
"Lesser Lights in Cornwall." *The Observer,* November 08, 1908, 4.
Norris, Gerald. *West Country Rogues and Outlaws.* Devon: Devon Books, 1986.
Peach, Alexander. "Book Review: The Irish in Victorian Britain: The Local Dimension by Roger Swift and Sheridan Gilley." *History in Focus: The Victorian Era,* May 2000. https://www.history.ac.uk/ihr/Focus/Victorians/peach.html. Accessed on 08/27/2017.
Pearce, Cathryn J. *Cornish Wrecking, 1700–1860: Reality and Popular Myth.* Suffolk: Boydell & Brewer, 2010.
Saintsbury, George. "New Novels." *The Academy,* June 25, 1892. British Periodicals.
Trezise, Simon. *The West Country as Literary Invention: Putting Fiction in Its Place.* Exeter: University of Exeter Press, 2000.
Vulliamy, Colwyn Edward. *Unknown Cornwall.* London: John Lane, 1925.

Piratical Identity, Antarctic Solitude and Stolen Treasure in *The Frozen Pirate*

MINKE JONK

William Clark Russell's 1887 two-part novel *The Frozen Pirate* is a curious mix of Victorian romance and maritime supernatural tale. It contains what is possibly the first fictional representation of cryonics (Leane 213), and Russell's sublime descriptions of the Antarctic landscape are both vivid and horrifying. It is also a novel that takes an ambiguous stance towards pirates and piracy. It presents the frozen pirate, Jules Tassard, as an evil figure literally and figuratively beyond the edges of society. On the other hand, the novel fails to notice its English protagonist Paul Rodney's acts of piracy. After his own ship is wrecked miles off Cape Horn, Rodney comes upon an old schooner frozen fast into an ice island. The ship, the *Boca del Dragon*, turns out to be a pirate ship containing vast amounts of piratical treasure. Rodney quickly realizes he would be set up for life if he were able to keep the treasure for himself. This means not only that he prefers not to share the treasure with Tassard, but also, after Tassard slips back into his frozen sleep, that Rodney needs to avoid the authorities upon his return to England. This conscious evasion of the law seems indistinct from piracy, as an "act of depredation, committed for private ends" against someone else's property on board a ship on the high seas, but the novel never names it as such.[1]

Rodney's character is presented in sharp contrast with that of the frozen pirate Tassard, whose scarred face, "with a singular diabolical expression of leering malice" reveal his savage character (Russell 88). The correspondence between his explicitly evil appearance and his placement beyond the edges of society is placed in contrast with Rodney's schemes on the south coast of England, which are never called piratical. At the same time, however, *The*

Frozen Pirate is acutely aware of the irony of its own unwillingness to name Rodney a pirate. This essay will consider the solitude of the Antarctic setting and the ways in which it resonates with descriptions of its occupant. In naming Tassard pirate, the narrative others him, and by exiling him in the desolate Antarctic reinforces the sense that he is an arcane relic who no longer has a place in society. It will then consider the characterization of Rodney and the implications of, in Hans Turley's phrase, the "heroicization of [the protagonist's] criminality" (205). The following reading will draw out the implications of the novel's confusing representation of the piratical figure.

Elizabeth Leane, in her 2009 "The Land That Time Forgot: Fictions in Antarctic Temporality," argues that Antarctica is "a place with its own distinct temporality" (200). Time stretches and narrows in Antarctica due to the simultaneous impossibility and vital necessity of accurate timekeeping in this place that has no time zone of itself. This strange temporality in fiction creates an atmosphere bordering on the supernatural, of uncanny horror and otherness. In *The Frozen Pirate*, the Antarctic setting is described as horrifyingly featureless and awe-inspiring. Andrew Nash suggests that "Rodney's descriptions of the blurred land and seascapes establish a mood that portends the supernatural events that follow. His narrative is charged with references to superstition and the supernatural. He sees "heads and bodies of monsters and giants in the cliff's face and imagines 'the souls of seamen drowned in these seas' flocking to the ice and haunting it" (Nash 95). Rodney asserts that "you cannot conceive how shocking to me was the appearance of that great gleaming length of white desolation. On the deck of a stout ship sailing safely past it I should have found the scene magnificent, I doubt not" (Russell 45). The naturally spectral Antarctic landscape creates an uncanny atmosphere saturated with superstition.

The maritime space around the Antarctic, remarkably bleak and featureless apart from floating icebergs, is separate and isolated and subverts the idea of the pirate as a communal figure. It is a far cry from the more typical piratical communities in the Caribbean: Tortuga and Port Royal are mentioned in *The Frozen Pirate* but are only distant memories, far out of Tassard and Rodney's reach in the Antarctic Ocean. The timing and setting of the novel are crucial here. *The Frozen Pirate* is set firmly in 1801. The *Boca del Dragon* has been encased in the ice for forty-eight years. That means Tassard and his fellow frozen pirates undertook their piratical exploits in the early 1750s. This is *after* what Marcus Rediker has called the "golden age" of piracy, which he places between 1650 and 1730 (8).[2] The name *Boca del Dragon* evokes the series of straits of the similar name, Bocas del Dragón, that separate Trinidad and Tobago from the Venezuelan mainland, and conjures up that much more familiar pirate territory: the Caribbean. Given that Anglo-American and European piracy was on the decline from the beginning of the eighteenth century, it is perhaps not a coincidence that the *Boca del Dragon*, such a late pirate, is found at the Antarctic circle rather than in the Caribbean heart of piracy. The Antarctic setting embodies the literary marginalization of the pirate as a figure now from the past.

The Antarctic is also a place "that appears to offer direct access to the past, its ice acting as a kind of archive of previous ages" (Leane 201). In *The Frozen Pirate*, the landscape literally contains the past. The ice island, floating a few hundred miles off the Antarctic coast, has preserved an entire mid-eighteenth-century ship, her stores, treasures, and occupants perfectly, creating a capsule which enables Rodney to temporarily travel back in time. The frequent references to timekeeping contrast starkly with the apparent unchanging nature of the desolate frozen island—yet the awareness that the island, which is slowly moving northwards, will melt, creates urgency in Rodney's attempts to clear the frozen vessel from the icy mass to regain mastery of the ship's course. Time simultaneously stretches indefinitely and is also running out. More importantly, perhaps, this race against time, and race to find time, reflects the eponymous frozen pirate's fate, whose suspended animation supernaturally lengthens his life, only for him to age quickly when he unfreezes.

Once Rodney's own ship, the *Laughing Mary*, has sunk and he is the sole survivor, he loses track of time, only registering the number of days he drifts around on his small boat. Rodney's first reaction to seeing the island of ice is one of disbelief: "It cannot be ice! 'tis too mighty a barrier. Surely no single iceberg ever reached to the prodigious proportions of that coast. And it cannot be an assemblage of bergs, for there is no break—it is leagues of solid conformation" (Russell 42). Rodney's failure to grasp the truth of what he is seeing suggests Rodney experiences the sublime, in the Burkean sense of being literally and figuratively "beyond our sight" (Glenn 166). The sublime, the invocation of pleasurable terror at the sight of overwhelming nature, pervades Russell's fiction, notes Nash, who argues that the author moves the sublime onto the ship for a first-hand experience of the beauty and terror of the ocean: "his elaborate evocation of the colours and movements of ocean panorama (which were often likened to [J.M.W.] Turner's paintings) were conducted from on board ship" (8). In *The Frozen Pirate*, Russell moves the experience of the sublime from the ship to the icy landscape of Antarctica and, ultimately, onto the body of the frozen pirate.

Though he recognizes the natural beauty of the ice island, the potential changeability of the ice fills Rodney with sublime horror. The Antarctic environment is unfamiliar and yet uncannily reminiscent of landed mountains and peaks, allowing "for the willing suspension of disbelief necessary for the supernatural events to be taken on board. The Atlantic Circle is presented as a world on the edge of dissolution" (Nash 94). The uncertain nature of the ice, which appears simultaneously in all three states of water, ice and vapor, implies a supernaturalness that pervades the island. The sense of horror always retains a focus on the physical nature of the supernatural phenomena; the physicality of the frozen island is horrifying, and the undoubted reality of the frozen pirates equally fills Rodney with terror. It is not the imagination that is frightening, but the horrific potential contained within the reality of the ice. The icy landscape is presented as the perfect natural habitat for the pirate. It is not only physically far from land-based society, but the landscape's supernatural atmosphere moreover suggests a different, further kind of remove from the laws of nature. The Antarctic landscape is just as strange and removed from middle-class British normality as its frozen occupant. The similarities between the environment and the pirate suggest piracy belongs in this place that is beyond the edges of society. The sublime sense of awe and fear remains as Rodney explores the island but the object of his sublime gaze quickly moves from the ice island to the frozen pirate himself.

Tassard's viability is discovered by accident when Rodney leaves him in front of the fire overnight. When the frozen body has inexplicably turned itself on its side, Rodney seizes the opportunity to rid himself of the oppressive loneliness and restores the frozen pirate from his suspended animation. It never becomes clear whether the other frozen pirates are also viable, as Tassard refuses to revive them. He suggests his old companions "would reward your kindness with the poniard that you might not tell tales against them or claim a share of the treasure in the vessel" (Russell 175). Ironically, it is Rodney who will let Tassard fall back into his frozen sleep so he cannot "tell tales" against Rodney and so claims the treasure for himself. Tassard disposes of the other frozen bodies before Rodney can interfere, but not before the pirate removes all valuables from their pockets. Tassard himself is described in unequivocally negative terms. He is cunning and deceptive from the moment he wakes up, and quite quickly Rodney realizes he feels "no joy in this man's company" (Russell 157). Tassard tells detailed stories of his violent piratical exploits, and his narration of what happened to the crew of the *Boca del Dragon* after the ship got stuck in the ice is punctuated with the cry, "'That is all! They are dead—Jules Tassard lives! The devil is loyal to his own!' and with that he lay back and burst into laughter" (Russell 166). Despite the ubiquitous "spirit of cruelty ... visible in every line" of his face, Tassard is also described as being cowardly and weak; a "white-livered creature" who whimpers and pleads at the notion of death (Russell 201). Both ferocious and cowardly, Tassard is presented as the opposite of Rodney, whose repeated assurances that he does not fear death stand in stark contrast with the pirate's handwringing anxiety.

Rodney is initially frightened of Tassard, and certain the pirate will not hesitate to get rid of him in order to keep the treasure for himself. Rodney describes how he "was sensible of a momentary fear of the man—not, let me say, an emotion of cowardice—but a sort of mixture of alarm and awe, such as a ghost might inspire" (Russell 210). Once again, Rodney experiences the sublime, although this time the object of his combined fear and awe is the ontologically disturbing pirate rather than the ice. Tassard's grisly stories repulse Rodney, who notes that

> the impression he had made upon me was not agreeable. To be sure he had suffered heavily, and there was something not displeasing in the spirit he discovered in telling the story.... But a professional fierceness ran through it too; it was as if he had licked his chops when he talked of dismissing the captured ship with her people confined below and her cabin on fire. He had been as good as dead for nearly fifty years, yet he brought with him into life exactly the same qualities he had carried with him in his exit [Russell 169].

Tassard is one of those who, Rodney theorizes, when raised from the dead, "exhibit their original natures, and pursue exactly the same courses which made them loved or scorned or feared or neglected before, which brought them to the gallows or which qualified them to die in peace with faces brightening to the opening heavens" (Russell 169). He is not a "misunderstood but noble [corsair] of the romantic era, [nor a] cynical, amoral, brutal [adventurer]" of late nineteenth-century fiction (Deane 693). He is an archaic souvenir of a largely forgotten past, strangely out of place and physically marginalized in a world that no longer accommodates him and his kin.

The representation of the cryonically frozen pirate Tassard suggests an invocation of Spiritualist notions that "sought to make the spiritual world visible, scientifically proven and technologically advanced" (Kontou and Willburn 2). Through séances, spiritualists attempted to prove the possibility of communication with the dead. In *The Frozen Pirate*, the supernatural and the scientific meet in cryonics, and Russell seems particularly to mediate the Spiritualist claim of "the survival and immortality of the spirit following bodily death" (Noakes 27). Tassard's lingering spirit ensures his emergence from suspended animation. Although he is technically supposed to be dead, the spirit of the frozen pirate remains intact and, importantly, unchanged. He is "after eight-and-forty years of insensibility as real a pirate at heart as ever he had been" (Russell 181). Tassard is literally and figuratively on the edge of humanity. He is a pirate who is *hostis humanis generis*, the enemy of all mankind, because he is completely and savagely different from the world in which he awakens. Acts of piracy take place outside the jurisdiction of any country, placing pirates outside landed laws (Buhler 65). They exist "beyond the natural scope of society" (Burgess 301). Tassard, more unnatural than other pirates, embodies the otherness resulting from this separation between pirates and other seafaring men.

Contrastively, Rodney is never named "pirate." Shannon Lee Dawdy and

Joe Bonni have pointed out that "the naming of who is a pirate and who is not—or whether piracy is a reprehensible crime against all humankind or not—depends on the vantage point of the namer" (Dawdy and Bonny 675). If we take Russell to be the namer of pirates in *The Frozen Pirate*, and given the hostile way in which he gives flesh to the epithet, it makes sense he reserves the term for the novel's antagonist; naming his protagonist "pirate" would stigmatize the noble English Rodney. That does not mean Rodney is not a pirate in a legal sense. In other words, even though he is not named pirate, he acts like one throughout the narrative. In his unwillingness to categorize Rodney as a pirate, Russell leaves his characterization of the piratical figure unfinished and ambiguous. Rodney's exclusion from the definition of piracy emerging from the narrative introduces a nationalistic element to the discussion. Through the decision to define "the pirate" as a savage other, and by failing to address its protagonist's acts of piracy, the novel allows Rodney's licensed form of piracy, and in effect makes him an English privateer.

Throughout the novel, it is suggested that Rodney acts in similarly morally ambiguous ways as Tassard. Rodney takes an expensive-looking watch off one of the frozen bodies, initially in order to keep track of time and calculate his position, but also because of the watch's potential as a trade item. He realizes the watch is valuable in financial terms, not only useful for practical survival. It is Tassard who points out that taking the watch was an act of piracy; Rodney calls it "the captain's watch" but Tassard laughs and tells the embarrassed Englishman that the "watch is yours, sir; and you mean it shall be yours" (Russell 174). The moment curiously mixes with Rodney's first introduction of himself to the pirate, whereby Rodney's name becomes wedded to what is essentially an act of theft.

Tassard reluctantly shows Rodney the treasure, which must be worth "between ninety and one hundred thousand pounds of your English money" (Russell 177). Piratical custom prescribes the treasure is divided equally between all crewmembers, and both men prefer to keep the treasure for themselves rather than share it. While Tassard's greed is perhaps unsurprising, as he is an unapologetically greedy pirate, Rodney's reaction is more remarkable. He admits that "the sight of the treasure had put a sort of fever into my imagination" (Russell 197). Rodney sees an opportunity to escape from the dreaded sailor life, making him more of a pirate in Rediker's terms, who characterizes piracy as a way of emancipating oneself from a dangerous and harsh work environment (*Deep Blue Sea* 258). Nevertheless, dismissed initially as "fancies," these thoughts of treasure become Rodney's main motivation for clearing the frozen ship from the ice. He realizes that "[h]ere was money enough to set me up as a fine gentleman for life, and I meant to save it and keep it too, if I could" (Russell 320). Rodney initially contemplates the treasure and its possibilities whilst "swinging in the darkness"; the context makes it clear he is in his hammock but the association with swinging from the gallows as punishment for piracy is unmistakable (Russell 197). He feels he has a strong claim to keep the treasure, and often repeats that he has an equal share in it. This logic only holds if he is identified and accepted as a member of the crew of the *Boca del Dragon*—if he becomes a pirate.

Rodney is warned by Tassard that it will be impossible to sail the *Boca del Dragon* into any English port. Tassard says they will be hanged if they attempt to bring it into port as the ship will be recognized as a notorious pirate. Despite Rodney's claims that everyone will have forgotten her existence after nearly fifty years in the ice, which Tassard does not believe, Tassard says the best course of action will be to bury the treasure on an island, "then head for the shipping highways, and obtain help from any friendly merchantmen we may fall in with" (Russell 237). Finding men in the Tortugas to dig up the treasure will ensure the pair can keep their treasure. Rodney's reaction to Tassard's plan is ambiguous. He remarks: "how much I relished this scheme you will imagine; but to reason with him would have been mere madness" (Russell 238). It is almost as though Rodney is tempted to visit the piratical epicenter in spite of himself, until the second clause suggests that reason prescribes another course.

After an evening contemplating how he will get his treasure to land without interference of customs officers on the Thames, Rodney awakes to find Tassard once again frozen, exhibiting no signs of life. The outside world briefly intrudes on the Antarctic through Rodney's contemplations, and seems to solidify his decision not to resuscitate Tassard. Rodney admits that "though it occurred to me to test if life was out of him by bringing him close to the fire and chafing him and giving him brandy, I would not stir. No, I would not have moved a finger to recover him, even though I should have been able to do so by merely putting him to the furnace. He was dead, and there was an end" (Russell 293–94). Without Tassard, Rodney can keep the piratical treasure for himself. He resembles the assumed-dead French pirate, who similarly could have checked whether his crewmates were still alive but does not out of greed. In devising extensive plans for keeping the treasure for himself, Rodney himself commits an act of piracy. Like Tassard, who advises against attempting to revive the other pirates in order to minimize the number of claimants for the treasure, Rodney refuses to bring Tassard back to life when the latter falls into a renewed frozen sleep. Rodney knows he is supposed to hand over the treasure to the authorities when he returns to Britain, but his extensive plan to avoid this suggests a conscious decision to break the law for his own benefit.

In the remaining chapters of *The Frozen Pirate*, Rodney concerns himself with freeing the frozen ship from the ice and securing the piratical treasure. He mans the ship by himself: he is now the *Boca del Dragon*'s only crew member as well as her captain and owner, which legitimizes his claim to the treasure. Nevertheless, he is relieved to encounter an American whale ship. Displaced in time, Rodney's ancient ship appears spectral to the American whalers: "superstition lay strong upon their imagination" and they are reluctant to go on board (Russell 331). In the cabin, the delegation of American whalers makes the frozen ship appear to be haunted, their presence "rendered the vessel a vast deal more ghostly than ever she could have shown when sailing along with me alone on board" (Russell 333). Eventually, the supernatural effect of the temporally displaced ship wears off, and Rodney manages to secure a few men to sail the ship to London. Rodney can keep the pirate treasure, argues Andrew Nash, because "[i]n the amoral world of adventure, heroic triumph against the elements brings its rightful reward" (97). In Rodney's eyes, he is rightly "rewarded for ... perseverance," but once again the veracity of this statement depends on who utters it (Turley 200).

The morality of the novel's end is more ambiguous than Nash suggests. Arranging for the piratical treasure to be smuggled onto land, Rodney ventures into illegal practices himself, once again resembling the assumed-dead frozen pirate. Turley Rodney's description is reminiscent of Defoe's description of Quaker William in *Captain Singleton*. William, and Rodney like him,

> refuses to shed blood, but is happy to join Singleton's gang and share in the booty. Defoe redefines the criminalized pirate [with this character].... William's sensible, business-like mind—as well as his enthusiastic though passive assistance—enables the gang to become richer and richer ... he is thus implicated in all of the criminal acts without participating in the actual violence ... [he] is constructed by a desire for profit [Turley 204].

Rodney, not-quite pirate nor smuggler, is a strange remnant of the golden age of piracy, focused on individual gain rather than the prosperity of a community. Rodney's solitude, which he dreaded initially, is ultimately the cause of his prosperity. He is the ultimate capitalist, the "ideal rational-choice individualist" rather than "a profit-sharing, utopian socialist" (Dawdy and Bonni 675). He is not interested in "the transgressive culture of piracy" but finds the "wealth he might accumulate" more alluring (Turley 202). In Dawdy's and Bonni's view, pirates tend to act on the "both/and principle between greed and sharing," but Rodney, never named "pirate," does away with the need to share and simply claims (Dawdy and Bonni 675). Once again, the narrative legitimizes its protagonist's act of piracy by refusing to categorize Rodney as anything but an English sailor.

Rodney plans to undertake his ultimate act of piracy in the small harbor town of Deal, England.[3] Although it was a port-town, it was not an Albion version of the Tortugas. Rodney's particular type of piracy, subtle and entitled, suits this environment in the same way Tassard's suit his Antarctic environment. Whereas Tassard is a figure on the margins, which is emphasized by his strange ontological status, Rodney's centricity and Englishness means he feels like he has a right to this treasure. Bradley Deane argues that in *Treasure Island* piracy and Englishness become equated with one another: "heroes are quick to behave piratically, while the pirates ... act out a parody of conventional middle-class rectitude" (696). In *The Frozen Pirate*, the two extremes do not meet in the middle. Nevertheless, Rodney's act of piracy introduces Tassard's archaic form of by-now marginalized piracy to the nineteenth-century English shores. Rodney imagines that "[t]here might be booty enough in the hold to make a great man, a fine gentleman of me ashore. It would be a noble ending to an amazing adventure to come off with as much money as would render me independent for life, and enable me to turn my back for ever upon the hardest calling to which the destiny of man can wed him" (Russell 169). It is implied the treasure will find its way into the English economy, thus ultimately and once again legitimizing Rodney's act of piracy. The appropriation of this piratical treasure, while beneficial for the English, is not exactly what Nash calls "rightful reward." An act of privateering, not "heroic triumph against the elements," concludes *The Frozen Pirate* (Nash 97).

The open ending and the novel's unwillingness to name Rodney a pirate point to a discomfort within the novel towards definitions of piracy. This discomfort, however, might as well be irony intended to be picked up by the reader. Even if Rodney does not realize his actions are piratical, an observant reader should, and thus begin to understand *The Frozen Pirate* confusing stance towards piracy. The novel remains ambiguous on how exactly it understands and represents piracy. In ways the novel is different from Stevenson's *Treasure Island*; like its 1883 predecessor, *The Frozen Pirate* "brings piracy home to England" too, but whereas Billy Bones represents a frightening and savage kind of piracy, the kind of piracy Rodney represents is understated, subtle and calculating (Deane 695). The novel revisits earlier literary notions of pirates as sea bandits that seize people or property by force, and places them beyond the physical edge of the known world. The old pirate world, represented by Tassard, is now archaic, "a place of libertine excess" disliked by its thoroughly Victorian protagonist who nevertheless benefits from the treasures it has accumulated (Turley 202). Rodney's unfortunate shipwreck ultimately makes him a rich man, in the right place at the right time to seize the piratical treasure. By no means an anarchist out for social equality, Rodney is the ultimate privateer who brings riches into the English treasure chest.

Notes

1. I use the definition of piracy found in the United Nations Convention on the Law of the Sea, Article 101:
    (a) any illegal acts of violence or detention, or any act of depredation, committed for private ends by the crew or the passengers of a private ship or a private aircraft, and directed:

(i) on the high seas, against another ship or aircraft, or against persons or property on board such ship or aircraft;
  (ii) against a ship, aircraft, persons or property in a place outside the jurisdiction of any State;
 (b) any act of voluntary participation in the operation of a ship or of an aircraft with knowledge of facts making it a pirate ship or aircraft;
 (c) any act of inciting or of intentionally facilitating an act described in subparagraph (a) or (b).

  2. In his 1987 *Between the Devil and the Deep Blue Sea*, Rediker presents contemporary records showing Anglo-American pirates were numbered between 1800 and 2400 at their zenith (1716–18) and steadily declined to fewer than 200 men between 1723 and 1726. He compares these numbers to those employed by the Royal Navy, an average of 13,000 men per year between 1716 and 1726 (256).
  3. Russell lived in the seaside resort town for a number of years before retiring to Bath.

Works Cited

Buhler, Phillip A. "New Struggle with an Old Menace: Towards a Revised Definition of Maritime Piracy." *International Trade Law Journal* 8 (1999): 61–71.
Burgess, Douglas R., Jr. "Hostis Humani Generi: Pirates, Terrorism and a New International Law." *University of Miami International and Comparative Law Review* 13 (2005): 293–343.
Dawdy, Shannon Lee, and Joe Bonni. "Toward a General Theory of Piracy." *Anthropological Quarterly* 85 (2012): 673–99.
Deane, Bradley. "Imperial Boyhood: Piracy and the Play Ethic." *Victorian Studies* 53 (2011): 689–714.
Glenn, Barbara. "Melville and the Sublime in Moby-Dick." *American Literature* 48 (1976): 165–82.
Jones, Stephanie. "Maritime Space as Law and Light: Retrieving William Clark Russell's *An Ocean Free-Lance* (1882)." *Journal of Colonialism and Colonial History* 15 (2014).
Kontou, Tatiana, and Sarah Willburn (eds.). "Introduction." *The Ashgate Research Companion to Nineteenth-Century Spiritualism and the Occult.* Farnham: Ashgate, 2012, 1–16.
Leane, Elizabeth. "The Land That Time Forgot: Fictions of Antarctic Temporality." *Futurescapes in Utopian and Science Fiction Discourses.* Ralph Pordzik (ed.). New York: Rodopi, 2009, 199–223.
Nash, Andrew. *William Clark Russell and the Victorian Nautical Novel: Gender, Genre and the Marketplace.* London: Pickering & Chatto, 2014.
Noakes, Richard. "Spiritualism, Science and the Supernatural in Mid–Victorian Britain." *The Victorian Supernatural.* Nicola Brown, Carolyn Burdett and Pamela Thurschwell (eds.). Cambridge: Cambridge University Press, 2004, 23–43.
Rediker, Marcus. *Between the Devil and the Deep Blue Sea: Merchant Seamen, Pirates and the Anglo-American Maritime World, 1700–1750.* Cambridge: Cambridge University Press, 1987.
_____. *Villains of All Nations: Atlantic Pirates in the Golden Age.* Boston: Beacon Press, 2004.
Russell, William Clark. *The Frozen Pirate.* Toronto: William Bryce, 1887.
Turley, Hans. "Piracy, Identity, and Desire in 'Captain Singleton.'" *Eighteenth-Century Studies* 31 (1997–98): 199–214. United Nations Convention on the Law of the Sea. http://www.un.org/depts/los/convention_agreements/texts/unclos/unclos_e.pdf. Accessed on 09/09/2017.

Pirates and Orphans in Literature
From Victorian Boys' Books to J.M. Barrie's Peter Pan

EURYDICE DA SILVA

"Dids't never want to be a pirate, my hearty?" Captain Hook asks one of the little boys from James Barrie's *Peter Pan*, to convince him to join the ranks as a pirate. To this question, most of us younger (and adult) readers would perhaps answer "yes," for we have learned from literature that whenever children and pirates are involved, there is the promise of great adventure ahead. Although we often picture them together in literary fiction, these two figures first appeared separately in novels. Originally, pirates were the heroes of historical accounts in the narratives of Alexandre Exquemelin, Charles Ellms or Daniel Defoe, before moving on to become romanticized figures in works such as *The Corsair* (1814) by Lord Byron or *The Pirate* (1836) by Captain Marryat. During the Victorian period, orphans were already depicted as heroes linked with the sea in Edgar Allan Poe's *The Narrative of Arthur Gordon Pym of Nantucket* (1838), W.H.G. Kingston's *Peter the Whaler* (1851), and *The Water Babies* by Charles Kingsley (1863). However, it is truly with *The Coral Island* (1857) by R.M. Ballantyne that pirates and orphans appear together for the first time. Following this landmark, the fruitful association of these two figures gave way to more novels with recurrent themes where they appear as complementary characters.

In *Orphan Texts: Victorian Orphans, Culture and Empire*, Laura Peters mentions the recurrence of the orphan figure in Victorian literature, in a society that sets family at its core. This rise in the orphan portrayal appears as a manifestation of the political and social context; the crisis of the central notion of family in the Victorian era being symbolic of the State's relation with a threatened British Empire. Charles Dickens qualified the eponymous character in the novel *Oliver Twist* (1838) as being "[d]espised by all and pitied by none" (5). The same could be written about pirates after the golden age of piracy. After the eighteenth century, privateers who served the Crown against foreign enemies were no longer allowed to attack countries that had become allies. While a number of them joined the Royal Navy, others chose to maintain their activity without the protection of the Queen and plundered illegally. In literature, pirates became the idealized figure from the fallen, golden age of piracy and the British Empire, while orphans stood for the evils of the time and embodied the victims of the same declining empire. Pirates and orphans were both seen as outcasts and as the symptom of the woes of society.

As Jacqueline Bratton writes in *The Impact of Victorian Children's Fiction*, the child was also suddenly seen as a "potential instrument of change" in a society prone to the industrialization and social revolution (13). Education improved for male children under twelve years of age along with their access to literature, which accounts for the rise of the "boy's book" genre, adventure novels of education, or *"bildungsroman"* for young boys with core values based on family, religion, and patriotism (Denisoff 174). It is in these boy's books, such as *The Coral Island*, that pirates and orphans together were mostly portrayed. Beyond the mere adventure tales, some of these boy's books explore darker, existentialist themes. The maritime world becomes entirely codified and pirates become key figures in the orphans' journey and in their education: they help the parentless children transition from the world of childhood to that of adulthood in a society that has failed them. In order to understand how the depths of the seafaring world convey this inner journey, this essay will focus on two Victorian boy's books or novels of apprenticeship, *Treasure Island* (1883) by R.L. Stevenson and *Moonfleet* (1898) by J.M. Falkner, and explore how these figures became entwined and evolved in a post–Victorian era, in J.M. Barrie's *Peter Pan* (1911), forging a lasting and evocative imagery for the reader. One of the unifying elements we can find in these stories is the seafaring landscape or the piracy world as a transformative space for the hero. The first instance of this occurrence takes shape in the presence of remote islands both in *Treasure Island* and *Peter Pan*, which seem to represent inner islands for the child, thus becoming a symbol of the hero's self.

Far from the idyllic representations of Caribbean islands in literature that can be found in Defoe's *Robinson Crusoe* (1719) or Ballantyne's *The Coral Island*, which are depicted as preserved Gardens of Eden, Treasure Island is described by Stevenson as being a disquieting and dark place. The funereal appearance of this island of death—also referred to as "Skeleton island"—foreshadows Jim Hawkins' trial to come and his killing of a man at the end of the novel. Despite the call for adventure, the very sight of the gloomy island provokes striking ambivalent feelings within the hero upon his arrival:

> perhaps it was the look of the island with its grey, melancholy woods, and wide stone spires ... although the sun shone bright and hot, and the shore birds were fishing and crying all around us, and you would have thought anyone would have been glad to get to land after being so long at sea, my heart sank, as the saying is, into my boots; and from that first look onward, I hated the very thought of Treasure Island [980].

Stevenson recurrently attaches a human characteristic, the word "melancholy" here, to the vegetation or other natural elements, whereas it is Jim, struck by angst, who is prone to melancholy at the sight of the island. This transfer contributes to conveying uncanny attributes to this living island, which mirrors the main character's inner state and transformation throughout the story. The island's influence also extends to the pirates, among whom "the very sight of the island had relaxed the cords of discipline" (80), as if something within the characters was about to be let loose as soon as they caught sight of the island. Claire Harman's biography of Robert Louis Stevenson indicates that the writer based the landscape of the island on the Monterey coastline. In Stevenson's essay titled "The Old Pacific Capital, The Woods and the Pacific," retracing his travels in California in 1879, the description of the coastline and its thick vegetation strongly resembles that of Treasure Island. "Tall trees of the pine family" populate the island, conveying the sense that the dark evergreen landscape is not subjected to seasons nor the passing of time, as if it existed in a different space, where the characters' true self is revealed (79).

This temporal suspension is revisited in *Peter Pan* with Neverland, the land of pending time and negation, as Peter refuses to grow up. Described by Barrie as being "more or less" an island, which accounts for its cinematic representations as a fluttering island, Neverland is a manifestation and a projection of Peter's mind. All children have their own Neverland and depending on the child, "Neverlands vary a good deal" (14). J.M. Barrie writes about the geography of this inner space in the first few pages of his novel, after introducing the Darling family. He describes how every child's mind works: "I don't know whether you have seen a map of a person's mind ... catch them (doctors) trying to draw a map of a child's mind, which is not only confused, but keeps going round all the time. There are zigzag lines on it, just like your temperature on a card, and these are probably roads in the island" (13).

Barrie then describes differently the Neverlands of Michael, John and Wendy: "John's for instance, had a lagoon with flamingoes flying over it ... while Michael, who was very small, had a flamingo with lagoons flying over it" (14). As for Wendy, who is very fond of sewing things, including Peter Pan's shadow, she lives "in a house of leaves deftly sewn together" (14). Each

Neverland matches the children's tastes, as it is described as being their inner land of imagination and adventure. Soon after these descriptions, Peter Pan arrives to take them to his own complex world, also called Neverland. No other child knows how to reach that distant place and Peter must teach the children how to fly to get there in chapter 3, titled "Come Away, Come Away!" Only Peter holds the key to this secret land and he explain that, in order to fly, "you just think lovely wonderful thoughts" (42). When Peter tries to convince the children to fly away to his land of never, where children never grow up, he describes his inner map in a manner that will please the other children, inviting them to make it their Neverland as well: he promises pirates and adventure for John, and orphans to take care of for Wendy, who is depicted as a motherly character. Therefore, the Neverland the children fly to and where the story takes place is in fact within Peter Pan himself, which is partly why the children must leave it eventually in the end, while Peter Pan chooses to stay.

The island as the main character's mind map appears as a revisit of the former juvenile literature imagery. In *Treasure Island*, the map plays a central part as its discovery sets the plot in motion, launching the treasure quest for Jim and his sailing to sea. The journey of self-discovery linked with the overcoming of trials and the loss of innocence when Jim is betrayed by those whom he trusts, brings Jim from the world of childhood to that of adulthood. The original map, which triggers the adventure in *Treasure Island*, becomes an internal, ever-moving map in *Peter Pan*, reflecting the hero's undergoing change. The moment the children leave Neverland, they forget how to fly back to that magical place within, and adulthood takes over. As for Jim Hawkins, once the adventure ends, he never returns to Treasure Island where the specter of his childhood lies, along with the man he killed.

The symbolism of life and death is present in the three novels through the violent waters that surround the main action's location. Indeed, there are no still waters around Skeleton Island and the sea is never quiet. Jim Hawkins himself narrates:

> the sun might blaze overhead, the air be without a breath, the surface smooth and blue, but still these great rollers would be running along all the external coast, thundering and thundering by day and night; and I scarce believe there is one spot in the island where a man would be out of earshot of their noise [137].

Even on land, the sea is ever-present. From the moment Jim sails towards the island, he is assailed by the sound of these rough, turbulent waters. There is nowhere to take refuge, no choice but to confront what comes ahead. With its perpetual motion, the constant breaking of waves and almost supernatural growling, Stevenson gives the ocean a distinct voice, reflecting the character's inner questioning and reminding the hero that change is afoot. Jean-Pierre

Naugrette comments that in Stevenson's work, the sea is constantly ambivalent: it is "the place of birth and death at the same time, of the return to the mother's amniotic fluid and of a terrifying dive into forbidden depths" (185, my trans.). In the three novels examined in this essay, the symbolism of the sea seems to be associated with life and death as well as with motherhood, bringing together images of birth or rebirth for the hero as a new self.

In his works about maritime history, David Cordingly, explores the link between women and the sea. Basing his analysis on Freud's work, he establishes a parallel between the maritime world and the possible psychoanalytical interpretations of this codified landscape. Cordingly points out that Freud established an association between women and water in a series of lectures given at the University of Vienna in 1915 and 1916. Freud observed that birth was represented in dreams by water. He reminded his audience that not only are we mammals, including man's ancestors, descended from creatures that lived in water, but every individual mammal, every human being, spent the first phase of its existence in water—namely as an embryo in the amniotic fluid in its mother's uterus, and came out of that water when it was born (Cordingly *Women Sailors* 156). Cordingly also notes that the sea had already been associated with the female body since Antiquity, and that ships were also referred to as being a "she" for centuries. Such evocative imagery can be found in our three novels. The vessels the characters embark upon are charged with feminine symbolism and they seem to take them through a metaphysical journey and a metaphorical rebirth. The main characters' transformation from child to adult is never peaceful, like childbirth, but they need to overcome difficult trials to be reborn as adults. These struggles either take place at sea or on the island. Jim's emancipation from childhood, as he leaves his mother behind at the Admiral Benbow Inn, operates gradually, culminating towards the end as he faces death. The journey through land and water together leads to the hatching of the egg and the age of adulthood. Therefore, the sea surrounding the island can be seen as this amniotic fluid and the island as a representation of the self. In the end, there must be parting from the sea or the island for the hero to come to fulfill his transformation. In *Treasure Island*, Long John Silver escapes at sea with a share of the treasure. In *Peter Pan* Captain Hook falls overboard and is devoured by crocodile/time while the orphans and the Darling children fly back home to grow up. As for Elzevir in *Moonfleet*, he also dies, drowned at sea. The pirates remain within their element, the seafaring world, permanently detaching themselves from the hero's fate as the grown child sails on to new adventures at the end of the novels. Only when this separation occurs do the children continue their journey as adults, following the natural course of time.

Detachment scenes occur repeatedly in *Treasure Island* and *Moonfleet*. In chapter 23 of *Treasure Island*, for example, Jim takes action in defeating the pirates. Despite the strong current, he jumps into a coracle to reach the *Hispaniola* in order to cut it loose along with the pirates on board. The motive of the rope can also be found in *Moonfleet*, where the ocean is also the ambivalent screen for projections of life and death. Although there is no island in *Moonfleet*, the coastline and the sea caves where the action occurs bear the same symbolism. The death of Elzevir, the contrabandist whom the hero, John, sees as a fatherly figure, holds the striking image of the rope as a severed umbilical cord: "he pulled me up the beach himself, and it was he that pushed me forward to the rope. 'Ay, he saved thee, and then the undertow got hold of him and swept him down under the curl'" (266). Like a mother dying in childbirth, the pirate gives up his own life to save the orphan. On the other hand, separation does not occur in *Peter Pan*, where the protagonist refuses to leave Neverland, choosing to stay on his inner island while the lost children decide to fly back to the adult world after fighting the pirates. Thus, Peter remains a child forever and hides deeper within himself, as he chooses to live in the hollow of a Neverland tree, where time can never get a hold of him. Peter is also scared of water, a fear that can also reveal his contentious relationship with his mother, whom he believes to have forgotten him. Indeed, when the tide comes up in the lagoon, Peter remains stuck on a rock, incapable of diving into the sea because he cannot swim. Unlike every newborn child, he is not familiar with the amniotic fluid, persistently refusing to hatch and grow up. The protective mermaids, half-female half-fish creatures belonging to the worlds of both land and water, come to save him, bringing him back to the island, as Peter is not ready to face adulthood. For him, there is no parting from Neverland.

    The maritime imagery also feeds these tales with links to motherhood. According to Cordingly, the vessels on which the heroes sail to reach the island can be seen as references to the female body and what it can evoke. Cordingly argues: "Freud also maintained that the female genitalia were symbolically represented in dreams by objects which enclosed a hollow space such as cavities, hollows, boxes, chests, cupboards, and rooms. Ships also fell into this category" (157). The words described to depict these heroes' journey seem to be regularly attached to these mental images. The ship carries the orphan in its womb like a mother during a gestation period.[1] As for the organic quality of the vessel in *Treasure Island*, it becomes clear in Stevenson's description of the *Hispaniola* as a living boat: "The *Hispaniola* was rolling scuppers under in the ocean swell. The booms were tearing at the blocks, the rudder was banging to and fro, and the whole ship was creaking, groaning, and jumping like a manufactory" (80). Precisely like the humanized ocean, the ship's sonorous manifestations grant it a voice that haunts the hero.

    From buried chests to caves or cellars, the treasure is always buried in a hollow space that can take different shapes. In *Moonfleet*, John goes down forbidden depths, deep into a well or a "black abyss" as he refers to it, where he hopes to find a hidden diamond (210). The well is described as unusual; it is not damp with stagnant waters or "dead waters" as Gaston Bachelard defines them in his essay "Water and Dreams" on the symbolism of water (78). Instead, the well is "dry and clean, for it is said that there are below hidden entrances and exits for the water, which keeps it always moving" (201). The mystery around the origin of these moving waters contributes to the singularity of this well as a figurative space.

The darkness of hollow spaces takes yet another form when John decides to sneak into an open tomb to seek Blackbeard's treasure in the cemetery. Falkner writes: "I believe there never was a boy yet who saw a hole in the ground, or a cave in a hill, or much more an underground passage, but longed incontinently to be into it and discover wither it led" (37). The child's excitement and first impulse is immediately followed by fear as "a horror of the darkness" seizes him (38). The appearance of the hole in the ground near the tomb is oddly described as a "patch of dark velvet" (42), much like the uterine wall. When John tries to enter the flooded family vault, the description of his entering the hole evokes a reversed childbirth and the movement of the water like breaths taken by the mother before the child comes to the world: "I settled within myself that I would count the water wash twenty times, and at the twentieth would let myself down into the hole" (43). John is at the origin of his own birth and this plunge into darkness to find the precious stone comes at a risk, as he is in danger of being trapped inside the vault. Life and death are yet again linked and the image of the umbilical cord returns in this crucial moment of effort and pain: "in despair I turned back to the earth wall below the slab, and scrabbled at it with my fingers, till my nails were broken and the blood ran out—having all the while a sure knowledge, like a cord twisted round my head, that no effort of mine could ever dislodge the great stone" (70).

Another cave by the sea bears a strong role in *Moonfleet*. When accused of murder, John and Elzevir hide by the shore in a cave that John describes as his second home. As John must recover from his wounded leg, Elzevir feeds him every day like a parent would nurse a child. Two months pass and within this gestation period John grows up. When Elzevir turns to him to say, "John, these two months have changed thee from boy to man" (153) he reveals the key to understanding the role of pirates in these seafaring worlds. They lead the child towards an understanding of human duality, the harrowing realization of their finitude and eventually their own impending death, turning the abandoned orphans from children to men.

The role of pirates is to steer the hero from innocence to experience, from childhood to adulthood through experience and trials, forcing them to choose sides for the first time: defending good over evil, joining the pirates or fighting them. Both friends and foes, pirates face them with the understanding that the world, along with human nature, is a complex ocean to navigate. As the child succeeds in sailing through these violent waters, the hero grows into his adult self. This natural evolution, which occurs at sea, can be seen as a rebirth or as the death of the hero's childhood. The strong references to life and death shape the hero's journey throughout these adventure stories. The experience of death has a fundamental importance in *Treasure Island*. The novel opens with the death of Jim Hawkins' father. However, this death is described by the hero/narrator almost impassibly: "my poor father died quite suddenly that evening, which put all matters on one side. Our natural distress, the visits of the neighbours, the arranging of the funeral, and all the work of the inn to be carried on in the meanwhile, kept me so busy" (18). Jim speaks of "our" natural distress, but not of his specifically, insisting on the extra work the death has provoked as the main cause for his anxiety rather than his natural grieving.

The subsequent death of Captain Billy Bones is described in much more vivid words, causing a marked difference between the previous death reported with seemingly detachment. This time, as soon as the captain is struck dead, Jim says that he "burst into a flood of tears. It was the second death I had known and the sorrow of the first was still fresh in my heart" (21). Had it not been for this second death, the manifestation of Jim's sorrow would have remained unnoticed. Stevenson writes: "it is a curious thing to understand," for Jim Hawkins did not even like Captain Billy Bones and his "dreadful stories" (4). However, the transfer occurs for the main character, as grieving Captain Billy Bones equals overcoming the distress provoked by his father's death. Suddenly, the captain's stories linger within Jim Hawkins, awakening a persistent desire to sail for adventures at sea. The quest for the treasure becomes intrinsically linked with the disappearance of the father, rapidly dismissed at the beginning but in fact more important than it seems. As Charles William Sullivan writes more generally about young adult literature, "the defection of the father becomes the principal motive force in the assertion of the youth's independence. It links him immediately with the traditional heroes of romance and folklore ... each of whom, fatherless, must make his own way resolutely through the forest of experience" (100). With his father's death, the hero is then free to assert his independence and pursue his quest for knowledge and experience.

However, the journey is long and perilous and the hero needs guidance, in spite of how ambivalent the mentor turns out to be. In *Treasure Island*, the illustrious one-legged Long John Silver brings Jim Hawkins to maturity and self-understanding by betraying him. Jim becomes aware of the pirates' duality when he overhears a conversation, hidden in the apple barrel, which reveals the treacherous nature of the formidable cook he greatly admired.

Although he takes action against Long John Silver, Jim keeps a sense of lingering respect for this man who manages to trick and fool others so swiftly. As proven by his friend's behavior, the realization that there is no man who is entirely good or evil is impending. Jim's understanding of the duality of human nature is part of his initiatory route, entangled with doubt and self-questioning. The pirate not only escorts the hero through this journey of self-discovery, he sets this evolution forth, keeping the child on board, urging him to fight and putting every other outcome, other than growing up, to rout.

In *Moonfleet*, the child also vows a lasting admiration towards the pirate he idealizes. Elzevir's resemblance with John's own deceased father is striking, as they are both contrabandists. This characteristic is downplayed by the child, who describes his father as being "given to roaming and to the contraband" (39). Despite this trait, he believes him to have been honest. Elzevir is depicted in similar terms as the child qualifies the pirate as "a prince among the Contrabandiers," granting him a nobility of character and betraying his reverence for the man who appears as a living substitute for the memory of his lost father (190). In the eyes of the hero, Elzevir truly appears as a parental figure, bearing the role both of a father—"I had come to lean in everything upon this grim and grizzled giant, and love him like a father" (146)—and of a loving mother—"all that time he nursed me as tenderly as any mother would her child" (143). Elzevir becomes the orphan's family base, but the nature of their relationship evolves throughout the story. When both are sent to jail, they are marked with a hot iron bearing the letter "Y" on their cheek, like Cain's mark, Biblically considered as the first murderer on earth. From father and son, the prisoners become equals in their punishment. When Elzevir dies, John does not leave the words of a son on his epitaph, but those of a dear friend: "greater move hath no man than this, that a man lay down his life for his friend" (283), revealing that John has freed himself from childhood and sees himself as an adult at the end of the novel. The role of the pirate is instrumental in this transformation as Elzevir devotedly stands by John's side throughout the trials guiding him with words of wisdom. Elzevir does so willingly as he too admits he wished John were his son.

In *Peter Pan*, James Barrie inverts the codes of the novel of apprenticeship at sea and warns the reader from the beginning that his hero will not change: "all children, but one, grow up" (9). Peter Pan will never become an adult and Captain Hook, who stands for adulthood, is defeated. The plot revolves around the quest for a different treasure: finding a mother for the lost children and live happily ever after in the world of childhood. Captain Hook himself is perhaps the only famous pirate who is not primarily interested in finding gold, but in capturing a little girl, Wendy, because he misses his own mother. Hook is subjected to adult afflictions: loneliness, the fear of the passing of time, and of his own death. Depicted as a profoundly melancholy character, Hook is assailed by metaphysical questionings and nostalgia, and characterized by the fact that he feels "so terribly alone" (137). Peter, on the other hand, does not understand the concept of death. When stuck on a rock in the middle of the lagoon, he believes that "to die will be an awfully great adventure" (98). Life and death are the same to Peter as he is unfamiliar with the notion of time. Consequently, Peter has no memory, or prefers not to remember. When he stays away from the orphans for too long, he forgets about them. The same occurs at the end of the novel, much to the reader's sadness, when Peter no longer seems to remember who Captain Hook is, nor his faithful friend Tinker Bell. This loss of memory can be linked with Peter's original wound, the loss of his mother's love, when he reveals that back in the grown-up world, his mother forgot about him and replaced him with another child. He tells the orphans: "I thought like you that my mother would always keep the window open for me; so I stayed away for moons and moons and moons, and then flew back; but the window was barred, for mother had forgotten all about me, and there was another little boy in my bed" (115), which led him to never wanting to leave Neverland.

In *Mourning and Melancholia*, Freud mentions that the wish of replacing what is lost by another object of love can bring a narcissist impulse. And indeed Barrie writes about Peter Pan that "to put it with brutal frankness, there never was a cockier boy" (33). The substitute object of Peter's love is not, to their great regret, Tinker Bell or Wendy, but himself. In fact, Peter does not want a substitute mother or father. If he flies back to the "real" world, it is only to find a mother for the orphans of Neverland. Having found his figure of substitution in himself, Peter never needs to leave his mental island. As for Captain Hook, his relationship with Peter is only defined through their endless fights. When Captain Hook bites him, Peter is surprised and vexed as "every child is affected thus the first time he is treated unfairly" (96). Peter should learn from these arguments, but since he has no memory, he forgets about the offense and never improves or evolves, thus never growing up.

Hook stands for everything Peter Pan hates. He stands for a world in which he would be subjected to the passing of time, eventually becoming an adult and Peter often expresses his full denial: "as soon as he got inside his tree he breathed intentionally quick short breaths at the rate of about five to a second. He did this because there is a saying in the Neverland that, every time you breathe, a grown-up dies; and Peter was killing them off vindictively as fast as possible" (116). In *Peter Pan*, Captain Hook does not stand for a fatherly figure, but rather for what an adult embodies in the eyes of Peter. He also stands for what the romanticized pirate figure represents: the promise to help the orphan reach the age of adulthood. However, Captain Hook does not succeed in bringing Peter to the adult world. In fact, for once, it is the world of childhood which prevails as Hook falls into the treacherous Neverland waters, ending up being devoured by the ticking crocodile, symbol of the greatest enemy of all, time itself.

With this post–Victorian novel, James Barrie plays with the codes attached to the novels of apprenticeship from the previous century, exploring and recognizing the depth of their hidden meaning, breathing new life into the seafaring imagery, crystallizing it from one century to the other and adding to its popularity and timelessness. The success of these novels beyond the Victorian era can perhaps be accounted for the fact that beyond the call of a simple adventure story for young boys, run darker, existential themes with a universal appeal. By confronting the children to knowledge and guiding them from innocence to experience, pirates not only address the hero, but also the young readers, urging them to set sail and find out that the treasure they are looking for is in fact within themselves. As for the thrilling adventure at sea, it is but the journey of their life that is still waiting ahead.

NOTE

1. The boat den, as a metaphor for a uterine cavity, can also be found in other seafaring adventure stories such as Edgar Allan Poe's *The Adventure of Arthur Gordon Pym* and Joseph Conrad's *The Secret Sharer* (1910).

WORKS CITED

Bachelard, Gaston. *L'Eau et les rêves*. Paris: Biblio Essais, 1942.
Barrie, James Matthew. *Peter Pan & Peter Pan in Kensington Gardens*. 1911. Hertfordshire: Wordsworth Classics, 2007.
Bratton, Jacqueline Susan. *The Impact of Victorian Children's Fiction*. London: Croom Help, 1981.
Cordingly, David. *Under the Black Flag: The Romance and Reality of Life Among the Pirates*. New York: Harcourt, 1995.
_____. *Women Sailors and Sailors' Women: An Untold Maritime History*. New York: Random House, 2001.
Denisoff, Dennis. *The Nineteenth-Century Child and Consumer Culture*. Hampshire: Ashgate, 2008.
Dickens, Charles. *Oliver Twist*. London: Penguin Classics, 2003.
Falkner, John Meade. *Moonfleet*. 1898. Hertfordshire: Wordsworth Children's Classics, 1993.
Freud, Sigmund. *Deuil et mélancolie: Extrait de Métapsychologie*. Club France Loisir, coll. Bibliothèque Classique du XXème siècle, 1989.
Harman, Claire. *Myself and the Other Fellow: A Bibliography of Robert Louis Stevenson*. 2005. New York: Harper Perennial, 2006.
Naugrette, Jean-Pierre. *Robert Louis Stevenson, L'aventure et son double*. Paris: Presses de l'Ecole Normale Supérieure, 1987.
Peters, Laura. *Orphan Texts: Victorian Orphans, Culture and Empire*. Manchester: Manchester University Press, 2000.
Stevenson, Robert Louis. *Treasure Island*. 1883. London: Penguin Popular Classics, 1994.
Sullivan, Charles William. *Young Adult Science Fiction*. Westport: Greenwood Publishing Group, 1999.

Really Romantic?
Pirates in Romantic Fiction

RACHEAL HARRIS

Despite being at odds with the historical reality, the image of the pirate and, to a lesser degree, the privateer, has long been used to conjure ideas of romance and adventure on the high seas. Historically at least, piracy denotes a life of crime, violence and, commonly, premature demise from illness, misadventure or murder. Strange, then, that for nearly as long as there have been romance novels, the pirate/privateer archetype has played a leading role as romantic hero. The primary reason for the selection of this prototype can be linked to the concept of forbidden love and, in the case of the romance novel, the idea of taming the untamable man—or "bad boy," as he might better be understood in modern culture. As any Google search of pirate-themed romances will reveal, the pirate figure has been sailing across the horizon of the genre for decades, casting a silhouette that is not only distinctly dangerous, but deeply sexual. For this reason, he has become one of fiction's most enduring romantic icons.

While the theme of forbidden love is certainly not uncommon within the romance genre, we might suggest that the use of the pirate as an expression of it first came to prominence with Daphne Du Maurier's 1941 novel *Frenchman's Creek* (Kania 4), before reaching a pinnacle in the so-called bodice rippers of the 1970s and early 1980s (Luther; Lee 55). Although the romance genre experienced a movement away from this style during the fiction of the late 1980s and 1990s, persistent themes specifically related to sex, sexual abuse, and virginal heroines illustrate that many of the more ingrained tropes persist into modern day plot lines. Presenting himself as hero and villain, the pirate allows readers to experience a wide range of romantic scenarios. In many instances, he becomes an avenue via which more taboo ideas around love, sex, and romantic entanglement can be considered and explored from the female perspective. The fact that these romantic interludes take place on board of a ship, and, as such, are divorced from the cultural and gender specific role expectations of society is also a key consideration of the genre. This is important in period romances (which pirate-themed narratives commonly fall into), because the class structure of a specific period is at odds with the exploration of gender dynamics and sexuality, which are key to the romance plot. For the modern audience, placing the core narrative at sea bridges these cultural gaps, allowing readers to identify with heroines (and heroes) who might otherwise be unrelatable. This identification has been highlighted by Stephanie Moody as a key concern for female readers, who seek out heroines with whom they can identify through similar personality traits, if not experiences (108–109). From the characters' point of view, being free of these same social constraints and expectations provides an exotic and dramatic setting in which to fall in love, while also allowing for an exploration of the physicality of that love, which would be impossible in other environments.

As a genre, romance fiction has long labored under the reputation of frivolous escapism. In this respect, it is perhaps well matched to the figure of the pirate, who, by his very nature, is an outcast among polite or educated society. Among its more highbrow fiction cousins, the romance novel is maligned, an outlet for bored housewives and single women to indulge in fantasies that are, at best, completely absurd and, at worst, flowery prose punctuated by unrealistic sexual encounters (Lee 52). Despite the negativity associated with such a stereotype, however, it cannot be denied that romance fiction has an enormous readership (Cabrera and Menard 241; Cox and Fisher 387; Clawson 462). Each year, the romance industry publishes a phenomenal volume of titles, across a highly specific thematic range and in both print and online media. Consulting the website for one of the most longstanding publishers of romance, Mills and Boon, it is evident that whether readers are interested in para-normal or period romances, cowboys, doctors or pirates, there is bound to be a title to please. Thus far, however, the genre continues to be under-represented in academic consideration for its role in shaping the cultural landscape. In the same respect, the pirate figure is often absent from studies of the romance genre, which tend to focus more on how female characters are portrayed and how stereotypical heroines have impacted the feminist and equality movements. When considering the history of the pirate figure within romance fiction, what one cannot also help but notice is that where once pirate-themed plotlines presented a thriving sub-genre, they have suffered something of a decline in recent decades. In its heyday, the pirate saga was the focal point of large scale romantic epics, which spanned multiple generations (and novels), featuring an inter-connected cast of (often) related characters. By contrast, in the current day, the pirate is conspicuously absent from much of the romance fiction market. While he does appear sporadically in any one of the many hybridized formats that are becoming popular, the traditional swashbuckling epics so beloved by previous generations are no longer commanding the same readership. This essay considers why that might be the case.

This essay has been based on ten pirate themed romance novels, written between 1972 and 2015. These were sourced from a selection of websites that discuss the "best" pirate themed romance fiction (as voted by readers), with others chosen simply for the year in which they were published (Bowling, Goodreads, Smart Bitches). The selection was based upon common titles, which featured across multiple "best pirate romance novel" lists. While there is a sub-section of pirate novels within the genre in which the female heroine is the pirate and while these also feature repeatedly among reader favorites, this essay focuses exclusively on the male pirate centered narrative to keep comparisons between plot devices and character tropes consistent. Of the titles selected, Marsha Canham's *Across a Moonlit Sea* (1996) was most frequently discussed on reader forums, with the general attitude being that the hero and heroine presented a fresh perspective on the genre, while also being the most equal regarding relationship dynamics.

Primary to the sub-genre of pirate romance are issues around the finite number of scenarios in which the pirate might believably appear. Secondary to this concern are questions of how to make the hero enticing to the heroine and to the reader, if he is indeed a true pirate. The first problem is most commonly solved through kidnapping or stowaway plot (in which the female lead is either the victim of a kidnapping or a restless free spirit that gains access to a ship as a stowaway or using a false identity). Similarly, the most common way of negating the issue of making the hero enticing is to bestow (either realized or unrealized) upon the pirate some form of class title. Frequently, pirate characters are either part of the English nobility, or have ties to it and, as such, fitting them with the title of Duke or Earle becomes a means of suggesting not only breeding, but a basic benchmark of education and manners. For stories in which the hero is an American, he is usually the son of a wealthy sugar baron or a descendant of English/Spanish nobility. This becomes relevant to establishing the pirate as a product of the romance genre as opposed to a historically accurate concept. While overall romance writing attempts to adhere to historical realism as much as possible, in the pirate there is the unique issue of melding the historical villain with the romantic hero. Adding nobility and class to the pirate figure removes elements of ill breeding and negates the need for unattractive behaviors which the reader would not be able to reconcile with the sexual relationship that needs to be established between the two leads.

Like the revelation that the pirate has a class title, common across romantic novels is the fact that the heroine understands herself to be undesirable to the male gender generally and to the pirate specifically. Only one novel, Karen Robards' *Island Flame* (1981), demonstrates the counterpoint of the trope. Unlike the other heroines, who use physical shortcomings (or the self-perception of these) as an excuse for an array of maladies, Robards' heroine, Catherine Aldley, is the beautiful *ingénue* who suffers the most once she had fallen into the path of her pirate lover. The victim of physical, emotional, and sexual abuse, Catherine's story seems to suggest that, as a self-assured and beguiling heroine, she must earn/pay for her perfect romance through other travails.

For the heroines who do not understand or acknowledge their beauty, it is through a series of developing liaisons with the "forbidden" pirate lover that these qualities are eventually realized. Frequently the heroine views herself as a spinster or ugly duckling (as is the case in Susan Wiggs' 1999 *The Charm School*). It is precisely because of this fact, though, that she is able to engage with the pirate as an equal. In traditional romance fiction fashion, this is the very trait which first attracts the hero to her. Romance is only reached after mutual misunderstandings between the pair, which often provide comedic relief within the plot. Similarly, genuine love is always declared before the relationship is consummated, leading to a more fulfilling emotional and sexual experience for both parties. In contrast, the heroine of *Island Flame* is raped by the pirate throughout.

If we are to consider the pirate as a reflection of the historical personality on which such a figure is based, however, we must conclude that he would likely be a man more prone to crime and cruelty than a romantic gentleman masquerading as a cad (Kania 8). It is on this point particularly that the pirate romance suffers greatly within modern readership, in that it struggles to maintain a character archetype which is faithful to the genre but also to the pirate's historical counterpart. As the traditional alpha-male and hero, the pirate must exhibit physical dominance over his lover. Outside of the physical abuse evident in *Island Flame*, sex, specifically the loss of virginity, is a primary vehicle through which this is explored. While two novels (Sabrina Jeffries' 1975 *The Pirate Lord* and Teresa Madeiros' 2007 *Thief of Hearts*) suggest that their heroes have endured a long period of celibacy, in all the novels under examination the pirate has a long and storied sexual history. So too, the pirate's skill at lovemaking is highlighted as a focal point of the relationship he develops with the heroine. Noteworthy is the image of her first sexual encounter being devoid of pain or awkwardness, along with the idea that the hero only experiences real pleasure after he has first bestowed it upon his virginal love interest. The setting of such unrealistic expectations for readers of the genre has been touched upon in previous considerations of romance fiction, which conclude that these scenes cause confusion and frustration for readers who are unable to reenact similar encounters in real life (Cabera and Menard 207–208). That the romantic experiences of romance heroines are unachievable in reality, though, does not appear to have had an impact on the writing styles of romance authors. Across all the books examined here, sexual encounters between the hero and heroine follow a similar formula.

The concept of the male hero being more sexually experienced and dominant than his diminutive heroine is a trope common across most traditional romance fiction, and is not specific to the pirate storyline. Owing to gender roles being so defined in the category romance, it is only in rare circumstances that readers would ever encounter a virgin hero at all, and then his virginity would be a sign of weakness, ill health or some other extenuating circumstance (Allen 5). In pirate-centered narratives the virgin male is non-existent. As in the wider collection of romance fiction, male virginity equates to lack of virility. In the case of the pirate themed romance specifically, the hero often dominates his lover sexually to prove himself attractive to her and, by extension, the reader (Dubino 108).

Comparatively, the female desires to dominate the pirate emotionally. Through love, she can undo his sins, making him whole by restoring his trust in women and giving him the courage to act gallantly and less "like a pirate." In many novels, the term "pirate" transforms throughout the narrative, used by the end as a term of endearment, marking the transformation of the hero from criminal rouge into acceptable gentleman. Considering the transformative qualities which physical and emotional intimacy have on both parties, it can be concluded that by introducing the heroine to sex, the pirate brings her femininity to full realization. The fact that their sexual encounters are frequently based on dangerous situations intensifies the passion and allows for the heroine to go beyond what is considered appropriate behavior for a lady. As such, she feels that she can only "be herself" when she is with the pirate. In being "bad" the pirate becomes an avenue through which his lover (and by extension the reader) can engage in fantasies that are against the grain of acceptable behaviors. For the hero, the innocence of his lover and the gift of her virginity remove his previous sins, allowing him to progress into the loving husband and trustworthy partner idealized and desired by the heroine/reader.

Among the novels examined in this study there were only two instances (Marsha Canham's 1996 *Across a Moonlit Sea* and Katie MacAlister's 2005 *Blow Me Down*) in which the heroine is not a virgin when she encounters her pirate lover. While in another example (Jennifer Haymore's 2012 *Pleasures of a Tempted Lady*), the heroine is not a virgin, she lost her virginity many years prior to the same sea captain that rescues her in later life. She has consequentially been celibate during the years of their separation and thus, in this instance, her virginity, while not being intact at the time in which the story takes place, belongs to the hero. As a result, their renewed affair is described in much the same way as those in which the heroine is a virgin.

In *Across a Moonlit Sea*, the female lead lives aboard her father's ship and has adopted the identity and traits of a stereotypical crewmate, as a direct consequence of a prior failed love affair. Her loss of virginity is then atoned for in the confession that the chosen man was not in love with her, but wanted her money. As a result, she, like many of the other heroines, turns away from the notion of romantic love and thus shuns the advances of the pirate who commandeers her father's ship. In this instance, the sexual relationship that develops between the two retains many similarities with the loss of virginity that is experienced by the other heroines. In taking her as a lover, the pirate "opens her eyes" to her hidden sexual desires. Experiencing sex with him and depicting it as very different from her previous encounter enables the heroine to understand herself on a deeper level. Through their sexual encounters both hero and heroine come to understand the importance of trust, equality, and companionship in a partner.

In contrast, Kesley Cole's *The Captain of All Pleasures* (2003) sees the pirate mistake the virgin heroine for a prostitute. Although he does not bed her at the first opportunity, his misconception allows for a certain degree of sexual interaction between the two, which feeds their later attraction. The revelation that the heroine is a woman of class and breeding but also the daughter of his sworn enemy allows the pirate to deny his love. Despite his attempts to disregard the heroine, however, the pirate is once again taken under the spell of her difference. As previously mentioned, this heroine sees herself as distinctly unfeminine and unattractive. From the pirate point of view, though, it is this difference that makes her so beguiling. Cole's novel prolongs the deflowering of the heroine for the longest time, using a series of "almost ... but not quite" sexual encounters to keep the reader entertained. Although it is difficult to imagine a man having the patience or the self-discipline to abstain from penetration as frequently as Cole's hero does, each interaction between the pirate and the heroine is clearly an avenue through which she might explore her emerging sexuality and he might come to accept his need for feminine love and tenderness outside of that which is purely sexual. Each interaction draws her closer to him and him further into "love"; which again communicates to the reader that forbidden romance is more fulfilling than the ordinary. Additionally, in their eventual sexual encounter, the reader is impressed with the idea that his prior sins as a pirate can be undone by her purity and that in their realized love both are made whole.

Perhaps the most unrealistic is the relationship between hero and heroine in Sabrina Jeffries' novel *The Pirate Lord* (1972), in which a convict ship bound for Australia is intercepted by pirates who are seeking women to make into wives, so that they can colonize their own island community. While the story, in its treatment of convict exile to Australia, is based on historical fact, the notion of the celibate band of pirates and their equally celibate captain is difficult to reconcile with the historic image of the pirate lifestyle. In this novel, the hero refuses to consummate his relationship with the heroine until he has legitimately won her love and her hand in marriage. While this eventually does occur, the larger plot highlights the improbability of a romantic relationship being played out historically. Although the plot is difficult for the modern reader to digest, the overwhelming reception of the novel from older fans and long-time readers of the romance genre suggests that it is not accuracy as much as style that endears these characters to readers. So too, the style of the writing is indicative of the era in which the book was published and suggests that during that period the romance fiction market was driven towards a very different set of thematic concerns than its modern counterpart. The quickly shifting nature of reader wants has been documented in academic considerations of the genre, specifically when examining titles and themes of romance novels from the last decade (Cox and Fisher 388). The evolutionary cycles of these titles, which move through specific genres and settings to mirror reader wants, provide further proof of how frequently the romance genre has changed in the nearly fifty years since *The Pirate Lord* was published.

Another integral part of such a change is how the hero interacts with the heroine, particularly in relation to their sexual relationship. Karen Robards' *Island Flame*, for example, uses rape as a means of establishing the connection between pirate and captive and this produces a different level of dominance between the romantic leads. This approach impacts the modern reader in a different way than it might have in 1981 when the book was published. While the rape trope presents difficulties for the modern reader because of its brutality and distinct lack of romance, it is certainly not a new trope within the genre historically (Toscano 1–3; Lee 55). Within the scheme of pirate fiction, the concept of rape is something that, for the sake of historical accuracy alone, must be considered as a possibility by the reader (Kania 8). This is difficult for writers of the genre in the modern era, however, because traditional ideas about gender roles within these novels are continuing to shift towards a more feminine, empowered focus. Using the rape of the heroine as a plot device risks turning potential readers away from the larger work or a lack of investment from the reader in the larger journey and romance the heroine experiences. Trying to balance historical authenticity then with a more feminist focus within the pirate setting becomes a task which is virtually impossible without being implausible, and this may account for some of the downturn in the number of titles published.

For the sake of the plot line, in *Island Flame* rape eventually develops into love between the two leads, with the act justified by Robards in her description of the heroine's arousal during her initial and all subsequent encounters with her captor. After having committed sexual and physical abuse on the heroine, it is little surprise that the hero must then encounter his own abuse in order to give the perception that he and his love interest are back on equal footing. In response, a tragic personal history, in which the hero has been abandoned by his parents, is introduced to provide his prolonged rapes with a context that the reader can use to justify and nullify his actions. Within this plot line is an undercurrent of the idea that if the hero marries his captive she is transformed into something new. Rather than a rape survivor, she becomes a wife and any trauma or wrong doing are erased. Similarly, the idea of marriage undoing the sinful act of sex and the enjoyment of the same is used to "set things right" by the end of the plot. This idea of "making it right" is present throughout many of the narratives, not just those involving rape, commonly coming into play upon the realization that the heroine is pregnant and thus must wed her lover so as to avoid becoming a social outcast.

Of the more recent examples of romance and relationship dynamics within the genre, MacAlister's *Blow Me Down* casts the romance between hero and heroine inside of a game. Not only does the updated setting provide the opportunity for the characters to behave in ways in which they normally would not, but the gaming platform also lends itself to scenarios which are beyond the bounds of the natural world. MacAlister's heroine is also not a virgin at the time of her romance; she has been through a divorce and, as such, she is mistrusting of men and of the idea of love. Perhaps to give the genre a modern update, it is the hero in this story that is the first to declare his love for the heroine. She rebuffs this declaration stating that she is not sure that she believes in love anymore. Both the hero and heroine become victims of self-doubts that are directly related to self-image, which is again indicative of the shifting wants of readers. In casting her hero as less than perfect, MacAlister removes many of the alpha-male qualities that make the romance hero attractive to the reader. Indeed, unlike heroes of other titles, Corbin is described as slightly overweight and not very well endowed. Although MacAlister attempts to make up for these physical short comings in her descriptions of Corbin's enthusiastic love making, it is evident that in her novel the heroine is in charge of her own pleasure. She is the dominant party, often dictating the rules of their liaisons. This, added to the fact that much of the action takes place in the virtual world, puts the novel at odds with the others used in this study, making it feel more like chick lit than traditional romance fiction. Unlike the traditional romance, chick lit is more commonly defined through its portrayal of the freethinking heroine who is in control of her own destiny. Frequently narratives which fall into this subgenre have a contemporary setting and characters which have more in common with the modern thirty-something woman (Ehriander 1–2). MacAlister, in her attempt to meld elements of both these styles, demonstrates the attempts that have been made to update pirate romance narratives for modern audiences. In doing so, however, her hero highlights the ongoing difficulties faced within the sub-genre, specifically when the characteristics of the established male and female roles are updated to reflect more modern reader ideals.

Adopting a more recognizable approach, Darlene Marshall's *Sea Change* (2011) demonstrates the dramatic shift in the relationship and power balance between hero and heroine by using the classic trope of mistaken identity. Rather than being a society lady, the heroine pretends to be a man, so that she can work as a surgeon. This charade is aided by her perceived ugliness, allowing for her to be mistaken for a male by most people whom she encounters. Even the pirate hero is oddly unaware of her true gender and identity, at one point contemplating his own sexuality as he struggles to reconcile the attraction he feels towards the ship's doctor. What this reconsideration of his sexuality and gender illustrates is the sub-genre of the pirate romance attempting to reinvent itself to mirror more modern attitudes towards romantic love and sexual attraction. How successful these reimagining will be, however, remains to be seen. Unlike other stereotypical figures within the romance canon, pirates are in many ways prisoners to specific traits and time periods. As a result, the characters in *Sea Change* revert to traditional gender roles before the conclusion, allowing for a stereotypical happy ending.

Pirate romance is not the only sub-genre within romance fiction to have suffered under the weight of modern reader wants. Academic studies of Gothic genre fiction have similarly highlighted that the traditional roles of supernatural creatures, such as werewolves and, more commonly, vampires, have likewise undergone updating to stay current within the romance market. Unlike the supernatural vampire or werewolf, however, the pirate lover, being based in history rather than fantasy, cannot be recast with as much ease as his vampire counterpart. Once the personification of repressed sexual desires and explorations of the female sexual nature, vampires have shed much of their "bad boy" imagery, morphing from figures of terror into something decidedly more appropriate to a Parental Guidance (Nakagawa 2–4). While in the case of the vampire this shift might be attributed to Young Adult (YA) fictions that have been adopted by a huge readership of soccer moms, in the case of the pirate the archetype struggles to reconcile itself to a historical ideal of what a pirate is. Where the vampire is able to lend itself to a variety of time and place settings, the pirate is largely a product of his era. While novels such as *Blow Me Down* attempt to update the pirate or bring him into the modern world, the recasting of the traditional character into an online platform removes much of the drama of the traditional setting. It is this same setting which makes the pirate genre so rich and such a distinctive sub-genre of romance. Without it, the pirate is virtually unrecognizable. Also, unlike the vampire or the werewolf, the pirate figure is intrinsically linked to a specific set of codes. He must live aboard a ship, he must pillage, and he must be a criminal. While the allure is still the same "bad boy" persona at the core of all three examples, because the vampire or werewolf stereotype is not reliant upon a specific setting in order for his archetype to be recognizable, he is more easily adapted to scenarios which will appeal to and be familiar for modern readers. In contrast, the pirate figure, being confined to his ship and stereotypical character tropes, has excluded his evolution into contemporary romance plotlines.

While the pirate figure may not be as malleable as the vampire, modern readers are witnessing an increase in pirate hybrid romances. These will combine the stereotypical character with another recognizable historical figure. One example would be the pirate/highlander. While the concept of a pirate that is also a highlander or a highlander who happens to be a pirate seems ridiculous, it is indicative of the ways in which cultural trends are quickly appropriated into the genre. In the case of the highlander, we might look to the recent success of the *Outlander* television series (2014–), based on the historical romance novels by Diana Gabaldon, as an inspiration around the increased use of hybrid characters within the romance genre. For the writer of the romance, combining two powerful archetypes into a single hero is beneficial in that it allows audiences a wider scope in which the adventure and romance can take place, giving writers the ability to pick and choose between the traits of these two male character types. Additionally, employing characters that are based on recent popular stereotypes attracts readers who are looking to indulge in romance-based plotlines which echo that of similarly popular texts.

Writers of the pirate romance have played an essential role in establishing the pirate figure as a cornerstone of popular culture. Although the pirates responsible for commandeering the hearts and bodies of their romance heroines bear little resemblance to their historical counterparts, they remain representative of a core section or romance fiction and pop-culture heritage. Despite a downturn in interest in the pirate themed narrative, the romance fiction genre as a whole is in no danger of going down with the ship. In fact, romance novels continue to move from strength to strength across all reading platforms, with new writers being published on a regular cycle. While there are likely to always be purists who keep the pirate sub-genre alive, in many instances the pirate depicted in recent romantic novels is merely a hybrid, blended with some other archetypal figure in order to make him more palatable to the modern reader. What the pirates of history would think of this development is perhaps a topic for another time.

Works Cited

Allan, Jonathan A. "The Purity of His Maleness: Masculinity in Popular Romance Novels." *Journal of Men's Studies: A Scholarly Journal about Men and Masculinities* 24.1 (2016): 24–41.
Bowling, Anna. "Ahoy, Maties: Top 10 Pirate Romances from Hoyt, Lindsey and More!" *HeroesandHeartbreakers.com*. https://www.heroesandheartbreakers.com/blogs/2014/09/ahoy-maties-top-10-pirate-romances. Accessed on 07/15/2017.
Canham, Marsha. *Across a Moonlit Sea*. New York: Bantam Doubleday, 1996.
Cabrera, Christine, and Amy Menard. "She Exploded into a Million Pieces: A Qualitative and Quantitative Analysis of Orgasms in Contemporary Romance Novels." *Sexuality & Culture* 17.2 (2013): 193–212.
Clawson, Laura. "Cowboys and Schoolteachers: Gender in Romance Novels, Secular and Christian." *Sociological Perspectives* 48.4 (2005): 461–79.
Cole, Kresley. *The Captain of All Pleasures*. New York: Pocket Books, 2003.
Cox, Anthony, and Maryanne Fisher. "The Texas Billionaire's Pregnant Bride: An Evolutionary Interpretation of Romance Fiction Titles." *Journal of Social, Evolutionary, and Cultural Psychology* 3.4 (2009): 386–401.
Dubino, Jeanne. "The Cinderella Complex: Romance Fiction, Patriarchy and Capitalism." *Journal of Popular Culture* 27.3: 103–18.
Du Maurier, Daphne. *Frenchman's Creek*. London: Hachette Press, 2012.
Ehriander, Helene. "Chick Lit in Historical Settings." *Journal of Popular Romance Studies* 5.1 (2015): 1–12.
Goodreads, Popular Pirate Romance Books. https://www.goodreads.com/shelf/show/pirate-romance. Accessed on 03/01/2017.
Haymore, Jennifer. *Pleasures of a Tempted Lady*. London: Hachette, 2012.
Jeffries, Sabrina. *The Pirate Lord*. New York: Avon Books, 1972.
Kania, Richard R.E. "Pirates and Piracy in American Popular Culture." *Romanian Journal of English Studies* 11.1 (2014): 183–94.
Lee, Linda J. "Reading Romance Novels as Reworked Fairy Tales." *Marvels & Tales* 22.1 (2008): 52–66.
Luther, Jessica. "Beyond Bodice-Rippers: How Romance Novels Came to Embrace Feminism." *The Atlantic*. March 18, 2013. https://www.theatlantic.com/sexes/archive/2013/03/beyond-bodice-rippers-how-romance-novels-came-to-embrace-feminism/274094/. Accessed on 07/07/2017.
Macalister, Katie. *Blow Me Down*. London: Penguin Signet Eclipse, 2005.
Marshall, Darlene. *Sea Change*. Colorado: Amber Quill Press, 2011.
Medeiros, Teresa. *Thief of Hearts*. New York: Bantam Doubleday, 2007.
Menard, A.D., and Christine Cabrera. "Whatever the Approach, Tab B Still Fits into Slot A: Twenty Years of Sex Scripts in Romance Novels." *Sexuality & Culture* 15.3 (2011): 240–55.
Mills and Boon. "About Us." https://www.millsandboon.co.uk/np/Content/ContentPage/5. Accessed on 09/05/2017.
Moody, Stephanie. "Theorizing Popular Romance Reading." *Pedagogy: Critical Approaches to Teaching Literature, Language, Composition and Culture* 16.1 (2015): 105–23.
Nakagawa, Chico. "Safe Sex with Defanged Vampires: New Vampire Heroes in *Twilight* and *The Southern Vampire Mysteries*." *Journal of Popular Romance Studies* 2.1 (2011): 1–17.
Robards, Karen. *Island Flame*. New York: Bantam Double Day, 1981.
Smart Bitches, Trashy Books. "Good Shit Vs. Shit to Avoid: Pirate High Seas Romance!" http:77smartbitchestrashybooks.com/2006/08/good_shit_vs_bad_shit_to_avoid_pirate_high_seas_romance. Accessed on 06/13/2017.
Toscano, Angela R. "A Parody of Love: The Narrative Uses of Rape in Popular Romance." *Journal of Popular Romance Studies* 2.2 (2012): 1–17.
Wiggs, Susan. *The Charm School*. New York: Harlequin Mira Books, 2008.

"Yo-ho-ho and a bottle of rum"

Representations of Drunkenness in Literary and Cinematic Narratives on Pirates

Antonio Sanna

Rum and drunkenness have been staple attributes of pirates and buccaneers since the seventeenth century. After briefly reconstructing the history of rum, this essay will examine testimonials detailing the truth behind pirates' abundant consumption and love of this amber drink, as well as trace the literary and cinematic representations of it over the past four centuries.

Served as a precious ingredient in such cocktails as the Mojito, Caipirinha, and Cuba Libre, and also used to prepare dishes such as some kinds of omelets and rum baba pastries, rum is an alcoholic beverage known as a "global spirit with its heart beating in the Caribbean" (Williams 14). The beverage is distilled from sugar cane, "either in the form of the raw juice or from molasses refined from sugar by boiling" (Foss 10). The extracted liquor, which can be either light or dark, either aged or unaged, was first documented 6,000 years ago in New Guinea, where sugar canes were cultivated and their syrup fermented. The plant itself was introduced by the Muslim traders in Egypt and Sicily during the Middle Ages, but the Mediterranean climate was not warm enough to allow a rich growth of it, because the plant requires lots of sunshine and water to flourish and is therefore more suitable to tropical weather (Williams 13). It was the Portuguese who started the first sugar plantations in their African colonies, especially in the island of São Tomé, where they imported slaves from Benin to work the plantations since 1490 (Williams 14). The Portuguese subsequently imported slaves for the sugar plantations in Brazil, whose first known canefields and sugar mills were documented during the sixteenth century. It was there that a crude version of what we now call rum was born (Foss 24–25).

Proper distillation and trade of rum began in the humid region of the Caribbean. The first mention of the beverage in the Caribbean was in 1651 and can be found in the report from a visitor to the British colony of Barbados, the first place where the liquor was commercialized and where superior distilling technologies emerged. The visitor mentioned a beverage known as "*Rumbullion*, alias *Kill-Divil*, and this is made of sugar canes distilled, a hot, hellish, and terrible liquor" (qtd. in Foss 28).[1] The quality of the first product coming from the distilleries was usually not very high, as several testimonies of the time confirm. Richard Lingon, for example, described rum as "infinitely strong, but not very pleasant in taste. It is common and therefore the less esteemed: the value of it is half a crown a gallon" (qtd. in Williams 44). Effective improvements in distillation techniques, which reduced the strongest odors and flavors of the beverage, came at the beginning of the eighteenth century and, with them, the beverage acquired also respectability (Williams 52). Rum was cheap because the raw materials were highly accessible (Toss 34–35). For this reason, the beverage was soon exported from the Caribbean across the globe, a process that was facilitated on the one hand by the fact that the distilled liquor became itself a currency in both licit and illicit trade. On the other hand, rum was at the center of a triangle based on the slave trade that functioned between the Caribbean (the site of plantations), New England (a center where rum was distilled and produced on an industrial scale since the seventeenth century) and Africa (where slaves were acquired and sometimes paid for with rum barrels).[2]

The historical association of piracy with rum originated in the actual use of rum as a currency during the seventeenth century, which made the liquor a valuable commodity in the eyes of the pirates who roamed the Atlantic and the Caribbean in search of treasure. Rum was then either exchanged as a currency or abundantly consumed aboard the pirate vessels. Indeed, there are several testimonies describing ships being wrecked or run aground by drunken crews (it happened to Sir Henry Morgan's flagship in 1669) and of pirates not being able to fight against the Royal Navy because they were exceedingly drunk when their vessels were boarded a fate was met by pirate John Rackham in 1720 (Williams 229). Drinking rum was an everyday habit on board pirate vessels, who inherited the custom of distributing it among the members of the crew from the Royal Navy. Indeed, since the seventeenth century, it was customary aboard Navy ships to distribute among the crew a small ration of rum. Such a ration was standardized in 1730 at half a pint per day (split between two servings), which was later mixed with water, weak beer, or lemon juice to create the beverage known as "grog" (Foss 60).

According to Robert C. Ritchie, the predilection for drink was partly related to the ancient habit of imbibing to overcome fear of battle and ultimately, of death (68).

Such a standardization and rationing of alcohol did not occur on board pirate vessels, where lack of moderation was typical and immoderate drinking occurred throughout the day. In his influential 1678 volume *The Buccaneers & Marooners of America*, for example, Esquemeling reports that during an expedition, the crewmembers under Bartholomew Roberts "had taken a considerable quantity of rum and sugar, so that liquor was as plenty as water, and few there were who denied themselves the immoderate use of it; nay, sobriety brought a man under a suspicion of being in a plot against the commonwealth, and in their sense he was looked upon that would not be drunk" (302). According to Esquemeling, Captain Bartholomew Roberts himself declared: "'a merry life and a short one!' shall be my motto! Thus he preached himself into an approbation of what he at first abhorred, and being daily regaled with music, drinking, and the gayety and diversions of his companions, these depraved propensities were quickly edged and strengthened, to the extinguishing of fear and conscience" (329). The almost constant state of drunkenness among pirate crews is echoed in Captain Charles Johnson's 1724 popular volume *A General History of the Robberies and Murders of the most Notorious Pirates*, which examines the tendency of many pirates to overindulge in alcohol. Johnson explained that rum was a most valuable commodity among the cargo of the vessels plundered by pirates, and it was a habit for villains to make abundant use of it (68). Johnson refers specifically to "the surgeon being tolerably drunk, as it was customary for everybody to be" (296) as an exemplary case of the life on board a pirate vessel. This is what occurred also on Captain Spriggs' ship, he adds, where "the day was spent in boisterous mirth, roaring and drinking of healths, among which was, by mistake, that of King George II for you must know, now and then the gentry are provoked to sudden fits of loyalty, by the expectation of an act of grace" (327).

Rum was therefore a source of gaiety for several historical pirates, who (ab)used it to celebrate their freedom from social and legal constraints and their libertine lifestyle. As B.R. Burg has noted, the consumption of the wine, rum, or brandy (and the resulting swearing, rioting, and debauchery) was also associated with celebrations following a vessel's sacking (155). Such a ritual was mentioned in some of the pirate codes, specifically in reference to the acquisition (but not necessarily the consumption) of alcohol on board the vessels. Indeed, according to the articles drawn by Bartholomew Roberts, "every man ... shall have an equal title to fresh provisions or strong liquors at any time seized, and shall use them at pleasure unless a scarcity may make it necessary for the common good that a retrenchment may be voted" (qtd. in Cawthorne 146).

Rum was also reported to be a source of discord among the members of the pirate crews. According to Captain Johnson, "when drinking together on board of [Captain] Davis, they had like to have fallen together by the ears, the strong liquor stirring up a spirit of discord among them and they quarrelled [sic], but Davis put an end to it" (143). Similarly, Esquemeling states, "being almost always mad or drunk, their behaviour produced infinite disorders, every man being in his own imagination a captain, a prince, or a king" (305). Life on board a pirate vessel therefore alternated between merry episodes of camaraderie and untoward occasions for brawling and misdeeds among the members of the crew.

Drunkenness did not merely occur on board pirate vessels; many ports in the Caribbean provided the dreaded seawolves with other occasions for both merriment and riotous behavior. The divided booty of the expeditions was often squandered once the pirate crew returned to a port. As Burg argues, "the conduct of buccaneers in port ... is well chronicled, and tales of fortunes squandered, riotous excess, maniacal gaming, and lewd and drunken conduct are all substantially true" (155). One of the major ports that pirates visited in between their expeditions was Port Royal, whose "superabundance of imported alcohol struck contemporaries as remarkable" (Preston 49). The city was renowned for the presence of "a huge quantity of cheap local rum, originally called 'rumbullion' and nicknamed 'Kill devil'" (49). Such a beverage was served in the many "taverns for men from every social level and occupational category" (Burg 95). Port Royal's name thus came to be associated with debauchery, drunkenness, and promiscuity. In the words of one cleric who visited the town, Port Royal was "the Sodom of the New World," inhabited mainly by "pirates, cutthroats, whores and some of the vilest persons in the whole of the world" (qtd. in Preston 50). When a violent earthquake destroyed much of the town, and many buildings sunk beneath the sea in the summer of 1692, the event was interpreted by some as God's just punishment for a wicked and impenitent town (Cordingly 167).

The actual historical accounts of drunken pirates were fictionalized in many literary narratives published since the seventeenth century. Literary works such as Frederick Marryat's *The Pirate* (1836), Robert Louis Stevenson's *Treasure Island* (1883) and Tim Powers' novel *On Stranger Tides* (1987) have further strengthened the relationship between pirates, rum, and drunkenness in the popular imagination. In Marryat's novel, the pirate captain blames his men for caring more about being drunk than for the safety of the sinking vessel and their own lives. He chastises them, "Shame upon you! Do you call yourselves men, when, for the sake of a little liquor now, you would lose your only chance of getting drunk every day as soon as we get on shore again? There's a time for all things; and I've a notion this is a time to be sober" (n.p.). Such a portrayal of the crew's immoderate passion for drinking certainly reflects the reality of those vessels that were lost at sea for the same reasons. Similarly, in Howard Pyle's short story "With the Buccaneers," from the posthumous collection *The Book of Pirates* (1921), the marauders under Sir Morgan are described as "drinking healths in raw rum as though it were sugared water" (59). In Pyle's tale, immoderate drinking is frequent among the crew of Captain Morgan. The latter even threatens his crew with death should they celebrate the victory over a Spanish vessel and its profitable cargo by getting drunk before they reach Port Royal, an occurrence that probably mirrors what actually transpired on board some pirate vessels.

Other literary works amplify the historical accounts, but frame them as an indictment against drunkenness. In Walter Scott's novel *The Pirate* (1822), for example, the captain of the second pirate vessel is "the old brute Goffe [who] gets drunk as a lord every day, swaggers and shoots, and cuts among the crew; and, besides, he has quarrelled with the people here so damnably that they will scarce let water or provisions on board of us, and we expect an open breach every day" (332). Scott heavily criticizes Goffe for his misbehavior with both the members of his vessel's crew and the local inhabitants of the Shetland Islands, and blames the character's drinking of alcohol for his infamy. Goffe is, for this reason, set against the protagonist of the story, Captain Cleveland, the redeemed and sober pirate who has fallen in love with the daughter of the local udaller and wants to abandon all his criminal activities. Such a severe judgment on drunkenness and its consequences also appears in William Clarke Russell's *The Frozen Pirate* (1887). In this novel, Paul Rodney distrusts and criticizes his companion, the unfrozen, malicious pirate Tassard, for being frequently drunk. In this tale, drunkenness accompanies the pirate's narration of his past evils: "added to all this was my dislike of my companion. He would half fuddle himself with liquor, and in that condition hiccup out twenty kinds of villainous yarns of piracy, murder, and bloodshed, boasting of the number of persons he had despatched, of his system of torturing prisoners to make them confess what they had concealed and where" (200). Later in the narrative the protagonist affirms, "I thought with loathing of the drunken ribaldry of the pirate and my own tipsy songs piercing the ear of the mighty spirit of this solitude" (233). Rodney is profoundly ashamed of himself for having toasted, drunk, and sang in the company of the pirate and having thus become almost like him. As Minke Jonk argues in the volume in your hands, this association has already been established by his theft of the captain's watch and later corroborated by his smuggling of the gold once he returns home.

The most notorious representation of drunkenness among pirates comes to light in Stevenson's *Treasure Island*. The story begins with the arrival of the brown, filthy, and scarred old seaman, Captain Billy Bones, at the Admiral Benbow Inn. During the subsequent weeks, Bones proves himself a very silent man during the day, scrutinizing the coastal horizon with a telescope, while he occupies the inn's parlor at nights, where he drinks great quantities of rum, savoring it as "a connoisseur, lingering on the taste" would do (4). As the young narrator of the novel surmises, "there were nights when he took a deal more rum and water than his head would carry; and then he would sometimes sit and sing his wicked, old, wild sea-songs, minding nobody" (6–7). Among the sea songs performed by the character in a state of drunkenness is the one that has now become closely associated to all fictional pirates: "fifteen men on the dead man's chest—Yo-ho-ho, and a bottle of rum!" (3). Bones terrorizes the inn's customers with his threatening presence (accentuated by his cutlass); he elicits their shock and awe with dreadful stories about his previous deeds. After the visit from his old shipmate Black Dog, the captain has a stroke and, oblivious to the doctor's advice, he continues to drink rum until he is visited by the blind beggar and is given the "black spot," which causes him a second—this time, fatal—stroke. Stevenson attributes the character's death, therefore, to his drinking habit.

More recent representations of pirates likewise provide readers with a negative depiction of drunkenness among the crew of a vessel. In Tim Powers' novel *On Stranger Tides*, the protagonist John Chandagnac finds himself forced to join the pirate crew, whom he describes as "a crowd of drunken murderers" (51). Such a negative characterization of the sea marauders, however, does not prevent him from becoming one himself for the sake of a beloved. Later on in the narrative, he falls into the same degraded state, abusing rum: "I'll stay here till I run out of money for rum, and then I suppose I'll move on, get some kind of work.... I don't know, it's a sunny day, and I've got rum—I'll worry about tomorrow's problems tomorrow" (285–86). This passage exemplifies a character's wasted life, with him finally drowning the many regrets with alcoholism. He personifies a destiny that was probably shared by many real pirates who did not die in battle or at the end of the rope.

In Michael Crichton's *Pirate Latitudes* (2009), drunkenness is used to further mar the reputation of the town of Port Royal, its inhabitants, and the Spanish enemy in favor of the brave conduct of the story's protagonist, Captain Hunter, a privateer who accepts the secret mission to assault the most dreaded Spanish stronghold in the Caribbean and capture a galleon transporting an immense treasure. At the beginning of the tale, the narrator reports that in Port Royal "the morning patrol of garrison soldiers was collecting drunks and dead bodies" (4). The story is set in 1665, when the town is said to have "grown from a miserable, deserted, disease-ridden spit of sand into a miserable, overcrowded, cutthroat-infested town of eight thousand" (9). Port Royal is infested with drunk citizens, some of them disrupting the proceedings of the church "with blasphemous shouts and oaths" (10), while others spend their mornings "vomiting in the streets" (24). The immoral atmosphere of the streets is matched by the corruption practiced in the Governor's mansion and among the town's officials, who do not hesitate to charge Captain Hunter with piracy near the end of the story in order to seize the precious prize he has acquired. Crichton deploys drunkenness to condemn both the populace and the government of Port Royal, further characterizing the story's protagonist and his motley group of accomplishes as heroic. Such a marked contrast is established between Hunter's men and the crew of his Spanish rival, the evil Cazalla. The latter are indeed incapable of properly defending their flagship because "their sleep was heavy with rum" (138).

Literary representations of drunken pirates are generally aligned with historical accounts. Cinematic representations of drunken pirates are, instead, more light-hearted and ironic. With the exception of Stevenson's *Treasure Island*, these adaptations do not represent drunkenness as the sole cause for misbehavior, and they rarely depict the most sordid and dirty aspects of such a condition. On the contrary, the cinematic portrayals of drunken pirates emphasize the celebratory nature of the act of drinking. Negative consequences, such as the crew's inability to guard their own vessel, only emerge as a means of discrediting the protagonists' adversaries. The latter is the case in Michael Curtiz's *Captain Blood* (1935), the story of an English physician unjustly condemned to be sold into slavery at Port Royal. In this film, the heroism of the title character and his men contrasts the debauchery of the Spaniards that attack the colony where the protagonist leads a slave revolt. On this occasion, the Spanish soldiers guarding the vessel during the plundering of the town are presented as drunk and merrily singing songs instead of attending to their duties. The Spaniards are therefore taken by surprise by Peter Blood's men and their vessel is lost in but a few minutes. Although drunkenness here seems jovial and not at all squalid or especially vulgar (there are indeed no close-ups on either the bottles of alcohol or the intoxicated faces of the guards), it sets the "good" pirates against the oppressive foreigners. Such a representation of drunkenness further contributes to the characterization of pirates as heroic, valiant, and righteous, a pattern of representation that is typical of films produced between the 1930s and 1950s.

On a similarly positive note, Henry King's *The Black Swan* (1942), Jacques Tourneur's *Anne of the Indies* (1951), and Roman Polanski's *Pirates* (1986) revel in the celebratory nature of drinking. *The Black Swan* introduces two of the film's major villains as they take advantage of a barrel laid on a beach after their victorious raid on a coastal settlement. Later in the narrative, the liberation of the protagonist by the members of his crew becomes another occasion for celebration through the uncorking of two bottles of wine. On both occasions, drinking alcohol marks a milestone and the characters are not depicted as either stuttering or staggering due to overindulgence. In *Anne of the Indies*, the gathering of different pirate crews becomes an occasion for the celebration of their victories at the Tavern of the Black Anchor. Such a sequence focuses on the pirates' feasting, merriment, and dancing, and does not linger on any negative aspect related to the consumption of alcohol. The character of Blackbeard is evidently drunk but jovial, festive, and affectionate with the female protagonist of the story, whom he treats on equal terms. Such a portrait of Blackbeard clearly defies the historical accounts on the character. In Raoul Walsh's *Blackbeard the Pirate* (1952), he is a heavy drinker who repeatedly brings a bottle to his mouth while sitting in his office. Walsh's film, however, depicts him as lucid and scheming in spite of his habit; he never babbles incoherently nor does he let down his guard. In Polanski's *Pirates*, Bartholomew Red and his cabin boy Jean-Baptiste lead a mutiny against the Spanish crew of a galleon carrying a very valuable cargo. After imprisoning the Spanish members of the crew, Captain Red and his new crew reach a small island, where they celebrate their victory by drinking enthusiastically from barrels taken from the vessel. The film emphasizes the ironic futility of the pirates' celebration and makes fun of drunkenness by representing it as the premise for the Spanish to escape imprisonment and retake possession of their galleon. When the pirates realize that the vessel has been re-taken, it is too late. The escape of the Spaniards is achieved by three armed men who cleverly hide inside the rum barrels; this comic planning underlines the direct relationship between being drunk and facilitating one's own demise through careless distraction.

A more humorous depiction of drunkenness may be found in the *Pirates of the Caribbean* saga (2003–17) through the representation of Captain Jack Sparrow (Johnny Depp) and his first mate Gibbs (Kevin McNally). The former spends several scenes complaining about not finding any rum on his vessel and feeling sick while sober. When stranded on a desert island in the first episode of the series, he opens a secret deposit built by rum smugglers and drinks abundantly from a bottle while singing piratical songs with Elizabeth Swann (Keira Knightley). The young woman, however, ruins his dream of an extended state of drunkenness by burning the whole reserve of rum while he is asleep in order to catch the attention of passing ships. In the fourth installment of the saga, *On Stranger Tides* (2011), Sparrow drinks from Hector Barbossa's peg leg while toasting to the latter's desire to seek revenge against Blackbeard. Each of these representations of drunkenness seeks the viewers' laughter above all else. This comic imperative recurs in the most recent episode of the saga, *Dead Men Tell No Tales* (2017), when the pirate captain surfaces from a vault in Saint Martin's Bank with a bottle of rum in his hand and with a precariously tottering gait. His first mate, Gibbs, enters the first scene of *The Curse of the Black Pearl* (2003) on a Royal Navy ship while secretly sipping alcohol from a tiny bottle. He does so to gain courage after seeing a wrecked vessel. This surreptitious drink is a historically accurate habit, one that he indulges in every time he is nervous, and he does so even after he becomes a pirate. Gibbs' tiny bottle then returns in the subsequent scenes when it is used in the place of a bullet for lack of ammunition, shot against Barbossa's ship and returned by Sparrow to its owner. In *Dead Man's Chest* (2006) Gibbs is introduced on a stormy night while hollering out Stevenson's famous pirate song with a bottle of rum in his hand. Both Gibbs and Jack Sparrow are no strangers to rum or drunkenness, but their representations are light-hearted and not intended to elicit the audience's disapproval.

In contrast, a judgmental representation of drunkenness finds expression in cinematic adaptations of *Treasure Island*. The various films utilize different techniques to criticize the act of drinking rum, whether it is by juxtaposing Billy Bones' manners against those of the inn's customers, by representing him as debilitated by his drinking habits, or by emphasizing the unhealthy nature of the beverage. In Victor Fleming's black and white *Treasure Island* (1934), Billy Bones' arrival at the Admiral Benbow Inn creates immediate unease in the customers and his abrupt manners, staggering walk (suggesting that he is perpetually drunk), rough voice, and arrogant tone starkly contrast the customers' polite composure. In spite of his vicious habit, Bones is full of energy until he receives the black spot, a note bearing a black circle sign that predicts his forthcoming death at the hands of his former comrades. Bones' requests for rum alternate with his threatening injunctions for the inn's customers to join him in song or listen to his obscene tales. The film focuses on the shock of the customers at the foul-talking and hard-drinking Bones, emphasized by close-up shots on their scared faces. The sentiment would likely have been shared by the audience of the film, who were, at the time, in the midst of the Prohibition era. The soundtrack also underscores Bones' contrast to the customers. A musical theme accompanies his piratical swagger. The song itself is introduced during the main titles and then is repeated several times throughout the film to accompany the actions of Long John Silver, thus highlighting the association between rum and pirates in the mind of the viewers.

The Disney version of Stevenson's novel, directed by Byron Haskin and released in 1950, presents Billy Bones as a weak pirate because of his drinking habits. The film begins directly with the arrival at the inn of an ill-tempered and cautious Black Dog, who asks young Jim for a double rum. After discovering the presence of a chest with Bones' initials carved on it behind the counter, Black Dog hastily leaves the inn. A hoary Captain Bones then confronts Black Dog without resorting to physical violence; he merely chases him away from the inn. He then asks for some rum, even though his degraded state of illness is evident and the doctor had previously barred him from drinking any of the amber poison. On this occasion, Bones staggers towards a chair and suckles avidly from the bottle. The Disney version focuses on the consequences of the character's drinking habit by depicting Bones as an aged, tired man who has been defeated by alcoholism even before being defeated by his former pirate comrades. A similar interpretation may be found in Peter Rowe's 1999 adaption of the story, which insists on the unhealthiness of alcoholic indulgence. In this version, Bones is a solitary character whose piratical song is sung out of loneliness. The film focuses on the doctor's recommendations for the pirate's health by alternating between medium shots of the two characters that set the doctor's gravity and firmness against the desperation of Bones' scarred face. Contrary to the original novel, the subsequent sequence is set in Bones' bedroom while he is recovering from the first fit rather than in the parlor; he never completely recovers and dies in bed while revealing Jim about the existence of the map.

Debilitation by alcohol is central also in Fraser C. Heston's 1990 version of the story, which juxtaposes the character's drunkenness with his combativeness and pride. Initially, during the main titles, Bones stands proudly erect on the boat that carries him to the small English port where the story begins. However, such a characterization of him as strong falters as soon as he enters the inn, where he helps himself to a bottle of rum in spite of the owners' protests. In the subsequent sequences, he is constantly drunk, shouting to the other customers, and singing uninvited. In spite of his questionable health, during the cutlass-wielding physical duel against his rival Black Dog, Bones uses all of his strength and beats his adversary with brutal efficiency. It is only at the end of the fight that he suffers from a violent fit of coughing, which he attempts to sedate by drinking rum. According to this version of the story, rum has eroded Bones' health but not his pride and fighting prowess.

Steve Barron's 2012 version of *Treasure Island* prioritizes Bones' addiction to alcohol by using a series of close-ups that frame the bottles and glasses used by the pirate before illuminating his very face. The fact that the character dies of a heart attack when he is drunk suggests that his health had already been irrevocably compromised by his drinking. Yet the film also associates the act of drinking alcohol with relief from desperation. Indeed, drinking allows some moments of relief for Bones, who is tormented by nightmares and visions about Captain Flint's previous betrayal of him and part of his crew, an exposition conveyed by flashbacks and some prefatory scenes. Drinking rum does not have a completely negative presence in this film; rather, Bones entertains both the inn's guests and Jim with his stories rather than scaring them. The guests even contribute to his songs, whereas Jim is clearly fascinated by the pirate's tales and dreams about becoming an adventurer himself.

Historical accounts of pirates dating back to the seventeenth and eighteenth centuries remarked upon the unhealthy and amoral nature of the villains' drinking habits along with their subsequent inability to perform their nautical duties or engage in battle against their enemies. Such negative representations of drunkenness have been recreated accurately in the literary versions of pirates, which insist on their immoderate passion for drinking, the riotous climate on board their vessels, and alcohol's association with the cruelties they commit against other men and settlements. Alcoholic overindulgence cannot be separated from an existential sense of uselessness and wasted time at the end of a pirate's life. Among the various cinematic depictions of pirates, however, only the adaptations of *Treasure Island* highlight the unhealthiness of drinking rum, whereas the majority of the films on pirates concentrate instead on its power as a celebratory tool and joyful premise for camaraderie and goodwill. As is the case with the figure of the pirate at large, modern representations have offered a more light-hearted, palatable version of historical pirates' lives. The actual effects of immoderate consumption of rum that characterized the daily existence of pirates have thus been "diluted" of their (im)moral extremes. By creating a sanitized narrative of drinking as occasional and celebratory acts, we witness a distortion of the contemporary figure of the pirate; he becomes someone jovial, fun-loving, and even pleasant, broadly effacing the more accurate understanding of these men as rapacious, violent, and ruthless marauders that infested the high seas centuries ago.[3]

Notes

1. According to Foss, "the origin of the name 'rumbullion' is hotly disputed, with some partisans alleging that the word 'rum' was rustic British slang for 'excellent.' Others point to an alleged link between the words 'rum' and 'scrum,' meaning fight, or 'rumbustious,' meaning exuberant, noisy and undisciplined" (29).

2. The subsequent history of rum includes records of many nations having banned it in favor of promoting morality and public health. Although such bans partly ensured that export were limited (Toss 48), numerous smugglers, bribed inspectors, and tax collectors managed to make it reach its destinations. Rum was notably used in voodoo rituals in Haiti and Santería rituals in Cuba. Instances where the beverage emerges in more recent pop culture history include the Portland rum riot of 1855, the founding of the Bacardi Company in 1862, the fire on the Thames caused by the destruction of a warehouse containing more than 6,000 barrels of it in 1933, and its presence in the famous nightclubs of 1950s Havana. Here, American novelist Ernest Hemingway uttered the famous sentence, "my Mojito in La Bodeguita, my Daiquiri in El Floridita" (qtd. in Williams 289).

3. I would like to thank Dr. Nancy Kang for her more than precious suggestions.

Works Cited

Anne of the Indies. Dir. Jacques Tourneur. Twentieth Century Fox, 1951.
The Black Swan. Dir. Henry King. Twentieth Century Fox, 1942.
Blackbeard the Pirate. Dir. Raoul Walsh. RKO, 1952.
Burg, B.R. *Sodomy and the Pirate Tradition: English Sea Rovers in the Seventeenth-Century Caribbean*. New York: New York University Press, 1995.

Captain Blood. Dir. Michael Curtiz. Warner Bros, 1935.
Cawthorne, Nigel. *A History of Pirates: Blood and Thunder on the High Seas.* Toronto: Arcturus, 2003.
Cordingly, David. *Life Among the Pirates: The Romance and the Reality.* London: Abacus, 2004.
Crichton, Michael. *Pirate Latitudes.* London: HarperCollins, 2010.
Defoe, Daniel. *The Life, Adventures and Piracies of the Famous Captain Singleton.* Champaign, IL: Project Gutenberg, 2004.
Esquemeling, John. *The Buccaneers and Marooners of America: Being an Account of the Famous Adventures and Daring Deeds of Certain Notorious Freebooters of the Spanish Main.* 2nd ed. London: T. Fisher Unwin, 1892.
Foss, Richard. *Rum: A Global History.* London: Reaktion Books, 2016.
Johnson, Charles. *A General History of the Robberies & Murders of the Most Notorious Pirates.* London: Conway Maritime Press, 2002.
Marryat, Frederick. *The Pirate.* Champaign, IL: Project Gutenberg, 2007.
Pirates. Dir. Roman Polanski. Carthago Films, 1986.
Pirates of the Caribbean: Curse of the Black Pearl. Dir. Gore Verbinsky. Walt Disney Pictures, 2003.
Pirates of the Caribbean: Dead Man's Chest. Dir. Gore Verbinsky. Walt Disney Pictures, 2006.
Pirates of the Caribbean: Dead Men Tell No Tales. Dir. Joachin Rønning and Espen Sandberg. Walt Disney Pictures, 2017.
Pirates of the Caribbean: On Stranger Tides. Dir. Rob Marshall. Walt Disney Pictures, 2011.
Power, Tim. *On Stranger Tides.* London: Corvus, 2011.
Preston, Diana, and Michael. *A Pirate of Exquisite Mind: The Life of William Dampier: Explorer, Naturalist and Buccaneer.* London: Corgi Books, 2005.
Pyle, Howard. "With the Buccaneers." *The Book of Pirates.* Champaign, IL: Project Gutenberg, 2007. 58–72.
Rediker, Markus. *Villains of All Nations: Atlantic Pirates in the Golden Age.* London: Verso, 2012.
Ritchie, Robert C. *Capitan Kidd e la guerra contro i pirati.* Luciana Stefani (trans.). Torino, IT: Einaudi, 1988.
Russell, William Clarke. *The Frozen Pirate.* Chicago: M.A. Donohue, n.d.
Scott, Walter. *The Pirate.* London: Adam and Charles Black, 1893.
Stevenson, Robert Louis. *Treasure Island.* London: Puffin, 1994.
Treasure Island. Dir. Victor Fleming. Metro Goldwin Meyer, 1934.
Treasure Island. Dir. Byron Haskin. Walt Disney Pictures, 1950.
Treasure Island. Dir. Fraser C. Heston. Agamemnon Films, 1990.
Treasure Island. Dir. Peter Rowe. Kingsborough Greenlight Pictures, 1999.
Treasure Island. Dir. Steven Barron. Parallel Films, 2012.
Williams, Ian. *Rum: A Social and Sociable History.* New York: Nation Books, 2006.

PART III: PIRATES IN CINEMA AND ON TV

The Image of the Pirate in Adaptations of *The Adventures of Tintin*

MICHAEL CHARLTON

In Belgian writer and artist Hergé's long-running adventure comic *The Adventures of Tintin* (1929–1976), the intrepid young reporter Tintin, his faithful dog Snowy, and his loyal but belligerent friend Captain Haddock face off against a succession of villains, from Communists to mobsters to forgers. Hergé often drew inspiration from popular subject matter for children, sending Tintin off to the sorts of "exotic" locales common in adventure books, films, and comics and experimenting in multiple genres, ranging from humorous mysteries to espionage to science fiction.[1] The pirate story would get its turn with 1943's *The Secret of the Unicorn* and its sequel, 1944's *Red Rackham's Treasure*. These books would be adapted into audiovisual form three times, first in 1957 for the animated television series *Hergé's Adventures of Tintin*, next in 1991 for the animated television series *The Adventures of Tintin*, and finally in 2011 for the animated film *The Adventures of Tintin: The Secret of the Unicorn* (which also contains plot elements from 1941's *The Crab with the Golden Claws*). This essay examines how the series depicts its pirates, focusing on the original story and the 1991 and 2011 adaptations. Hergé and his adapters seem to have slightly different ideas about the piratical Rackham and his more traditionally heroic counterparts, Sir Francis Haddock and his descendant Captain Haddock, and these differing ideas are eloquent about how the image of the pirate has shifted and changed over the last decades. Specifically, while Hergé plays around with both the positive and negative aspects of the pirate, adaptations have tended to portray the pirate as much better or much worse than in the original stories.

Since these two books were written during the Nazi occupation of

Belgium, there have been attempts to read them as either pro- or anti-fascist in their politics, though noted Tintin critic Michael Farr has pointed out that there is only the faintest allusion to the war in either (*Companion* 112).[2] It is difficult to form a coherent picture of Hergé's politics as reflected in the series. Benoit Peeters has noted the artist's willingness to conform to censorship standards was parodied even by fellow cartoonists (160). Pierre Assouline has attributed part of the series' preoccupation with political targets to one of its early editors while Harry Thompson pointed out that Tintin becomes increasingly apolitical as the series progresses, with the early muckraking reporter being replaced by a more straightforward adventurer (11, 112).

Later critical reception and analysis of the story has tended to view it as having little political relevance. Phillippe Goddin has praised it for its careful melding of past and present in its storytelling and Tom McCarthy for what he sees as its focus on the series' overarching themes of resolving puzzles and "reading" enigmas (110, 18–21). Serge Tisseron mentions it in his discussion of how family lineage and memory are represented in the series. Jean-Marc Lofficier and Randy Lofficier point to it as the story in which the series comes to be more about Captain Haddock than Tintin himself (53). Neither the television shows nor the 2011 movie have attracted much critical attention outside of fansites and general reviews, with many writers on the movie focusing primarily on the motion-capture technology used to create it (for example, see Scott Foundas's article in *Film Comment*).

The main pirate character was inspired by a story Hergé read about female pirates Marie Read and Anne Bonny and their sometime ally John Rackham and involved extensive historical research into pirates and ships (Farr *Companion* 108–112; Farr *Company* 37). Assouline has also noted the clear influence of Robert Louis Stevenson's *Treasure Island*, whereas Peeters traces the influence of Jules Verne (particularly *The Children of Captain Grant*, which also involves puzzle-solving, globe-trotting, and piracy), and Jean-Marie Apostolidès underlines certain parallels with Daniel Defoe's *Robinson Crusoe* (88, 143, 138). In many ways, *The Secret of the Unicorn* and *Red Rackham's Treasure* are two of the purest adventure stories in the entire series, borrowing heavily from preexisting classics in the genre and melding them with history and lore about piracy.

Many readings of pirates, both historical like Read and Bonny and fictional like Stevenson's Long John Silver, tend to stress the relationship between the image of the pirate and the question of authority, whether to present a revisionist view of how "free" the pirate ever actually was or to explain why the pirate remains a romantic, attractive image centuries after the so-called golden age of piracy ended. Erin Mackie summarizes this appeal:

in part, the dream for this particular brand of liberty has its origins in notions of absolute individual sovereignty that arose even as absolutism came under assault in the political sphere. A law unto himself, the outlaw asserts the ultimate aristocratic privilege of sovereign will ... for those who have never had power, the taking of criminal liberties needs to be seen as an utopian as well as a nostalgic gesture; such gestures are more purely nostalgic, however, when embraced by those who have power, secured in part by the disavowal of such liberties [25].

In other words, the romantic and nostalgic appeal of the pirate as a being of absolute freedom who creates his or her own world is inescapably intertwined with the darker realities of the era, including the shadows that violent criminality, the slave trade, and colonization cast over the present day. The pirate claims freedom by denying it to others and his or her actions are covered with a haze of nostalgia and idealism to disguise this fact.

Captain Haddock is often considered the series' most popular character, though the source of that popularity is somewhat puzzling. He is not introduced until the ninth story and from the moment he arrives he proves to be a "hero" with few traditionally redeeming qualities—an angry, stubborn drunk of little apparent intelligence prone to fits of euphemistic cursing and bouts of hypocrisy about alcohol. With the exception of an incident in *The Red Sea Sharks* (1958), where he successfully captains a tramp steamer, he does not appear to be even a competent sailor. The easiest explanation for his paradoxical popularity is that he provides a necessary comic foil to the ever-sincere, ever-stalwart Tintin and proves to be a loyal, if misguided, friend.

This preexisting relationship is one of the driving forces of the plot in the original comics story, as a gift intended for Haddock to celebrate their friendship becomes the catalyst for everything else. One of the major changes in the Spielberg adaptation will be the erasure of this friendship, so that Haddock becomes an unlikely ally met along the way rather than Tintin's trusted companion. The main conflict in *The Secret of the Unicorn* begins almost at once, when Tintin spots a model sailing ship and buys it for Captain Haddock before being accosted by Ivan Sakharine, a collector insistent on purchasing it. Haddock arrives and immediately drags Tintin off to examine a portrait of his ancestor Sir Francis Haddock, who captained the *Unicorn* during the reign of Charles II. After his apartment is robbed twice, Tintin discovers a cryptic piece of parchment that came from the model's broken mast and jumps to the conclusion that the parchment must be part of a clue toward finding treasure. He goes to see Haddock, who has dressed up in the hat and cutlass of his ancestor after uncovering an old sea chest that also contains a manuscript written by Sir Francis. Haddock recounts the adventures of his ancestor, who was sailing his ship home from the West Indies when he ran afoul of pirates. The story then switches back and forth between the encounter with the pirates and the present day as the captain excitedly acts out a sea battle between the two ships, which ends in the *Unicorn* being boarded by the crew of infamous pirate Red Rackham. Rackham gloats over the captured booty before Sir Francis escapes, fights a duel which leaves the pirate dead, and rigs an explosion which sinks his own ship. The reader then discovers that at his death Sir Francis left each of his three sons a model, which leads Tintin to realize that each of the models must contain a piece of parchment much like the one he found. The rest of the story involves the reporter and his friend trying to recover all three pieces, learning in the process that the collector Sakharine is innocent of the thefts and has been robbed himself.

Tintin is kidnapped and brought to Marlinspike Hall, the ancestral home of the Haddocks, by the criminal Bird brothers, who are the actual villains. After being rescued, he intuits that the final parchment was accidentally taken by a pickpocket and reunites all three pieces of the puzzle to discover a message containing the coordinates for the sunken treasure. *Red Rackham's Treasure* is instead a much less complicated story in which Tintin and Haddock travel to the West Indies to recover the titular prize. They fail to find it there even after using a submarine designed by Professor Calculus and discovering Sir Francis's island and the wreck of the *Unicorn*. Calculus buys Marlinspike Hall for Haddock after selling the plans to his submarine. Tintin solves a riddle and reveals the pirate treasure hidden inside an old globe, which proves rich enough to allow Haddock to retire.

Summarizing the story reveals how little the captain actually contributes to the plot. Tintin is the one who finds the model in the first place, makes the connection to a treasure map, reunites all three pieces, and solves every riddle along the way (including one involving differences between types of sea charts which should logically be more obvious to a sea captain). Professor Calculus develops the crucial submarine and provides the funds to purchase the Haddock estate. What Haddock offers is a familial connection to Sir Francis and his encounter with Red Rackham. In his own ridiculous fashion, he seems to embody the spirit of his dashing ancestor, from "play-acting" with his hat and cutlass to shouting the very same curses which will be heard on Sir Francis's island refuge (144). The reader is clearly meant to see the flashback as within the captain's imagination and it contains some of the most strikingly detailed, sweeping images in the entire series—exchanging Haddock's grubby quarters for vast vistas with sailing ships and cannon-fire. Haddock makes a fool of himself imitating his ancestor, smashing his own table, chairs, and chandelier while trying to be as heroic as Sir Francis.

Red Rackham actually does not get much attention even though these two books revolve entirely around the booty he captured from another boarded ship. In contrast to Sir Francis, Rackham is almost a visual stereotype of a pirate: he hoists the Jolly Roger and wears a feathered hat and a cloak with a skull affixed on it. He is hardly a dashing figure, either, with most of his dialogue consisting of gloating and threats to turn the heroic Haddock over to his crew. Red Rackham loses his life, his ship, and his treasure fewer than ten pages after being introduced. In short, Rackham is a pathetic excuse for a pirate. He is certainly an outlaw but contains none of the positive qualities often associated with the pirate captain in fiction. Instead, these positive qualities—courage, freedom, cleverness—are all associated with his opponent, the legally sanctioned Sir Francis. One could dismiss this as Hergé not wanting to celebrate violent criminality in a story consciously aimed at younger readers, though this would introduce the question of more attractive pirates for juvenile audiences up to and including Captain Jack Sparrow in the *Pirates of the Caribbean* saga (2003–17). Another solution is more complicated and related to the earlier question of why Haddock is appealing to some readers. Many of the traits associated with pirates are actually projected onto him. He is obsessed with rum, fixated on treasure, destructive, loyal to his "crew" (primarily Tintin) but hostile to the outside world and authority, loves the romance of the sea but resists anything like a military occupation, curses in a way more associated with a common sailor (or pirate) than a commander, and even ends the story rich off of what is primarily the cleverness and labor of others.

Perhaps that is part of the enigma of Haddock's enduring popularity: he has the impulses of a pirate but far too good a heart to act on them. He "play-acts" being a scoundrel in the same way he "play-acts" being the supposedly more honorable Sir Francis. Haddock is a paradox, a socially acceptable rascal who can be pirate-like without carrying the transgressive stigma of the pirate. This also calls into question the heroism of his ancestor, who procures a stolen treasure for himself by sacrificing his own ship. In pirate fiction it is not normally the stalwart, moral heroes who leave treasure maps behind. The story itself emphasizes over and over that the only path to these riches is through theft, whether through its claim by Red Rackham or through the cycle of stolen models. The dashing, nostalgic image of Sir Francis is imposed on the narrative to give the appearance of legitimacy to the treasure in the same way that Captain Haddock's loyalty and basic benignity provide an excuse for his more piratical traits. While on the surface the books draw a stark contrast between the two, with one being the sad and satirical shadow of the other, perhaps both ancestor and descendant are more like Red Rackham than they at first appear.

The figure of the pirate has therefore always been a symbol of both positive and negative social transgression. Hans Turley finds this in the depiction of the pirate as libertine as early as Defoe's 1720 novel *Captain Singleton*. Bradley Deane traces the figure of the pirate in Victorian literature post–*Treasure Island* and describes a persistent mirroring of boyhood and piracy, stressing how often piracy is depicted as a type of playground where boys and pirates reflect issues of empire and trade off conventional values for new sets of rules. Shannon Lee Dawdy and Joe Bonni's "Towards a General Theory of Piracy" points out that the pirate is characterized by binary oppositions— both pro-capitalism and anti-capitalism, both individually and collectively minded, both organized and anarchist. Returning to the immediate inspiration for Hergé's story, Rob Canfield discusses an early account of Anne Bonny, Mary Read, and their male companion Jack Rackham as an example of an author struggling to both condemn piracy and pirates and "glorify the pirate as a counter-heroic role" (51). To many writers, readers, and viewers, the pirate thus seems to be at once horrifying in his or her violent rejection of society and its rules and perversely attractive for the very same reason.

In terms of plot the 1991 three-episode adaptation of *The Secret of the Unicorn* and *Red Rackham's Treasure* is remarkably faithful to the original books.[3] *Unicorn* introduces the villainous Bird brothers slightly earlier and deletes a couple of minor characters; *Red Rackham* omits a couple of scenes during the treasure hunt in the West Indies. Haddock is equally aggressive in this adaptation, yelling at Tintin when the reporter refers to his ancestor as "Francis" instead of "Sir Francis" and swinging his sword, pounding on the table, and smashing furniture with great violence. The flashback engages in a clichéd montage of high seas action that includes hauling on ropes, climbing the rigging, setting the sails, loading shot, but also copies some panels exactly. As in the book, Sir Francis is drawn to be identical to Captain Haddock and is also given the same voice, though the adaptation does not call as much attention to the captain's alcoholism as the original book does. In a much more significant change the episode transforms the duel between Sir Francis and Diego the Dreadful, the pirate's first mate, into a duel between Sir Francis and Red Rackham. In the novel the two do not meet until Sir Francis has been knocked out and tied up. From there the adaptation follows the original book almost panel-for-panel, with the one major change being a *Robinson Crusoe–like* shot of Sir Francis standing on his new tropical island home with a tattered uniform and an umbrella. At the end of the second episode, after Tintin and Captain Haddock have discovered the latitude and longitude on the assembled parchment, the two characters dance for joy as in the original but exclaim "Yo-ho-ho and a bottle of rum," which seems a rather peculiar thing for the descendant of a pirate-hunter to do. As noted before, the two major sequences left out of *Red Rackham's Treasure* both involve the hunt on Sir Francis's treasure island, a scene in which the submarine gets in trouble and a scene in which the treasure hunters dig underneath a wooden cross on the island which they mistakenly believe is the eagle's cross mentioned in Sir Francis's clues (and in which the ever semi-piratical Captain Haddock promises a bottle of rum to whoever finds the treasure).

Insignificant as these alterations may seem, they indicate a shift in the story's representation of pirates. Hergé depicts Red Rackham as a devious, hateful man who taunts the more heroic Sir Francis only after his crew has been disposed of and he has been tied up. By giving them a duel prior to the pirate's complete victory and Sir Francis being knocked out of commission, Rackham becomes a subtly bolder, more dashing figure. The added shot of Sir Francis in *Robinson Crusoe* garb also leaves a different final impression of the spirited, aristocratic captain—more primitive, less bound by society and laws, closer in dress and appearance to the pirates than to his own former officers. The "yo-ho-ho" at the end of the second episode finds Tintin and Captain Haddock drifting closer to the world of pirates—identifying them with Rackham rather than Sir Francis. Furthermore, omitting the wooden cross scene in the third episode serves to downplay the religious imagery that subtly runs through the story, culminating with the discovery of the actual treasure at the feet of a saint (in fact, Tintin never mentions St. John by name in the TV adaptation). The overall effect is to make all three characters closer to the traditional image of the pirate. While Hergé's original novel introduces shades of ambiguity by comparing Rackham, Sir Francis, and Captain Haddock in ways that make it clear that there are similarities among all three, this telling emphasizes the dashing, romantic side of piracy without also emphasizing the social and religious restrictions associated with the nostalgic image of Sir Francis as an ideal, faithful aristocratic captain.

Steven Spielberg's *The Adventures of Tintin: The Secret of the Unicorn* is a much freer adaptation. The basic skeleton of the plot is from *Unicorn*, though the entire middle act of the movie—in which Tintin is kidnapped, taken prisoner on a ship, escapes with Captain Haddock, and crashes in the desert—is taken from the unrelated story *The Crab with the Golden Claws*. The only element of *Red Rackham's Treasure* to survive somewhat intact is the discovery of the globe (though this discovery is rewritten so that it is a fraction of the treasure, with the rest yet to be found). Perhaps the largest change is the transformation of the collector Sakharine into the suave, diabolical villain of the film. While *Red Rackham* lacks anything like a traditional antagonist, *Crab* and *Unicorn* both have one in the form of an opium-smuggling operation and the Bird brothers. These are cast aside in favor of a complete overhaul in which Sakharine is not only the mastermind behind the theft of the models, the criminal search for the treasure, and the illicit activities abroad the *Karaboudjan*, but also a direct descendant of Red Rackham.

The Sakharine reimagined by Spielberg and the screenwriters (Steven Moffat, Edgar Wright, and Joe Cornish) is a modern-day pirate, with his own pirate ship in the form of the *Karaboudjan* and his own crew of mercenaries, and yet he is markedly different from his physically identical ancestor. He is elegant, sophisticated, intelligent, and diabolical, with a taste for the finer things and a gift for convoluted plans filled with betrayals and double-crosses. Thus he makes an interesting contrast with not only the drunken, belligerent Haddock but with his own ancestor. This version of Sakharine is unmistakably aristocratic, using the privilege of wealth to hide the brutality and criminality he shares with Red Rackham. Making him the occupant of Marlinspike Hall may introduce questions of plot logic (why has he never searched his own cellar?), but it also demonstrates that he is the outwardly respectable face of modern piracy. Indeed, while the Haddocks have declined into poverty and obscurity with nothing but nostalgia for the past glories of their ancestor, Sakharine has modified the methods of his ancestor to assert his own privilege and freedom from a position of power while maintaining the appearance of respectability. In essence he has resolved the paradox of piracy, which offers a sort of liberty that can only be defined in opposition to a regulated society, by keeping the violent methods and greedy motives of piracy but doing so from within the very society which once would have outlawed him. He does so primarily by having others do the dirty work. At the end of the film, when he finally embraces his full ancestry enough to engage in a direct duel, he violates the terms of the social contract, which allows him to be a pirate as long as he does not publicly act like a pirate. He is punished both legally and financially for doing so.

Making Sakharine a direct descendant of Red Rackham changes the meaning of the flashback. In the original book and in the TV adaptation the flashback is primarily a means to provide exposition and to show how closely Haddock identifies with his ancestor. The flashback sequence in Spielberg's film is radically different, taking place in the Moroccan desert instead of Haddock's apartment and in some ways being presented as half-mirage/half-delirium from alcohol and alcohol withdrawal. It begins with one of the film's most striking images, in which the *Unicorn* appears and sails over sand dunes as if they were waves. This sets the tone for Haddock's narration, which is far more fantastical and melodramatic than the version in the original book or the TV adaptation—raging seas instead of calm ones, swelling orchestral music, an extended battle sequence in which the camera sweeps through the hold and through the burning sails, a pirate crew which boards the ship as their own swings entirely across its deck, a Sir Francis who performs acrobatic feats worthy of actor Errol Flynn, and a Rackham who appears from amidst flames like a demonic force.

While the book and TV adaptation present this flashback as a recording of historical fact straight from the journals of Sir Francis, in the 1991 adaptation it is presented as a story Haddock only fully remembers under the influence of alcohol and in a berserker rage. This Sir Francis and Red Rackham instantly begin to duel, with the pirate being a dashing and powerful fighter. It also makes the treasure not booty plundered by Red Rackham but booty recaptured from the pirates Sir Francis was sent to hunt. The naval captain escapes with the help of a knife hidden in his hat, duels Rackham as usual, and blows up the ship only after seeing the pirate unmasked for the first time, revealing to Haddock that Sakharine is the villain's descendant and that Rackham pledged that the Haddocks would be forever cursed. It is an odd adaptation of the book's central sequence, at once casting it as more conventionally exciting and dramatic and making it possible to be read as a fantasy rather than history. Both Red Rackham and Sir Francis receive upgrades in terms of fighting ability and general swashbuckling appeal. The original book and the TV adaptation both contain hints that Captain Haddock is viewing his ancestor through the lens of pirate literature and popular culture—making him conform to the cinematic image of the swashbuckler rather than the truthful account of an historical figure—but this is the first version of the story which seems to suggest that the entire sequence might be the captain's delusion.

The film invents a climax that has no original in Hergé but serves as a mirror image to this flashback sequence, in which the descendants of Red Rackham and Sir Francis face off against each other onboard ship much like their ancestors once did. The climactic fight at the end of the film begins with enormous dockside cranes and escalates to Sakharine using a sword cane much like his ancestor's weapon and descending the crane wreckage in a manner identical to Red Rackham boarding the *Unicorn*. This serves to reinforce the idea of Captain Haddock as a legitimate swashbuckler in the tradition of his ancestor rather than the bumbling alcoholic who accidentally stumbles into a victory but it again introduces the question of reality versus fantasy. Haddock casts himself in the role of the dashing adventurer he sees in his ancestor down to a modernized but otherwise almost exact recreation of the old duel. Whether he really is as heroic as Sir Francis—indeed, whether Sir Francis was as heroic as his descendant imagines—is a question that the film leaves somewhat ambiguous.

The film has an interesting relationship with piracy, creating its own elegant, sophisticated modern-day pirate and depicting the golden age pirate as far more dashing but also far more loathsome than he is in either the book or the TV adaptation. While the book and the TV adaptation play with ambiguities around the character of Captain Haddock, showing qualities and sympathies more closely associated with pirates than with the more traditionally heroic Tintin and making him a sort of socially acceptable brigand, Spielberg's film makes sure to provide Haddock with more conventionally redeeming qualities. Haddock is forced to learn a lesson about believing in himself and even gives Tintin a morally uplifting lecture on the same topic. He is responsible for uncovering the true villain and fights him directly in the romantic, swashbuckling tradition of his ancestor. There are suggestions that he will give up or at least moderate his drinking in his uncharacteristic self-loathing at how alcohol cost him his ship. He even solves one of the film's final puzzles, using his naval knowledge to point out a non-existent island on the globe and so reveals the key to the treasure, and there is an implication that he will buy the ancestral home back for himself. Having proven himself worthy, he puts on his ancestor's hat and sets off on a new adventure. The treasure is scrubbed clean of ethical questions, because in this adaptation it is explicitly the product of raided pirate ships rather than the ill-gotten gains of a recently plundered ship.

In some ways making Sakharine not only the villain but a descendant of Red Rackham and a pirate himself throws the story out of balance. Rather than containing piracy to the past, where it can be viewed with enough historical distance to seem romantic or appealing through a nostalgic lens, it insists on presenting piracy as a clear and present danger. Having Red Rackham and his descendant be identical and active threats to the protagonists leaves no room for Captain Haddock to reveal his more piratical tendencies. He cannot be the same ambiguous figure with both piratical and heroic traits when his opponent is viewed as completely villainous and explicitly a pirate. In this situation his heroism comes from rejecting piracy entirely. While Hergé and the TV adaptation tease the notion that violence, criminality, and social transgressions at least have their appeal, *The Adventures of Tintin: The Secret of the Unicorn* attributes those qualities only to its clearly villainous pirates and leaves its protagonists as wholly, unquestionably good. It changes the story from a deliberate throwback to Verne and Stevenson filled with fun puzzles to be solved, a treasure to be found, and the vicarious thrills of piracy to a psychodrama in which Haddock has to resolve his issues with family, low self-esteem, and drinking and imposes a clear moral in place of romantic yearnings. This has the ironic effect of making the most modern of the adaptations feel the most old-fashioned. Rather than embracing the moral and social ambiguities of the pirate, it makes piracy entirely negative and defines heroism as the rejection of anything that pirates would do. No pirates are allowed in this club.

Notes

1. Dates given are the year of first publication in book form.
2. A much stronger case could be made against 1942's *The Shooting Star*, which Hugo Frey has accused of the types of anti-Semitic views published by *Le Soir* during the occupation and which arguably recur in later Tintin stories.
3. All three episodes were directed by Stéphane Bernasconi. *Unicorn* was adapted by J.D. Smith, Christophe Poujol, and Robert Réa. *Red Rackham* was adapted by Alex Boon and Réa.

Works Cited

The Adventures of Tintin. Eclipse/Nelvana, 1991–1992.
The Adventures of Tintin: The Secret of the Unicorn. Dir. Steven Spielberg. Paramount, 2011.
Apostolidès, Jean-Marie. *The Metamorphoses of Tintin.* Stanford: Stanford University Press, 2010.
Assouline, Pierre. *Hergé, The Man Who Created Tintin.* Oxford: Oxford University Press, 2009.
Canfield, Rob. "Something's Mizzen: Anne Bonny, Mary Read, 'Polly,' and Female Counter-Roles on the Imperialist Stage." *South Atlantic Review* 66.2 (2001): 45–63.
Dawdy, Shannon Lee, and Joe Bonni. "Towards a General Theory of Piracy." *Anthropological Quarterly* 85.3 (2012): 673–99.
Deane, Bradley. "Imperial Boyhood: Piracy and the Play Ethic." *Victorian Studies* 53.4 (2011): 689–714.
Farr, Michael. *Tintin and Company.* London: Egmont, 2011.
_____. *Tintin: The Complete Companion.* London: Egmont, 2001.
Foundas, Scott. "Boy Wonder." *Film Comment* 48.1 (Jan/Feb 2012): 38–41.
Frey, Hugo. "Trapped in the Past: Anti-Semitism in Hergé's *Flight 714.*" *History and Politics in French Language Comics and Graphic Novels.* Mark McKinney (ed.). Jackson: University Press of Mississippi, 2008, 27–43.
Goddin, Phillippe. *The Art of Hergé, Inventor of Tintin.* Michael Farr (trans.). San Francisco: Last Gasp, 2009.
Hergé. *The Adventures of Tintin.* Leslie Lonsdale-Cooper and Michael Turner (trans.). London: Egmont, 2007.
Hergé's Adventures of Tintin. Belvana, 1957.
Lofficier, Jean-Marc, and Randy Lofficier. *The Pocket Essential Tintin.* London: Pocket Essentials, 2002.
Mackie, Erin. "Welcome the Outlaw: Pirates, Maroons, and Caribbean Countercultures." *Cultural Critique* 59 (2005): 24–62.
McCarthy, Tom. *Tintin and the Secret of Literature.* London: Granta, 2006.
Peeters, Benoit. *Hergé: Son of Tintin.* Tina Kover (trans.). Baltimore: Johns Hopkins University Press, 2012.
Thompson, Harry. *Tintin: Hergé and His Creation.* London: Hodder and Stoughton, 1991.
Tisseron, Serge. "Family Secrets and Social Memory in 'Les aventures de Tintin.'" Barbara Harshav (trans.). *Yale French Studies* 102 (2002): 145–59.
Turley, Hans. "Piracy, Identity, and Desire in 'Captain Singleton.'" *Eighteenth-Century Studies*, 31.2 (1997): 199–214.

Masculine Ideal/ Cultural Treasure
Long John Silver in Treasure Planet

SUE MATHESON

> Like a Candarian zapwing overtaking its prey, Flint and his band of renegades swooped in out of nowhere. And then, gathering up their spoils, vanished without a trace. Flint's secret trove was never found but stories have persisted that it remains hidden somewhere at the farthest reaches of the galaxy stowed with riches beyond imagination the loot of a thousand worlds.... Treasure Planet.
> —Ron Clements and Jon Musker's *Treasure Planet*

Glittering treasure troves have fascinated young men for centuries. As David Head remarks, in *Howard Pyle's Book of Pirates: Fiction, Fact and Fancy Concerning the Buccaneers and Marooners of the Spanish Main*, "[b]oys love pirates and they have loved pirates for a long time" (93). Presenting "an alternative model of manliness" (Eastman 99), the figure of the pirate has been a role model for boys since Alexandre Exquemelin's *Bucaniers of America* rocketed off the press in 1678. In late nineteenth-century America, adventure stories about pirates (with little of the lust and rapine found in Exquemelin's tales) were written to allay parental fears that middle-class boys were becoming soft and weak. First encountered by young readers in genteel magazines that promoted middle-class gender ideals and ensured children's reading habits were guided toward the right ends, pirate stories were designed to appeal to the "natural savagery" of children and encourage boys to experience what G. Stanley Hall termed "their primitive stage in the proper dose" (qtd. in Head 111).[1] Pirate stories, filled with "violence and gushing blood" (qtd. in

Head 95), by authors like Robert Louis Stevenson and Howard Pyle, were thought to instill in young men the masculine vigor that child psychologists thought they needed to become forceful adults.

Written for its author's stepson, *Treasure Island* first appeared in serial form as *The Sea Cook* in *Young Folks* magazine (1881–82). Later, the story was republished as a best-selling juvenile novel. Filled with masculine vigor, *Treasure Island* was Stevenson's first financial and critical success. Frequently dramatized, the story has been adapted to the screen over fifty times. To date, Hollywood studios have released twenty-one versions of Stevenson's swashbuckling money-maker. No print exists of *The Story of Treasure Island*, a one reeler produced by Vitagraph in 1908 or Thomas Edison's 1912 rendering of Stevenson's novel. A six reeler, directed by Sidney Franklin and released by Fox Film Corporation in 1918 is the earliest surviving version of *Treasure Island*. The most recent film adaptations of Stevenson's desert island romance include Leigh Scott's *Pirates of Treasure Island* (2006), a direct to DVD film by Asylum, Alain Berberian's *L'ile aux tresors* (2007) from FIT Productions/ Bac Films (France), Steve Barron's *Treasure Island* (2012) from RHI Entertainment, and Sam Miller and T.J. Scott's TV series *Black Sails* (2014–17) from Starz. Notably, Walt Disney Productions has cashed in on *Treasure Island*'s enduring allure, having adapted Stevenson's tale of "buccaneers and buried gold" to film three times. In 1950, *Treasure Island* was Disney's first completely live-action film, starring Bobby Driscoll as Jim Hawkins and Robert Newton as Long John Silver. In 1996, the Muppets successfully set sail with Long John Silver (Tim Curry) in *Muppet Treasure Island*. Then, in 2002, Disney's reworking of *Treasure Island* in outer space, *Treasure Planet*, depicted "alien worlds and other galactic wonders," in 2-D and 3-D animation.

The success or failure of Disney's adaptations of Stevenson's wildly popular masterpiece has depended on their faithfulness to the original. In 1950, *Treasure Island* was a moneymaker at the box office, grossing $1.85 million in the first year of its release (*Top Grosses* 58). Loyal in most respects to Stevenson's story, this movie was also a critical success. On the 16th of August, the *New York Times* reviewer found "the greatest pirate story of 'em all" to be "a grand and glorious entertainment" and "a splendid escape into the land of adventure" designed for spectators aged six or sixty who were sure to be "caught up in the magic of this thrilling quest for fabulous wealth" before closing with the comment, "pity the heart that is so worn and tired that it will not respond to the timeless fascination of 'Treasure Island'" (*THE SCREEN*). Critical reaction to the Disney and The Jim Henson's Muppet Company's spoof of *Treasure Island* in 1996, which grossed $34,327,391 million at the domestic box office (*Box Office MTP*), were also very positive. On the 16th of February, the *New York Times* reviewer Stephen Holden approved of *Muppet Treasure Island* as "intelligent nonsense." The fun in this version of

Treasure Island, he says, is found "in watching the Muppets defuse the swashbuckling tale of its scariness" (Holden). Curiously, Disney's *Treasure Planet*, released in 2002, did not appeal its critics and audiences. Judged on the 27th of November by the *New York Times* to be "less an act of homage [to Stevenson and his tale] than a clumsy and cynical bit of piracy, designed to steal time and money from schoolchildren and their harried, Pottered-out parents during this very long holiday weekend" (Scott), *Treasure Planet* bombed at the box office. Made for $140 million, the movie strayed from Stevenson's popular account of piracy to yo-ho-ho a lifetime domestic gross of only $38,176,783 (*Box Office TP*).[2]

Complaining that Jim (Joseph Gordon-Levitt) and his companions "set out in search of loot and adventure and wind up learning lessons about friendship, loyalty and self-esteem," Scott effectively pinpoints why *Treasure Planet* has been under appreciated. Very little conflict drives the film narrative. *Treasure Planet* is not an action adventure filled with popular stereotypes of pirates from the imagined Caribbean of the eighteenth century. An art film that broke animation barriers, *Treasure Planet* contains extremely complex characters and focuses on the complicated trajectory of Jim Hawkins' transition to manhood. Ron Clements and John Musker's high seas adventure (in outer space) is a 70/30 hybrid that modifies the character of Long John Silver (Brian Murray), one of the most popular pirates ever to sail the Spanish Main.

To begin, Clements' 70/30 Law ensures that 70 percent of the film's material remains true to the spirit of Stevenson's high seas adventure while the remaining 30 percent (being the sci-fi or modern) updates the tale. As Andy Gaskill, *Treasure Planet*'s Art Director, points out in the film's visual commentary, any given image will feel essentially traditional. You will look at [*Treasure Planet*] and say: "oh that's an eighteenth century sailing ship." And then on second take you will realize: "oh, wait a minute. It's different. It's new. It's odd." Also updated, the film narrative offers an altered version of the Hawkins family. Jim's father (a faithful family man in Stevenson's version) abandons his young son. On the *Legacy*, Clements and Musker's Sea Cook acts as a surrogate father, addressing problems created by the absence of Jim's father and guiding the boy to maturity.

Silver's uncharacteristic fondness for the boy alters the presentation (and the character) of the pirate in *Treasure Planet*. Hunting for hidden loot, fictional pirates in the desert island romance adhere to rigid plot conventions, being colorful catalysts for the narrative's young hero who turns away from lawlessness. "Capturing Spanish galleons, burying glittering treasures, punishing miscreants with marooning or walking the plank, [and seeking] a new adventure on the blue Caribbean seas" (Avery 1), pirates are romantic figures accompanied by "a certain lurid glamour of the heroical" (Head 94). One of the most iconic, fictional pirates populating the popular imagination, Long

John Silver is a cunning, charismatic opportunist in *Treasure Island*. But as Disney's "first and (so far) only cyborg" (Davis 193) Long John Silver lacks the ruthless drive of the deep-sea desperado. When he is not in pursuit of Flint's treasure, he displays genuine affection for Jim Hawkins. Generally, fictional pirates serve as negative examples from which the boy hero turns away in the desert island romance, but on board the *Legacy*, Silver becomes a positive role model for the boy. Replacing Jim's father, who was "the taking-off-and-never-coming-back sort," the Sea Cook spends much of his screen time discouraging unruliness while developing in Jim the masculine vigor expected of boys in the late Victorian period. "[L]ike it or not," he tells his charge, "I'll be pounding a few skills into that thick head of yours to keep you out of trouble."

Neophytes are often tortured during their initiations (Eliade 189), but Jim does not experience mutilation, tattooing or scarring to represent his symbolic death as a child and resurrection as an adult on the *Legacy*. As a surrogate father, Silver teaches Jim how to work (to stick to a job and finish it), how to pick his fights, and how to chart his own course throughout life. He also keeps his promise not to do his student "any favors." Training the teenager to scrape space barnacles off the *Legacy*'s hull and unsatisfied with the work, he shouts: "put your elbow into it." Insisting the boy does his job well, the Sea Cook makes Jim to experience the true dimension of a man's existence and compels his charge to assume "the responsibility that goes with being a man" (Eliade 191–92). In "Learning About Manhood: gender ideals and the middle-class family in nineteenth-century America," E. Anthony Rotundo points out that coupling hard work with moral fiber was a refrain that ran through father-son correspondence in the nineteenth century—and while middle-class fathers taught their sons to work, they instilled ethics in their offspring (45). Showing Jim how to work hard, Silver becomes the boy's moral tutor. A series of scenes illustrate how different Silver is from Jim's deadbeat dad. Next, as the boy puts his elbow into scrubbing the deck, a flashback introduces the viewer to Jim as a very young child attempting to show his father a toy and being ignored. In the next shot, as Silver casts off from the *Legacy*'s hold in a solar surfer, Jim remembers waking early, running downstairs to find his mother sobbing, and chasing his father, who is leaving for the last time, along the dock only to be ignored again and left behind when the boat sails. When this memory fades, Jim finds Silver inviting him to come on board. After sailing, Silver compliments Jim's ability to handle the craft: "[i]f I could manoeuvre a skiff like that at your age," he says, "they'd be bowing in the streets when I walked by today."

In *American Manhood: Transformations in Masculinity from the Revolution to the Modern Era*, Rotundo points out that the difference between a boy and a man is found in "frivolous behavior, the lack of worthy aims, and the want of self-control, for what underpins the contrast between boyhood and manhood is a set of assumptions about how to control the aggressive passions that were considered a male birthright. In nineteenth-century America, boys were thought to be driven by their passions and their "eager, impulsive, 'almost brutish'" natures, and to become a man, a boy needed to transform his impulsive passions into "the purposeful energies of the man" (Rotundo *American Manhood* 21–22). Academies and colleges were devised to serve this purpose; apprenticeships were also considered to build character and maturity (Rotundo *American Manhood* 21). Jim's apprenticeship as Silver's cabin boy on the *Legacy* serves this purpose, transforming his character and enabling him to transition to manhood at the movie's end. At the beginning of *Treasure Planet*, Jim's arrest and warning not to solar surf in a restricted area demonstrates his lack of direction and self-control. This activity contrasts sharply with his purposeful use of the solar surfer to change door of Flint's portal at the movie's end. Jim's effectiveness (ensuring the treasure hunters escape "total planet destruction") prompts Captain Aemelia's (Emma Thompson) promises to recommend him to the Interstellar Academy. "They could use a *man* like you," she says (italics mine).

Here it should be noted that social representations of manhood "are not edicts determined on high and enforced by law.... American manliness itself is a learned, used, and reinforced cultural construct that is reshaped by individuals in the course of life" (Rotundo *American Manhood* 7). Aptly, throughout *Treasure Planet*, masculine gender ideals change according to characters' situations and circumstances, for the transition from boyhood to manhood is a very complicated trajectory. Silver's complicated, 70/30 characterization not only exhibits two popular and diametrically opposed models of nineteenth-century manliness, it also displays the plastic nature of masculine gender ideals. Fundamentally, Silver is a Masculine Primitive who cares only for Flint's treasure. At times, however, he becomes a Christian Gentleman who possesses "the ability to love, and do the right thing by the boy to whom he becomes a father and a true friend" (Davis 197). He is at once villain and a hero—a positive and a negative role model for Jim.

Privileging the needs of the individual over those of society and celebrating mental and physical toughness and the "male" competitive, assertive drives, the Masculine Primitive is an important figure as Jim matures on board the *Legacy*. As Rotundo remarks, natural passions and instincts suddenly became a valued part of a man's character in the late nineteenth century: and in response to the notion that all males, civilized or not, shared the same primordial instincts for survival a new pattern of male behavior arose in popular literature in which one finds the evaluation of men according to their physical strength and energy, the view of man as the master animal who could draw on primitive instincts when reason would not work, and the popularity of the metaphor in which a man's life was a competitive jungle struggle (Rotundo "Learning About Manhood" 40–41). "Gentlemen of fortune," Stevenson's Silver and his pirates are Masculine Primitives, living "tough" and eating and drinking "like fighting cocks" (103). The only man whom Flint feared, the Sea Cook easily keeps company with "the roughest crew afloat ... [indeed] the devil himself would have been feared to go to sea with them" (104). Aboard the *RSL Legacy*, Captain Aemelia may think Silver and his crew are "a ludicrous parcel of driveling galoots," but Billy Bones (Patrick McGoohan) is correct when he warns Jim at the Benbow Inn that Silver is to be feared. Silver often expresses manliness that celebrates the "violence, savagery, and aggression" that Victorian parents believed boys had to experience in order to become men (Head 111). After Bones gasps "beware the cyborg," Silver arrives at the Benbow Inn. Even though he only appears as a cast shadow, his vigor, his strength, and his personality convey his aggressive primitive masculinity. Silver is clearly in charge throughout this scene, breaking down the door of the inn and ordering the pirates to find Bones' map.

Being the source and provider of food, Silver is also a powerful, aggressive figure on the *Legacy*. Notably, the Masculine Primitive's kitchen is not a gentle, domestic, feminized sphere. When Silver chops, dices, and sets fire to the ingredients of his famous bonzabeast stew with the "hunk of hardware" that is his right hand, viewers are reminded that fathering is not like mothering. Preparing food to be eaten in Silver's galley is an aggressive, messy, and violent activity that satiates the appetites of others. As Margaret Visser remarks in *The Rituals of Dinner*, "violence is necessary if any organism is to ingest another. Animals are murdered to produce meat; vegetables are torn up, peeled and chopped; most of what we eat is treated with fire; and chewing is designed remorselessly to finish what killing and cooking began" (8). Similarly, as Eileen T. Bender points out in "The Woman Who Came to Dinner: Dining and Divining a Feminist 'Aesthetic,'" "images of food are rarely neutral" (316).

In *Treasure Planet*, food and the treatment of it serve as indicators of character, revealing another example of the 70/30 Law at work. In the *Legacy*'s galley, the modified Masculine Primitive is shown to be only partly domesticated. Emphasizing the savage nature of life, an eyeball, one of the ingredients of Silver's "old family recipe" bobs about in the bowl of stew that Silver gives to Delbert Doppler (David Hyde Pierce), Jim's traveling companion. Doppler loses his appetite when the eyeball floats to the surface of his meal. A civilized intellectual, he is unable to put it in his mouth. Silver, on the other hand, jokes that the eyeball is "a part of the old family," and does not hesitate to swallow the revolting morsel. At base, the Sea Cook remains a primitive, self-interested force. "Now mark me, the lot of ya," he says, dominating Scroop (Michael Wincott) who accused him of having a "soft spot" for the cabin boy, "I care for one thing and one thing only, Flint's trove. Do you think I'd risk it all for the sake of some nose-wiping little whelp.... I cozied up to that kid to keep him off our scent, but I ain't gone soft." Much later, on Treasure Planet, Silver reveals the softer side of his personality that he did not show to the mutineers to his surrogate son. "Whatever you heard back there, at least the part concerning you," he says to Jim, "I didn't mean a word of it. If that blood-thirsty lot thought I'd gone soft, they'd have gutted us both."

An ethic of compassion that directed a man's attention to the needs and concerns of others in nineteenth-century America, the ideal of the Christian Gentleman is also a significant element of Silver's character in *Treasure Planet*. As Rotundo notes, this ideal stresses love, kindness and compassion as "worthy attitudes for a man," because they form "the basis for right actions on his part" ("Learning About Manhood" 38). Unlike the Masculine Primitive solely bent on self-gratification, the Christian Gentleman fosters social good and privileged the needs of society over those of the individual—via philanthropic activities, acts of self-sacrifice and a deep involvement in family life ("Learning About Manhood" 38). Aptly, this gender ideal emphasizes impulse control on the part of the individual. Because his band of primitive cutthroats are incapable of self-control, Silver, capable of reason and restraint, has to constrain them, preventing Scroop and the crew from killing Jim once after the *Legacy* has begun its journey. As he takes on the work of parenting Jim, the Sea Cook becomes a Christian Gentleman.

Today, the Christian Gentleman is readily recognizable as "a media creation ... that etched itself into the collective unconscious in American culture" after the Second World War (Newman). From 1957 to 1963, the Christian Gentleman appeared as the American father in the popular series, *Leave It to Beaver*, Ward Cleaver (Hugh Beaumont). The Christian Gentleman was also foregrounded in *My Three Sons* from 1960 to 1972 in the character of Steven Douglas (Fred MacMurray). Other television husbands and fathers, dependable, caring family men, include Darrin (Dick York) in *Bewitched* (1964–1972) and Ricky Ricardo (Desi Arnaz) in *The Lucy Show* (1962–1968), Wilbur Post (Alan Lane) in *Mr. Ed* (1961–1966), Jim Anderson (Robert Young) in *Father Knows Best* (1954–1960), and Dick Van Dyke (Dick Van Dyke) in the *Dick Van Dyke Show* (1961–1966) all household heads. These popular representations of the caring American father remind us that "a man's obligations to his sons were not only instrumental and worldly; he was also encouraged to love and cherish them" (Rotundo *American Manhood* 27).

On board the *Legacy*, Silver fulfills his paternal obligations and grows to cherish his surrogate son. An important measure of a man's public usefulness and success, fathering involves a number of duties. Fathers are expected not only to be protective of their children; they are also supposed to prepare their sons in a practical sense for entry into the world: being not only in charge of their sons' educations, they also impart the values associated with work, achievement, and property and teach them "the importance of perseverance and thrift, of diligence and punctuality, of industry and ambition" (Rotundo *American Manhood* 26–27). Demonstrating public usefulness, Silver teaches Jim to care for himself and others by maintaining and caring for the ship. As a prime example of the good father, Silver is pleasant, mild-mannered and devoted to the good of the community on board. He performs his duties as a sea cook faithfully, governs his passions rationally when Jim becomes difficult (leaving Morph to keep an eye on the "pup"), submits to his fate and to his place on board by obeying Captain Aemelia, and treats his dependent crew and cabin boy with firm, but affectionate wisdom.

Jim's fiercely competitive personality is tempered under Silver's tutelage as he acquires the strength of character necessary to follow orders. As Jim learns to do his duty, he becomes a man, a socially useful citizen *and* a powerful individual on board ship. Doing "the right thing" is an important marker of the manhood that Jim acquires during his "character-building months in space." Before he boarded the Legacy, he was unable to do anything right— "messing up" and disappointing his mother. On board, he excels, working conscientiously without supervision. Silver comments one night: "thank heaven for little miracles. Up here for an hour and the deck's still in one piece." Notably, Jim becomes a Masculine Achiever as he learns from Silver. As Rotundo remarks, the Masculine Achiever, a standard of manhood generally linked with the economic forms of the nineteenth century, emphasized self-advancement via accomplishment, autonomy, and aggression. Hard work and persistence were not the only qualities needed for self-advancement. Ceaseless effort and independent action and thinking on the part of the individual were also necessary (Rotundo "Learning About Manhood" 36–37). Jim's hard work and dedication to duty earns him the respect of his captain and crewmates. He is trusted to safeguard his crewmates' lifelines during a solar storm, to scout ahead and find a defensible position on Treasure Planet, and to save the ship at the end of their adventures.

Caring in *Treasure Planet* not only guarantees that the work at hand is accomplished; it also ensures that the right thing is done and self-sacrifices are made. The importance of altruism, another marker of the Christian Gentleman, therefore cannot be overlooked when considering masculine gender ideals in *Treasure Planet*. In the end, it is Silver's altruism that enables him to give up Flint's loot in order to save Jim. As the planet explodes around him, Silver discovers that he can either have Flint's loot or bring Jim to safety. Doing the right thing, he rescues Jim even as he damns himself as "for a fool." As Silver runs through the portal that leads from the interior of the planet, he tells the boy not to worry about the sacrifice that he has just made. "Just a life-long obsession, Jim," he pants ironically, "I'll get over it." *Treasure Planet*, however, is not simply an updated version of the TV series *Father Knows Best* (1954–60) set in outer space. Silver's selflessness redeems him, but it does not reform his nature. At their adventures' end, he asks his surrogate son to "ship out.... You and me, Hawkins and Silver, full of ourselves and no ties to anyone." Having acquired self-control and reason himself, Jim turns down Silver's offer and instead enters the Interstellar Academy. He appears in uniform as an Interstellar cadet at the story's end, validating "the American belief that the autonomous person is the basic unit of society and the ultimate source of cultural value" and confirming the "modern notion that the core of each individual is an inner essence, a unique combination of temperament, passion, and personal experience untouched by society" (Rotundo *American Manhood* 279, 285).

Jim's decision to not accompany Silver privileges John Locke's concept that the individual "exists in relation to the state, the law, the economy as a citizen and a public actor" over Jean-Jacques Rousseau's spiritual and emotional definition of the individual in terms of "the passionate or 'romantic' self" (Rotundo *American Manhood* 279). His choice of a socially sanctioned, vigorous masculinity offers a satisfying nineteenth-century conclusion, identifying law, order, and good behavior as the markers of the well-mannered adult. However, as Rotundo remarks, the balance of bourgeois values for men in America has tipped from nineteenth-century standards of self-discipline to the modern emphasis on self-expression, from self-denial to self-enjoyment throughout the twentieth century (*American Manhood* 279). As Chris Land points out in "Flying the black flag: revolt, revolution and the social organization of piracy in 'the golden age,'" the pirate is "a figure in full sympathy with the Zeitgeist of the early 21st century" (170). Promoting the male virtue of independence, Clements and Musker's Silver points out that he and Morph cannot go to jail and exist in "a cage—because they are free spirits." Ensuring the survival of the Masculine Primitive, the Sea Cook is freed, and in harmony with the spirit of the twenty-first century, Silver's storyline resists closure at the movie's end.

As in the traditional pirate story, Silver's self interest and emphasis on individualism in *Treasure Planet* is linked with poor choices and wrong actions. Here, however, it should be noted that primitive masculinity in this movie also acts as a positive catalyst for the hero. Voyaging with the pirate creates Jim's "true manliness and cement[ed] it in place" (Head 110). Without the Sea Cook, Jim could not have developed the strength of character necessary to win back the map and the treasure at the film's end. Without Silver's help, Jim could not have constructed a solar surfer and saved the *Legacy*. As Roger Clements notes in the audio commentary accompanying *Treasure Planet*, at the end of the film Jim "had to go through the experience to get to where he's at now. He had to have met Silver. He had to have a father to help him mature."

Revealing that manliness is inseparable from the duties that a man owes others, *Treasure Island* ends, striking a happy balance between individual and community. Reunited with his mother, Delbert Doppler, Captain Aemelia, and B.E.N (Martin Short), Jim celebrates community at the rebuilt Benbow Inn. Having earned approval, made friendships, attained power, and won love, he has changed the perceptions of those who earlier considered him Other. Because this celebration of family and friends would be incomplete without Jim's father, Silver also appears at the celebration. When the young man looks up into the sky, the pirate's smiling face is seen outlined in the clouds above the Inn. A free spirit, a felon, *and* a father, the Sea Cook is included in the family gathering, watching from a distance over the son he has fathered. Redeemed and sanitized, Long John Silver in *Treasure Planet*'s joyous, highly sentimental finale does not resemble Stevenson's Sea Cook's in his departure at the closing of *Treasure Island* at all. In *Treasure Island*, Silver sneaks away from the *Hispaniola* as the social outcast he is, a "gentleman of fortune," "a prodigious villain and imposter" (Stevenson 105, 329). After his departure, Jim dismisses the pirate out of hand, saying "I think we were all pleased to be so cheaply quit of him" (Stevenson 339). In *Treasure Planet*, Jim's reaction to Silver's leave-taking is intensely emotional: he chokes back tears as he says goodbye to his surrogate father.

As Rotundo points out, masculine gender ideals are closely related to the broader values of the culture in which they develop, and represent a series of cultural choices out of the vast range of qualities possible for a man. A distinct and powerful code that offers a set of values, manliness determined ideals, forged identity and defined reality for Victorian boys and men ("Learning About Manhood" 36). "Recommended by arbiters of genteel taste as appropriate reading for children, especially for boys" (Head 100), pirate tales by writers like Howard Pyle and Robert Louis Stevenson offered boys, encouraged in the nineteenth and the twentieth centuries to acquire masculine vigor, manly vitality. In final analysis, Long John Silver in *Treasure Planet* imparts a distinct and powerful code of masculinity that Victorian readers would have recognized as their own and that explains the allure of the pirate. Remarkably, it seems the Primitive Masculine has also acted as an important surrogate father throughout the twentieth century. In all, masculine gender ideals do not seem to have altered much since 1883. As Hollywood's success with the Sea Cook points out, Long John Silver is cultural treasure. And in *Treasure Planet*, the Masculine Primitive, the Masculine Achiever, and the Christian Gentleman are alive and well—and living in the twenty-first century.

Notes

1. For more information, see G. Stanley Hall's comments regarding civilizing boys on page 796 of "Corporal Punishments." *The Intelligence: A Semi-Monthly Journal of Education* 19 (December 15, 1899).

2. According to *Box Office Mojo*, *Treasure Planet*, released in theaters for only 79 days, closed February 13, 2003. The film's foreign lifetime gross totals only $71,401,332.

Works Cited

AVI. "Foreword." *Treasure Island*. New York: Aladdin, 2000, xi–xviii.
Bender, Eileen T. "The Woman Who Came to Dinner: Dining and Divining a Feminist 'Aesthetic.'" *Women's Studies: An Interdisciplinary Journal* 12.3 (1986): 315–33.
"Box Office Business for *Muppet Treasure Island*." 1990–2017. *IMDb*. http://www.imdb.com/title/tt0117110/business?ref_=tt_dt_bus. Accessed on 08/11/2017.
"Box Office Business for *Treasure Planet*." August 11, 2017. *Box Office Mojo*. http://www.boxofficemojo.com/movies/?id=treasureplanet.htm. Accessed on 08/11/2017.
Davis, Amy M. *Handsome Heroes and Vile Villains: Men in Disney's Feature Animation*. New Barnet, Herts: John Libby Publishing, 2013.
Eastman, Carolyn. "'Blood and Lust': Masculinity and Sexuality in Illustrated Print Portrayals of Early Pirates of the Caribbean." *New Men: Manliness in Early America*. Thomas A. Foster (ed.). New York: New York University Press, 2011, 95–115.
Eliade, Mircea. *The Sacred and the Profane: The Nature of Religion*. New York: Harcourt, 1987.
Head, David. "Howard Pyle's *Book of Pirates*: Fiction, Fact & Fancy Concerning the Buccaneers and Marooners of the Spanish Main." *The Washington & Jefferson College Review* 58 (2010): 93–112.
Holden, Stephen. "FILM REVIEW; Those Muppet Puppets as Wacky Swashbucklers." *New York Times* February 16, 1996. http://www.nytimes.com/movie/reviewres=9C00EFD91239F935A25751C0A960958260. Accessed on 05/10/2017.
Land, Chris. "Flying the Black Flag: Revolt, Revolution and the Social Organization of Piracy in 'The Golden Age.'" *Management & Organization History* 2 (2007): 169–92.
Newman, Andrew Adam. February 5, 2006. "Changin' in the Boys' Room." *New York Times*. www.sundaystyles/25DIAPERS.html?pagewanted=print&_r=0. Accessed on 05/10/2017.
Rotundo, E. Anthony. *American Manhood: Transformations in Masculinity from the Revolution to the Modern Era*. New York: Basic Books, 1993.
_____. "Learning About Manhood: Gender Ideals and the Middle-Class Family in Nineteenth-Century America." In *Manliness and Morality: Middle-Class Masculinity in Britain and America, 1800–1940*. J.A Mangan and James Walvin (eds.). New York: St. Martin's Press, 1987, 35–51.
Scott, A.O. "FILM REVIEW; 'Treasure Island' Flies into Neurosis." *New York Times*, November 27, 2002. http://www.nytimes.com/2002/11/27/movies/film-review-treasure-island-flies-into-neurosis.html. Accessed on 04/12/2017.
"THE SCREEN: TWO FILMS HAVE THEIR PREMIERES; 'Treasure Island,' with Bobby Driscoll and Robert Newton, Featured at the Mayfair Pictorial Review of Pilgrimage to Rome, 'Holy Year, 1950,' Is Presented by Fox at the Embassy." *New York Times*, August 16, 1950. http://www.nytimes.com/movie/reviewres=9400E4DE133DE03BBC4E52DFBE66838B649EE. Accessed on 04/12/2017.
Stevenson, Robert Louis. *Treasure Island*. New York: Aladdin, 2000.
"Top Grosses of 1950." *Variety* January 03, 1951. https://archive.org/stream/variety181-1951-01#page/n57/mode/1up:58. Accessed on 04/12/2017.
Visser Margaret. *The Rituals of Dinner: The Origins, Evolution, Eccentricities, and Meaning of Table Manners*. New York: Harper Perennial, 2008.

"What would the world be like without Captain Hook?"
A Freudian Analysis of Our Love for (Anti-)Villains.

TIAGO A.M. SARMENTO

> I'm going to tell you a story about a boy who would never grow up. About the pirate who wished to kill him. About the island where fairies roamed. But this isn't the story you've heard before because, sometimes, friends begin as enemies and enemies begin as friends. Sometimes to truly understand how things end we must first know how they begin.
>
> —Wendy, *Pan* [2014]

One of those cultural icons that have longed in folklore and myths are pirates. Their adventures in the unknown following an alleged marginal code created a popular fascination whose equivalent is present only in a few other popular culture and fiction characters such as Robin Hood, King Arthur, and the Olympian deities. Like everything that is popular and widespread, the culture industry and major corporations have taken ownership of such icons and sold them at whatever manner they see fit to generate profit. And like everything that is popular and comes from narration, some of the fictional pirates have been subverted, reimagined, and reinstalled both as heroes and villains. An illustrative example is offered by J.M. Barrie's *Peter Pan*[1] and his adventures against his archenemy Captain Hook, which is one of the most popular stories of the twentieth century. Barrie's story lends itself to many psychoanalytical interpretations that reflect Freudian theories. However, it is Steven Spielberg's cinematic adaptation, *Hook* (1991), and the latest version of the story, Joe Wright's *Pan* (2015), that perfectly illustrate many of the psychoanalytical theories elaborated by Freud and, particularly, the concept of the *unheimlich*,[2] the Oedipal Complex, and the spectator's identification with both good characters and villains.

When using Freudian theory to analyze fiction and characters, one must be cautious not to let its concepts fall under popular knowledge in a potentially distortive way. Unlike Jungian's archetypes, it is not possible to define to the letter what a character represents, because its representations lie within the single individual's psyche. An individual's affections are what make unconscious drives come forth and allow him/her to identify with a particular character, and not the opposite. Although it is possible to recognize certain cultural traits and common psychic processes, to reduce the individual's associations to representations "external" from one's psyche is a mistake that has long prevailed. And by "external" we also mean the Jungian collective unconscious, which suggests a previously given meaning not solely achieved by subjectivity.

Freud describes the *unheimlich* as an occurrence in which the subject is suddenly flooded by a heavy dose of anxiety/anguish[3] in the face of something seemingly unknown, but that is deeply familiar to the unconscious as a consequence of the process of *Verdrängung*[4]—translated into English as "repression" (a term that is very debatable in the field since it is not a literal translation). As the repressed material tries to resurface, the anguish causes an unpleasant sensation. Freud explains that the *unheimlich* is related to strong desires that have been repressed because external reality made them impossible to realize. The repressed desires thus provoke anguish[5] but this sentence's original meaning got lost in its various English translations. This point is of the uttermost importance because the English version states that the *unheimlich* relates to what is terrible, to everything that arouses dread and creeping terror (Freud "The Uncanny" 217). However, the original German version actually uses different terms, including "angst" (anxiety in English) and horror. Although the words may appear close in meaning, they indicate that the *unheimlich* is not only related to what is terrible, but also to what causes anguish and frightens. Highlighting these discrepancies is imperative considering that various translations in a methodology such as psychoanalysis, and thus distinct interpretations of Freudian theory, may generate misunderstandings. The *unheimlich* is not solely related to what causes dread and terror, but also to what brings anguish, which might not necessarily be a monster or a killer. It could be anything that speaks directly to an individual's repressed and/or unconscious desires.

Moreover, according to Freud the *unheimlich* is related to the primacy of psychic[6] reality and the realm of fantasy, desires, and affections within the individual as measured against the external reality ("The Uncanny" 249).

The *unheimlich* happens when psychic reality defies what external reality made us believe and accept, such as the desire to fly or to be invulnerable. If the world outside instills doubt about that reality, the *unheimlich* may occur, through the re-emergence of repressed desires and a temporary shock to the ego. This re-emergence manifests through Freudian slips, dreams, wits, humor, symptoms, pure anguish, and the *unheimlich*, to name a few of the most important effects. Throughout his work, Freud often remarks how the unconscious retains all the sensations and desires we have ever felt, some of them having been displaced, condensed, and even fragmented into other ideas, but its source material is retained and able to resurface. In "The Interpretation of Dreams," Freud argues that to dream is in fact to enter the realm of the child where we retain many feelings we previously experienced but were forced to repress (485). In its essence, the unconscious remains infantile and our earliest desires and repressions may come forth especially when dreaming, when the "ego"—another ill-translated term from the original in German, "Ich," the "I"—rests and keeps resistance at a minimum. On the other hand, Freud also mentions some specific ideas that are not retained by the unconscious: the idea of time, "negation" (*Verneinung*), the absence of contradiction, and one's own death ("The Unconscious" 187). Time is irrelevant in the unconscious because what happened in the past may still affect us today. The idea of negation implies that the denial, the "no," is nothing but a way of the repressed material to come to consciousness without causing anguish. And, finally, Freud believes that we are unconsciously convinced of our immortality ("Thoughts for the Times of War and Death" 295). This is epitomized by the fact that, in dreams, we cannot die and when we imagine our death we are somehow still present at the scene.

J.M. Barrie's play and its novelization are illustrative of many of the Freudian theories we have examined here. Primarily, this occurs because *Peter Pan* evokes the language of dreams. Many human delusions commonly present in dreams are evoked throughout the narrative, such as flying and being forever young. These abilities of Peter Pan can be considered as a cultural reference to the most common desires of all human beings. Amongst children's many fantastic desires, in fact, flying is always constant. Of course, this desire could only be understood under analysis and dream interpretation and in no way it could be considered as universal. Peter's ability to fly comes from a repressed desire or unconscious wish, according to Freud's theories, which argue that the unconscious realm of dreams is infantile and retains the drives that have been repressed.

On the other hand, it would be rather unpleasant for a regular individual to see another one flying out of nothing. This would bring him/her anguish caused by the strong desire the person was once forced to renounce due to its impossible realization. Therefore, as soon as something challenges an individual's beliefs about the external reality, the *unheimlich* arises (Freud "The Uncanny" 248). What separates a simple unknown and strange event from the uncanniness of the *unheimlich* is the fact that the latter is related to an innermost desire attached to high levels of affection, otherwise the unfamiliarity of something unknown would not cause a disconcerting effect. Yet, as Freud asserts ("The Uncanny" 249), it is easier to achieve the fantastic effect in fiction and, due to our "acceptance" of that realm, not experience uneasiness or anguish when it occurs. Fiction "suspends" reality: when we watch *Hook*, we tend to ignore the fact that a human being cannot fly in the real world, because flying is part of the reality of the fictional universe onscreen. The movie *Hook* exemplifies the effects of the *unheimlich* through its depiction of an adult Peter Banning (Robin Williams) who has forgotten that he had been Peter Pan. Once he returns to the fantastic dreamlike place that is Neverland, he is able to remember his forgotten abilities. It is therefore the return of the character to a realm of dreams that allows him remembrance (and resurgence) of his infantile desires.

In the film, the resurgence of Peter's abilities occurs only through the great angst that the protagonist experiences for losing his children, who have been kidnapped by Hook. That is his motivation to try and re-acquire the ability to fly. Simultaneously, thinking about his children and their happy moments together is the same factor that brings Peter joy, allowing him to fly—which apparently triggers the rest of his abilities. Once those abilities have returned, he forgets his serious duties and acts childishly, just as the young Peter Pan used to. This is comparable to the "child within our unconscious" that is brought back every night while sleeping, which belongs to the realm of dreams, where time stands still, where mermaids and crocodiles obsessed with a single human being are credible, and flying is possible. This is the realm where every boy that lost his parents may find parental figures, as it occurs in the original story to Wendy when she becomes Peter's mother or even when she expresses her desire to be acknowledged as his "pretend-to-be" wife. This is the realm where nothing is really lost or forgotten, unlike the daily, busy lives of contemporary society, which have caused Peter Banning to grow up and forget about his lust for adventure and his childish lightheartedness as adults usually do. The difference between the realm of dreams and daily reality is epitomized in the film by the sequences that depict the return of the repressed through the phobia of airplanes in Banning's life and his problem with heights on Hook's ship. When growing up Peter has repressed his ability to fly, which now resurfaces through his fear and anguish.

The Freudian theory on the *unheimlich* is manifest in the film *Pan* as well. When the boy Peter (Levi Miller) is condemned by Blackbeard (Hugh Jackman) to walk the plank and fall to his doom, he stupefies the ruthless villain and hundreds of his slaves (the orphans he has been kidnapping for decades) by suddenly floating before hitting the floor hundreds of feet below. This moment produces the effects of the *unheimlich* in the fictional spectators of the event, especially in Blackbeard. The pirate captain had previously seen fairies, mermaids, and other fantastic creatures, but he reacts with anguish to Peter's ability to fly. The narrative justifies such a reaction by explaining that the appearance of the "flying boy" fulfills a prophecy about an orphan, born to a fairy prince and a woman girl, who would return to Neverland when he reached a certain age and would then overthrow the cruel pirate. Nevertheless, this sequence from *Pan* also illustrates Freud's theory that an *unheimlich* feeling might arouse when the lines between imagination and reality are blurred, when something regarded as imaginary appears, or when a symbol takes over the functions of what it symbolizes ("The Uncanny" 244). The same happens when a legend or a prophecy, which we were forced to understand as either a fantasy or an impossibility—and, as consequence, were obliged to repress—comes to life. Freud names them "sourmounted beliefs" or primitive ideas ("The Uncanny" 249). This would explain why Blackbeard's reacts with fear and angst: the prophecy of a flying-boy that would defeat him comes to life right in front of him. His subsequent interview with the boy depicts him as deeply troubled and demonstrating kindness in front of his future adversary. This scene reveals a more intimate aspect of the pirate's personality, his weakness in the face of a possible defeat and death. The realization that a boy can actually fly and that the prophecy could be true produce the effects of the *unheimlich* in him.

Another Freudian concept that can be easily traced within the story of Peter Pan and its cinematic adaptations is the Oedipal Complex. In Barrie's play, it is epitomized by the presence of a villain who has the appearance both of a beloved and feared father (pirate captain Hook), a loving mother (Wendy), and a possessive and jealous mother (Tinker Bell). The Oedipal Complex is all the more evident in those versions of the play and in those illustrations of its novelization in which Captain Hook has the same face as Mr. Darlings, Wendy's father—a detail that has been faithfully reproduced in P.J. Hogan's *Peter Pan* (2003), the only film in which an actor (Jason Isaacs) portrays both characters. Spielberg's film seems to initially validate a psychoanalytical interpretation of the story in the sequence in which, when first meeting Tinker Bell, Pan ironically states:

> you're a complex Freudian hallucination having something to do with my mother, and I don't know why you have wings, but you have very lovely legs, and you're a very nice tiny person, and what am I saying, I don't know who my mother was, I'm an orphan, and I've never taken drugs because I missed the 60's—I was an accountant.

This passage is an explicit example of how the Oedipus Complex is treated in the 1991 movie, either in its references to the hallucination bringing repressed material on the surface and to the desire for one's own mother. Subsequently, the film applies a reversed version of the Oedipal Complex by representing Peter as a father whose daughter Maggie (Amber Scott) seems to be the only one who misses her family and whose son Jack (Charlie Korsmo) experiences a rivalry stage, during which he is angry against his parent's prohibitions, his occasional severity, and his frequent absences. The ambivalence of the Oedipal Complex towards the Father is clear: although Jack identifies with him, Peter is still perceived as someone who denies him his wishes. It is for this reason that the eccentric Captain Hook becomes appealing to Jack's eyes. After being subtly convinced by the pirate captain that his father Peter does not love his children, Jack identifies with Hook (he even dresses like the elegant pirate captain) and comes to hate Peter. The two adult figures, although inverted, exemplify the different faces of a father, the severe, hated father and the affectionate, loved one.

The film *Pan* as well exemplifies the Oedipal Complex, specifically through its depiction of the relationships between the young protagonist and the two male adult figures he interacts with. Indeed, the two men that Peter meets in Neverland fulfill both the roles of the dreaded and the loving Father: Blackbeard, the villain, is the rival-father, the one who threatens the child with castration and rules by fear, whereas Hook (Garett Hedlund)—an inmate in Blackbeard's prison camp, who, like the usual "master/apprentice" dichotomy, helps and guides the boy to achieve his fullness—represents the father whom the child may identify with, love, and elevate to an ideal to be followed. According to Freudian theories, later in life, those "two fathers" become the superego altogether, but usually the child, unable to develop a hatred towards his father, is forced to repress these aggressive drives—which leads him to displace this sentiment to another object or animal that may be a symbolic representation of that anger towards his parent ("Group Psychology and the Analysis of the Ego" 150).

Not only can the characters of the two films be examined through Freud's theories of the *unheimlich* and the Oedipal complex. Their very functions within the narrative are symbolic of the opposite life and death impulses of the human psyche explained by Freud. This, as we shall see, allows for the identification of the spectator with both the hero and the villain. In "Group Psychology and the Analysis of the Ego" Freud treats heroes as creations dear to our psychic lives, often representing what the individual seeks to achieve but simply cannot. He argues that they function as a safe escape against the struggles of living. The antagonist usually dies or gets punished as a metaphoric triumph of the superego, but the hero must live to reassure us of that immortality that children once believed in. The feeling of invulnerability is recognized and projected, and the hero represents the narcissistic quality of the ego, thought to be a "majesty" (Freud "Creative Writers and Day-

Dreaming" 150). The ego—the I—thus becomes a hero(ine) and the individual identifies with him/her. This identification actually represents the longing of early fantasies and daydreams that had been repressed (Freud "Creative Writers and Day-Dreaming" 147).

In his acclaimed "Civilization and Its Discontents," Freud argues that the hero represents the superego and the villain represents the Id (in German the original term used by Freud is *Es*, which means "it") (144). This means that the conservative superego manifests in the individual's psyche as a voice of conscience cultivated by laws, cultural norms, which tries at all costs to keep the impulses of the id repressed because of the perils that fulfilling those urges may bring to a person's life. The unconscious contains not only sexual desires, but also aggressive and destructive ones. The individual therefore carries within him/herself both life and death drives, the second being the most primordial impulses of all. Our desire to create life and union is overshadowed by our desire to destroy whatever is foreign to the ego—and, more frequently than one might think, to destroy even what derives from one's own ego (Freud "Civilization and Its Discontents" 122). Aggression is one of the first instincts of the human being, according to Freud, and that must be properly kept under control if we want to live in a civilized society. As he notes,

> the element of truth behind all this, which people are so ready to disavow, is that men are not gentle creatures who want to be loved, and who at the most can defend themselves if they are attacked; they are, on the contrary, creatures among whose instinctual endowments is to be reckoned a powerful share of aggressiveness [112].

However, Freud explicitly states that humankind found a way to sublimate these desires through fiction and art:

> it is an inevitable result of all this that we should seek in the world of fiction, in literature and in theatre compensation for what has been lost in life. There we still find people who know how to die—who, indeed, even manage to kill someone else. There alone too the condition can be fulfilled, which makes it possible for us to reconcile ourselves with death: namely, that behind all the vicissitudes of life we should still be able to preserve a life intact.... In the realm of fiction we find the plurality of lives that we need. We die with the hero with whom we have identified ourselves; yet we survive him, and are ready to die again just as safely with another hero ["Thoughts on War and Death" 290].

It is in fiction that we may reconcile with that "forbidden" part of our drives through identification with the villains.[7] Our psyches reveal that we are driven by opposite drives that actually reflect those governing the relationship between heroes and villains. Indeed, the superego and the ego aim to preserve life, thus keeping humankind united and alive, whereas the Id represents our impulses, especially the aggressive impulses. The superego acts as a jury of those impulses, usually suppressing them through guilt and shame even before they reach consciousness. However, the superego only acts after those impulses are launched (Freud "Civilization and Its Discontents" 141).

The same could be argued about the relationship between a character and his/her villain in a fictional narrative. As Richard Reynolds affirms, indeed, villains are the real stars of comic books, whereas heroes are passive and only called upon when the status quo is being challenged by those who want to change it (51). Such an argument could be applied to all fictional representations of the conflicts between heroes and villains: the antagonist is a character who is not satisfied with the world as it is and tries to modify it. The hero-protagonist, on the other hand, is conservative and defends the status quo. Whoever is against the preservation of the status quo becomes his/her enemy. Heroes exist because they represent collective interests and aspirations, because they guard the status quo, as the very meaning of the word "hero"—from the Greek *héros*, meaning "guardian," "keeper" (Brandão 15)—demonstrates. We could therefore argue that cinematic villains enact those desires that the superego tends to repress in each individual. The identification with villains on the part of the audience does not imply a willing refusal of the moral codes and social norms that govern our society. Identifying with the Joker, for example, does not imply that a person desires (and will act upon his/her drive) to blow up a truck or mass shoot a crowd—at least those people who do not fall under psychosis. But to agree with some of the Joker's thoughts is not a certification of madness. Identifying with a villain satisfies those urges and drives that have been repressed by the superego.

Although villains, pirates, monsters, and misfits have their own moral codes, the ones they display are incompatible with present (and past) cultural, legislative, and social norms of conduct. It is for this reason that they are outcasts. However, as is the case of Dustin Hoffman's Hook, villains may offer us more than just a transgression of societal norms and a feud with the hero. Spielberg's Hook is, indeed, a convincing fatherly figure; he is charismatic, funny, and relatable, even though he is also threatening, mischievous, and evil. This is clearly determined in the first appearance of the character, when the pirate captain kidnaps Peter's children, and is confirmed in the course of the filmic narrative, in which he is dreaded by both pirates and lost boys. On the other hand, in his moments of intimacy and confidence with his subordinate Smee, Hook is depicted as an old and jaded pirate who has no will to live without his counterpart Pan, almost to the point of dramatizing an alleged suicide. In a plan to kidnap and turn Banning's children evil, he becomes a humoristic and joyful, albeit manipulative and cynic, fatherly figure for them, especially for Jack. His intentions are to become an ideal parent for the kid to look upon. Hook's depiction as a complex, "round" character with both positive and negative drives allows for an identification on the part of the spectator. Identifying with his figure and sympathizing for his character therefore does not demonstrate intimate urges on the part of an individual that need to be cured.

Identification with both heroes and villains could be seen as legitimate. Just as both life and death drives do not exist without one another (Freud "Civilization and Its Discontents" 66) and appear always as a dialectical condition, so heroes and villains are symbiotic. Pan and Hook certainly reflect such a condition, each of them being perennially looking for the other, although with opposite intentions, in all versions of the story. Nevertheless, in Spielberg's film the two opposite rivals present traces of both drives: Pan is impulsive, violent, and even tyrannical towards the lost boys, whereas Hook is charismatic, joyful, and, although his primary goal is to erase Pan from existence, he is loving and caring for Peter's children.[8] Identification with both characters is then easier for the members of the audience, who interpret the two characters as more realistic because closer to their own experiences.

This does not happen, however, with Hook from the movie *Pan*, where the character is not relatable. Hedlund's interpretation is not as charismatic as Dustin Hoffman's and the script ventures far away from the original play by presenting a prequel story in which Peter and the pirate-to-be become close friends. *Pan* distorts the dichotomy between the title character and his antagonist by presenting the two of them as friends, rescuing orphan boys from London, and fighting together to beat the "more evil" character Blackbeard. Hook is a resented prisoner who changes his life thanks to the boy's help. Although moved by selfish interests and self-preservation, Hook becomes affectionate towards the boy and the film does not hint at any possible motive for future disagreement and enmity between the two characters. Hook's future as a beloved yet dreaded captain bent on revenge against Peter Pan is therefore not very credible. Contrary to the film *Hook*, in which the believable and "round" characters manage to capture the spectator's affection (the absent and workaholic father becomes the joyful hero and the jaded and evil villain suffering from depression becomes a beloved father), the Hook represented in *Pan* is rather a poorly relatable and "flat" character. On the other hand, Blackbeard is presented as the ultimate evil: he is a threatening presence for his dark armor and his authoritarian attitude, which reveals from his first appearance on the screen his lack for compassion and severity. Blackbeard is the tyrannical creator of a new society based on slavery and extermination of indigenous cultures. In an unexpected reversal of the original story's contents, it is the pirate captain here that does not grow old by using a machine that vaporizes a mineral from Neverland that rejuvenates him through inhalation. He is a murderer who never hesitates to fire a weapon and his selfish pursue of immortality is based on the suffering of the people under him. Undoubtedly, he is represented as "more evil" than the Hook depicted hitherto by Barrie, Disney, Spielberg, and Hogan.

The representation of a renowned villain as good and amiable in a past that precedes his evil actions is part of a tendency of many contemporary films, which narrate the prequel stories of the villains' friendly relationships with the heroes. The public has demonstrated for decades his affection towards Dracula, the Wicked Witch, Darth Vader, Frankenstein, and Hook. But this love has been subverted in the past two decades through the transformation of the villains into (anti-)heroes. According to contemporary cinema, in fact, Dracula only becomes a vampire to save his people in Gary Shore's *Dracula Untold* (2014); the Wicked Witch is a loving and charming character who is fooled by her "more evil" sister in Sam Raimi's *Oz the Great and Powerful* (2003); Frankenstein becomes a monster hunter in Stuart Beattie's *I, Frankenstein* (2014); Darth Vader becomes an annoying child and a troubled teenage hero who sacrifices his integrity for the love of his wife in the *Star Wars* prequel trilogy (1999–2005). And, in each of these stories, a "more evil" character is introduced. Such a tendency has emerged also in the case of the *Pirates of the Caribbean* saga (2003–17), in which Geoffrey Rush's Captain Barbossa becomes one of the good characters at the end of the second installment and faces "more evil" characters such as Lord Cutler Beckett, Davy Jones, Blackbeard, and Captain Salazar.

Such a tendency could be explained as an attempt on the part of the industry of cinema to deny a spectator's identification with a villain as dictated by the prejudice that to identify oneself with a malevolent character such as the Joker or Captain Hook implies necessarily also to become Evil, to commit crimes and heinous acts. That could explain why after years of love for Captain Hook and his panic of clocks, especially after Dustin Hoffman's treasured performance, the film industry upgraded the character to reveal his good side. Introducing another villain, Blackbeard, who is even "more evil" than Hook, is a cultural attempt to deny our identification with the characters who enact a form of behavior that is contrary to social norms, with the image of the pirate as a malevolent being who is an enemy of all mankind. Yet, the human psyche tells us a different story, one that is fluid and not pinned in extremes. Maybe to love a villain like Hook is something that an individual needs in order to release his/her own aggression, to purge the drives repressed by the superego. Portraying Hook as an amiable character, on the other hand, could result in a lack of identification on the part of the spectator who has grown affectionate towards the character's "darker side" or, at least, to a mixture of positive and negative traits. Perhaps it is time for the cinematic industry to accept that we can love monsters, villains, and pirates without necessarily making them heroic too or revealing their past history as righteous characters. It is time to abandon the pixie dust of never growing up and accept that the public may want a pirate's life after all.

NOTES

1. I cannot but proudly remember the Peter Pan play I participated in during my late teens. Nobody could perform Pirate n. 4 or Tree n. 2 like I did.
2. We have defined the term this way to differentiate the Freudian psychic phenomenon by the contemporary uses of its English correspondent, *uncanny*. Many of Freud's concepts, including the *unheimlich*, have been appropriated by scholars from different fields and have been used mainly by authors from outside the psychoanalytic theory in a way not always faithful to Freud's original concept.
3. Some terms that Freud used were translated to English following a series of criteria. However, the term *angst* was translated to *anxiety*, when, in its essence, it represents *anguish*.
4. It is worth to note how the term *Verdrängung* relates not to *repression*, as the author used *Untertrucken* for *repression*, but to a term that has not yet met its correlation in English— just like *Trïeb* (instinctual drive), *Es* (Id) and the *Über-ich* (the "above-the-I").
5. At that point, Freud believe that was the case. Later, in an essay from 1926, "Inhibition, Symptom and Anxiety," he describes repression as being a consequence of angst.
6. The term *psychic* is related to what derives from the human psyche; it does not relate in any way to psychic phenomena like mind-reading, clairvoyance, and other uncanny events. These occurrences are common in fantasies, and may be a part of the unheimlich if they ever come to reality.
7. According to French psychologist Gustave LeBon, the unreal has almost as much influence over the crowd as the real, and they have a tendency of not being able to distinguish between them. LeBon affirms: "the creation of the legends which so easily obtain circulation in crowds is not solely the consequence of their extreme credulity. It is also the result of the prodigious perversions that events undergo in the imagination of a throng.... Our reason show us the incoherence there is in [the images that fascinate the crowds], but a crowd is almost blind to this truth, and confuses with the real event what the deforming action of its imagination has superimposed thereon. A crowd scarcely distinguishes between the subjective and the objective" (33).
8. *Hook* was released back when the necessity of turning bad guys into good ones had not emerged yet, so the identification of the spectator with the pirate captain tends to work even better than in the original play. Everything Hook does is ultimately evil; but the actor Dustin Hoffman made him so charismatic that the spectator might even feel "sad" for his death.

WORKS CITED

Bandão, Junito de Souza. *Mitologia Grega*. Vol. 3. Petrópolis: Vozes, 1980, 15–71.
Baudrillard, Jean, and Morin, Edgar. *A Violência do Mundo*. Rio de Janeiro: Anima, 2004.
Freud, Sigmund. "Civilization and Its Discontents." 1930. *The Standard Edition of the Complete Psychological Works*. Vol. 21. James Strachey (ed. and trans.). London: Vintage, 2001, 58–147.
_____. "Creative Writers and Day-Dreaming." 1908. *The Standard Edition of the Complete Psychological Works*. Vol. 9. James Strachey (ed. and trans.). London: Vintage, 2001, 41–153.
_____. "Group Psychology and the Analysis of the Ego." 1921. *The Standard Edition of the Complete Psychological Works*. Vol. 18. James Strachey (ed. and trans.). London: Vintage, 2001, 65–143.
_____. "The Interpretation of Dreams." 1900. *The Standard Edition of the Complete Psychological Works*. Vols. 4–5. James Strachey (ed. and trans.). London: Vintage, 2001.
_____. "Negation." 1925. *The Standard Edition of the Complete Psychological Works*. Vol. 19. James Strachey (ed. and trans.). London: Vintage, 2001, 235–42.
_____. "Thoughts for the Times of War and Death." 1915. *The Standard Edition of the Complete Psychological Works*. Vol. 14. Trans. James Strachey (ed. and trans.). London: Vintage, 2001, 273–301.
_____."The Uncanny." 1919. *The Standard Edition of the Complete Psychological Works*. Vol. 17. James Strachey (ed. and trans.). London: Vintage, 2001, 217–55.

_____. "The Unconscious." 1915. *The Standard Edition of the Complete Psychological Works.* Vol. 14. James Strachey (ed. and trans.). London: Vintage, 2001, 159–215.

LeBon, Gustave. *The Crowd: A Study of the Popular Mind.* London: Filiquarian, 2005.

Reynolds, Richard. *Superheroes: A Modern Mythology.* Jackson: University Press of Mississippi, 1992.

"Take what you can…"
Disney's Jack Sparrow and His Indebtedness to the Pirate Genre[1]

Susanne Zhanial

Before the Disney studios released the first installment of their movie series *Pirates of the Caribbean* in 2003, film critics mildly smiled at the idea to turn a theme park ride into a summer movie. A similar attempt by the same studios, Peter Hastings' movie *The Country Bears*, which is based on a theme park attraction as well, had met with mixed reviews a year earlier. Additionally, the genre of the pirate film was generally shunned by production companies after a number of expensive flops in the 1980s and 1990s, including Roman Polanski's *Pirates* (1986) and Renny Harlin's *Cutthroat Island* (1995). The Disney studios nevertheless embarked on this risky venture, and the success proved them right: until today, the studios have released five successful *Pirates of the Caribbean* movies and generated immense profits from the lucrative franchise. A decisive factor in the series' success was the employment of actor Johnny Depp for the role of the lead pirate, Captain Jack Sparrow. His portrayal was praised by films critics and viewers alike, and even earned him a nomination for Best Actor at the Academy Awards in 2004. Roger Ebert, screenwriter and film critic, claimed after the release of the first installment that "there has never been a pirate, or for that matter a human being, like this in any other [pirate] movie." To a certain extent, Ebert is right: never before has there been a male pirate captain with kohl-rimmed eyes, dreadlocks and a braided beard, staggering through the plot of a pirate movie as if he were (or maybe is) constantly drunk. And yet, the question of Jack's "originality" is a difficult one to answer. On the one hand, Johnny Depp himself revealed possible inspirations for his character's development in various interviews. On the other hand, the representation of Jack Sparrow is also indebted to, and relying on, his literary and filmic pirate predecessors, of whom Jack is both a pastiche and parody. In particular, in the following pages, Disney's main pirate captain will be compared and contrasted to the three major manifestations of the pirate motif in the last two hundred years—the Byronic hero, the Victorian villain, and the Hollywood's swashbuckler—before returning to a final assessment of the "originality" of his character.

Stories with and about pirates have excited readers since antiquity, but only at the beginning of the nineteenth century the figure of the pirate transformed from a lower-class criminal into a literary motif (Moore 1). In the Romantic era, authors merged the pirate motif with the archetype of the Byronic hero, which developed at the same time, and thus the pirate captain transformed into a dark anti-hero, capable of violent deeds, but simultaneously an attractive and educated man. The Byronic pirate had typically been wronged by society in his youth and in his rebellion against society and his unfair treatment he turns to piracy. He is thus an outlaw by his own accord, but never depicted as law-less. He still follows his own, self-defined code of honor, which leads him, among other things, to protect women. Therefore, he is, if not by birth, then at least a gentleman in behavior, and often perceived, especially in the eyes of female readers, as an ideal(ized) lover.

In his poem *The Corsair* (1814), Lord Byron produced with the protagonist Conrad the first, and until today, most impressive, combination of the Byronic hero with the pirate motif. Surrounded by an air of mystery, Conrad is presented as an ascetic and lonely man, who keeps apart from his pirate crew "but to command" (Byron 1.63) and enjoys a fearsome reputation among foes and friends. In the poem, the pirates attack the palace of their enemy, the Pasha Seyd, but Conrad causes their defeat and his own imprisonment when he hears the cries of the female slaves in the burning harem and orders his men to not only rescue the women, but to leave them unharmed: "so well could Conrad tame their fiercest mood, / And check the very hands with gore imbrued" (Byron 2.219–20). Due to his compassion towards the women and capability to restrain his men, Conrad comes across more like a chivalric knight than a ruthless pirate captain. A further aspect that underlines his extraordinary character and his men's respect and loyalty, is the fact that, although Conrad is responsible for the pirates' overthrow, they set sail in the third and final canto to either save their captain or revenge his death.

At a first glance, Jack Sparrow can only be regarded as a parody of the Byronic pirate captain. Jack is neither the undisputed leader that Conrad is, nor does his name inspire fear in his enemies. Although other characters admit that they "have heard of him" (*Curse*), his reputation as fearsome pirate is undermined by the fact that he constantly has to insist on being referred to as "captain." This position is further called into question by the fact that

Jack often lacks a ship and a crew. Also in his outward appearance and behavior, Jack notably differs from Conrad, who possesses the facial attributes, most notably the dark eyebrows, piercing eyes, and rising lip, as well as the melancholy air typical of the Byronic hero (Byron 1.196–206). In direct contrast to Conrad—and despite the fact that his fights and especially his escape attempts are mostly unsuccessful—Jack never broods over his fate. Instead, *Pirates of the Caribbean* cleverly turns Jack's incompetence as a pirate into an integral part of the series' comedy. This is recognized by film critic James Berardinelli, who notes:

> Cap'n Jack Sparrow (Johnny Depp) is a pirate who's infamous for his ineptitude. After rescuing a damsel, Elizabeth Swann (Keira Knightley), he finds himself thanked by her father (Jonathan Pryce) and her would-be betrothed (Jack Davenport) while simultaneously being arrested for piracy. He escapes, but after losing a duel with the heroic blacksmith Will Turner (Orlando Bloom), who pines for Elizabeth, he is sent back to jail.

Nevertheless, there are several similarities between Jack and the Byronic pirate Conrad: as in Byron's poem, where Conrad's crew decides to inquire after, and if necessary, revenge, their leader's fate, Jack's friends also set sail to rescue him after he has been swallowed and dragged to Davy Jones' Locker by the kraken at the end of *Dead Man's Chest*. Another parallel is that both Conrad's and Jack's past remain mysterious. In the first installment, Joshamee Gibbs (Kevin R. McNally) points out to William Turner (Orlando Bloom) that "not a lot's known about Jack Sparrow before he came to Tortuga" (*Curse*). In fact, only the fifth installment of the franchise, *Dead Men Tell No Tales* (2017), finally offers viewers an insight into Jack's youth by explaining how he acquired his magical compass, his nickname "Sparrow," and some other personal items, like his hat, sword, and the bead chain for his dreadlocks, in a battle against the Spanish pirate hunter Armando Salazar (Javier Bardem). The flashback, however, is brief and rather aimed at providing some necessary background information on Salazar's hatred of Jack, rather than being aimed on exploring Jack's history at length.

Apart from these narrative parallels, Jack Sparrow could also be compared to the creator of Conrad, because Lord Byron's lover, Caroline Lamb, famously declared the poet to be "mad—bad—and dangerous to know" (Wolfson and Manning xv). The phrase was later often extended by critics to speak about other Byronic heroes, as, for example, Charlotte Bronte's Rochester, Emily Bronte's Heathcliff or the character Q, who appears in various *Star Trek* series (Stein 14; 24–28; 135), but it can also be used to describe Jack Sparrow. First, according to society's rules, as a criminal and pirate, Jack has to be regarded as a bad character; however, he apparently enjoys his outlaw status, which offers him the freedom to disregard rules, cheat in duels, indulge in love affairs, and the pleasure of rum drinking. Second, he never contradicts other characters when they declare him mad; instead, when William wonders whether it is "madness or brilliance" to use an upturned boat to walk on the bottom of the sea, Jack's answer "It's remarkable how often those two traits coincide" (*Curse*) highlights how difficult it is to apply such categories to a character/person. As regards the third aspect, "dangerous to know," it has to be said that both William Turner and Elizabeth Swann (Keira Knightley) start to disregard society's rules and slowly transform into outlaws after meeting Jack. In the first movie, *The Curse of the Black Pearl*, Jack frees Elizabeth from the corset, which symbolizes patriarchal society and the prescribed position she would have to occupy in it as the governor's daughter and future wife of a British navy soldier. Afterwards, Elizabeth is constantly drawn closer to Jack and to piracy. In the second installment, *Dead Man's Chest* (2006), Jack correctly predicts that she "won't be able to resist" (20) the lure of piracy, and he finally plays a part in her election into the pirates' king in the third film, *At World's End* (2009). Similarly, through his friendship with Jack, William learns to accept that his father has been a pirate as well and that therefore "the pirate is in [his] blood" (*Curse*).

While Lord Byron was notorious for his love affairs, his protagonist Conrad is presented as a married man and a faithful lover of one particular woman. This construction of the Byronic pirate captain as a passionate lover contributed largely to his appeal (Lutz 23–5, 30), but it was also soon criticized. In Walter Scott's historical novel *The Pirate* (1821), for example, the female protagonist Minna is forced to realize that pirates are not Romantic heroes, and that by falling in love with an ideal, who transpires to be an outlaw and criminal, she "has built the fabric of her happiness on a quicksand instead of a rock" (Scott 492–3). Minna's re-evaluation of the pirate foreshadows a similar re-assessment of the motif in the Victorian era. With the continuous growth of the British Empire, pirates were turned into the stories' villains and viewed as a threat to the Empire's expansion. In order to emphasize their criminal nature, contemporary theories of degeneration were utilized for the portrayal: the pirates' weather-beaten faces, scars, and mutilations, as well as their violent behavior were presented as signs of a return to a more uncivilized and primitive state of being (Moore 169–172). In addition, pirates shifted from being the protagonists of literature written for adults to stock characters in juvenile stories. Only few of these "penny dreadfuls" are still known or read today,[2] but their depiction of pirates as ruthless cutthroats culminated in the creation of the best-known pirate villain of (Victorian) fiction: Long John Silver, the main pirate in Robert Louis Stevenson's *Treasure Island*. The novel, as both historians and literary critics emphasize, had an undeniable impact on the pirate motif (Cordingly 5; Emeljanow 236; Deane 694). Its influence has been so far-reaching that also Disney's *Pirates of the Caribbean* still borrows elements from it, such as the two famous lines of the pirate song "Fifteen men on the dead man's chest—Yo-ho-ho, and a bottle of rum!" (Stevenson 3; *Chest* 2), the black spot, and the speaking parrot.

As in the case of the Byronic pirate, there do not appear to be a lot of similarities at a first glance between Stevenson's one-legged pirate Long John Silver and Jack Sparrow. While Long John Silver is a cruel and greedy traitor and cold-blooded murderer, Jack is neither depicted as mutilated nor as a vile cutthroat. Nevertheless, both of them are difficult to classify as either villain or hero: in *Treasure Island*, Long John Silver betrays the narrator Jim, raises a mutiny on board the *Hispaniola*, and even kills some of his own men, but, in spite of these deeds, Jim still speaks of him in admirable terms towards the novel's end: "Silver ... looked as cool as ever I saw him. He was brave, and no mistake" (Stevenson 182). In a similar manner, in all the films of the Disney cinematic saga Jack seems to shift sides depending on the situation and in order to gain the greatest profit for himself. However, by the end of the single movies he always contributes to the victory of the good characters.

Another character trait Silver and Jack share is that both of them distract their listeners from their true intentions, but they achieve this in slightly different ways. Long John Silver has a silver tongue, which is confirmed by several speeches that he carefully adjusts to his respective listeners in order to persuade them of a certain point. Jack's strategy, in comparison, is to distract and confuse his listeners. For example, in *The Curse of the Black Pearl*, when Barbossa is about to discover that William is the person necessary to lift their curse, Jack (unsuccessfully) tries to prevent the revelation by babbling that William is "no one. He's no one. Distant cousin of my aunt's nephew twice removed. Lovely singing voice. Eunuch" (*Curse*). In other instances, Jack's (conscious) slurring of vowels distracts his listeners, and adds to the movies' comedy: when Barbossa's undead crew is threatening him with pistols and swords, Jack appears like a drunkard searching for the right word: "Pearlie... . Palu-li-la-la-lulu.... Parlili.... Parsnip.... Parsley.... Partner," until Ragetti (Mackenzie Crook) helps him out with "Parley" (*Curse*).

Both Jack and Silver are still alive at the end of the narrative and are given the chance to continue their criminal careers. Silver's exemption from justice is extraordinary in the context of the late nineteenth-century negative perception of piracy. It is true that Conrad and other Romantic pirates survive as well, but they are normally allowed to do so because they abandoned the society of their fellow outlaws. In Victorian narratives, instead, the evil pirates typically die, like J. M. Barrie's Hook in *Peter and Wendy* (1904/1911), or they sincerely have to repent their crimes, like Gascoyne in Ballantyne's *Gascoyne, the Sandal-Wood Trader* (1865). In the case of Long John Silver, neither of the two options applies: the treacherous pirate slips away with a bag of the treasure, and yet, the narrator Jim hopes that he is able to comfortably spend the rest of his life with his black wife (Stevenson 190). Similarly, Jack always emerges triumphant and with something precious in the end: the *Black Pearl* is handed over to him three times, twice in her full beauty (*Curse* and *Dead Men Tell No Tales*) and once in a magic bottle containing a reduced version of it (*On Stranger Tides*), and *At World's End* we see Jack sailing away in possession of the map guiding him towards his next goal, the Fountain of Youth. Only in *Dead Man's Chest*, Jack seems to be on the losing side, because he is swallowed by the kraken. However, a few moments earlier, Jack triggers Elizabeth's final crossing into outlawry by inducing her to betray him. The broad grin he displays when he officially declares her a "pirate" signals that he has enjoyed another, even though short, triumph.

With the turn from the nineteenth to the twentieth century, the figure of the pirate was successfully transferred to the new medium of film. As a subgenre of the adventure movie, pirate films generally work with a dialectic opposition of good and evil, and quite often split the pirates themselves into villainous and heroic crews. Along with the shift in media, the portrayal of the "good" pirate captain was once again adapted to fit cultural and aesthetic needs. In Hollywood's classic studio era, the pirate captain is portrayed in positive terms and as a swashbuckler, who outwits his evil opponents with his intelligence and physical skills. His fitness is demonstrated by breathtaking stunts and sword duels, and the swashbuckling pirate is visually recognizable by his broad smile, which he displays in moments of victories. Similarly to the Romantic era, Hollywood's swashbucklers typically act according to a personal code of honor that demands protecting weaker victims and women, while the darker character traits of the Byronic outlaw are softened or assigned to their evil opponents in the movies (Richards 12).

For the pirate movies in the early and mid-twentieth century, the Hollywood studios engaged good-looking male actors, including Douglas Fairbanks, Errol Flynn, Tyrone Power, and Burt Lancaster and thus fostered the production of an image of the male pirate captain as an attractive, heroic, and heterosexual outlaw. Rather than being a direct descendant of this cinematic tradition, Jack Sparrow is an ironic comment on it. As Heike Steinhoff argues in her study *Queer Buccaneers*, Jack is a "dandified version of the hypermasculine pirate" (48) produced by Hollywood. In fact, the series offers an ambiguous representation of the pirate captain's sexuality, providing viewers with clues about both his heterosexuality and homosexuality (Steinhoff 47–52). On the one hand, Jack is interested in women and has most likely had some affairs, as the slaps in his face by several women in Tortuga indicate; thus, he definitely has his admirers among the female characters—and, certainly, among his (female) viewers. On the other hand, as critics note, he also appears to be "a peacock in full display" (Ebert), who repeatedly seems to check his good looks by "wielding his 'compass that doesn't point north' like a compact mirror" (Martin; Steinhoff 48). Furthermore, there are scenes between Jack and Will, which according to Steinhoff, can be read as "tentatively homoerotic" (49). In the end, however, Jack rejects both the advances of his former lover Angelica and of other women; his primary love object remaining the *Black Pearl*. It is this ship that, as Jack himself points out, gives him the freedom to roam the seas, and as Steinhoff correctly points out, "eventually turns him into a potent pirate" (Steinhoff 52). By preferring the ship to a real woman, Jack does not need to renounce his piratical life in order to marry and/or re-integrate into society. Such a "happy ending" was typical of the pirate films produced in Hollywood during the classic studio era: in these movies, the good male pirate captain and hero typically won the heart of the female protagonist over the course of the movie, and for their love—signaled by the couple's kiss in the movie's final minutes—relinquished his outlaw life.[3] One such example is Michael Curtiz's *Captain Blood* (1935), in which the hero Peter Blood (Errol Flynn) wins the hand of Arabella Bishop (Olivia de Havilland) and is established as Port Royal's new governor.

Jack's unusual behavior also parodies the athletic skills of Hollywood's movie pirates. Despite the fact that the viewer sees him engaged in a number of sword duels and participating in battles and chase scenes throughout the series, his stunts are never entirely serious in tone and often explicitly exaggerated. Repeatedly, we see him preparing his exit with the sentence "You will remember this as the day on which you almost caught Captain Jack Sparrow" (*Curse*) but Jack's heroic escapes always fail: he stumbles over the wall and falls down into sea (*Curse*), or the final words of his sentence are swallowed by a wave that clashes into his face (*Chest*). By exaggerating Jack's action scenes, the *Pirates of the Caribbean* saga draws attention to the implausibility of many stunts performed by the pirate protagonists in earlier movies. Jack's use of a rope and cannon to fire himself back on board of the *Black Pearl* in *At World's End*, for example, is a homage to a famous action scene in Douglas Fairbanks' *The Black Pirate* (1926), where the hero uses a cannon as a counterweight to lift himself up to the yard. However, by depicting Jack as wildly wind-milling his arms while being flung through the air, the seriousness of such an attempt is comically subverted (*At World's End*). In addition, Jack never heroically wins his sword duels or is able to leave a duel scene elegantly. In *Dead Man's Chest*, for instance, a lengthy and funny action sequence develops around Jack, Will, and Norrington's fight over the key to Davy Jones' Chest. The battle involves some sword fighting, but it also hilariously depicts the three men as fighting inside a spinning water wheel. In the sequence Jack repeatedly fails to recover the key and slip away with it, once even stumbling into an empty grave (*Chest*).

Nonetheless, Jack cannot be considered only as a parody of earlier filmic pirate captains, because he is given heroic moments in the movies as well.

The *Pirates of the Caribbean* series rather questions whether he really wants to take over this role or not. In some instances, Jack rather seems to be forced against his will to play the hero in order to ensure the victory of the good characters and his friends, but strikingly, he does so without difficulty: with a steady hand, he fires the necessary shot in the middle of the most chaotic battle, whether it is aimed at the cursed Barbossa in the first film or at the barrels of gunpowder prepared to kill the kraken in *Dead Man's Chest*. Yet Jack is also and primarily presented as a trickster, who sincerely loves to outwit his opponents instead of overcoming them in a physical battle. It is exactly at such moments that he displays the roguish smile typical of Hollywood's most glorious swashbucklers. In the first installment, for example, Jack smiles victoriously when he manages to steal the *Interceptor* from the British Navy and when he convinces Barbossa that he is the only one who definitely knows whose blood can lift the curse. Remarkably, the roguish smile is seen less frequently in the succeeding installments, which increasingly focus on Jack's mishaps and exploit them for parody. Nonetheless, as pointed out before, the movies' final minutes always grant Jack his triumph. By re-establishing him as a successful pirate, the Disney studios have managed to keep their series always open for a possible continuation.

Jack Sparrow is therefore neither a straight descendant of the dark Byronic anti-hero and the Victorian villain, nor of Hollywood's swashbuckler. Instead, he shares some character traits with all of them. Like the Byronic pirate, Jack is a defiant, and largely anti-heroic outlaw, who prefers to keep apart from his men and his past a secret. From his Victorian ancestor Long John Silver, Jack takes over the capability to use words to manipulate listeners. Furthermore, like Silver, Jack is an ambiguous character whose true intentions and affiliations are difficult to determine. His filmic predecessors serve as an inspiration for tricks and stunts, and for the representation of the male pirate captain as a love object for (female) characters. One further possible source for Jack Sparrow's character was revealed by Johnny Depp himself: in interviews after the release of the first installment, the actor admitted to having based his character on Rolling Stone guitarist Keith Richards (Lee; Morrison). Depp's consciously intended homage to Richards was admired by film critics, who claimed that it "com[es] across clearly in his slurred speech, swaying swagger and slack, waving arms (Cadorette). Literary critic Andreas Rauscher takes up this reference and argues that in the same manner in which Keith Richards constructed his image as twentieth-century rock star, the role of "Jack Sparrow" should be understood as a performance (203; Steinhoff 54). In fact, the idea that the infamous pirate captain is a constructed identity performed by Sparrow at certain moments is supported by the fact that the plots of the movies sometimes seem to be interrupted in order to allow Jack/Depp to give a solo performance, while the other characters are forced to occupy the role of—and thus, double—the viewer. Through this "highly theatrical representation of the pirate" (Steinhoff 53), the movies draw attention to their own artificiality, but also highlight the fact that for at least the last two hundred years, the pirate has primarily been a literary and filmic— and thus a fictional and highly stylized—figure.

The emphasis on the figure's performance finally leads us back to the question of Jack's origin(ality). In this essay, the analysis revolved around similarities and differences of Jack Sparrow to earlier representations of the pirate motif, as well as on the explicitly highlighted parallel to rock star Keith Richards. The high number and diversity of references demonstrate that Jack Sparrow's character is best regarded as postmodern: the references produce a double-coded text, in which "an utterance or representation is applied in such a way that it can and should be understood (at least) in two different ways—as a quotation as well as an independent, non-citing form of communication; as 'verbatim' and 'serious' as well as ironic and self-reflective" (Eder 17, my translation).[4] According to this argument, double-coded, postmodern texts can always be read in two ways: they can be enjoyed straightforwardly, or a comparison can be made to earlier texts that then contributes to the pleasure of watching (and analyzing) the movie. This definitely applies to the *Pirates of the Caribbean* series: Jack Sparrow can be interpreted as an ironic parody of earlier literary and filmic representations of the pirate, and/or as a homage to Keith Richards, but one can also enjoy his representation without recognizing, and/or paying attention to, these references. Nonetheless, the pirate captain one encounters always remains one that eludes a clear definition. Therefore, Jack's popularity and originality is intrinsically bound up with his postmodern nature and the inability to pin him down, whether as mad or ingenious, as heroic or villainous. In the end, it is the dense web of references that offers Jack to numerous readings and readers, and nevertheless allows him to appeal to everyone of us.

NOTES

1. This essay is based on research completed for my Ph.D. thesis entitled "Postmodern Piracy: An Analysis of Disney's Pirates of the Caribbean and Its Exploitation of the Motif of the Pirate from the 19th to the 21st Century" (University of Vienna, 2017); in particular, the chapters revolving around Jack Sparrow's connection with earlier stages in the history of the pirate motif.

2. In his book *Desert Isles and Pirate Islands*, Kevin Carpenter offers an extended analysis of a number of these stories. Some examples of penny dreadfuls published in the nineteenth century are Edwin J. Brett's *Boys of England*, the Emmett brothers' *Sons of Britannia*, and Charles Fox' *Boy's Standard*. Two stories featuring pirates published in *Boys of England* are *Alone in the Pirates' Lair* (1866) and *Rovers of the Sea* (1872–3). Furthermore, in the mid- to late Victorian era, a number of authors, such as William Henry Giles Kingston (*The Pirate of the Mediterranean: A Tale of the Sea*, 1851), or R.M. Ballantyne (*The Coral Island*, 1857) published novels revolving around pirates. *The Coral Island* is one of the few books still widely known and read today.

3. The first pirate movie to partly abstain from this typically romantic conclusion is Henry King's *The Black Swan* (1942). Although it still unites the female protagonist Margaret with the pirate captain Jamie and depicts them as kissing in the final scene, the question whether they stay at sea or return to Jamaica is left open.

4. "Eine Äußerung oder Darstellung ist so angelegt, dass sie auf (mindestens) zwei verschiedene Wiesen verstanden werden kann und soll—sowohl als Zitat als auch als eigenständige, nicht-zitierende Kommunikation; sowohl als 'wörtlich' oder 'ernst' gemeint als auch als ironisch oder sich selbst kommentierend" (Eder 17).

WORKS CITED

Ballantyne, Robert Michael. *Gascoyne, the Sandal-Wood Trader*. 1865. Project Gutenberg, Ebook #23384, www.gutenberg.org. Accessed July 30, 2015.
Barrie, James Matthew. *Peter Pan in Kensington Garden* and *Peter and Wendy*. 1906/1911. Peter Hollindale (ed.). Oxford: Oxford University Press, 1991.
Berardinelli, James. "Rev. of *Pirates of the Caribbean: The Curse of the Black Pearl*." *Reelviews*, n.d., www.reelviews.net/php_review_template.php?identifier=521. Accessed April 8, 2010.
The Black Pirate. Dir. Albert Parker. United Artists, 1926.
Brooker, Peter. "Postmodern Adaptation: Pastiche, Intertextuality, and Re-Functioning." *The Cambridge Companion to Literature on Screen*. Deborah Cartmell and Imelda Whelehan (eds.). Cambridge: Cambridge University Press, 2007, 107–20.
Byron, George Gordon. *The Coral Island: A Tale of the Pacific Ocean*, 1858. Jacqueline S. Bratton (ed.). Oxford: Oxford University Press, 1990.
_____. *The Corsair*. 1814. *Lord Byron Selected Poems*. Susan J. Wolfson and Peter J. Manning (eds.). London: Penguin, 2005, 248–307.
_____. *The Madmen and the Pirate*. 1883. Project Gutenberg, Ebook #21813, www.gutenberg.org. Accessed July 30, 2015.
Cadorette, Guylaine. "Rev. of *Pirates of the Caribbean: The Curse of the Black Pearl*." Hollywood.com, July 9, 2003. www.hollywood.com/review/Pirates_of_the_Caribbean_The_Curse_of_the_Black_Pearl/1721427. Accessed April 8, 2010.
Captain Blood. Dir. Michael Curtiz. Warner Bros., 1935.
Carpenter, Kevin. *Desert Isles & Pirates Islands: The Island Theme in Nineteenth-Century English Juvenile Fiction: A Survey and Bibliography*. Frankfurt: Peter Lang, 1984.
Cordingly, David. *Under the Black Flag: The Romance and the Reality of Life Among the Pirates*. New York: Random House, 2006.
Cutthroat Island. Dir. Renny Harlin. Carolco/Forge, 1995.
Deane, Bradley. "Imperial Boyhood: Piracy and the Play Ethic." *Victorian Studies* 53.4 (2011), 689–714.
Eder, Jens. "Die Postmoderne im Kino: Entwicklungen im Spielfilm der 90er Jahre." *Oberflächenrausch: Postmoderne und Postklassik im Kino der 90er Jahre*. Jens Eder (ed.), 2nd ed. Münster: Lit Verlag, 2008, 9–61.
Emeljanow, Victor. "Staging the Pirate: The Ambiguities of Representation and the Significance of Convention." *Pirates and Mutineers of the Nineteenth Century: Swashbucklers and Swindlers*. Grace Moore (ed.). Aldershot: Ashgate, 2011, 223–41.
Ebert, Roger. "Rev. of *Pirates of the Caribbean: The Curse of the Black Pearl*." July 9, 2003, rogerebert.suntimes.com/apps/pbcs.dll/article?AID=/20030709/REVIEWS/307090301. Accessed April 8, 2010.
Lee, Alana. "Johnny Depp. *Pirates of the Caribbean: The Curse of the Black Pearl*." Interview, *BBC Movies*, August 4, 2003. www.bbc.co.uk/films/2003/07/29/johnny_depp_pirates_of_the_caribbean_interview.shtml. Accessed January 20, 2009.
Lutz, Deborah. "The Pirate Poet in the Nineteenth Century: Trollope and Byron." *Pirates and Mutineers of the Nineteenth Century. Swashbucklers and Swindlers*. Grace Moore (ed.). Aldershot: Ashgate, 2011, 23–39.
Martin, Marianne. "Rev. of *Pirates of the Caribbean: Dead Man's Chest*." *Reverse Shot. Museum*

of the Moving Image, July 15, 2006, reverseshot.org/reviews/entry/514/pirates_2. Accessed April 8, 2014.
Moore, Grace. "Pirates for Boys: Masculinity and Degeneracy in R.M. Ballantyne's Adventure Novels." *Pirates and Mutineers of the Nineteenth Century. Swashbucklers and Swindlers.* Grace Moore (ed.). Aldershot: Ashgate, 2011, 165–79.
Morrison, Alan. "Rev. of *Pirates of the Caribbean: The Curse of the Black Pearl.*" *Empire Magazine*, August 8, 2003, www.empireonline.com/reviews/ReviewComplete.asp?FID=9271. Accessed April 8, 2010.
Pirates. Dir. Roman Polanski. Cannon, 1986.
Pirates of the Caribbean: At World's End. Dir. Gore Verbinski. Walt Disney Pictures, 2007.
Pirates of the Caribbean: The Curse of the Black Pearl. Dir. Gore Verbinski. Walt Disney Pictures, 2003.
Pirates of the Caribbean: Dead Man's Chest. Dir. Gore Verbinski. Walt Disney Pictures, 2006.
Pirates of the Caribbean: Dead Men Tell No Tales. Dir. Joachim Ronning and Espen Sandberg. Walt Disney Pictures, 2017.
Pirates of the Caribbean: On Stranger Tides. Dir. Rob Marshall. Walt Disney Pictures, 2011.
Rauscher, Andreas. "Das Meer als Manege. Vom Fluch des klassischen Piratenfilms zu den *Pirates of the Caribbean*." *Das Meer im Film: Grenze, Spiegel, Übergang*. Roman Mauer and Richard Boorberg (eds.). München: Edition Text + Kritik, 2010, 190–203.
Richards, Jeffrey. *Swordsmen of the Screen: From Douglas Fairbanks to Michael York*. New York: Routledge, 1979.
Scott, Walter. *The Pirate*. 1846. Leipzig: Elibron Classics Replica Edition, 2005.
Stein, Atara. *The Byronic Hero in Film, Fiction, and Television*. Carbondale: Southern Illinois University Press, 2009.
Steinhoff, Heike. *Queer Buccaneers. (De)Constructing Boundaries in the PIRATES OF THE CARIBBEAN Film Series*. Transnational and Transatlantic American Studies. Vol. 10. Berlin: LIT Verlag, 2011.
Stevenson, Robert Louis. *Treasure Island*. 1883. John Seelye (ed.). London: Penguin, 1999.
Wolfson, Susan J., and Peter J. Manning (eds.). Introduction. *Lord Byron Selected Poems*. London: Penguin, 2005, ix–xxi.
Zhanial, Susanne. "Postmodern Piracy: An Analysis of Disney's Pirates of the Caribbean and Its Exploitation of the Motif of the Pirate from the 19th to the 21st Century." Dissertation, University of Vienna, 2017.

Civilization's Monsters

The Doomed Queer Anti-Imperialism of Black Sails

JESSICA WALKER

In the third episode of the Starz series *Black Sails* (2014–17), Benjamin Hornigold (Patrick Lyster), one among many pirate captains holding sway over Nassau, laments growing unease among his crew as Britain's colonial powers begin to take measures against pirate activity in the Caribbean: "They're coming to terms with a very uncomfortable truth.... That no matter how many lies we tell ourselves or no matter how many stories we convince ourselves we're part of, we're all just thieves awaiting a noose" ("III."). Historically, piracy was considered at odds with investment in the future, as pirates "did not expect to live long, nor did their criminal reputations allow them to settle down and invest in real estate, family, or the future" (Dawdy and Bonni 679). But there is an extratextual layer to Hornigold's fatalistic pronouncement: any viewer familiar with the series' source material already assumes its characters are doomed. Taking place in 1715, *Black Sails* is both a historical drama set during the golden age of piracy and a prequel to Robert Louis Stevenson's *Treasure Island*: historical pirates such as Hornigold, Edward Teach, Charles Vane, Jack Rackham, Anne Bonny, and Mary Read interact with Stevenson's Billy Bones, Israel Bissel, Ben Gunn, Long John Silver, and *Black Sails'* protagonist, Captain Flint. A pall hangs over the series as both a historical drama and prequel: the end of this period dooms many of its historical characters to execution, while *Treasure Island*'s Flint is dead, his former comrades shadows of their former selves. Viewers are likely, therefore, to expect a conclusion that portrays, or at least implies, the triumph of colonial rule over piracy.

That the pirates' exploits are doomed is further underscored by the series' association of piracy with queer relationships. Throughout its four seasons, heteronormative relationships are tied to colonialism's greed and abuses, while queer relationships are linked to the idealism, adventure, and freedom from social constraints valued in the pirates' "New World." The series prominently features two polyamorous relationships between characters of different sexual identities and social backgrounds, joined both by their love for one another and their resistance to the pressures of imperialism, just as cooperation and equal treatment regardless of status were vital to a functioning pirate crew.[1] When joined together, these characters are able to resist the forces of imperialism; when separated from their queer partners, they not only become subject to but perpetuate its evils, driven by their own self-interest rather than by the good of the group. These relationships include the historical pirates Jack Rackham (Toby Schmitz) and Anne Bonny (Clara Paget), who join with brothel madam Max (Jessica Parker Kennedy) to form a successful romantic and economic triangle that allows them to circumvent the restrictions of class, gender, and race enforced by English society. Most predominant among these is *Black Sails*' central storyline, in which the series' bisexual protagonist, James Flint, hopes to establish a secure future for Nassau through his political and sexual relationship with married couple Thomas (Rupert Penry-Jones) and Miranda Hamilton (Louise Barnes), only to lose both his lovers to the homophobia and greed of the English elite (Toby Stephens).

Even in its most hopeful moments, the series hints at the eventual dissolution of the pirates' utopia and the queer love stories that hold it together: not only do queer relationships all too often meet with bad ends in historical narratives, but the historical record concerning Rackham and Bonny, *Treasure Island*'s statements concerning Flint, and Flint's belief that Thomas is dead suggest that these relationships, like the pirate world they represent, are doomed. Yet *Black Sails* ultimately rejects the literary and historical narratives that shape it; these characters, in open contradiction of their literary and historical sources, end the series alive, happy, and continuing to resist colonial rule, sailing past the boundaries of the show's narrative to flourish indefinitely.

The show's refusal to constrain its pirates within the bounds of its source material is in keeping with its exploration of piracy as a queer enterprise. The term *queer* here does not simply connote non-heteronormative sexual relationships (though such relationships are the series' most prominent symbol of piracy's queer nature); rather, in this essay it bears the sense of queer theory's resistance to assimilation and binary categorization, its defiance to dominant ways of thinking, its "potential to challenge normative knowledges and practices" (Sullivan 44). Inhabiting both land and sea, adept at eluding the authorities and circumventing the laws that sought to constrain their activities, legally labeled *"hostes humani generis*—enemies of all mankind" and "denied ... the protections and rights enjoyed by '"legitimate' citizens," pirates existed in a geographically and socially queer space (Leeson 448). Our current view of piracy, popularized by historian Marcus Rediker, characterizes it as a sort of queer alternative to imperialism: a quasi-democratic response to the social strictures of eighteenth-century life, in which men were valued for skill and dedication rather than social class and where even women, in cases such as the historical Anne Bonny and Mary Read, could find freedoms denied them on land. As discussed elsewhere in this volume, crew members were treated better by far on pirate ships, where prizes were divided fairly among the crew, than on navy and merchant vessels under tyrannical captains (Rediker '"Under the Banner'" 214, "Review" 355). Close quarters and long voyages required cooperation, resulting in a surprisingly forward-thinking "shipboard democracy" (Dawdy and Bonni 680) in which rules, rewards, and leadership were subject to vote and the risk of "captain misconduct" was curbed (Leeson 454). The Empire's response to such a radical arrangement was a focused public relations campaign of "sermons, proclamations, pamphlets and the newspaper press to create an image of the pirate" that justified hanging them by the hundred; England branded piracy its queer other, a shapeshifting monster defined against the rulebound Empire (Rediker '"Under the Banner'" 226).

Black Sails' chief storyline, that of Captain James Flint's war against the British Empire, initially appears to be the kind of anti-imperialist resistance characteristic of that narrative. Our introduction to the *Walrus* sounds very much like the characterization of democratic piracy discussed above: that being familiar with the abuses associated with sailing under a "tyrant captain," subject to "his whims, his violence, his shit wages, his insufferable stupidity," the crew seeks instead "a different life where we don't rely on wages, we own a stake" ("I."). Yet it soon becomes apparent that though Flint, the *Walrus*' captain, condemns England's imperial control of the seas, he nevertheless behaves in a tyrannical manner, forcing his men into high-risk, low-profit ventures in pursuit of a "hidden agenda" ("IV."). His motives gradually come to light in flashbacks in Season Two: ten years previously Flint, then known as James McGraw, was a Navy lieutenant in England, tasked with working with aristocrat Lord Thomas Hamilton to defeat piracy and establish a successful British colony on New Providence Island. Both Hamilton's radical politics and the revelation of Flint's affairs with both Hamilton and his wife, Miranda, lead to Hamilton's confinement to an asylum and (supposed) death, while Flint and Miranda flee to Nassau in disgrace. His acts of piracy throughout the series are driven not by a yearning for adventure, freedom, or wealth, but from a desire for vengeance for Thomas's death against all those he deems responsible—including England itself. By tracing Flint's progression from

Thomas's partner in an idealistic plan to reform Nassau to a dangerous pirate hell-bent on revenge, the series troubles the binary between imperialism and piracy, instead contrasting idealism and cooperation (in the form of the political and romantic partnership between Thomas, Flint, and Miranda, and the successful pirate democracy to which the *Walrus* aspires) with the violent self-interest evident both in the British Empire's colonial abuses and in Flint's deadly retribution.

While contrasting imperialism and piracy relies on the issue of legality, the contrast of cooperation versus self-interest does not; the parties on either side can participate either within or outside of the law. Such is the case with Thomas Hamilton, who is part of the British aristocratic elite and does not seek to undermine colonialism itself; he is hoping to make Nassau a successful part of the empire. His ideals, however, are those of democratic piracy. He is a passionate idealist who preaches a "need to rethink things, systemic things" and recognizes the harm wrought by colonialism, declaring that "the New World is a gift, Lieutenant, a sacred opportunity to right our wrongs and begin anew" ("X."). Thomas realizes that the problems facing Nassau are caused not by the rebellious pirates, but by the exploitative behaviors of those in power; he views pirates' practices as a "symptom" of the real "root causes" of Nassau's ills, the corruption and incompetence of the city's lawmakers and landowners ("X.").

As the series hints at Thomas's homosexuality for several episodes before finally confirming his affair with Flint, his political passions frequently serve as code for his romantic ones: Miranda coyly calls him a "very special man, a man of ideas—about the world, about the order of things" ("VI."), while the British elite are scandalized by his desire for reform: "my God, do you know anyone in the world who talks that way?" Flint's superior asks. "Is it possible he's fully mad? Half of Whitehall whispers it" ("X."). Thomas himself uses romantic allusions to describe his political union with Flint, likening the two of them to Adam and Eve: "the moral of the story everybody needs a partner. You are the partner assigned to me.... Strange pairs.... They can achieve the most unexpected things" ("X"). Thomas's idealism, however, is not merely a symbol of but the driving force behind the polyamorous relationship that develops between himself, Flint, and Miranda. He is a man of lofty ideals and lofty language to match, and the ceaseless optimism with which he approaches his task binds the three together by their love for him and his vision. Flint is attracted to Thomas because of his passionate promise to "save Nassau before she's lost forever," and attracted to Miranda because of her praise of her husband's "relentless pursuit of a better world." Likewise, Miranda is drawn to Flint because of his admiration of Thomas: "I remember what it was like the first time I met him. There's a feeling one gets when in the presence of the truly great men. It's something quite indescribable. I imagine you're having it as we speak" ("IX.").

The series links Thomas's sexuality and his politics by contrasting both his private actions and political views with the rigid code of behavior dictated by British imperialism. The seeds of this contrast are planted early on by verbal parallels, beginning with the first episode, in which a minor character (a British captain) comes to arrest Nassau's governor for the sale of pirated goods. This captain names shame as the most important weapon in imperialism's fight against piracy: "Do you have gossip here [in Nassau]?... I've often wondered if it can survive in so remote a location. You see, gossip is what holds civilization together. It reinforces shame. And without shame, the world is a very dangerous place" ("I."). A few episodes later, Miranda says of her husband's skill for philosophical debate: "everything you hold sacred, he'd leave in tatters. Not from malice or hate, but from love. From a desire to see the yoke of shame lifted from your shoulders" ("VI."). Later, the romantic nature of Flint's relationship with Thomas comes to light through a copy of the writings of Marcus Aurelius with the inscription "James, my truest love, know no shame.—TH" ("XIII.").

Imperialism, therefore, relies on enforcing a binary division between civilized and uncivilized behaviors; those who threaten to fall out of bounds must be kept in check through shame for civilization to survive. Thomas, whose conception of right and wrong does not rely on what is considered acceptable or unacceptable by society but, rather, on what is best for the communal whole, sees shame as the problem rather than the solution. His plan to reform Nassau, by issuing a general pardon of those convicted of piracy and therefore remove the mark of shame from them so that they can work to establish Nassau's future, relies on this belief: "[Nassau] needs men and women vested in its interest. Don't these men fit that description? Couldn't they become part of the solution?" ("XII."). Like a successful pirate ship, this solution requires cooperation and compromise from all parties involved, from Thomas, Miranda, and Flint's efforts to sway prominent aristocrats, to the British Empire's willingness to forgive the crimes against it, to the pirates' willingness to cease their operations.

When their venture falls apart after Thomas's father learns of his affair with Flint, however, Flint is unwilling to pursue the path of cooperation that Thomas set before him, finding that any resolution that results in his reconciliation with England "requires an intolerable sacrifice.... They took everything from us. And then they called me a monster. The moment I sign that pardon, the moment I ask for one, I proclaim to the world that they were right. This ends when I grant them my forgiveness, not the other way around" ("VII."). The word *monster* here echoes Flint's assertion, in the first episode, that the Crown "doesn't mean to make [pirates] adversaries. He doesn't mean to make us criminals. He means to make us monsters" ("I."). Flint's options, as he sees them, are to seek reconciliation, in which case he will be labeled a monster for his sexuality (a negation of himself, of Thomas, of Thomas's dedication to eradicating shame); or to seek revenge against those responsible (as he does by using his crew to locate and murder Thomas's parents and then acquire the wealth he hopes to use to secure Nassau's freedom as a pirate nation), in which case he will be labeled a monster for his piratical acts.

He considers the latter the more acceptable of the two courses, unable to imagine any other outcome. At this stage in the narrative, Flint cannot conceive an identity for himself outside how the Empire labels him, which means he cannot be anything but a monster. A rebellion on such terms can only serve to help his enemy, by reinforcing the Empire's perception of itself as a force for order against Flint's chaos. He is fully aware of this, or *should* be, as revealed in a flashback scene in which he takes Thomas to witness the public execution of pirates, specifically so he can hear the bloodthirsty cheers of approval from observing Londoners. Pirates, Flint explains, are a necessary cultural scapegoat; Nassau will never truly be reformed because "civilization needs its monsters" ("IX."). His potential for monstrosity is foreshadowed in another scene taking place in this earlier timeline, in which Flint's captain warns him of "that thing which arises in you when passions are aroused.... All men have it, but yours is different—darker, wilder.... [W]hen exposed to extremes, I could not imagine what it is capable of" ("X."). Now, in the face of such "extremes," we see the full extent of Flint's grief and rage.

The resulting monstrosity of his acts exposes the contrast between abusive imperialist and free pirate as a false binary, showing that the tyranny of an Empire seeking to overthrow piracy is equally visible in the pirate seeking to overthrow an empire. When he and Thomas had worked together in pursuit of Nassau's interests, Flint said of the colony's corrupt governors: "put a man on an island, give him power over other men, and it won't be long before he realizes that the limits of that power are nowhere to be seen. And no man given that kind of influence will remain honest for very long" ("XI."). Now, without Thomas's partnership, still devoted to his memory but divorced from the sense of justice that drove his partner's actions, increasingly resistant to (and ultimately without, after her death) Miranda's mitigating levelheadedness, Flint is that man on an island, and he begins to exploit his own power just as much as the empire he hates does. Although he contrasts England's "God-fearing, taxpaying subjects" with pirates who "keep what is theirs and fear no one," he goes on to assert that "[i]f we are to survive, we must unite behind our own king.... I am your king" ("I."). He invokes imperialistic values to appeal to his men, promising to make them "princes of the New World," and compares himself to a king "ly[ing] to [his subjects] for their own good" ("I."; "VII.") Unlike the pirates of the historical golden age, who came into conflict with merchants and the law but typically "did not prey on one another," Flint spends more time at war with his own world than with

Britain, clashing with other pirates throughout the series and sacrificing every intimate relationship—with not only Miranda but fellow pirates Gates, Billy Bones (Tom Hopper), and John Silver (Luke Arnold)—in the course of seeking revenge (Rediker "'Under the Banner'" 219). He uses force and manipulation to bend men to his will, exploiting his crew and risking their lives in hopes of amassing wealth and controlling property; he is all too willing to endanger even those closest to him to reach his goals, and even quick to kill them if he deems it necessary. That he seeks wealth and power in pursuit of revenge for his lost love, rather than as ends to themselves, invites the viewer's sympathy, but, ultimately, Flint's desires are no more honorable than the Empire's. His actions expose the piratical monster and the imperialist tyrant as two sides of the same coin: one makes the rules, the other breaks them, but both do so in the service of getting what they want, regardless of the human cost.

However far he strays, Flint always finds himself returning to the plans he and the Hamiltons once hoped to set in motion. In contrast to colonialism and piracy's thievery of property, the utopia Thomas envisioned is supported by honest labor, in which pardoned pirates are put to work "[t]illing, harvesting, coopering, building, smiting, fishing" ("XII."). Flint, likewise, hopes to use the gold taken from the *Urca de Lima* to establish New Providence Island as a "nation of thieves" where men could "work the land, grow crops and raise cattle" ("II."). This idealized farm is a self-sufficient, cooperative, non-exploitative space, safe from the corruption of London, the violence of Nassau, or danger of the sea. The farm is placed in contrast with the spaces that represent the Empire's oppression and Flint's chaotic violence. In the flashback scenes, Thomas's house—actually owned by his father, Lord Alfred Hamilton—serves as a symbol of imperialist control over "uncivilized" behavior. After Flint and Thomas begin their affair (shortly after Flint quarrels with Thomas's father and ejects him from "his own house" ["X."]), Miranda becomes increasingly concerned that people will discover "what's been going on in this house" ("XIII."). When their relationship is finally exposed, Alfred Hamilton confronts Flint: "you thought I wouldn't hear what you'd done? In my own house?" ("XIII."). After Flint embraces piracy and takes to the seas, his domestic haven, the small house and farm he shares with Miranda, is destroyed, and he is pushed further out into increasingly wild spaces: the doldrums where he and his crew narrowly escape starvation, the Maroon Queen's island where he and his men are held captive, its jungles filled with traps, and finally Skeleton Island, the future setting for Stevenson's tale, a harrowing place "not on any chart, not on any civilized one, at any rate" ("XXXVI.").

Early in the series, expressing his hope of establishing agriculture in New Providence Island, Flint recounts the tale of Odysseus, who is told that in order to rest, he must "pick up an oar and walk inland. And keep walking until somebody mistakes that oar for a shovel. For that would be the place that no man had ever been troubled by the sea. And that's where he'd find peace. In the end, that's all I want. To walk away from the sea and find some peace" ("II."). He finally arrives on that peaceful farm far from the sea in the series' final episode, after his closest companion, John Silver, learns that Thomas is not dead but working as a laborer on "an estate in the wilderness, north of Spanish Florida" ("XXXII."). Silver uses the knowledge to finally put a halt to Flint's campaign of violent revenge, dividing him from the imperialist identity that will only allow him to see himself as civilization's monster: "I did not kill Captain Flint. I unmade him. The man you know could never let go of his war, for if he were to exclude it from himself, he would not be able to understand himself" ("XXXVIII."). Instead, he "return[s] him to an earlier state of being, one in which he could function without the war, without the violence" ("XXXVIII."). This peaceful "earlier state of being" suggests an Edenic innocence, as when Thomas characterized the two of them as Adam and Eve—which is precisely as their story ends, as two lovers in a garden. Flint arrives at the plantation to find Thomas tilling a field; like a guiltless Adam and Eve before the Fall, they embrace and kiss in the sight of the other inmates, both now without wealth or power that the Empire had once provided them, but also without the shame it hoped to engender in them.

Pirates, Rediker writes, were "as far removed from traditional authority as any men could be in the early eighteenth century" ("'Under the Banner'" 227). Sailing out beyond the Empire's reach, they "carried out a strange experiment" in which their "aspirations and achievements" could flourish untouched by the "power relationships of everyday life" (Rediker "'Under the Banner'" 227). From our position on the other side of history, to call the golden age of piracy an "experiment," an intriguing but ultimately temporary set of circumstances, seems appropriate. *Black Sails*, however, is a text utterly defiant of endings. It rejects the long, unfortunate literary and cinematic history of denying, particularly in historically homophobic settings, happy endings to queer characters. Not only does it avoid this trope, but blatantly subverts it by miraculously saving both Thomas from his supposed death in the asylum and Flint from his terrible end as recounted in *Treasure* Island.[2] And although Thomas and Flint have retired to their secluded corner of a world that they are no longer trying to either change or destroy, the series suggests that the vision they shared with Miranda of a thriving Nassau built on equality and cooperation will survive. The show closes on another group of polyamorous queer lovers, the aforementioned Anne, Jack, and Max, who have not only defied the historical record to survive but have expanded their successful partnership to include another queer figure, cross-dressing pirate Mary Read (Cara Roberts), who joins their crew in the last episode. In the series' final moments, the story of piracy refuses to end, portraying instead a *beginning*, the start of a new adventure: Jack Rackham unfurls the Jolly Roger for the first time, declaring, "Get us underway" ("XXXVIII.").

NOTES

1. I use *imperialism* here as a term to connote the use of exploitation, oppression, or force to increase one's own power, wealth, or landholdings; this term could encompass many of the oppressive structures at work in eighteenth-century Britain that support it, including colonialism, patriarchy/misogyny, racism, homophobia, and classism, all of which deeply affect the lives of the series' pirates and their allies. While "kyriarchy" or "hegemony" may be more apt, "imperialism" seems a better fit for the system of oppression in play here, one whose abuses manifested most obviously through the expansion of the British Empire. I will employ the term, therefore, in reference to characters such as Flint, who wields his power in an oppressive manner very similar to the British Empire, even though the Empire itself is his enemy. The term *colonialism* will be used when more specifically discussing Britain's political control of the New World.

2. *Black Sails* not only subverts the trope that same-sex relationships lead to death, but goes so far as to suggest that opposite-sex relationships are hazardous: Miranda's involvement with Flint, Vane's involvement with Eleanor Guthrie and, most significantly, Eleanor Guthrie's involvement with Governor Woodes Rogers lead to their deaths. Though beyond the scope of this essay, Eleanor's storyline is a sort of mirror for, and reversal of, Flint's: she rejects sexually and socially queer partnerships in favor of retaining her power by submitting herself to heteronormative patriarchy, resulting in her becoming the only queer character in *Black Sails* to die.

WORKS CITED

Black Sails. Jonathan E. Steinberg and Robert Levine (creators). Platinum Dunes and Quaker Moving Pictures, 2014–17.
Dawdy, Shannon Lee, and Joe Bonni. "Towards a General Theory of Piracy." *Anthropological Quarterly* 85.3 (Summer 2012): 673–99.
Deane, Bradley. "Imperial Boyhood: Piracy and the Play Ethic." *Victorian Studies* 53.4 (Summer 2011): 689–714.
Fletcher, Loraine. "Long John Silver, Karl Marx and the Ship of State." *Critical Survey* 19.2 (2007): 34–47.
Leeson, Peter T. "The Calculus of Piratical Consent: The Myth of the Myth of Social Contract." *Public Choice* 139.3/4 (June 2009): 443–59.
Rediker, Marcus. "Review: Pirates and the Imperial State." *Reviews in American History* 16.3 (Sept. 1988): 351–57.
_____. "'Under the Banner of King Death': The Social World of Anglo-American Pirates, 1716 to 1726." *The William and Mary Quarterly* 38.2 (Apr. 1981): 203–27.
Stevenson, Robert Louis. *Treasure Island*. New York: Airmont Books, 1962.
Sullivan, Nikki. *A Critical Introduction to Queer Theory*. New York: New York University Press, 2003.

PART IV: PIRATES IN OTHER MEDIA

The Servant, the Sinner and the Savior
The Pirate in Early Nineteenth Century Italian Opera

ALEXANDRA V. LEONZINI

As stated by Frederick Burwick and Manshag N. Powell in their 2015 *British Pirates in Print and Performance*, the term "pirate" is as much a social term as it is a legal one, and is in many ways culturally conditioned (16). While in some historical contexts a true pirate was considered *hostis humani generis*, the enemy of all mankind, the act of piracy very often proved to be a matter of perspective, a determination informed by the political and social contexts of the actors and their audiences. Considered a violent enemy of the people in some quarters while simultaneously viewed as a freedom fighter in others, the history of the public's perception of the pirate figure is an uneven one, and is epitomized in the diverse treatment of piracy on the early nineteenth century Italian opera stage. Although largely dismissed as an outmoded art form today, opera has at all times closely reflected the concerns and activities of the audiences that have patronized it (Willier 7).

Unlike in England, where *opera seria* and *opera buffa* provided entertainment solely for the upper-class audience of the King's Theatre, opera in Italy was a far more democratic art form, enjoyed by a wide cross-section of the urban public (Williams 145; Ebers 117). Although most people could not attend the theater in person, it was common for the most famous arias or scenes to be performed in the street by town bands and traveling musicians, or, in Venice, sung by gondoliers as they navigated the city (Leydi 314–42). "A form of expression and mode of collective sensibility which conditioned an entire period," Romantic stereotypes and narratives tropes were diffused throughout the librettos of early nineteenth century Italian operas, helping to shape Italian society by "envoicing" the passionate emotional tone of the *Risorgimento* (Sorba 483; Ginsborg 5–67). In the wake of the French Revolution, audiences were drawn to the tales of popular heroes, champions of the people who stood in opposition to tyrannical authority. Of these heroes, none was more popular than the pirate or sea-robber.

Discussing the representations of the pirate in Gioachino Rossini's *L'italiana in Algeri* (1813), Vincenzo Bellini's *Il pirata* (1827), and Giuseppe Verdi's *Il corsaro* (1848), this essay will examine the political and social conditions which shaped the portrayal of pirates and piracy in Italian opera of the early nineteenth century, and investigate why, in less than forty years, the sympathetically constructed pirate, a stateless servant of the Ottoman Empire, was transformed into a murderous sinner, a ruthless enemy to all mankind, only to emerge by mid-century as a figure positively charged with revolutionary intent—a leader of men and savior of the emerging Italian nation, guiding Italian peoples to throw off the shackles of oppression and claim political freedom. Adopting a historical perspective, Haly, the pirate figure in *L'italiana in Algeri* will be considered in the context of the Italian Peninsula's tumultuous relationship with the Ottoman Empire in the first half of the nineteenth century, drawing on the pirate's status as *Capitano dei Corsari Algerini* and the function of his only solo piece, "Le femmine d'Italia," to highlight his role as a stateless mediator within the opera—a privateer loyal to gold over nation or ideology. Following this, the Italian public's reconceptualization of the Mediterranean pirate as a wholly irredeemable sinner following the Second Barbary War (1815) will be discussed, and the deplorable actions of Gualtiero, the tragic hero of Bellini's *Il pirata* highlighted. Finally, the construction of Corrado, the protagonist of Verdi's *Il corsaro*, will be analyzed and the connection between the pirate figure and Giuseppe Garibaldi in the early years of the Risorgimento considered. Consequently, it will be argued that, far from the mercenary or cutthroat of old, the pirate figure of mid-nineteenth century Italian opera, tempered in the fire of the rapidly transforming political and social climate of Italy, emerged as a champion of revolution, self-determination, and liberation: a figure worthy of emulation and respect.

While pirates are not the protagonists of Rossini's *L'italiana in Algeri*, they are sympathetically constructed secondary characters who ultimately assist the heroes of the piece. Premiering at the Teatro San Benedetto in Venice on May 22, 1813, *L'italiana* is a work which was inspired by the kidnapping of a young Milanese woman named Antonietta Frapolli-Suini in 1805, and tells the tale of a clever and beautiful Italian woman who is taken by pirates to the court of an Algerian *Dey* while on a mission to rescue her captured lover. Underplaying the reality of the tumultuous relationship between the Italian peoples and the pirates of the Mediterranean at the time of the opera's composition, Rossini's depiction of pirates as stateless mediators coerced into acting on behalf the Ottoman Empire identifies the later as posing a more direct threat to the Italian peoples than the former, particularly in light of the kidnapping of Italian women such as Frapolli-Suini which many in Italy believed to be orchestrated by Ottoman agents.

Little is known of Frapolli-Suini's abduction. The most credible source available is the private diary of the then vice-president of the Government of Lombardy, Don Giovanni Bazzetta, who died in Milan in 1827. His account reveals the extent of public interest in the case, recalling how the general population of Milan continued for over three years to hold the Milanese government accountable for their lack of success in bargaining for Frapolli-Suini's freedom, feeling concerned that pirates could kidnap a Milanese "person of quality" and the government be proved powerless to intervene (Bazzetta de Vemenia). After her eventual safe return to the city in 1808, the exact date and circumstances of which are still unknown, the citizens of Milan continued to express their disappointment in the inaction of their government, lamenting the fact that the pirates who took Frapolli-Suini remained at large, escaping the grasp of the Milanese authorities (Bazzetta de Vemenia). It was the general consensus that they should be found and punished for their actions to ensure the safety of the "innocent" women of Italy (Bazzetta de Vemenia). The gossip surrounding Frapolli-Suini's story romanticized her ordeal, replicating the "rescue opera" plotline outlined above, with some suggesting that she, being an intelligent and cunning Italian woman, tricked her captors into releasing her, allowing her to return to her beloved homeland. This interpretation grew in popularity as the events of the *Risorgimento* unfolded, and it is this narrative, transcribed and produced as a libretto by Angelo Anelli in 1808, that Rossini decided to dramatize to great public acclaim.

L'italiana in Algeri has at its core a narrative form which was immensely popular in the early nineteenth century; the rescue opera. Pirates often played a pivotal role in this hugely popular Romantic subgenre, "as almost all such theatricals begin with a heroine being abducted by corsairs and transported to the court of some sultan, who falls in love with her directly" (Burwick and Powell 32). A product of the French Revolution, rescue operas would traditionally end with a happy dramatic resolution in which the captured heroine would be rescued by her beloved, and lofty humanistic ideals, such as resistance to oppression and the political power of the individual, would triumph. The concept of nationhood was integral to the success of the genre, as demonstrated by Rossini, who pits the Italians against the Ottomans for his audiences' amusement by utilizing the increasingly popular nationalist discourse that emerged in Italy as a response to Napoleon's interventions in the region.

In his original version of *L'italiana*, the female protagonist Isabella sings a *Rondo* in the second act titled "Pensa alla patria, e intrepido il tuo dover adempi [Think of your country, and fearlessly do your duty]" to motivate herself to find an escape. While some have indicated this as proof of Rossini's nationalist sentiments, John Rosselli claims otherwise, identifying the aria as a propaganda piece aimed at exhorting young subjects of Napoleon's Kingdom of Italy to fight in the German campaign that followed the leader's retreat from Moscow at a time when the Napoleonic regime was deeply unpopular in Venice. As such, Rossini was, in the words of Rosselli, "an ironic conservative," first and foremost interested in attracting a public rather than pushing any particular political ideology, and therefore comfortable with manipulating nationalist discourse for financial gain (Rosselli 185).

In *L'italiana* this is evident in his portrayal of the main pirate figure Haly, whose primarily function is as a narrator or neutral observer "guiding" the audience's reactions throughout the opera. Caught between the "heroic" Italians and "antagonistic" Ottomans, Haly is depicted as sympathizing with the "good" despite working in the interest of Mustafà, the *Dey* of Algiers, an Ottoman provincial governor. In the opera's *libretto*, Haly is listed as being "Capitano dei Corsari Algerini" [Captain of the Algerian Corsairs], a contrast to the later English and French translations in which he is listed as being something akin to "Captain of the Royal Guard" (Rossini and Anelli). This difference is significant in understanding why Italian audiences could sympathize with Haly, as it speaks to the nature of his relationship with the *Dey*. In the English and French translations, it is implied that he is a highly esteemed member of the court, while in the original Italian he is essentially a mercenary, a true "*corsaro*," acting purely in self-interest. When he captures Isabella, for example, he is doing so as he has been instructed to find an Italian woman for Mustafà's harem within six days on pains of being impaled. It is in his own interest to search the sea despite expressing discomfort at the prospect of kidnapping anybody. He is thus relieved when Isabella all but falls into his lap, happy to accompany him to Mustafà's court to eventually be united with her lover Lindoro, Mustafà's other Italian slave, and the man she has left Italy to find. It is because of Haly's status as a corsair, occupying a space outside of the politics of the court, that he is able to observe and admire Isabella's cleverness in her attempts to free herself and Lindoro from Mustafà's control. He acts as narrator, communicating the complex nature of Isabella's plan directly to the audience while appealing to their vanity. Haly's one solo piece is an *arietta* entitled "Le femmine d'Italia" in which he praises the cleverness of the women of Italy after having observed Isabella ply the palace guards with drugged wine so she can escape. Despite witnessing this and guessing her plan, Haly does not stop her. Rather, he communicates to the audience his appreciation of her intellect and bravery.

At the opera's premiere, this musical piece, dubbed an *aria di sorbetto*, was performed at the critical moment of the evening when street vendors would sell frozen ices inside the theater. There was an expectation of the performers of *aria di sorbetto* to engage their audiences directly and "break the fourth wall," providing a reprieve from the heavy drama of the opera, and explaining any convoluted developments in the plot. As we have no sources which directly comment on the audience's reception of this piece during its premiere in 1813, it is uncertain as to how captivating they found Giuseppe Spirito, the creator of the role of Haly. Sources we do have for this period, however, explicitly detail the Italian peoples' tremendous appetite for ice cream at the theater, and their enjoyment of *aria di sorbetto* as a result (Cronin 48–49). One can therefore assume that during the performance of his piece, Spirito would have capitalized on the audience's good humor, engaging directly with them to create an atmosphere in which, away from the influence of his employer, Haly could communicate exactly how he felt about the situation in which he had found himself. This would have reinforced the audience's perception of Haly as a sympathetic character, a trustworthy and neutral observer who was highly entertained by the unfolding drama, signaling the audience to be so as well. Thus, the pirate figure was not only central to the development of the narrative, but was also instrumental in guiding the audience's positive reception of the story, cheering with them as they witnessed the defeat of the buffoonish Algerian *Dey* at the hands of the clever, spirited, and beautiful Italian prisoner.

As the century wore on and pirate attacks became more frequent along the Italian coast, the Italian opera-going public's perception of the pirate as a neutral, apolitical, or even mediatory figure, began to alter. Tarnished by the violence of reality, the pirate emerged as the embodiment of sin; an irrational and tortured individual capable of courting nothing but grief. This shift in the construction of the pirate figure reflects the ever-changing political situation in Europe, which from the beginning of the nineteenth century saw a dramatic increase in the policing of Mediterranean piracy by Europe's largest naval powers. While the two Barbary Wars fought between the United States of America and the Barbary States of North Africa from 1801 to 1805, and 1815 to 1816 respectfully, did much to destabilize the region and alter the public's perception of the pirate figure, it was the massacre of 200 Corsican, Sicilian, and Sardinian fishermen at the hands of men loyal to the Dey of Algiers in 1816 which led to calls to end piracy in the Mediterranean, and the Bombardment of Algiers by British and Dutch forces in August of that year (Parkinson 160). As such, the pirate figure underwent a dramatic metamorphosis in the eyes of nations vulnerable to corsair attack, a metamorphosis aided by cultural products which identified the pirate as an enemy to all. Vincenzo Bellini's *Il pirata* is the most representative example of this.

Il pirata was first performed on October 27, 1827, at Teatro alla Scala in Milan and was "an immediate and then an increasing success" (Weinstock 40). The source of the *libretto* was the three-act *mélodrame Bertram; ou, Le pirate* by "Raimond" (real name Isidore J. S. Taylor), which was derived from a French translation of Charles Robert Maturin's five-act verse tragedy, *Bertram; or, The Castle of St. Aldobrand* (1816). Incorporating many Gothic tropes of the late 1790s, Maturin's *Bertram* is the tragic tale of an exiled Sicilian count who, overthrown by an aristocratic tyrant named Lord Aldobrand, becomes captain of a band of sea pirates, haunted by the loss of his betrothed, Imogine, who Aldobrand forces into wedlock. After his ship sinks in a terrible storm, the pirate captain and Imogine are reunited, beginning an illicit and blasphemous affair which only ends when Bertram murders Aldobrand in a fit of rage, and, driven by grief, Imogine goes mad, murdering her son in the cave where she and Bertram would meet. She falls dead at Bertram's feet as he is being taken to the gallows, and he, upon seeing this, grabs a dagger and kills himself. Performed at Drury Lane, the play was both extremely popular and hugely controversial, running twenty-two nights in succession before being canceled due to public outcry (Willier 10).

Adapted into French by Charles Nodier in 1821, Bertram found greater success in Paris, running for fifty-three nights in 1822, and coming to the attention of Felice Romani who would use it as the source of his libretto for *Il pirata*. Finding the piece "provided several passionate and dramatic situations ... [and] ... Romantic characters [that] were then an innovation on the operatic stage," Bellini readily agreed to use Romani's libretto which "italianized" the English names to make it easy for the singers to pronounce (Galatopoulos 62). Bertram became Gualtiero, the Count of Montalto, Aldobrand became Ernesto, the Duke of Casldora, and Imogine became Imogene. The character dynamics, however, remained largely untouched, with the biggest differences in characterization occurring in the depiction of the pirate.

Unlike Maturin's Bertram, whose crew is a constant presence throughout the play, reinforcing the notion of the pirate captain as a strong leader inspiring the loyalty of his men, Bellini and Romani actively distance Gualtiero from this image of fraternal devotion, presenting him throughout the opera as a solitary figure. Because his pirating ceases at the beginning of the opera, there are no scenes in which Gualtiero "actively" plays the role of the pirate, and when telling Imogene of his previous life, he describes how miserable he was, painting the experience of piracy as wholly unpleasant, singing "Nelle stragi del pirata, quell'imagine adorata si presenta al mio pensier? [Amidst the violence of the pirate's life, what adored image comes to mind?]" The difference between the two protagonists' perceptions of their pirating is central to the audience's reception of them as men of character. While Maturin's Bertram begrudges the circumstances that have led to his becoming a pirate, he proves himself to be resilient, strong, and clever, capable of commanding great respect despite his status as an exiled aristocrat. Gualtiero, in contrast, wallows passively in his misery and misfortune. Bellini and Romani's intentions in depicting Gualtiero as such may have been to disassociate him from the suggestion that his character was negatively affected by his time as a pirate, portraying him, at least initially, as a more tragic figure than Bertram so as to illicit greater sympathy from their audience.

Yet, despite this, Gualtiero is no more positive a character than the murderous Bertram. Both Imogine and Imogene are treated increasingly callously by their respective partners as their stories progress. This behavior, while tragic, would have been expected of Bertram "the sinful pirate" but would have been wholly unexpected of the tragic lover that Gualtiero is initially depicted as in the opera, shocking audiences and emphasizing the tragedy of Imogene's situation. Bertram's actions reinforce the notion of the pirate as amoral; the very embodiment of sin. Gualtiero, however, is a figure of madness, of self-delusion. His belief that he can fight his inner demons and redeem himself through the power of sinful love makes him appear even weaker than Bertram, whose behavior, while deplorable, remains consistent throughout the play. Bertram wishes to seek revenge and reclaim Imogine at all cost, committing suicide upon the realization that the ultimate cost of this revenge is the sanity and life of his beloved. Gualtiero's behavior, in contrast, is anything but consistent, becoming increasingly erratic as he is consumed by a jealous rage, and his treatment of Imogene, the woman he claims to love, becomes callous and cruel. As Friedrich Lippmann has observed, "from the mouth [of Gualtiero] we hear not one word that expresses a rational proposition" (qtd. in Rosselli 50).

While Gualtiero is driven by madness, Bertram is driven by his need for revenge. In both cases, the "reclamation" of Imogine/Imogene is their ultimate objective. Adultery had provided the plot for many popular plays of the period, yet what audiences witnessed in *Bertram* was an adulterous relationship unlike any previously portrayed on a British stage: in previous plays, the sin was accompanied by guilty remorse; in *Bertram*, the sin was accompanied by more sin. Bertram and Imogine knowingly commit their adultery multiple times throughout the course of the piece despite expressions of guilt and calls for forgiveness and redemption. Their blasphemous passion for one another consumes them both and they, unable or unwilling to control their desires, inevitably meet with tragedy. More so than Bertram, it was the portrayal of Imogine as an adulterous heroine that shocked audiences; the depiction of a willingly adulterous woman was thought to be beyond acceptable limits. That she continued to crave her former lover despite being married to another was abhorrent to many. *New Monthly Magazine and Universal Register* condemned the play in the strongest terms in 1817, as did Samuel

Taylor Coleridge, who launched a scathing attack on *Bertram* in the conclusion of his *Biographia Literaria* (285).

Burwick, among others, places the responsibility for Imogine's corruption solely in the hands of Bertram, highlighting the pirate captain's delicate manipulations of the fragile woman's feelings as reason for her conduct (147). Likewise, Bellini and Romani emphasize Gualtiero's callous treatment of Imogene to explain and excuse her sinful behavior. This is particularly evident in the finale of Act I when Gualtiero informs Imogene that he wants to meet her in a deserted place of her choosing one last time before he leaves the island. It is in this moment that the irrationality of Gualtiero's character becomes apparent to the audience, for rather than appeal to her love for him, he threatens the life of her son: "Se tu ricusi per te deh! trema, per te, per lui, per figlio [If you refuse, then tremble, for yourself, for him, for your son]" (Willier 16). Out of concern for her child, Imogene agrees to meet the pirate, and, in doing so, rekindles their affair. Unlike Gualtiero, Bertram "the sinful pirate" never threatens Imogine, nor does he intentionally do her bodily harm. While his manipulations of her fragile mental state are apparent and reprehensible, his delicate treatment of her never wavers.

At the conclusion of *Il pirata*, Gualtiero delivers an ultimatum to Imogene: Either she flees with him, thereby punishing Ernesto, or he stays and fights his rival to the death. Placed in an impossible position, Imogene pleads to be killed instead. Her cries, however, are ignored and, after an offstage altercation, Ernesto is murdered by the pirate and Imogene goes mad, ranting and imagining she has saved her son from an evil assassin as Gualtiero is lead away for execution. True to Maturin's *Bertram*, Romani's original libretto concluded with the pirate's suicide, an ending Bellini chose not to stage in order to emphasize the tragedy of Imogene's demise by highlighting her victimization at the hands of the pirate (Willier 19). In doing so, Bellini denies Gualtiero the "honourable death" Maturin grants Bertram, for, although one can argue that there is no honor in suicide, it suggests of Bertram a personal and moral accountability that Gualtiero lacks. Bertram is thus "romanticized" by Maturin, constructed for a British audience whose only exposure to Mediterranean piracy was in the pages of adventure novels and at the theater. Bellini, on the other hand, writing for an Italian audience for whom the realities of piracy were of daily concern, chooses ultimately to portray the pirate as irrational, morally corrupt, without honor, and entirely irredeemable: as the very embodiment of sin.

As the century wore on, the pirate figure was once again transformed in the eyes of the Italian public, emerging as a champion of revolutionary opposition to tyrannical authority (Moore 4). The popularization of Lord Byron's *The Corsair* (1814) in Italy from the 1830s, a piece perpetuating the now well-established myth of the pirate or bandit as the redresser of wrongs by idealizing the pirate's ability to operate outside the legal and moral constraints of mercantile bourgeois society, was central to this reconceptualization of the pirate figure. Depicting these "men of blood" as "persons of the highest sentimental cast; who, in short, if it were not for the exclusive spirit of our laws in respect to person and property, marriage and succession, might possibly live among their fellow creatures without crime or reproach," *The Corsair* portrayed the life of the pirate as one of sacrifice and freedom (Burwick 117–39; Roberts 391–400). Strongly anti-clerical, "a covert republican, hence a liberal, and perhaps even a democrat," Verdi first expressed interest in staging *The Corsair* as early as 1844 (Rosselli 186). After completing several other projects, Verdi again considered staging *The Corsair* in 1846, even going so far as to enlist the services of the librettist and ardent nationalist Francesco Maria Piave to work with him on the project. This enthusiasm did not last long, however, and Verdi soon abandoned the opera, returning to it in February 1848 to finish, after which he essentially wiped his hands of the project, leaving all decisions as to where, when, and how the work would be performed up to the publisher. The opera was eventually premiered on October 25, 1848, at Teatro Grande, Trieste, but was poorly received by both the press and the public, leading it to "vanish from the repertoire after three performances" (Budden 363–66).

Despite following Byron's plot closely, Verdi's endowment of the rebellious slave Gulnara's murder of her captor with positive revolutionary force, imbues his pirate-protagonist Corrado with a "savior-like" quality missing in the original text. While, in *The Corsair*, Conrad's rescue of Gulnare from the burning harem is "the first step in [her] liberation … [freeing] her spirit to rebel" (Hadlock 48), Gulnare's strike for freedom, particularly her murder of Seyd, her captor, is not considered heroic as she lacks the pirate's honor, murdering her enemy in his sleep and feeling no shame for having done so. In contrast, Verdi's Gulnara is a female avenger endowed with a ferocity tempered in a positive prerevolutionary light. At her transgression, the sight of her guilt moves Corrado to pity as he sympathizes with her plight. This is reflected in the score as a musical storm accompanies the off-stage murder, a storm representative of the tumultuous emotions coursing through Gulnara's mind as she commits the murder. This "storm" *leitmotif* is heard earlier in the score, foreshadowing the event, developing, and becoming more present as the piece builds to this moment of bloody climax, peaking when the deathblow is struck. It then breaks almost instantly in an indication that Gulnara's murderous rage is situational; it is a product of her cruel treatment at her captor's hands, and thus requiring sympathetic reflection rather than judgment. In the words of Hadlock, "the storm fulfils a promise of revolutionary violence that has been brewing in Gulnara over the course of several earlier numbers" (Hadlock 54).

That Verdi's remaking of Gulnara posits her as a revolutionary figure inspired by the pirate to violently seek freedom from her oppressor is evident in Verdi's treatment of her ethnicity. In Byron's poem Gulnare is distinctly racially "other" and her violent action is thus interpreted as innate, as an essential aspect of "the fire that lights an Eastern heart" (III, III). In Verdi's opera, however, while she remains nominally "eastern," her music bears no "orientalist" markers and she is further distanced from the "oriental" character so familiar to western audiences by declaring, as her first words no less, Seid to be a "vile Muslim [O vile musulmano]" (Act II, Scene 1). While it is never explicitly stated that Verdi's Gulnara is, like Isabella, a captured Italian woman, it is suggested in the non-orientalist music accompanying her actions, particularly the use of a barcarolle rhythm as a *leitmotif*. As such Gulnara's tempestuous personality seems less a cliché of "oriental" character than a product of her situation as a woman oppressed by a man, and a subject oppressed by a tyrant. As such, Hadlock writes, Verdi "envoices" Gulnara as a liberator, a revolutionary, and a Romantic heroine: "Verdi's Gulnara is a murderess ... but she is also a freedom fighter, an oppressed woman avenging her own 'stained' honor. If she is guilty, so was her tyrant-victim" (56). While Verdi and Piave "envoice" Gulnara as a revolutionary figure, it can be argued, however, that her actions, or rather, the inspiration for her actions, are the result of her interaction with Corrado. Until she meets him she is a passive figure, unhappy with her life, suffering terribly under slavery and unable to envision an escape from her situation. Corrado's failed rescue attempt is what spurs her into action. As such, the scene can be read allegorically, with Gulnara, the beautiful yet oppressed slave representing the Italian people, the tyrannical pasha representing the Austrian Empire and the Kingdom of the Two Sicilies, and Corrado, the pirate captain who inspires the slave to action and liberate herself, representing Giuseppe Garibaldi, a central military leader in the Italian *Risorgimento*.

Known as "The Hero of Two Worlds," the first image of Garibaldi presented to the Italian public was that of pirate or sea-robber. The Italian people were enthralled by his rumored exploits as a corsair in South America, attacking Brazilian ships for the rebels of Rio Grande do Sul during the Ragamuffin War (1835–1845) and proving himself to be an experienced military commander and strategist. The exoticism of his time in America was highly appealing as the Americas were a favorite theater for Romantic narratives and images in Italy, being so far removed from the Mediterranean. The images of the free frontiersman and brave adventurer, unconstrained by law and close to nature, were popular and lasting configurations of heroism in the Italian imagination, and Garibaldi's followers were quick to accept this image of the man many believed would lead a nationalist revolution (Lyttelton 39). The pirate, ever the heroic individualist, was a particularly potent image to those seeking a revolutionary figure who embodied extreme passion at odds with society and its laws. In Italy, the Romantic myth of the bandit and pirate became increasingly popular as the 1848 movements toward revolution and rebellion gained momentum (Zamovski 34). The "self mastery" of the pirate was seen as an essential attribute of the hero, and the true democratic hero was one who accepted that he was one of the people and that his political authority rested on their investiture. Garibaldi was thus seen as the amalgam of these attributes, imagined as a figure of resistance to all tyrannical power structures.

The depiction of piracy on the early nineteenth century Italian opera stage was conditioned by the Italian audience's lived experiences of piracy in the Mediterranean during this period, seeing a rapid reconceptualization of the pirate figure. Local and regional interactions with Barbary pirates, such as the kidnapping of Antonietta Frapolli-Suini in 1805, and the Barbary Wars, transformed the public's perception of the pirate from one of nationless mediator, such as Haly in Rossini's *L'italiana in Algeri* of 1813, to one of irredeemable sin, madness, and malice, as displayed by Gualtiero in Bellini's *Il pirata* of 1827. It is only with the rise of Garibaldi in the 1840s that the pirate figure is redeemed, depicted as a savior in Verdi's *Il corsaro* 1848, a reference to the Italian general's past as a corsair resistance fighter in the Rugamuffin War (1835–1845). Yet while the pirate image was highly successful in attracting the support of Europe's increasingly politically minded young people, it also provided a target for Garibaldi's opponents in Italy and abroad, proving itself to have its political disadvantages. He was often depicted as a brigand, uneducated, and "loutish" and his character and moral judgment were questioned. *The Times* even described him as a "'chieftain' at the head of foreign freebooters" in 1849 (Lyttelton 38).

To counter such critique Garibaldian propaganda began to depict him as an "adventurer" rather than a pirate, distinguishing one from the other by emphasizing his "devotion to a cause that [transcended] any personal motives of offended honour or vendetta" (Lyttelton 38). Despite this, criticism continued, with fellow-politician and nationalist Guiseppe Mazzini drew attention to the limitations of the sort of Byronic heroic individualism that Garibaldi's pirate image embodied, believing that the new revolutionary hero must be the expression of collective will and faith (Migliorini 158). As such, Garibaldi modified his image after he was exiled to the Americas following the unsuccessful First Italian War of Independence of 1848 and 1849, leaving his "bandit persona" behind him and developing "an image more in keeping with Anglo-Saxon ideals of manliness, marked by modesty, courtesy, and steadfastness" (Riall 114). It is, perhaps, for this reason that Verdi's *Il corsaro* failed disastrously in Italian theaters, as revolutionaries distanced themselves from the pirate figure on their march to revolution. Nonetheless, his opera

198 Part IV: Pirates in Other Media

suggests the pirate to be a "savior-like" figure, a catalyst for revolution, self-determination, and liberation—an opinion which is still held by some to this day.

Works Cited

Bazzetta de Vemenia, Nino. *Luci e penombre di Lombardia: donne ed amori, ville e misteri di Milano e del Lario*. Como, IT: Libreria Editrice Omarini Vittorio, 1921. http://opera.stanford.edu/Rossini/Italiana/Frapolli.html Accessed on 09/11/2017.
Bokina, John. *Opera and Politics: From Monteverdi to Henze*. New Haven: Yale University Press, 2004.
Budden, Julian. *The Operas of Verdi, Volume 1: From Oberto to Rigoletto*. London: Cassell, 1984.
Burwick, Frederick. *Playing to the Crowd: London Popular Theatre, 1780–1830*. Basingstoke: Palgrave Macmillan, 2011.
_____. *Romantic Drama: Acting and Reacting*. Cambridge: Cambridge University Press, 2011.
Burwick, Frederick, and Manushag N. Powell. *British Pirates in Print and Performance*. New York: Palgrave Macmillan, 2015.
Campbell, Mel. "Pirate Chic: Tracing the Aesthetics of Literary Piracy." *Pirates and Mutineers of the Nineteenth Century: Swashbucklers and Swindlers*. Grace Moore (ed.). Burlington: Ashgate, 2011, 11–39.
Coleridge, Samuel Taylor. *Biographia Literaria, Or, Biographical Sketches of My Literary Life and Opinions: Volume 2*. London: Rest Fenner, 1817.
Cronin, Charles P.D. "Stefano Pavesi's *Ser Marcantonio* and Donizetti's *Don Pasquale*." *Opera Quarterly* 11.2 (1995): 39–53.
Davis, Robert C. *Christian Slaves, Muslim Masters: White Slavery in the Mediterranean, the Barbary Coast, and Italy, 1500–1800*. London: Palgrave Macmillan, 2003.
Ebers, John. *Seven Years of the King's Theatre*. London: W.H. Ainsworth, 1828; rpt. New York: Benjamin Blom, 1969.
Galatopoulos, Stelios. *Bellini: Life, Times, Music: 1801–1835*. London: Sanctuary Publishing, 2002.
Ginsborg, P. "Romanticismo e Risorgimento: l'io, l'amore e la nazione." *Storia d'Italia*: Annali 22, *Il Risorgimento*. A.M. Banti and P. Ginsborg (eds.). Turin, IT: Einaudi, 2007, 5–67.
Grout, Donald Jay. *A Short History of Opera*. New York: Columbia University Press, 2003.
Hadlock, Heather. "'The firmness of a female hand' in *The Corsair* and *Il corsaro*." *Cambridge Opera Journal* 14.1 (2002): 47–57.
Idman, Niilo. *Charles Robert Maturin: His Life and Works*. London: Constable and Company, 1923.
Kimbell, David. "Il pirata." *The New Penguin Opera Guide*. Amanda Holden (ed.). New York: Penguin Putnam, 2001, 47–48.
Leydi, Roberto. "The Dissemination and Popularization of Opera." *Opera in Theory and Practice, Image and Myth*. L. Bianconi and G. Pestelli (eds.). Chicago: University of Chicago Press, 2003, 314–42.
Lutz, Deborah. "The Pirate Poet in the Nineteenth Century: Trollope and Byron." *Pirates and Mutineers of the Nineteenth Century: Swashbucklers and Swindlers*. Grace Moore (ed.). Burlington: Ashgate, 2011, 23–40.
Lyttelton, Adrian. "The Hero and the People." *The Risorgimento Revisited: Nationalism and Culture in Nineteenth-Century Italy*. Silvana Patriarca and Lucy Riall (eds.). London: Palgrave Macmillan, 2012, 37–55.
Marcus, Steven. *The Other Victorians: A Study of Sexuality and Pornography in Mid-Nineteenth-Century England*. Piscataway, NJ: Transaction, 2008.
Moore, Grace. "Introduction." *Pirates and Mutineers of the Nineteenth Century: Swashbucklers and Swindlers*. Grace Moore (ed.). Burlington: Ashgate, 2011, 1–10.
Osborne, Richard. "L'Italiana in Algeri." *The Grove Book of Operas*. Stanley Sadie and Laura Macy (eds.). Oxford: Oxford University Press, 2006, 310–12.

Pacini, Giovanni, and Jacopo Ferretti. *Il corsaro: melodramma romantico, posto in musica pel Nobile Teatro di Apollo in Roma.* https://archive.org/details/ilcorsaromelodra00paci. Accessed on 09/11/2017.
Parkinson, C. Northcote. *Britannia Rules: The Classic Age of Naval History 1793–1815.* London: Weidenfeld and Nicolson, 1977.
Riall, Lucy. *Garibaldi: Invention of a Hero.* New Haven: Yale University Press, 2007.
Roberts, William. "The Bride of Abydos, a Turkish Tale. By Lord Byron. London. 1813." *British Review* 5 (1814), 391–400.
Rossini, Gioachino, and Angelo Anelli. *L'Italiana in Algeri: Dramma Buffo per Musica.* Florence: Presso Giuseppe Fantosini Eviglio, 1814.
Rosselli, John. *The Life of Bellini.* Cambridge: Cambridge University Press, 1996.
_____. "Music and Nationalism in Italy." *Musical Constructions of Nationalism.* Harry White and Michael Murphy (eds.). Cork: Cork University Press, 2001, 181–96.
Sorba, C. "Il 1848 e la melodrammatizzazione della politica." *Storia d'Italia*: Annali, 22, *Il Risorgimento.* A.M. Banti and P. Ginsborg (eds.). Turin, IT: Einaudi, 2007, 481–508.
Turley, Hans. *Rum, Sodomy, and the Lash: Piracy, Sexuality, and Masculine Identity.* New York: New York University Press, 1999.
Weinstock, Herbert. *Bellini: His Life and His Operas.* New York: Knopf, 1971.
Williams, Michael. *Some London Theatres Past and Present.* London: Sampson, Low, Marston, Searle & Rivington, 1883.
Willier, Stephen A. "Madness, the Gothic, and Bellini's *Il pirata*." *Opera Quarterly* 6 (1989): 7–23.
Zamoyski, A. *Holy Madness: Romantic, Patriots and Revolutionaries 1776–1871.* London: Weidenfeld & Nicolson, 1999.

The Humorous, Sarcastic Case of the Pastafarian Pirates

Jeff Parish

What would a pirate do? The answer depends on what kind of pirate you ask. A historical pirate might respond with a rampage of violence and plunder, alternately hunter and hunted on the high seas. The more modern ideal, however, would respond with something much different. Despite (or perhaps because of) the dangers of a buccaneer lifestyle, the pirate has become hopelessly romanticized in the collective consciousness. From *Treasure Island* (1950) to *Treasure Planet* (2002) and the *Pirates of the Caribbean* franchise (2003–17) to *The Pirates Who Don't Do Anything* (2008), these maritime marauders have become the hero of virtually every tale they inhabit. Their outlaw status has become a symbol of freedom—freedom to live how they want, take what they want, and exact whatever measure of justice or revenge they want without any discernible, lasting consequences. Pirates have become loved and lovable; this corsair affection has escaped the screen and printed page to entangle itself in popular culture. The modern pirate would be a hero. And in the case of the Church of the Flying Spaghetti Monster, what the pirate would do is become a religious (if satirical) icon. This essay examines Henderson's *Gospel of the Flying Spaghetti Monster*, the crowdsourced *Loose Canon*, and the official FSM website (www.vengaza.org) and explores how this parody religion makes ready use of pirates' pop culture status as a humorous wedge into public discourse over intelligent design versus evolution and the ways in which this use of the pirate figure informs the unique Pastafarian sense of satire.

The Church of the Flying Spaghetti Monster, also known as Pastafarianism, began as a "response to the debate over teaching evolution in schools, an issue that has persisted since the 1925 Scopes Trial" (Laycock 24). The religion traces its origins to a 2005 open letter to the Kansas State Board of Education that Bobby Henderson published on his site as the board debated including intelligent design alongside evolution in science classes. Multiple viewpoints are important, Henderson argued, and if intelligent design "is not based on faith, but instead another scientific theory, as is claimed, then you must also allow our theory to be taught, as it is also based on science, not on faith ("Church of the Flying Spaghetti Monster"). Henderson maintains that observable evidence ("science") is unreliable because the Flying Spaghetti Monster (FSM) made the world to appear older than it really is as a means of testing (or maybe simply messing with) humanity. Students need to be taught the truth, he said, and should be done so properly, as it "is disrespectful to teach our beliefs without wearing His chosen outfit, which of course is full pirate regalia" ("Church of the Flying Spaghetti Monster"). Henderson's letter captured the attention of netizens almost immediately. At first, Pastafarianism drew "support primarily from atheists and college students," but has since spread throughout the world to become "perhaps the most successful parody religion of all time" (Laycock 24). Several countries have officially acknowledged the Church of the Flying Spaghetti Monster as an official religion, and New Zealand became the first to recognize Pastafarian weddings in 2016.

Henderson and his fellow FSM followers acknowledge the satirical nature of their faith but say that should not disqualify it as a "real" religion. Unwavering believers form a minority of any religion, he says, so the only real "difference is that Pastafarians are more honest when they don't hold a literal view of their religion" ("Church of the Flying Spaghetti Monster"). The subject of their worship is equally farcical, living up to its designation as a monster and sharing "the transgressive qualities of other monsters, mixing familiar categories of human and nonhuman, internal and external, animate and inanimate, organic and inorganic" (Van Horn and Johnston). The FSM has more in common with Muppets or Fraggles than it does werewolves or zombies, relying "on humor to transgress ... boundaries" (Van Horn and Johnston). Renderings vary, but the most common image presents hovering, oblong mass of noodles wrapped around a pair of meatballs to the left and right, a pair of eyestalks rising from the top, and noodly appendages coming out of the sides and bottom. The overall effect is of something relatively harmless, if strange.

That very absurdity lies at the heart of the Pastafarian approach to a sensitive subject. Intelligent design remains a matter of faith as much as science for many Americans, which can lead to sharp debate on the matter. There is, however, more room for debate than may be apparent at first. Many creationists accept a sort of hybrid scenario whereby Someone set the universe in motion and let evolution take its course, indicating the dichotomy between intelligent design and evolution may not be quite as polarized privately as portrayed in the public arena. As with much discourse these days, however, sharp divides dominate media attention and the ensuing public debate. Because Henderson's FSM is so patently silly, the "Monster (and the mythological and soteriological narrative it inhabits) may be a much more effective tactic than tackling advocates of intelligent design head on, calling attention to the absurdity of certain creation-oriented 'theories' through a mimesis of absurdity" (Van Horn and Johnston). Pastafarianism frames the debate through satire and uses humor to sidestep a potential horn-locking grudge match that would run counterproductive to the discussion. The religion further helps to deflect criticism and encourage participation by incorporating an image currently beloved in popular culture—the pirate.

Historical figures such as Blackbeard and Captain Kidd still have power to capture the imagination centuries after their deaths, but perhaps even more well-known are "other pirates, such as Long John Silver and Captain Hook, although those pirates never lived at all. So there have been two kinds of pirates—real and imaginary" (Rennie v). These seagoing marauders have long found themselves embedded in our popular culture; American writers in "the early-to-mid nineteenth century felt in need of a respectable historical dimension, and of legends of a supernatural kind, and pirates served such needs" (157). Their modern popularity can be seen as an extension of America's love for frontier outlaws, which "is colored by a nostalgia for a kind of fully licensed machismo already becoming outdated by the turn of the eighteenth century and yet one that still, at the beginning of the twenty-first century, remains active in fantasies of masculinity" (Mackie 24–25). Nostalgia derives not so much from reality as it does from a wishful recollection that, even "as it laments an irrevocable past ... evokes and so revives the past, or a desirable version of that past, in the here and now" (24). Nautical marauders have existed for almost the whole of human history, but today's pirate is more the subject of myth than reality. By the advent of film, the "pirate ingredients were well-established" in American culture; they "were sea-faring outlaws and gangsters ... but were obviously historical, probably European, and no longer American national heroes like the frontiersman" (Rennie 220). Indeed, those "ingredients" have become so ingrained that "there are formal ways of being a pirate that are profoundly influential to the American audience. Such formal patterns offer audiences 'equipment for living.' They instruct us on how to live in the midst of conflict" (Hartelius 174). Pirates found onscreen, such as those in *Pirates of the Caribbean* saga, are based less on history than an image that "Disney and others hope the public to take as historical fact" (Petersen 63).

A similar mechanism is found in graphic novels, where rather than constantly reboot franchises, artists simply rewrite the past to reflect a new, present reality—known as "retroactive continuity," or simply a "retcon." One of the most famous examples arises with Batman, who frequently made use of firearms against his foes from his inaugural appearance in *Detective Comics #27* (1939) through *Batman #4* (1940), where he explicitly states that he does not use any kind of gun. Since then, the "no gun" rule has been a defining characteristic for the Dark Knight. Another example can be found in Spider-Woman, who first appeared in *Marvel Spotlight #32* (1977) as a spider that the High Evolutionary had mutated into appearing human. When she appeared in her own series the following year, writers retconned her first origin story into a lie she had been told and made her a superhuman rather than a spider that looked human. In some cases, the same detail may get several adjustments. The parents of the super-powered twins Quicksilver and the Scarlet Witch were said to be Miss America and The Whizzer in *Giant-Size Avengers #1* (1974), but writers retconned their father to Magneto in *The Vision and Scarlet Witch #1* (1982)—which was itself further retconned in *Uncanny Avengers #4* (2015) to make them experiments created by the High Evolutionary. This sort of revision occurs outside the pages of comic books as well. Pirates offer a prime example: Americans love the image of a lovable scallywag and honest thief, and the pirate changes to fit this desired image in the American consciousness. The contradicting history of murder, rape, and pillage gets ignored—or at least conveniently forgotten for the present.

While pirates have arguably never gone completely out of style—Captain Hook and Long John Silver have maintained devoted literary and cinematic fans since their inceptions—they have seen a resurgence in popularity since 2003. The modern fascination with pirates largely owes its success to the *Pirates of the Caribbean* franchise and the charismatic scofflaw Captain Jack Sparrow, played by Johnny Depp. The public imagination has found something to latch on to with these make-believe pirates. At a time "of declining governmental power and growing corporate influence, the *POC* films formally reflect how Americans are managing everyday life" (Hartelius 155). Cinematic pirates live in a world of gray. They thrive on their own terms, and if some of their activities are technically illegal, they remain acceptable since almost no one gets hurt, and those who do usually have it coming. Piracy as a trope "has always been highly mobile, a marker of the very instabilities of those lines that define social and ethical standards" (Mackie 29). From Jack Sparrow to Jack Harkness, modern renditions of the pirate retcon away the violent history of their historical counterparts and focus instead on their freedom as individuals outside the system; "the dream for this particular brand of liberty has its origins in notions of absolute individual sovereignty that arose even as absolutism came under assault in the political sphere. A law unto himself, the outlaw asserts the ultimate aristocratic privilege of sovereign will" (Mackie 25). The pirate's independence becomes an act of acceptable transgression, offering a figure that meshes well into the Church of the Flying Spaghetti Monster, itself a religion that attempts to satirize and subvert contemporary ideology.

Pastafarian doctrine tends to be rather loose, but written texts can be found in three primary sources: Henderson's *The Gospel of the Flying Spaghetti Monster* (2005), an electronic tome compiled by the online FSM community entitled *The Loose Canon: A Really Important Collection of Words* (2010), and Henderson's website at www.venganza.org ("venganza" being Spanish for "revenge"). The religion started as a reaction against what Henderson perceived as a Christian intrusion into scholastic and scientific matters. Small wonder, then, that although Pastafarian adherents can now be found worldwide, Western culture and Christianity—particularly American—remain the primary target for the Church of the Flying Spaghetti Monster's satire. As with many religions, FSMism begins with an account of human origins. According to the *Loose Canon*, "midgets" (who were bald) and later "midgits" (with hair) were created first as the Flying Spaghetti Monster's chosen people and a source of source entertainment. Eventually, "Big People" were introduced as a means to keep the smaller people in check; their "first words in praise of their noodly master were: 'Shiver me timbers. O'im off ta' collect some pieces of eight.' And they were given the gift of politically incorrect putdown. And their maritime, rumdrinking, and bird-handling skills were unsurpassed" (11). These "Big People" were not created in the image of their god, Henderson writes, but in "His ideal image: that of the Pirate" (Henderson 41). The use of changing "chosen people" marks strong parallels between Pastafarianism and Christian doctrine, where the Israelites were first the chosen ones during the Old Testament, a mantle Christians later claim via the New Testament. Not only are the followers of the Flying Spaghetti Monster his elect, but Henderson and his followers paint a picture where the chosen come from their particular self-reflecting view of the ideal Pastafarian. FSMism starts with a pirate and works its way backward into a supposition that the figure must be god's favorite. In doing so, the religion skewers a tendency for many American Christians to see Jesus as a white, Western figure despite his Middle Eastern origins.

As the Pastafarian account continues, pirates eventually, "tired of all the wowsers, did ... depart the lands of Noodle Earth to seek adventure and treasure," and the FSM decided to follow their adventures because "these guys have fun" (*The Loose Canon* 13). Thus began the "Golden Age of the Pirate lifestyle. Millions, possibly hundreds, of Pirate ships roamed the world's oceans and maybe lakes, searching for a good time, spreading joy and maybe VD to whomever they came into contact with" (Henderson 53). Pirates declined into arrogance over time, smug in the knowledge that they were their god's chosen people. In their heyday, the FSM's buccaneers (used interchangeably with "pirate" for Pastafarian purposes) would bury treasure so others would not succumb to greed, but they later began instead to keep "the gold and jewels for themselves. They no longer sailed around distributing candy to young children. They forced their religion on others, demanding that nonbelievers follow the FSM" (*The Loose Canon* 42). This behavior runs contrary to one of the central tenants of FSMism, as espoused by Fearsome Pirate Pete: Pastafarians "must be understandin' and tolerant of others beliefs and practices, and sometimes we just need t' go with the flow" (32). Henderson remains true to the pop culture origin to his piratical priests as he toys with the "good pirate" trope in his mythology. As characters created directly by a god as his chosen people, the pirates get pushed to an extreme to where they become holy figures beyond the likes of ordinary humans. They fall from grace, but find a balance in their modern Pastafarian incarnation—a trajectory frequently found in religions stories. By foregrounding the pirates' arrogance and calls for tolerance, Pastafarians (many of them atheist) subtly put themselves forward as better followers of the "judge not" ideal than many professing Christians. The fact that a pirate epitomizes the peaceful, accepting figure only adds to the satire.

Not all of the Flying Spaghetti Monster's parallels with Christianity are quite so subtle. Pirates play a key role in many "Old Pastament" stories that bear a striking resemblance to accounts found in the biblical Old Testament. One of the first is the tale of Steve the Pirate, who survives the FSM's plan to destroy the world with pasta sauce because it "was no longer a tasty place. And the Flying Spaghetti Monster said, I will destroy all this untastiness that I have created from the face of the earth; man and beast, beer and brothel, and all the creeping things that are less than savory" (*The Loose Canon* 15). However, Steve finds "grace with the Flying Spaghetti Monster," who gives him instructions to build a pirate ship of bay leaves "several hundred cubits in length and pretty wide in cubits as well and high enough that thou doest not feel hemmed in. Useth thou thy best judgement" (15). Steve, instructed to collect two of every kind of spice, stays aboard the vessel for "41 days and 40 nights (allowing for cooling)" (16). Once the saucy deluge abates, he sends out a parrot "to see if the sauce had receded, but the parrot found no place to roost and returned to the ship. So Steve waited and after seven days he sent forth the parrot again to see if the sauce had abated and the parrot returned not to him again but instead found refuge beside a large beer volcano" (16). As a derivative of the biblical Flood story, the tale of Steve repeats a tendency in Pastafarianism to borrow ideas from the intelligent design camp and recast them in absurd territory. Henderson has taken this approach ever since his letter to the Kansas State Board of Education, but the accounts in *The Loose Canon* are not Henderson's work. The initial satire continues through thousands of proselytes, pirates and all.

Another important Pastafarian religious figure is Abe, a human drinking buddy to the Flying Spaghetti Monster. Intoxication leads to shenanigans that include Abe circumcising himself, so the FSM offers the human and his descendants the sea as their "promised land." The sea would be theirs, and "'you get the whole thing, but only on the condition that you and your descendants are pirates. I like pirates. Cool?' ... And so the Pastament was made" (*The Loose Canon* 23). Generations later, Pirate Mosey finally leads Abe's descendants to the sea after years of wandering because they were often "back seat wanderers" who suggested turns instead of going in a straight line as Mosey suggested (23). Mosey himself could not go into the promised land because the FSM "provided them with a keg and told Mosey to tap it. But Mosey, still frustrated, hacked it with his cutlass. Beer splattered everywhere, getting the pirates sticky and spilling all out onto the ground" (23). The account parallels the story of Abraham and his descendants, to whom the Bible says God promised the land of Canaan. According to Exodus, the Israelites were led to their promised land by Moses, but they were forced to wander through the desert as a punishment for a lack of faith. Moses, like Mosey, could not enter Canaan because God instructed him to speak to a rock to provide water, but Moses struck it instead. FSMism frequently pokes fun at the idea of a vengeful god, instead preferring to focus on humanity's own foibles as the cause of our misfortunes. Even the Mosey account becomes more lighthearted—the Flying Spaghetti Monster becomes miffed more because of a mess than for how the liquid was retrieved.

The tale of David and Goliath gets its Pastafarian version as the tale of Dave and Kyodai. Dave is "the son of an Englishman named Jesse," one of Captain "Dead Sole" Paulson's crew (*The Loose Canon* 39). Kyodai, a ninja from Osaka, stands "six cubits and a span tall, as he was unholy and was never touched by His noodly appendage" (39). Their one-on-one battle takes place (where else?) on the island of Tortuga. Dave says he can defeat the giant ninja because he had saved spaghetti in the kitchen from "the rat and the seagull, and this ninja will be like one of them, because he has killed the people of the FSM" (40). Dave defeats Kyodai by using spaghetti as a sling and hurling a "meatball at the ninja, shooting it right down his windpipe. Choking, the ninja fell to the ground" (40). Ninjas are frequently presented as the natural enemy of pirates. Not only are the famed assassins as absurd a figure in this context as pirates but pitting the two against each other reflects an "us versus them" mentality frequently found in the Western world—East vs. West, Christianity vs. Islam, Democracy vs. Terrorism.

This sort of duality is found in most religions, where each deity has its equal and opposite. For the Flying Spaghetti Monster, one devil comes in the form of the Anti-Past, whose "balls are ersatz soy-meat and don't even ask what his appendages are made of" (*The Loose Canon* 26). Another anti–FSM is the "Dark Lord Darwin," who uses the "four dark powers of Science"—observation, reason, experimentation, and evidence (42). This Dark Lord designed the theory of evolution to "destroy the faith of the pirates and prevent them from gaining new converts" (43). In one story, Darwin encourages ninjas to destroy the pirates and Pastafarianism, which proves to be easily accomplished because not only had the Flying Spaghetti Monster forsaken them, but pirates "have never been the most skillful fighters. They are peaceful men and had mostly held off attempted purges by the ninjas in the past by divine intervention from the FSM" (43). The slaughter apparently continues well into modern times. Hari Krishnas, "who are descended from Ninjas," nearly wiped out the pirates; the survivors "retreated to hidden coves where they could keep a lookout for the bloodthirsty Krishna bastards" and "quite pissed off for several centuries, and the textbooks reveal every detail of the looting and pillaging but are suspiciously quiet about the fact that Pirates were well known for passing out candy to children" (Henderson 55).

Historical accounts that portray them as violent seafaring thieves arose from jealousy; since pirates were "His Chosen People, the ones who listened and followed His divine plan.... The commonly propagated myth that Pirates were thieves can be traced, unsurprisingly, to the Christian theologians of the Middle Ages" (53). According to the *Gospel*, history abounds with other heretics, "non–Pastafarians who have dared to rock the boat, challenging the limits of religious and scientific dogma alike" (80). Notables include Aristotle, Leonardo Da Vinci, Charles Darwin, John Scopes, and Dolly the Sheep. All such figures have drawn criticism from religious experts and authorities at one point or another in history as espousing ideas contrary to Church dogma and upsetting the understood balance of the universe—or, in the case of Dolly, representing humans playing God and creating something contrary to nature. Henderson simply takes the same idea and applies them to his own satirical religion.

Salvation may be at hand, however. *The Loose Canon* predicts a coming Pastafarian messiah who will "raise the colors for all ships and will assemble the dispersed outlaws of the seven seas. He will be the Jolly Roger for all pirates and will unite all Pastafarians as one crew. We will face the coming doom together. Together we will man the cannons of our faith. Together we will hoist our sails to cruise to calmer waters" (108). As with most religious promises of a better tomorrow, the Church of the Flying Spaghetti Monster offers no specific date or era in which these pirate-laden metaphors will come to pass. The faithful must simply maintain their faith until it happens.

In much the same way that Pastafarianism parallels stories from other religions in a sort of funhouse-mirror fashion, the Church of the Flying Spaghetti Monster's religious trappings mirror those of other faiths, particularly the "big three"—Christianity, Judaism, and Islam. FSMism is similarly monotheistic with religious celebrations designed to encourage a connection with its deity and reflection on one's own faith and beliefs. As a satiric religion, Pastafarianism eschews creating its own celebrations in favor of cobbling together a system that arises from imitation and parody of the other faiths' observances. Pastafarians have their own communion "consisting of a large portion of spaghetti and meatballs" (Henderson 38). Holidays include Pastaover, where Pastafarians dress as pirates and eat spaghetti or other pasta to celebrate "the time when the Flying Spaghetti Monster first began touching people with His Noodly Appendage" (123); Ramendan, when adherents eat nothing but Ramen noodles for a few days and learn "to be happy about what they've accomplished, and if they haven't accomplished anything yet, to at least be happy that they are Pastafarians" (124); Halloween, a time when many of the faithful dress as pirates to distribute candy, just as "the original Pirates were well known for passing out candy to children, but that practice grew less common as they became persecuted" (124); and International Talk Like a Pirate Day, which happens September 19. The holiest Pastafarian holiday is Friday, a day "to take it easy and, if possible, try to find some sun. Fridays are dedicated to the ideals beholden in the Beer Volcano and the Stripper Factory [the Pastafarian heaven], and one can do no more to honor His Noodly Appendage than to observe Fridays with the utmost of piety" (124–25). There's also "Holiday," which "encompasses pretty much all of the big commercial holidays celebrated by the other religions. Holiday stretches over most of December and January" (125). Pastafarianism shows its colors as a parody through these holidays as an act of "appropriating traditions from established religions and rendering them absurd" (Laycock 24). The pirate theme dominates each holiday, keeping the buccaneers front and center throughout religious observances.

The faithful celebrate other events and holidays in similarly unique ways. In December 2006, Eric Martel submitted an account of the "Christmas Pirate" making an appearance at an office party. The pirate—decked out with hook, tricorn hat, eyepatch, and jolly roger bandanna—asked people if they wanted a new present or would "rather steal another one's gift that was already given; if the person chose the latter, he would then use his mighty weapon to threat the other poor chap to give away his gift (but was offered a new gift from his lot as a replacement)" ("Church of the Flying Spaghetti Monster"). The same year, the Hunger Artists Theater Company in Fullerton, California, presented the Flying Spaghetti Monster Holiday Pageant. Another chose to celebrate the holidays with a three-minute animated video pitting Santa against the Flying Spaghetti Monster. Unable to defeat one another in single combat, the foes summon help—Santa calls in elves (in the form of Link from *The Legend of Zelda*) while the FSM produces piratical fishlike skeletons with arms and legs. The video fades to black as the two forces meet, but no follow-up has been made. As noted on the FSM website, Pastafarian "Jo Selwood" demonstrated on Parliament Square in London in 2006, protesting the Serious Organised Crime and Police Act (SOCPA), which he said contained a provision curbing the rights of people to protest near Parliament. Dressed as a pirate, Selwood held a sign encouraging people to "stop global warming—become a pirate." He also used his platform "to spread the truth of His Noodliness to the people in and around Parliament Square," which resulted in "smiles, but there were enough 'yars' from people to make me think there are a lot of closet pirates in London" ("Church of the Flying Spaghetti Monster"). And in May 2007, Missouri State University Chapter of the Church of the FSM staged a free outdoor concert called Noodlefest to raise money for breast cancer research. In 2008, "GmanTerry" submitted a picture to the FSM website of himself wearing pirate regalia for Halloween, passing out candy under a red FSM flag. A post two years later show people dressed as pirates or even as His Noodliness Himself under the heading "Halloween Evangelism."

The website has an entire category of posts related to "pirates." The seven-page section contains announcements about events and media reports about Pastafarians in religious regalia. The first announces International Talk Like a Pirate Day for 2006. Because of FSM's belief in a correlation between the number of pirates in the world and global warming, Henderson says he expects "to see a considerable drop in temperature worldwide ... due to the widespread pirate activity taking place" ("Church of the Flying Spaghetti Monster"). In all, #Pirate posts to the site show the most activity in 2006 and 2007, with nearly three pages of material found on the site. The next two years consume less than a page, as do 2010 and 2011. Posts in this category apparently stop in mid-2016, with the final page containing sporadic postings from 2012 forward, although Talk Like a Pirate Day gets a mention every year. More recent entries fall under the #General category.

As a modern religion, Pastafarianism seeks to reach the unenlightened through a variety of means. The church's official website offers visitors the opportunity to become ordained as a minister of the Church of the Flying Spaghetti Monster, and "we are not above devising certain fund-raising schemes to ensure that we can obtain as big and as glorious a Pirate Ship as possible. The sale of T-shirts helps. Also, coffee mugs and bumper stickers are effective" (Henderson 122). An online game entitled "Quest for Englightenment ... and Pasta" has the player sail the world as Italian pirate 'Al Dente' seeking to obtain the Holey Colander of St. Lindsay, touch the Golden Noodle of the prophet Bobby, and bask in the glory of the FSM. Along the way, players dig for gold and artifacts in ruins, locate treasure chests, and seek rumors at inns along the way. A meter counts how many days the player has been a pirate, while another counts down how much rum is in his or her possession—

if the counter hits zero, then "yer outta rum … yer dead." More rum can be obtained in inns or found floating in bottles in the ocean ("Quest for Englightenment"). In another game, the player acts as His Noodliness to "convert as many people into Pastafarians as you can before time runs out" by extending "your noodly appendage toward the scurrying people" while being careful "not to make contact with the darkly-clad school administrators" ("Church of the Flying Spaghetti Monster"). Converts take the appearance of pirates while the administrators repel the FSM. Although modern video games often strive for cinematic realism, the graphics and gameplay of both FSM games have been kept simple. A more immersive, "gritty" style would be out of character for the humorous Pastafarian style.

Echoing the sort of cries that periodically arise from Christians in America, Pastafarians often claim religious discrimination and persecution for their beliefs. *The Loose Canon* offers the tale of faithful Pastafarian Bach, who wanted to participate in Talk Like a Pirate Day and "decided to assemble regalia and wear it throughout this most holy day, regardless of the consequence" (121). The regalia brought about some persecution as Bach was told to remove the hat even though he argued that "'it be permitted fer 'ats t'be donned fer relugous [*sic*] reasonin'" (121). He removed the headgear, but replaced it later in the day. When told to remove it again, he replied that was something he "shan't be doin'. This be me Regalia, and I shan't be takin' it off. It be a divine decree that I should be wearin' it. Shouldst I need to be speakin wit' a man higher up 'an yerself to rectify this problem, I be glad to comply" (122). In order to wear his religious hat, Bach had to get a letter from a representative of the religion, so he turned to Henderson for documentation. The story has no conclusion, stating that Henderson had not yet supplied the letter.

Another account is found online of a high school student in North Carolina named Bryan Killian, who was "suspended for coming to school dressed as a pirate" per his identifying as a member of the Church of the Flying Spaghetti Monster. When the story broke in late March 2007, Henderson noted that the news was so popular that he faced "a lot of problems keeping the server running" ("Church of the Flying Spaghetti Monster"). A similar tale in *The Loose Canon* tells of Tristan the Martyr, a 13-year-old student assigned to write a letter about his religion to someone in the future. Tristan wrote his letter about the Church of the Flying Spaghetti Monster, but his teacher "thought it was dumb and that he was just screwing around and took ten points off" (*The Loose Canon* 123). Tristan's letter states that

> being pastafarian I belive [*sic*] in the Flying Spagetti Monster to be the one true and only god. Usually when I tell people that I am pastafarian they laugh at me and say "No seriously." This really offends me. I thought that everyone was religiously accepting in this country apparently I was wrong. Yes this is seriously what I totally & completely belive in to be true, Ramen [124].

The boy's father contacts the teacher and insists that FSMism is "legit," and the teacher regrades Tristan's paper. The text relates this as a cautionary tale and bemoans that "persecution and inequality is a fate worse than dancing the hempen jig. Maybe some day [sic] we will be accepted" (123). Religious apparel in particular has become a hot-button topic in many circles, including the right to wear crucifixes and burqas in public or in official identification photos. The Pastafarian satirization of these debates is not merely theoretical. Aside from these school-related stories, many people in various countries have fought for (and won) the right to wear Pastafarian religious gear in ID photos. Most wear colanders on their heads, although a few have decked themselves out in full pirate regalia, as well.

Henderson himself coopts the WWJD phenomenon, but for a Pastafarian, the question is not "What would the Flying Spaghetti Monster do?" but "What would a pirate do?" The list includes: drink grog, get a parrot, find a band of marauders, build or steal a ship, find a wench, and plunder. The real key, however, is to "accept the Pirate life is to accept the eternal Arrrgh!!! Without it, you're just another landlubber" (Henderson 69). An odd combination, given that pirates have about as much in common with pasta as they do ninjas. Such absurd juxtapositions form the core of the Church of the Flying Spaghetti Monster. The religion started as a satirical commentary on what many see as an anti-science argument for intelligent design in American classrooms. Pastafarianism has not lost sight of those roots, but it has grown into something akin to a societal movement found in several nations worldwide. The one feature that Pastafarianism has held onto the hardest is its own human ideal: the pirate. Henderson could have chosen almost anything that would have come across as absurd to serve his purposes equally well—lectors, milkmen, whirling dervishes, elevator operators. Instead, he picked an image that stands out as both incorrigible and beloved, outsider and hero. The Pastafarian pirate may not be a historical artifact, but it is a popular culture figure "allowed" to subvert cultural norms and almost guaranteed—in a day when Renaissance fairs and Victorian-themed events feature about as many swashbucklers and Jack Sparrows as they do knights and Dickensian characters—to garner support while doing so. These pirates are as much a work of satire as the religion they support, invading once-sacred celebrations and institutions and using humor in a broadside attack to expose cracks in its target. In the realm of the Flying Spaghetti Monster, this is what a pirate would do.

WORKS CITED

"Church of the Flying Spaghetti Monster." *Church of the Flying Spaghetti Monster*, www.venganza.org. Accessed on 08/15/2017.

Hartelius, E. Johanna. "Weathering the Storm: *Pirates of the Caribbean* and Transnational Corporatism." *Uncovering Hidden Rhetorics: Social Issues in Disguise*. Barry Brummett (ed.). Los Angeles: Sage Publications, 2008, 155–75.

Henderson, Bobby. *The Gospel of the Flying Spaghetti Monster.* New York: Villard, 2006.
Laycock, Joseph. "Laughing Matters: 'Parody Religions' and the Command to Compare." *Bulletin for the Study of Religion* 42.3 (Sept. 2013): 19–26. *EBSCOhost,* doi:10.1558/bsor.v42i3.19. Accessed on 05/23/2017.
The Loose Canon: A Really Important Collection of Words. 1st ed. www.loose-canon.info/Loose-Canon-1st-Ed.pdf. Accessed on 06/04/2017.
Mackie, Erin S. "Welcome the Outlaw: Pirates, Maroons, and Caribbean Countercultures." *Cultural Critique* 59.1 (2005): 24–62. *Project MUSE,* doi:10.1353/cul.2005.0008. Accessed on 05/21/2017.
Petersen, Anne. "'You Believe in Pirates, of Course...': Disney's Commodification and 'Closure' vs. Johnny Depp's Aesthetic Piracy of 'Pirates of the Caribbean.'" *Studies in Popular Culture* 29.2 (2007): 63–81. *JSTOR,* www.jstor.org/stable/23416141. Accessed on 06/23/2017.
"Quest for Enlightenment ... and Pasta." *Quest for Enlightenment and Pasta—The Game of Noodly Goodness.* www.fsmgame.com. Accessed on 08/12/2017.
Van Horn, Gavin, and Lucas Johnston. "Evolutionary Controversy and a Side of Pasta: The Flying Spaghetti Monster and the Subversive Function of Religious Parody." *Golem: Journal of Religion and Monsters* 2.1 (2007). lomibao.net/golem/article.php?id=36. Accessed on 06/14/2017.

"Gay and brisk"
Constructing a Pirate's Image for Children

WILLIAM NEWTON

The golden age of piracy was a period of sea-robber activity that occurred in the Caribbean Sea, Atlantic, and Indian Oceans, from the mid-sixteenth century until the first quarter of the seventeenth century. Piracy in this period was not a sustained activity, it took place in bursts promoted by economic downturns and by changes made to national navies during and after wars between European powers. The self-organized piracy of the latter part of the golden age caused significant disruption to commercial shipping. It has been estimated that as many as 4000 pirates sailed in the period 1715–1726 (Rediker 29–30). We know from the weight of pirate-related literature that people have for a long time been interested in the deeds, misdeeds, and exploits of pirates. However, that does not answer the question of why we, and especially children, in the twenty-first century are more enthralled by pirates than ever before. Many people in the western world could probably draw, or at least describe, a pirate's stereotypical attributes: the hat, the wooden leg, the parrot, the eyepatch, the tattoos, and the crude manners of speech. Few, however, could explain where these features stemmed from.

Several historians, most notably Marcus Rediker, have produced work on the subject of pirates' manners of dress and speech. Pirates in children's literature have provided a rich source of research for dozens of articles and chapters, with notable recent work having been done on this topic by Alexandra Phillips. This essay aims to be the first (albeit, brief) study of pirates in children's culture as a whole, taking into account a wide range of representations from, for example, literature, toys, and television. In its conclusion this essay will consider these representations and will propose how pirates as characters in children's culture could be interpreted for children in the twenty-first century, in the context of a museum exhibition.

Famous names and noteworthy physical characteristics have outlasted most concrete details about real-life historic pirates. This is due in part to these pirates' acute awareness of the importance of their image and reputation. Historic pirates created their own image: affecting a frightening and often grand appearance was one of the keys to successfully capturing prizes, for forging a sense of unity and for enjoying the liberties allowed by their way of life. Famous pirates' appearances were often remarkable and memorable, hence their perpetuation, through a few primary and more numerous secondary sources, into the popular imagination. A great example is the oft-quoted account of Captain Edward Teach (also known as "Blackbeard") from Captain Johnson's *A General History of the Pirates*, in which he was described as having a fiendishly creative appearance, designed to impress and intimidate both his crew and his victims (37–38). However, at another point in the text, when referring to pirates more generally, Captain Johnson notes that they appeared "gay and brisk, most of them with white shirts, watches and a deal of silk vests" (111). This image is different from the one typically found in children's literature, particularly in the twenty-first century, where pirates are most often portrayed as being roughly dressed and somewhat oafish, as it occurs in Sue Fliess' *How to Be a Pirate* (2014), and Val McDermid and Arthur Robins' *My Granny Is a Pirate* (2012). Conversely, pirates have also been portrayed in fiction as favoring fine clothing, like J.M. Barrie's creation, Captain Hook, whose physical appearance seems to have been influenced by Johnson's descriptions of Bartholomew Roberts (113) and, to a lesser extent, of Blackbeard. Indeed, both Roberts and Hook wore very fine clothing, Roberts' "rich crimson damask waistcoat and breeches" (Johnson 113) having much in common with Hook's "attire associated with Charles II" (Barrie 81); and Hook's eyes, which lit up horribly (Barrie 80), are evocative of Blackbeard's, which were "fierce and wild" (Johnson 38).

Captain Johnson and Alexander Exquemelin's *The Buccaneers of America* are the only robust primary sources for pirates and buccaneers, written by men who seem to have had first-hand experience of pirates and piracy, so inevitably they have had a huge influence on subsequent works of fiction. Robert Louis Stevenson is known to have extensively referred to Johnson when writing his classic-of-the-genre adventure novel *Treasure Island*, bidding for an atmosphere of authenticity. In the novel, Stevenson referenced several real pirates and even integrated one, Israel Hands, into Captain Flint's crew (Colvin 378), as well as he used the name of another real pirate, Ben Gunn, for a key character (Johnson 105).[1] It is also thought that Stevenson based Long John Silver in part on a description of a formidable member of Edward England's crew, found in Johnson's work, "a man with a terrible pair of whiskers and a wooden leg, being stuck round with pistols, like the Man in the Almanack with Darts, comes swearing and vapouring upon the Quarter-Deck" (53). Such a particular seems to be confirmed by the fact that, in Stevenson's novel, Silver claims to have sailed with England (66). The depiction of pirates in works like *Treasure Island* has been so influential that it has frequently displaced what little is actually known about how pirates really looked. The creation of certain fictional characters has meant, generally, that there have been few opportunities for, or advantages in, literary invention when it has come to writing pirates' physical appearances.

Not only the appearance of pirates has therefore contradicted the historical reality, but their behavior as well has been exaggerated since the earliest news reports, either to emphasize their violence, cruelty, or godlessness, or to underscore the romance of their way of life, personal bravery, or the great charisma possessed by some individuals. For children, fictional pirates can provide the exciting notion of a life of adventure and reward, but can also offer a safe way to feel frightened, in the same manner as traditional fairy tales. In literature, pirates were initially used as moral counterpoints to the protagonists, something that began to change with the ambiguous, charming, and seductive Long John Silver. Early pirate fiction was often very violent, although the trend toward the sanitation of the more unsavory aspects of a pirate's life increased throughout the twentieth century. This evolution is thought by Alexandra Phillips to have begun with Captain Hook, the antagonist of J.M. Barrie's *Peter Pan*, who was portrayed as being something of a buffoon, despite his fearsome reputation.

In the eighteenth and early nineteenth centuries, most pirate-themed publishing was targeted at an adult audience. Probably the earliest accounts of pirates to which children would have been exposed were word of mouth reporting on the street, and semi- (or entirely) fictional sung ballads. It is easy to understand how, through these informal methods of exchange, the appearance of the pirates could easily have been exaggerated. In the early nineteenth century, chapbooks and penny dreadfuls were printed in great numbers. These cheap, mass-produced thrillers and adventure stories sometimes featured tales about morally questionable characters, such as pirates and highwaymen. Although not strictly intended for children, it is known that chapbooks were very popular with young people who were drawn to the exciting, often humorous, and sometimes bloody content (Richardson). Many chapbooks recycled existing stories and folk tales. A good example of this can be found in a chapbook of 1814, published by M. Angus and Son of Newcastle-upon-Tyne, held in the Victoria and Albert Museum's National Art Library. The text of this work is lifted directly from Captain Johnson's account of Blackbeard from his *General History*.[2] However, many eighteenth- and early nineteenth-century physical depictions of pirates were "stiff, bland

and static. They offered little in the way of dramatic anecdote, compelling narrative, or romantic charisma" (Lublin 167) which is at odds with what readers were encouraged to imagine, and with the non-fiction of Johnson and Exquemelin.

The accepted image of a pirate is anything but "stiff, bland and static," and generally consists of several easily identifiable elements. The next part of this essay will take several of the most important of these in turn and look at their stories within children's culture. Parts of a seventeenth- or eighteenth-century pirate's appearance and mannerisms would have been common to many sailors since the overwhelming majority of pirates were seamen before they turned to piracy (Rediker 42–46), but this fact is often lost in children's culture. Clothing was considered an important prize among pirates, as men who had boarded a captured vessel would be entitled to a "shift of clothes" as part of their reward. Clothing was auctioned to the crew from a common chest by the ship's Quartermaster, and those who took clothing without permission could expect to be soundly punished, as it was clearly stated in the second article of Bartholomew Roberts' Code (Johnson 96). Many of our ideas about pirate fashion, their penchant for bandannas, earrings and rich sashes, were actually the invention of the American illustrator and author Howard Pyle (1853–1911) and his pupil N.C. Wyeth (1882–1945). Pyle based his image of pirates on drawings he had made of Spanish Romani men whilst he traveled in Europe. These men wore long sashes at their waists, gold earrings, and headscarves, all of which became key distinguishing marks for fictional pirates through Pyle's work. Pyle was prolific in his painting of pirates: he produced nearly sixty illustrations for his own stories and those of fellow adventure writers (Loechle 60). He gave some insight into the contemporary American youth's mind-set, and reasons for the then-popularity of pirate stories, when he said, "would not every boy ... rather be a pirate captain than a member of parliament?" (Pyle16).

Before Pyle, the notion of what a pirate actually looked like was not so established, although references to rich clothing are found in printed fiction, to allude to their ill-gotten riches. A personal insight into how pirates were imagined to look *by* children may be found in a unique story book, found in the archive of London's National Maritime Museum.[3] The volume, JOD/247/1, dating from 1879, contains three seafaring tales, written and illustrated in watercolors by a young boy. The third story (Ye Pirate) describes a violent encounter with a pirate ship. The pirate crew are depicted in a colorful and rich array of dress: some wear coats with gold tassels, piping, and stripes, some wear breeches with them. Many, including the captain (or Ye Pirate Chief) wear long caps, perhaps Monmouth caps to show that they are sailors, or Phrygian caps to signify their liberty. The words "liberty, equality and fraternity" are inscribed on their Jolly Roger, possibly supporting their Phrygian candidacy. Monmouth caps were commonly worn by sailors, from at least as early as the sixteenth century, until as late as the mid-nineteenth century (uniforms for ratings were not introduced in the Royal Navy until 1857). They would, therefore, have been worn by some real pirates, but this detail has not survived Pyle's working of the pirate image.

The typical types of headwear worn by fictional pirates were felt hats (either a cocked hat or tricorne), or a colorful headscarf. Cocked hats, or bicorns, would not have been worn by real pirates of the golden age since the style dates to the end of the eighteenth century. However, cocked hats have commonly been seen in many depictions of pirates, often as a means to display a large, white skull and crossbones motif. The cocked pirate hat seems to have a long history, possibly stemming from theatrical productions where it, combined with a skull and crossbones motif, would have been used to distinguish pirate characters on stage. This could have been an accident of the era, as cocked hats were worn on formal occasions in many navies until the First World War. Thus, they would have been more easily obtainable to theatrical costumers than a tricorne, and would have appeared recognizably "maritime" to many audience members. The Pirate King wore a large bicorn emblazoned with a Jolly Roger in the 1884 production of *The Children's Pirates of Penzance*, as evidenced by the numerous photographs, illustrations and playbills in the V&A's Theatre and Performance collection.[4] The use of this motif on a hat is an apocryphal detail, there was no enforced standard design for a pirate's symbols, and these were used exclusively on flags. In literature, an example of the association between pirates and cocked hats is provided by S.G. Hulme Beaman's *Tales of Toytown* (1928), in which wannabe pirate Captain Peter Brass gives the order "You go and collect the Scum of Toytown while I buy myself a cocked hat and a cutlass" (86). In the collection of the V&A Museum of Childhood, there are a number of varied objects dating from the 1920s through to the 1980s which represent pirates' hats as cocked hats, usually with skulls and crossbones.[5] Another well-known example of a pirate in a cocked hat is offered by the Lego Group's Captain Roger Redbeard, who first appeared in 1989.[6]

Scarves or lengths of cloth worn about the head would have been a cheap, practical method of keeping hair and sweat from sailors' eyes while on duty, and may have been worn historically. In pirate fiction, headscarves or bandannas are typically used to indicate rank, and are worn by all crewmembers except captains. This relationship can be clearly seen in the late twentieth-century examples of Lego and Playmobil, two manufacturers who are well known for their large pirate ship playsets. It is also seen in the works of Howard Pyle, N.C. Wyeth, *Peter Pan* and in most illustrated versions of *Treasure Island*, including a number of comic book versions of the story.[7] An exception to this can be seen in the designs for the main characters from

John Ryan's celebrated *Captain Pugwash*, a mid-century British book and television franchise about the adventures and mishaps of a cowardly yet greedy pirate, Captain Horatio Pugwash. In the stories, his nemesis, the villainous pirate Captain Cutthroat Jake, wears a red and black striped scarf on his head.

Body piercing amongst pirates is commonly explained as having been a means for a pirate to store precious metal on their persons, or for reasons related to sailing prowess, or folk magic and superstition (Remy). However, there is little evidence that pirates actually wore large, gold, hooped earrings, although this is very much the stereotype. Nonetheless, Howard Pyle's use of lavish jewelry in his work could have been rooted in fact: Captain Johnson's account of Bartholomew Roberts' last stand refers to a particularly fine jeweled cross that he wore around his neck.[8] Showing pirates wearing jewelry was a note of conspicuous wealth, which made an "easy referent to [successful] thievery" (Loechle 66). Pirates wearing earrings and jewelry have been depicted many times, albeit inconsistently. Cecco, the "handsome Italian" member of Captain Hook's crew, wore pieces of eight in his ears (Barrie 79). However, none of the pirates, good or bad, wore earrings in the *Captain Pugwash* books or television shows, until its 1998 relaunch introduced the new character Jonah, who wears a single large hoop in his right ear. In the numerous versions of *Treasure Island*, Long John Silver is drawn sometimes with and sometimes without earrings, the most conspicuous version being probably the striking work done by Mervyn Peake in a 1949 edition published by Eyre and Spottiswoode. With toys, late twentieth- and early twenty-first-century Playmobil sets often have pirates wearing earrings, as do several Lego pirate characters from the Pirates line after its relaunch in 2009. A plastic Pedigree pirate doll in the V&A Museum of Childhood, dating from 1954–55, wears a plastic ring on either ear.

Among the accessories usually associated with the figure of the pirate the talking, cursing parrot is one of the most recurrent. It descends from Long John Silver's bird, Captain Flint, whose screams of "pieces of eight!" punctuate his scenes in the novel. There is no reason to suppose historical pirates would not have picked up exotic pets on their travels, but Captain Flint may have been inspired by Robinson Crusoe's talking parrot, Poll, who was for many years his only speaking companion during his exile. Mainly, these birds are used in fiction as another symbol of a character's status as a pirate, and to denote the exoticism of their lifestyles. Parrots in children's fiction are often used to denote a pirate's status as a captain, yet another symbol which has been inherited from *Treasure Island*. This can be seen in books such as *Pearl Fairweather Pirate Captain* (Jayneen Sanders and Lesley Danson), *Pirates Love Underpants* (Claire Freedman and Ben Cort), *My Granny Is a Pirate* (Val McDermid and Arthur Robins), and *How to Be a Pirate* (Sue Fliess and Nikki Dyson).

Working aboard a sailing ship would have been very dangerous, so it would not have been uncommon for sailors to suffer crippling injuries or the loss of limbs. A few historic pirates are known to have been amputees,[9] or to have in some way have been disabled,[10] and pirate codes often made provision for crewmembers who were injured in the course of performing their duties.[11] The loss of a body part is a common cliché in literary narratives on pirates as well, starting with Long John Silver's one-leggedness and Captain Hook's one-handedness (a detail which was directly inspired by Silver). This element is found across pirate-themed stories and objects, usually disconnected from the violent and gory means by which the loss might have happened, utilized as an identifying means to show that a character is a pirate. Its use seems to be more prevalent on pirate captains, perhaps to indicate prestige to show they are the most fearsome. The eyepatch is an even more common distinguishing feature than prosthetic limbs. Within the V&A Museum of Childhood, its use is fairly synonymous with pirate characters; examples of eyepatches are found in fancy dress items from the 1920s to the present day,[12] in fancy goods like coin banks,[13] toys like *Fighting Furies* action figures and accessories dating from the mid-1970s[14] and cereal packets, such as a Kellogg's *Puffa Puffa Rice* box from the early 1970s.[15]

Marcus Rediker has successfully argued that real pirates had a distinctive "dialect," characterized by colorful oaths and excessive swearing (Rediker 97–98). Any doubts about the veracity of his claim may be eased somewhat by the Royal Navy's current usage of centuries-old terminology and lively slang for everyday nautical items, shipmates, and situations. In nineteenth-century fiction, pirates often used rough language, usually written in a semi-phonetic manner, to signify their status as members of the lower class. Conversely, the villainous, aristocratic, and elegant Captain James Hook, who first appeared in 1904, was an eloquent Eton-educated fop. The "elegance of his diction, even when he was swearing" (Barrie 81) is traditionally pirate-esque, according to Rediker's research, but his upper-class origin is not. The idea of a gentleman pirate, like Hook, is an old one, and one that gained increased traction in the twentieth century. However, the only confirmed historical example was Stede Bonnet (1688–1718), a Barbadian landowner and former army officer who turned to piracy in 1717. For another case in the question of speech, the marked differences in speech between the more finely dressed Captain Pugwash and his enemy, Cutthroat Jake, confirms one as the hero and the other as the villain.

Undoubtedly the main twentieth-century source for a pirate's manner of speaking was Robert Newton's (1905–1956) portrayal of Long John Silver in Walt Disney's 1950 production of *Treasure Island*. Newton used a composite accent drawn from his native West Country, where several historical pirates are thought to have been born.[16] This is also where, in Bristol, Silver is first encountered in the novel. The now-generic growling "pirate accent" evolved from Newton's interpretation, much as the general format and content of many subsequent pirate stories originated with Stevenson's original novel. Today, and for the past few decades, the "pirate accent" has become an accepted fact which continues to perpetuate. For example, the pre-school television program *Swashbuckle* promotes "talking like a pirate" as entertaining, musical, and educational.[17] Similarly, Painty the Pirate, Patchy the Pirate and the Flying Dutchman, characters in the animated television show *SpongeBob Squarepants*, all speak (or sing) with strong "pirate accents." Captain Hector Barbossa, a major character in Disney's *Pirates of the Caribbean* film franchise (2003–17), as both an antagonist and a protagonist, speaks in a "traditionally" pirate-like manner. The writers of the adventure video game series *The Secret of Monkey Island* (1990) provided a humorous update to pirates' use of language during the dueling sequences, where enemies must be defeated through superior use of insults and retorts. The "pirate accent" has made pirates participatory, for both adults and children; a growl of "argh, me hearties" can be instantly identified as an attempt to sound like a pirate. Indeed, 19th September has now been recognized as International Talk Like a Pirate Day, an annual occasion upon which, according to its website, observers may "let the world see the buccaneer inside" (Baur). The accent (and the accouterments) of a pirate also marks them out as being distinctly "other," as fantasy figures like witches and vampires.

We could now consider how the image of the fictional pirate might be interpreted for children in the context of a museum exhibition. In the twenty-first century, young children (say, aged under eight years old) are the primary audience for pirate stories, toys, and other products, so it would make good sense for an exhibition to be similarly targeted at this age group, with accompanying family members as a secondary audience. The aim of the project must be to convey the importance of imagination, and to promote aspiration for children to be who they want to be. As a key message, the exhibition would need to emphasize the importance of personal image and creativity for conveying meaning, as well as recognizing that the image of the pirate has been standardized, is rooted now only in part in historical fact, and is therefore so distant from the reality of history that the cheeky, often incompetent, and mostly harmless, possibly supernatural, adventurer represented in popular culture could now be the main accepted truth. Lastly, a pirate exhibition would need to promote the importance of storytelling as an influence on, and a key element within, pirate fiction. The effective realization of such a project for young children would present a challenge, particularly when trying to maintain an institution's intellectual rigor, and whilst attempting to keep adults engaged. A good approach could be to introduce a child visitor to the various elements of a fictional pirate lifestyle, perhaps in the form of an immersive experience to find buried treasure, along the lines of a classic pirate adventure in the mold of *Treasure Island*. For very young children, key messages communicating simple, easily understood concepts would be helpful, for example how pretending to be villainous can be fun, what a map is, and what a treasure is. Then the exhibition should provide many opportunities to enable families to learn together and to interact constructively with one another, which could be achieved in the show through providing simple challenges and choices at certain points in the exhibition.

The exhibition would commence in a coastal inn. In this space we would create the start of an experiential adventure, and offer a feeling of discovery to begin the visitor's journey. The "inn" should be a slightly unsettling space, akin in its appearance and its sights and sounds to the Admiral Benbow in *Treasure Island*, with the aim that it should increase the visitor's alertness and curiosity. This location would be utilized to convey the importance of storytelling within pirate fiction. A mixture of interactivity, an immersive environment, and concise displays of objects would enable the topic to be unlocked, and would introduce its history and origins. Crucially, there would need to be some form of discovery for visitors to make, receiving a map to guide the rest of their visit toward the ultimate goal of finding treasure. This could be done through the telling of a story within the space, or by finding clues in each display to find the map, which would lead them through the subsequent sections of the exhibition to their eventual prize.

The visitor would then move on to a sort of pirate "high street," or a single "department store," where the archetypal trappings of piracy could be "purchased." Real pirates, of course, would not have bought their peg legs "off the peg," but environment of a shop is a useful method to bring a variety of items together. Most museum budgets (at least in the United Kingdom) would not stretch to providing fancy dress items for every young visitors to try-on, although the practice of dressing-up, establishing a ferocious reputation, and mimicking "pirate speech" would be of utmost importance for allowing children to understand the importance of pirates' creation of their own image. The retail-themed environment would work well for themed displays, such as of pirate hats and weapons, whilst playfully introducing the notion of a carefully constructed image. Digital interactives could be usefully employed here to allow visitors to, for example, see themselves on-screen with projected pirate features, or to use voice-changing software, combined with an amusing glossary of terms, to give visitors a distinctive pirate growl, and therefore to learn how to communicate like a pirate. They could also answer the conundrum of how to represent a shopping trip when you are not able to buy anything: through provision of a digital shopping basket for pirate goods.

The journey would next lead the visitor to a representation of a quayside, where they would learn about crews and how they were composed, pirate codes, and the value of working as a team toward a common goal. In this section we would discuss the characteristics of specific real and fictional pirates, such as Jack Sparrow, Anne Bonny, Captain Pugwash, and Elaine Marley. Working with recognizable characters would be useful for visitor engagement, particularly for adults, to eke out feelings of nostalgia and recognition, and therefore to promote intergenerational conversations. This would allow the possibility of a selection activity, where visitors could choose whose crew from the characters presented they might like to be part of, and in what capacity (boatswain, cook, gunner, quartermaster, etc.). This section would demonstrate some pastimes, music, and games, which are commonly associated with pirates and sailors. To interpret the characters, the museum would use concise displays of objects, probably pop-cultural but preferably also including some original design material as well as utilizing audio-visual technology to introduce sea shanties and games.

After assembling a crew, visitors would next find themselves on a pirate ship. The centerpiece would be a large play structure representing a vessel. This should be visually impressive, fun, and versatile as well as easy to disassemble and then reassemble elsewhere, should the exhibition tour. This structure would enable children to learn about some of the aspects of historical seafaring in a playful manner, such as setting flags and sails, steerage, knot-tying, and spotting other ships through telescopes. Ideally, the ship structure would include both external and internal areas, with the inside perhaps utilized for games, storytelling, and singing. Outside of it, perhaps "spotable" by telescopes mounted on the structure, should be displays about various fictional pirate ships, such as Captain Pugwash's *Black Pig* and Captain Jack Sparrow's *Black Pearl* as well as other toy ships. Digitally, there might be opportunities for the designing of flags and ships, perhaps with an overall competition to design the best one of each. This may also provide a model for remote participation with these elements of the exhibition via the Internet.

The fifth and final section of the exhibition should be its most exploratory, looking at island environments and the seas surrounding them, concluding with the discovery of buried treasure. An experiential environment could allow pre-school children to learn about the differences between the land and the sea, and what sorts of creatures and objects can be found in each of them. An atmosphere of rest and relaxation would be created, offering opportunities for story-telling and child-led activities. The "island" environment could be made through a combination of graphic imagery, differing textures, built structures like caves, and sounds effects. Also, a funny method of engaging children in thinking about sea creatures might be to display a variety of objects representing undersea animals, such as ceramics, sculpture, puppets, and woodwork from across the centuries. Displayed creatively, this "fish tank" could make an imaginative and entertaining scene. The display could be used as the basis of a guessing game, as many of the objects included might not accurately represent the creatures they were intended to. It would also introduce a variety of materials and techniques, which are not discussed elsewhere in the exhibition, enabling this section to have a further didactic element. For the treasure-finding, along with displays interpreting some of the commonly-held notions about buried treasure, there could be a large digital sandbox. Participants could "dig" down in it, through randomly appearing "X"s, until they "uncover" the treasure. Clearly, this would have to be of an adequate scale to satisfy large number of visitors, and also be complex enough to be effective. Both of these factors would create implications regarding cost and space.

As far as possible, this exhibition would be best composed of original objects rather than of graphic reproductions. Access to originals is what museums are best placed to uniquely offer. The childhood material could be displayed alongside "real-life" contextual items, such as cannons or flags, to emphasize the fact that pirate stories are old, and that pirates really existed. This exhibition would be best realized as an experiential show, and thus would require a strong design and a convincing, theatrical build. To furnish the exhibition project with an ambition of building developmental skills in young children, each section could be accompanied by an activity encouraging imagination and creativity, mapped to a particular type of play.

As demonstrated by this essay, the depiction of pirates has taken place in a fairly consistent way over more than two centuries, with a tendency toward sanitizing their image, and making them into more heroic figures than historically was the case. The hackneyed attributes given to them occasionally have some basis in historical fact, but more often have been the invention of a small number of later writers, artists, and directors. Interpreting pirates in a museum for children would be difficult as one must first try to understand what it is that makes them so appealing, and it would inevitably come with a considerable start-up cost to create the immersive environment that this type of show would require.

Notes

1. Specifically, see "At Rio Pongo, Benjamen Gun" (Johnson 105).
2. "He was Blackbeard's bo'sun," John whispered huskily. "He is the worst of them all. He is the only man of whom Barbecue was afraid" (Barrie 69).
3. See JOD/247/1.
4. See V&A Museum no. S.146.153–2007, a cabinet photograph of the cast. These were a series of matinee performances by children of Gilbert and Sullivan's comic opera of 1879, performed between 23rd December 1884 and 14th April 1885.
5. For several examples see V&A museum nos. MISC.336-1978, MISC.49–1982, MISC.425–1982, MISC.402–1991, B.64–2000, B.13–2017.

6. Completing the archetype, this character also boasts a wooden leg and hook for a hand, as well as having the appended nickname "-beard."
7. For three examples see: *Classics Illustrated* no. 64. New York: Gilberton Company, 1949; *Marvel Classics Comics* #15. New York: Marvel Comics Group, 1976; *King Classics*. New York: King Features Syndicate, 1977.
8. "Roberts himself made a gallant figure, at the time of the engagement … a gold chain round his neck, with a diamond cross hanging to it" (Johnson 113).
9. John Fenn, who lost an arm or hand, as well as the formidable member of Edward England's crew who had a prosthetic leg.
10. John Taylor, who was "lame of his hands."
11. See article VIII of John Phillips, article VI of Edward Low and George Lowther, article IX of Bartholmew Roberts and article III of the Buccaneers, as related by Alexander Exquemelin.
12. See MISC.336-1978, a child's fancy dress costume from the 1920s-1930s.
13. See B.12-2017, a child's coin bank.
14. See B.631-2016, *The One-Eyed Sailor Adventure* accessory set for Matchbox *Fighting Furies*, Lesney Products & Co., 1974.
15. Kellogg's *Puffa Puffa Rice* box, 1970, part of the Renier Collection of Children's Literature.
16. Examples are: Edward Teach, probably Bristol; Henry Avery, Devon; Samuel Bellamy, Devon.
17. *Swashbuckle*, series 4, episode 11 (BBC/CBeebies, 2016).

WORKS CITED

Barrie, Sir James Matthew. *Peter and Wendy*. 1911. New York: Charles Scribner's Sons, 1911.
Baur, John. "Today Is Talk Like a Pirate Day!" http://talklikeapirate.com/wordpress/. Accessed on 09/19/2017.
Beaman, Sydney George Hulme. *Tales of Toytown*. Oxford: Oxford University Press, 1928.
Colvin, Sidney. *The Letters of Robert Louis Stevenson to His Family and Friends, Vol. 1*. New York: Charles Scribner's Sons, 1899.
Fliess, Sue. *How to Be a Pirate*. New York: A Golden Book, 2014.
Freedman, Claire. *Pirates Love Underpants*. London: Simon & Schuster, 2012.
Johnson, Captain Charles. *A General History of the Robberies and Murders of the Most Notorious Pirates*. Amazon (CreateSpace), 2014.
Lubin, David M. "The Persistence of Pirates: Pyle, Piracy, and the Silver Screen." *Howard Pyle: American Master Rediscovered*. Delaware Art Museum, 2011, 167–80.
McDermid, Val. *My Granny Is a Pirate*. London: Orchard Books, 2012.
Melina, Remy. "Why Did Pirates Wear Earrings?" http://www.livescience.com/33099-why-did-pirates-wear-earrings.htmal. Accessed on 06/07/2017.
Phillips, Alexandra. "The Changing Portrayal of Pirates in Children's Literature." *New Review of Children's Literature and Librarianship* 17.1 (2011): 36–56.
Pyle, Howard. "Introduction." Alexandre O. Exquemelin, *The Buccaneers and Marooners of America: Being an Account of the Famous Adventures and Daring Deeds of Certain Notorious Freebooters of the Spanish Main*. Howard Pyle (ed.). London: T. Fisher Unwin, Popular Edition, 1905, 15–41.
Rediker, Marcus. *Villains of All Nations*. London: Verso, 2012.
Richardson, Ruth. "Chapbooks." http://www.bl.uk/romanticsandvictorians/articles/chapbooks. British Library, May 14, 2014.
Sanders, Jayneen. *Pearl Fairweather Pirate Captain*. Macclesfield, Victoria, Australia: Educate2Empower, 2016.
Stevenson, Robert Louis. *Treasure Island*. New York: Penguin, 1946.
The Voyages and Adventures of Edward Teach, Commonly Known as Black Beard, the Notorious Pirate. Newcastle upon Tyne: M. Angus & Son, 1814 [National Art Library reference no. Forster 1523].

Being a Pirate
The Use and Purpose of a Piratical Setting in Rum & Bones

Nicholas Moll

Piratical undead battling brave buccaneers amid ancient sea-witchery with the threat of the mighty Kraken looming ever-present: *Rum & Bones* offers its players the thrill of brutal ship-boarding combat in the thematic board game format. The game's narrative is piratical in focus, presenting two crews who compete to possess the mystical treasure of Davy Jones. The gameplay of *Rum & Bones*, however, is derived directly from Multiplayer Online Battle Arena (MOBA) video games. Herein, rank-and-file standard figures move directly towards their objective, while titled characters may undertake a liberal range of actions. Game mechanics and features such as board layout draw on a mixture of MOBA format as well as design features common to the wargame type. Thus, the game formats *Rum & Bones* draws upon are not explicitly nautical in orientation, with MOBA video games typically high fantasy in genre and the wargame largely a generic presentation.

Yet, *Rum & Bones* maintains a sense of fidelity to its piratical theme, drawing on both existing and current popular cultural legacies. The game presents a caricatured mixture of historical stereotypes mingled with a liberal selection of broad literary associations, blending varied nautical themes together into a single setting. But there is little of this legacy or theme in the statement of the rules themselves. While it is a common feature of thematic board games to articulate narrative undertones in their rules, there is no explicit link between game rules and the diegetic world in which the game of *Rum & Bones* is set. With the link between rules and theme implicit rather than explicit, this essay argues that the evocation of the pirate figure constitutes a middle ground between instruction and narrative that is essential to the communication of gameplay in *Rum & Bones*. Thus, throughout the game, the figure of the pirate provides a fundamental translation of the rules into narrative format for the players. This communicative role of the pirate figure is demonstrated, firstly, in the use of the crew format to distinguish between generic and titled characters, which helps contextualize the player's use and control, alternating between game pieces with both limited and expansive ranges of action. Secondly, the communicative role of the pirate figure is demonstrated by the use of the ship-deck setting, which fundamentally articulates the limited geographic scope within the gameboard design. In exploring the use of the pirate figure in the tabletop game format, this essay draws on theories of genre, design, and gamification:

> The age of piracy is at hand!
> Davy Jones is dead, his treasure scattered to the Seven Seas. And whosoever can seize it all, will claim the forbidden power of Davy Jones' Locker itself. Run out the guns, and prepare to board! Accept no quarter, for there's none to give! [Shinall].

Rum & Bones was released in 2015 from Cool Mini or Not, along with a host of supporting companies (Five Houses, Edge Entertainment, and Pendragon Game Studio). From the initial game box, a number of expansions were released with varying game pieces and boards, the former depicting varied crews and the latter representing distinctive ship-types. In 2017, a second edition of the game—*Rum & Bones: Second Tide*—was released, which both revised the rules and provided new content. Both versions of *Rum & Bones* maintain the same, piratical theme and focus. The game itself presents players with nautical-themed historical stereotypes from its very first onset, with images of piratical crews battling on one side of the box and the short narrative noted above on the opposite. Operating within the thematic wargame format, the gameplay itself sees players move figures depicting various members of piratical crews back and forth across interlinked game boards. The game operates from the premise of a "pirate story"—with a quest for treasure and other typical tropes. Yet, the rules themselves are not directly connected to the narrative, but rather take a generic form and draw heavy inspiration from Multiplayer Online Battle Arena (MOBA) video games. In mechanism and practice, the rules and narrative exist as two distinct portions of the game, connected implicitly by the depiction of piratical and nautical themes within the game pieces themselves.

It is thus the historical stereotype of the pirate that is the most prominent theme within the narrative and the basis for game pieces such as character figures. The figure of the pirate is central to the communication of gameplay, connecting the hypothetical series of actions within the rulebook to actual action on the part of the player.

Rum & Bones presents players with an elaborate board game experience. This experience consists of numerous game pieces and boards that represent ships, crew, captains, the kraken, sea-dragons, treasure, and countless other narrative elements. Due to its intricate presentation, *Rum & Bones* can be classified as a thematic board game. A subset of the broader type of the tabletop game, thematic board games can be differentiated largely by their level of articulation. This articulation typically takes the form of "a strong theme which drives the overall game experience" (*BoardGameGeek*). Where traditional games such as *Chess* or *Snakes & Ladders* are extrapolations or have a metaphorical relationship to their concept, the thematic board game attempts to create some level of literality in the portrayal of its narrative or action. *Chess*, for example, depicts the action of medieval war but represents each piece in terms of a metaphorical function. Pawns are peasants and thus have a limited range of movement and value, while the Knight is highly maneuverable and complex in its motion. Likewise, *Snakes & Ladders* reflects Indian and Tibetan spirituality, with snakes representing negative karma and the ladders positive (Schlieter 113). Translated through the colonial process into a commercial product, these aspects of the game exist only though an extrapolation of ideas into board game form (Schlieter 113).

Compared with traditional board games, thematic board games do not feature a sense of extrapolation or metaphorical relationship to their subject matter. Rather, thematic board games attempt the pronunciation of some sense of literality in the gameplay and narrative they undertake. Games such as *Monopoly* or *Arkham Horror* are prime examples of the thematic style of board game. *Monopoly*, for example, sees players move pieces through streets as they travel across the board, exchanging in-game money for property deeds. Similarly, *Arkham Horror* positions players in the town of Arkham, with the board itself also a map of the civic area and pieces depicting both player-controlled characters and their foes. In terms of situation, the expansive presentation of *Rum & Bones* aptly fits the thematic board game format. The play area consists of multiple boards—each depicting a different player's ship or group of ships, both of which are populated by figures that depict ship's crew and officers serving as game pieces. The game's articulation is further elaborated by tokens that are designed in representation of gold doubloons. Due to its elaborate level of evocation, *Rum & Bones* can be classified within the thematic board.

The gameplay of *Rum & Bones* can be further classified as occupying wargame status. A wargame can be defined as a tabletop game whose focus is on combat and confrontation (*BoardGameGeek*). Games such as *Risk* and *Axis & Allies*, are both examples of the wargame type, with players using armies to control multiple regions of a world-map board in a tactical confrontation. Herein the confrontation focuses on control of strategic regions such as continents or production centers. *Rum & Bones* features a slighter scale than that of *Risk* or *Axis & Allies*, but the focus on confrontation and control remains central to the game. Multiple boards, depicting decks and ships, are pushed together prior to the game's onset with gangplank pieces positioned to facilitate movement from one ship to another. As players play *Rum & Bones*, they must maneuver their crews and officers to occupy and destroy key features of other vessels. There is no set path, movement or tactic to achieve this objective. Rather, different figures have distinct abilities and capacities based on their role on the vessel. The Brute, for example, is generally slow but capable of sustaining and dealing damage in close quarters while standard Deckhands are fodder to be sacrificed.

While a wargame in gameplay, the style of action *Rum & Bones* engages is one that draws heavily from computer game influences. Specifically, the gameplay is adapted from the Massive Online Battle Arena (MOBA) format as credited on the publisher's website (*CoolMiniOrNot*). The form itself is modified from real-time strategy video games, with the first MOBA—*Defence of the Ancients*, published in 2002—deriving itself from *Warcraft 3* (Minotti). Within the MOBA format, players control individual avatars who move across negotiated pathways on the map, entitled lanes, to assault the enemy base on the other side. Each avatar is equipped with a role and a range of abilities. In *League of Legends*, for example, the Marksman specializes in dealing Attack Damage to the enemy while the Tank absorbs damage.[1] In this sense, players work together in competing teams to accomplish their objective and each is composed of a range of different abilities and compositions that both aid and offset different styles of play and distinct strategies based on the array of abilities assembled.

A MOBA game additionally provides both aids and obstacles to respective teams in the form of minions, non-player characters with limited abilities, and defensive guard towers. Minions are created by the game at regular intervals in groups, with specialized minions occurring as a reward for various side-objectives. For instance, in *Defence of the Ancients 2* minions are referred to as Creeps and come in a variety of forms. Melee Creeps specialize in close-combat attacks, Ranged Creeps deal less damage but attack from a distance and Siege Creeps do additional damage to buildings. Creeps are spawned from various barracks and if one team manages to destroy their opponent's barracks, they gain the ability to create Super Creeps—essentially high-powered variants of existing minions. When created, minions move towards the enemy base, automatically engaging opponents and obstacles such as avatars and watchtowers. Generally, player actions can influence but not directly control minion activity. The MOBA format can be understood as characterized by the use of teamwork through player controlled avatars to navigate and manipulate a computer-managed field of play.

In contrast with the similarity of gameplay aspects, unlike the nautical and piratical theme of *Rum & Bones*, the High Fantasy genre dominates successful examples of the MOBA type. The two most popular and enduring examples of the MOBA type—*Defence of the Ancients 2* and *League of Legends*—present High Fantasy settings. In *Defence of the Ancients 2* a pair of opposite celestial gods—the destructive Dire and divine Radiant—were trapped inside a moon. Dire and Radiant's conflict caused the moon to explode, showing the planet below with the rocks that caged both beings. The moon rocks hold magical properties, but also infected those near them with the conflict—prompting a series of wars (*DOTA2 Wiki*). Similarly, *League of Legends* is situated on the supercontinent of Valoran wherein magical city-states engaged in limited and controlled forms of warfare on agreed terms. These proxy wars are conducted via representatives characterized by the player's Avatars (*League of Legends Wiki*).

This narrative method of a creative fantasy space for limited conflict is followed by other examples of the MOBA throughout the format's history. This includes *Demigod, Heroes of Newerth, Guardians of Middle-earth* (a *The Lord of the Rings* adaptation) and *Dawngate*. While there have certainly been examples of other genres engaged in the format, such as the DC Superhero based *Infinite Crisis* and the genre-blending *Heroes of the Storm*, fantasy remains a close association of the MOBA. In each case, however, there are a number of common themes shared between distinct examples. The presence of lanes and watchtowers, for example, is a common trope of the MOBA genre, as is the differentiation of minion and avatar, and the division of avatars into distinct categories based on ability. Thus, there is an association of High Fantasy with the MOBA style that is not replicated in *Rum & Bones*.

While *Rum & Bones* does not address the narrative genre closely associated with the MOBA, the board game does adapt the video game style of gameplay to the thematic wargame format. The multiple gameboards featured in *Rum & Bones* do not feature the iconic lanes of the MOBA format. However, the ships depicted on *Rum & Bones'* game boards present a limited space. This limitation of space provides a relatively linear path for the player's pieces to move across—mirroring the lanes of the MOBA format. The pieces themselves are divided into Deckhands and Officers. Deckhands act akin to the MOBA's minions and move on a linear path towards the objective each turn, unless they encounter an opponent or obstacle in which case they stop and engage. Officers are provided with an expansive array of actions that allows the player a selection of tactical options and combinations, engaging the function of the Avatars. While the boards themselves do not feature an enemy base as its main objective, on each ship there are the ship's wheel, its central mast, and main rigging lines that serve as goals for players to destroy. Thus, *Rum & Bones* serves as a MOBA styled gameplay in board game form.

As is expected in the adaptation process, concessions and alterations are undertaken based on the nature of the mediums and their differences.

Most notably for *Rum & Bones* as a physical articulation of a typically digital format, the layout of boards is flexible. Players can choose to re-arrange the alignment or quantity of ships, quantity of gangplanks used, and other features to engage in official or unofficial alternative game modes. Likewise, the quantity of players is flexible, ranging from two to ten. This in itself varies the experience with one player controlling five Officer figures (two players) or each controlling one (ten players). Yet the central premise and aspects of gameplay remain entrenched with those adapted from the MOBA format. In this sense, the MOBA format functions as a template for *Rum & Bones* as well as an inspiration for the rules aspect of the game in a manner that allows distinctive settings to be extrapolated. The setting itself, however, is not linked to the MOBA form.

While the rules of *Rum & Bones* adapt MOBA styled gameplay, the setting itself is distinct from the high fantasy genre that dominates the format. The narrative of *Rum & Bones* as presented in the game is limited to a confrontation between two crews of cinematically styled pirates who compete for "the fabled Treasure of Davy Jones" (Shinall 7). These crews include the original game box's Wellsport Brotherhood under Captain Daniel Pale who enjoy a life of "piratical delights; ale, women (and men), song, and feasting," and the Bone Devils who are "undead pirate lords" under Captain Albrecht the Thrice-Damned (Shinall 23). No year, location or other distinguishing feature are mentioned in the rulebook's description of the setting, but the use of Elizabethan clothing on figures (such as poet's shirts, tricorns or Cavalier boots) draws on popular associations of time and place, as does liberal use of peg-legs, hook-hands and eyepatches in the depiction of individual characters. In this sense, *Rum & Bones* can be seen to occur within a nebulous golden age of piracy that liberally blends fictive and imaginative aspects in a manner that evokes the popular notions of the time, but bears little resemblance to the events and activities of the seventeenth-century Atlantic that inspired the swashbuckling genre.

Thus, while it is clear that *Rum & Bones* is not set in the strictness of history, it nonetheless engages "Historical Stereotypes" in the manner that Jameson employs the phrase to draw on the broader popular cultural interpretations of the time period (279). The style of historical representation Frederick Jameson discusses is less concerned with "facts or historical realities" than the evocation of "stereotypes" associated with the period. Historical stereotypes can be defined as ideas associated with a time period expressed repeatedly through popular cultural forms such as film and literature (Jameson 279). For the maritime early modern period (mid-seventeenth to early-eighteenth centuries) popular culture perpetuates the concept of a time of flamboyant piracy. These figures serve in fiction as mercenary free-traders and cultural deviants from the restrictive morality of the time. However, the board game and its action express nothing of the link between the increase of maritime travel, colonization, and the global slave trade, for example, with growth of naval conflict via privateering noted in Gabriel Kuhn's history of seventeenth-century piracy (66). With little of the history itself present in the historical stereotype, Jameson elaborates that "realism" in terms of the primary sources and information of a time period is distinct from the presentation of the past (279). In this sense, *Rum & Bones* is saturated with extraordinary elements (zombies, sea monsters, magic, anthropomorphic creatures, etc.) that are presented in a whimsical, Saturday morning cartoon style artwork. *Rum & Bones* does not draw on history in articulating the figure of the pirate. Rather, it draws on historical stereotypes associated with mass cultural representation.

The use of historical stereotypes situates the game of *Rum & Bones* into a broader series of literary works. The various Captains and crews within the game's setting draw on common themes throughout current and enduring nautical fiction. The undead Bone Devils of Captain Albrecht evoke images of Hector Barbossa's crew from *Pirates of the Caribbean: The Curse of the Black Pearl* (2003). Yet the Bone Devils likewise bring to mind the groaning, walking dead sailors of Samuel Taylor Coleridge's 1978 poem *The Rime of the Ancient Mariner*. Similarly, the Deep Lords of Captain Carcharius with their fish-like bodies draw on the general milieu of anthropomorphized aquatic life in literature including H.P. Lovecraft's "The Shadow Over Innsmouth," Hans Christian Anderson's *The Little Mermaid*, and *SpongeBob SquarePants*. Human crews, such as the Wellsport Brotherhood or the Marea de la Muerte, demonstrate individually a variety of literary nautical character types. The harpoon-wielding Don Santiago draws recollections of Ahab from *Moby Dick*, for instance. Likewise, the Peg-legged and eye-patched "Stumper" Pete recalls the image of Long John Silver from *Treasure Island*. Thus, while the narrative as presented through the premise of *Rum & Bones* is limited to a violent confrontation, the story itself is expanded and further articulated in the game pieces themselves and the evocation of a wide series of influences liberally drawn from nautical literature.

While these narrative elements are not connected directly to the rules of *Rum & Bones*, José P. Zagal, Jochen Rick, and Idris His argue that games require a style of narrative and story in order to give gameplay a "flow to be entertaining to the players" (33). Zagal, Rick, and His further elaborate that a "good game" is required also to function as a "good story," providing narrative and tension (33). In this sense, it is important to note with *Rum & Bones* that the game pieces themselves only tell part of the story. While this part is told through the articulation of theme, setting, and character type, it is further expanded in the game's rulebooks. Aside from the rules of gameplay, the books outline the individual histories of the various members of each crew. The Wellsport's Gunner, "Blackout" Bart, for example, is a "Royal Navy washout" whose "love of rum and spirits overcame his devotion to duty" (Shinall 24). The story aspect of the game is likewise featured in prose narratives, also featured in the rule book that help evoke the apt literary tone. Yet these aspects leave numerous plot holes open to the interpretation of the players—specifically why each Crew seeks the Treasure of Davy Jones. Players are thus provided with the opportunity to place as much or as little additional detail in to the game, its narrative and characters, as they wish in order to craft a satisfying storyline (Zagal, Rick, and His 27). A wide variety of literary influences are therefore integrated into *Rum & Bones*, with the purpose of crafting narrative.

There is a functionality to the narrative and its articulation within *Rum & Bones* that serves as explanation for both the rules and gameplay mechanisms. The function of narrative in providing a rationale is reflected in the design of the game and its play space allocation, drawing on *Rum & Bones'* MOBA roots and the pirate historical stereotype jointly. Where a MOBA generally offers expansive maps with limited movement space, defined by lanes, *Rum & Bones* grants players a relatively confined space for their characters and movement. The combined play area of both original (pre–*Second Tide*) edition boards totals forty-four zones or squares arranged in six rows. Each of these rows is divided across two graphics, depicting ships, with the middle row of each vessel containing two additional squares to represent "prow" and "stern" spaces. Both graphics represent larger, "galleon" styled vessels. The *Second Tide* edition of the game adds smaller, "sloop" style vessels that contain two rows of eight squares. Objective markers placed on the boards represent masts, the ship's wheel, and key points of rigging—placed in the center rows of each board. The effect of both minimalized space and centrality of objective is an orientation for the player, directing their command of game pieces (Whalen). Players move their pieces in such a way that encounters the objective. Indeed, given the size of the board they cannot reasonably avoid confrontation and nor can their opponent. The limitation of movement spaces creates a sense of individual and shared space, encouraging competition regardless of which side of the board players operate from (Whalen). The board is a ship and the objective markers are key points on each vessel which must be assaulted or defended.

Used to communicate narrative, the pirate historical stereotype occupies a middle role between rules and narrative in *Rum & Bones*. In engaging nautical themes, *Rum & Bones* displays the most common "use of story in games" to propel players into action (Fullerton 113). The Deep Lord's Quartermaster figure, for example, depicts an anthropomorphic crocodile wearing a clock around its neck titled Tick Tock. The title and shape of the figure instantly draws association with the clock-swallowing crocodile of James Matthew

Barrie's *Peter Pan*, exaggerating the character's name and appearance with themed abilities such as Time Freeze (the ability to reduce the speed of enemy figures (Shinall). While officer figures such as Tick-Tock possess a range of themed capabilities that provide tactical advantage to the player in certain situations, these are largely inconsequential to the figure themselves. Herein the abilities possessed on each figure play sheet could easily be swapped from one to another, retitling them for appropriate thematic effect. In this sense, the main role of the game figures themselves is not to communicate rules to the player but to drive gameplay forward. By providing a thematic alignment of tactical option with the distinctive officer figures and character narrative, *Rum & Bones* grants players a context for the kind of actions a player might undertake (Fullerton 114). The narrative aspect of the game pieces themselves thus further disguises the sensation that these motions or action possibilities are hampered by rules restrictions. Rather, the restrictions imposed on players, designed for gameplay reasons, are justified narratively as a storytelling exercise (Fullerton 114). Throughout a game session, then, the board dictates largely how *Rum & Bones* is to be played, and why certain pieces should be moved to key locations. However, the game pieces themselves repeatedly emphasize the tactical elements of the game through the use of narrative.

The historical stereotype of the piratical figure is integrated into the rules component of *Rum & Bones*, serving as a key explanation for the manner in which gameplay both functions and restricts player activity. While the game does draw explicitly from the MOBA genre of computer game in terms of these same rules and functions, common nautical themes such as ship and deck, officers and crew are engaged in the actual communication and articulation of those mechanisms. *Rum & Bones* engages the figure of the pirate to communicate rules and gameplay. The use of historical stereotypes in this sense articulates popular ideas associated with the mass cultural representation of the golden age of piracy and popular concepts of the pirate. And in this sense, while not historical, the popular concept aptly reflects the cultural phenomenon surrounding nautical adventures, represented by the liberal manner in which *Rum & Bones* draws on piratical literature. The setting and nature of the game is essentially a small-scale battle simulation between two ships. This concept is distinct from the rules as written but clearly integrated into the design of the game. Thus, while the board itself dictates how the game pieces are to be moved, the narrative element indicates why they are moved in this manner to the players with the presence of decks, rigging, and guns becoming both key features of the board and occupying a key feature of gameplay, as is the differentiation of crewman and officer, and the division of officers into distinct categories or classes based on ability. Narrative and historical stereotypes are integrated with rules and gameplay in *Rum & Bones* with concepts such as "crew" and "officer" engaged to heighten the sense of nautical theme. Thus, while the game pieces themselves do not help dictate the rules, they do emphasize the narrative elements of the game through the use of piratical figures. While it is a common feature of thematic board game to articulate literary undertones in their rules, there is no explicate link between game rules and the diegetic world in which the game of *Rum & Bones* is set. With the link between rules and theme implicit, this essay argues that the evocation of the pirate figure is essential to the communication of gameplay in *Rum & Bones*. The figure of the pirate provides a fundamental translation of the rules into narrative format for the players. This communicative aspect is seen, firstly, in the use of the crew format to distinguish between generic and titled characters (the latter framed as the ship's officers). The contextualization of the game pieces further helps players consider their use in a tactical sense. And, secondly, such a communicative aspect is evident in the use of the ship-deck setting, which fundamentally articulates the limited geographic scope within gameboard design.

Note

1. Attack damage is defined as "the amount of damage dealt by a basic attack excluding the applicable damage modifiers" (*League of Legends Wiki*).

Works Cited

BoardGameGeek. 2000. www.boardgamegeek.com. Accessed on 07/20/2017.
CoolMiniOrNot. 2001. www.coolminiornot.com. Accessed 07/20/2017.
Darrow, Charles B. 1934. *Monopoly*. Parker Brothers, 1997.
Dawngate. Electronic Arts, 2014.
Defence of the Ancients 2. Valve Corporation, 2013.
Demigod. Gas Powered Games, 2009.
DOTA2 Wiki. 2017. https://dota2.gamepedia.com/Dota2Wiki. Accessed on 07/20/2017.
Fullerton, Tracy. *Game Design Workshop: A Playcentric Approach to Creating Innovative Games*. 2004. Amsterdam: AK Peters/CRC Press, 2014.
Guardians of Middle-Earth. Monolith Productions; Zombie Studios, 2012.
Heroes of Newerth. S2 Games; Frostburn Studio, 2010.
Heroes of the Storm. Blizzard, 2015.
Infinite Crisis. Turbine; Warner Brothers Interactive Entertainment, 2015.
Jameson, Fredric. *Postmodernism, or, The Cultural Logic of Late Capitalism*. Durham: Duke University Press, 1999.
Kuhn, Gabriel. *Life Under the Jolly Roger: Reflections on Golden Age Piracy*. Oakland: PM Press, 2010.
Launis, Richard and Kevin Wilson. *Arkham Horror*. Fantasy Flight Games, 2005.
League of Legends. Riot Games, 2009.
League of Legends Wiki. 2017. http://leagueoflegends.wikia.com/wiki/League_of_Legends_Wiki. Accessed on 07/20/2017.
Minotti, Mike. "The History of MOBAs: From Mod to Sensation." *VB*. 2016. https://venturebeat.com/2014/09/01/the-history-of-mobas-from-mod-to-sensation/. Accessed on 07/20/2017.
Schlieter, Jen. "Simulating Liberation: The Tibetan Buddhist Game *Ascending the [Spiritual] Levels*." *Religions in Play: Games, Rituals, and Virtual Worlds*. Philippe Bornet and Maya Burger (eds.). Scheßlitz: Rosch-Buch, 2012, 93–116.
Shinall, Michael. *Rum & Bones*. *CoolMiniOrNot*; Five Houses, 2015.
_____. *Rum & Bones: Second Tide*. *CoolMiniOrNot*, 2017.

Whalen, Tara. "Playing Well with Others: Applying Board Game Design to Tabletop Display Interfaces." UIST 2003. Vancouver, November 2–5, 2003, 4–5.

Zagal, José P, Jochen Rick, and Idris His. "Collaborative Games: Lessons Learned from Board Games." *Simulation & Gaming* 30:1 (2006), 26–40.

Pirate as *Homo Ludens*
Analyzing the Humorous Outlaw at Play in One Piece

ARTUR SKWERES

Common to popular pirate narratives is the portrayal of piracy as an aspiration of the young hero in search of adventure and fortune. While undeniably alluring with the vision of a life of ease and pleasure at the expense of others, piracy carries a stigma because of the danger it brings to anyone involved. In narratives about pirates that have a lighthearted tone the brutality is often defused through slapstick and comic relief. As a result, the pirate tends to be effectively depicted as a clown, comically following his desires wherever they lead him or her. An especially compelling object of study that is representative of such a trend is the anime series *One Piece*, adapted from the manga under the same title created by Eiichiro Oda (1997–). A monumental work spanning over 86 volumes of manga and 800 animated episodes to date, it is regarded as one the most popular and significant works of Japanese popular culture as well as the best-selling manga series ever written. This essay will consider the reasons for the popularity of a story that focuses on the swashbuckling adventures of the unlikely group of pirates who seem to be more at play than actively robbing and pillaging the innocent.

It can be argued that *One Piece* is representative of the adventure genre for young viewers. Target audience is varied, but Oda stated that when he writes he has fifteen-year-old boys in mind (as an example of the Japanese *shōnen* manga, it can be defined as a comic book written specifically for young male readers), hence the stress on action and fighting between strong characters (Oda "ONE WORLD"). Nonetheless, his manga is enjoyed by the young and adults of both sexes, his fans including many Japanese celebrities such as the musicians Takuya Kimura, Mari Yaguchi or Olympic medalist Kousuke

Kitajima (Oda "Vicky the Pirate"). Oda also admitted that he prefers to avoid serious topics or "deep messages," focusing rather on delivering an engaging pastime (Oda "A Manga"). Yet the series' themes are universal and concern notions wider and more complex than simply the categories of friendship and masculine rivalry. Indeed, due to the pirate setting they also concern freedom, solidarity between social outcasts, responsibility for others, class inequality and racism, and, finally, a deep distrust towards authorities. In his monograph on historical adventure movies, Taves argues that the idealistic belief in righteousness and valor are typical of the adventure genre regardless of the context, "[r]anging from exploration of the world's remote regions to Robin Hood–like rebellions against totalitarianism ... follow[ing] a pattern of despotism, subversion, and the establishment of a governing system to protect the rights of its citizens" (11). As this essay will demonstrate, all of these classic elements of adventure films can be found in *One Piece*. However, another major quality of the series is the wider notion of piracy as a means of fulfilling one's dreams.

As in the case of most popular *shōnen* manga, *One Piece* follows the adventures of a young male character with one great ambition: the protagonist Monkey D. Luffy wants to become the king of pirates. His wish is not without precedent, as he is following in the footsteps of the man who engaged in a war with the World Government and managed to start the pirate era during his own execution. He divulged to the crowds that he hid all of his amassed riches, the eponymous One Piece, at one location which they first have to find.[1] Each episode of the series starts with the recollection of the great pirate's defiant call for everyone to travel the world and search for the treasure—to take part in the adventure, which can be analyzed in terms of an invitation to play. Hence, the world of pirates depicted in *One Piece* can be analyzed in terms of a playground for the characters, in which rules that are different than in normal life are applied and the pirates themselves are examples of a "homo ludens."

The term "homo ludens" was coined by Johan Huizinga in 1938 and denotes the "playful human," the quality of the human being as willingly and freely engaged in play as separate from normal life, often clearly detached from reality through its placement within the arena of a "magic circle" (10). Huizinga's theory of play was further developed by Roger Caillois, who distinguished between four basic categories of play: *agon* (competition as in chess or boxing), *alea* (play of chance, as in gambling by means of a slot machine), *mimicry* (role playing as in acting), and *ilinx* (play which induces a feeling of vertigo, as in rollercoaster rides) (12). The relation between the player and the environment outside of play led to the introduction of two additional categories: *pragma* (practical or pragmatic approach to play) and *óneiros* (immersion in the world of play at the cost of contact with reality outside of play) (Skweres 11–15). All of these categories are helpful in analyzing the representation of pirates in the world of *One Piece*.

The world created by Eiichiro Oda can be seen as a space of play, an enchanted circle, where the heroes can achieve their dreams and desires, living a life of adventures. Luffy's band of Straw Hat Pirates (named after this signature element of their captain's attire), for example, represent almost all kinds of players: the fighters are mostly interested in *agon* and *ilinx*. The less powerful Usopp and Nami turn to role play (*mimicry*) and trickery. *Alea* as an aspect of play is visible in the gamble which all devil fruit-eaters take when they eat the forsaken fruit. Since each of them is unique and can give highly useful as much as seemingly useless powers, the decision to eat one is a great risk. An exception to this rule can be seen in the actions of Blackbeard Teach, who cheats by killing two men for their fruits and takes over their powers. Hence, he is clearly depicted as a dishonorable pirate: he and his companions are criminals who do not abide by any rules. The cinematic and kinesthetic quality of action depicted both in the manga and in the animated series are testament to the *ilinx* as an aspect of the adventures of the Straw Hats. Luffy, the main character, is constantly shown while enjoying the vertigo of speed— always running and jumping through the air at high speed and height, he enjoys himself due to the feeling of *ilinx*. This is evident when he abducts Rebecca and flies with her above the city, falling from great heights—she cries in terror while he laughs gleefully (Episode 742). Similarly, during the Punk Hazard arc, when all protagonists escape from the island facility in a wagon, Luffy enjoys the ride like the other children, sitting not just at the front of the cart speeding through the underground, but in front of it (Episode 620). In episode 757, when Luffy first sets foot on a suspension bridge, he cannot help himself but to immediately start rocking it dangerously, scaring everyone. He inadvertently scares everyone out of their wits also when he embraces his group and suddenly jumps with them off the top of the giant elephant in Zou to their utter dread (one of his companions, the skeletal musician Brook actually gives out his ghost out of fear). To the amazement of the onlookers, Luffy laughs as they fall from the immense height (Episode 776).

In its depiction of piracy, *One Piece* seems to be constantly balancing the relations between harsh reality and carefree fantasy. This is consistent with Huizinga's notion of a magic circle, which requires the players to "suspend their disbelief" and engage in a flight of fancy. The viewers are to perceive the world depicted in *One Piece* as such an area of play, however, to keep clear the high stakes of the games the heroes of the series engage in, there is always a clear relation drawn between their actions and real-life consequences. To facilitate the perception of the real relevance of events occurring in the story, the author consistently alludes to reality outside of the fictional world he created. The dichotomy starts at the level of aesthetic design. Oda's distinctive visual style, while remaining close to the traditional manga style with the simplified facial features and expressive backgrounds, also consistently simplifies the anatomy of the characters to the point of exaggeration or parody (Clarke 120–121). The design of many characters seems to be based on celebrities, especially actors and musicians, as the resemblance between Steven Tyler and Jango, Freddie Mercury and Peeply Lulu, Al Capone and Capone Bege, Michel Polnareff and Don Quixote Doflamingo, or God Enel and Eminem demonstrates. Throughout the series, Oda also skillfully alludes to certain anime conventions. For example, Luffy is idolized by a younger pirate, Bartolomeo, who blushes like a girl seeing Luffy as a handsome character with large eyes straight out of *shōjo* manga for girls that usually focuses on romances (Episode 658), signifying Bartolomeo's adoration for a more accomplished and famous pirate as divorced from reality. In another instance, Oda alters his style to mockingly mimic classical Western art: one of the characters, Jora, uses her devil fruit powers to change everything into abstract or cubist art. As a result, she makes all objects or weapons useless and broken, while rendering her enemies helpless and much less attractive (on one occasion she transforms the skeletal member of the Straw Hat Pirates, Brook, into a live Munch painting and causes Nami to lose all her feminine shapes) (Episode 646). Hence, Oda playfully parodies the Western art world as pretentious and corrupting.

However, the author also often alludes in his oeuvre to other works of popular culture. Hence, two of the Straw Hat Pirates are literary allusions: Zoro is a master swordsman, though he bears very little resemblance to McCulley's Zorro, while Usopp is a lying and quite cowardly character whose storytelling abilities could match the ingenious imagination of the Greek fabulist, Aesop, while his long nose brings to mind Collodi's Pinocchio. Less prominent characters also sometimes resemble classical stories, as the "Three Musketeers" on the island of Zou, which is divided between two rivaling leaders, Ruler of the Night (Master Nekomamushi) and Ruler of the Day (Duke Inuarashi), in conflict like King Louis XIII and Cardinal Richelieu in Alexandre Dumas's *The Three Musketeers*) (Episode 756). While some characters are completely unrelated to the literary or film counterparts, as in the case of the villainous Donquixote Doflamingo (possibly alluding to Cervantes' masterpiece), others resemble them to a great degree, as in the case of the blind swordsman Zatoichi portrayed in many fine details in Admiral Issho/Fujitora (Episodes 630–631), or other Admirals, who are an allusion to the Japanese legend of Momotaro. Among numerous others, in the world of *One Piece* the Land of Wano is a clear allusion to Japan itself, with its representative warriors—an old-fashioned samurai, an artist, and a ninja, attempting to defend their country from a foreign invasion and at the same time struggling with the idea of opening it to outside influences.

Parody and allusion constitute a part of the concept of play, which lies at the heart of the *One Piece*'s plot. Apart from the theme of following their desires at all costs, linking it to the *Pirates of the Caribbean* (2003–17) or Roman Polanski's *Pirates* (1986), the story also introduces the element of the fantastic. Many of the heroes gain special, magical abilities after having eaten a "devil fruit": hence, while Luffy can stretch his body as if it were made out of rubber, others can transform their bodies or environments, wield the force of the elements, or become human-animal hybrids. Despite possessing such superhuman abilities, the many powerful characters of *One Piece* choose the life of piracy as a means of achieving their dreams or desires. This is caused by the social and political conditions, which are oppressive in nature. Seemingly serene and well-organized, the marine-based world of *One Piece* is governed by corrupt and merciless World Government, World Nobles (known as the Celestial Dragons), and the powerful Navy. Adding to the sentiment of injustice are the many local conflicts caused by usurpers, often silently backed by the officials, who disrupt and conquest smaller countries. They do so at the cost of ordinary people's lives, and are driven by the desire to control others. Their tyranny is established through force and revolutions caused by small, elite groups. It is only when a group of pirates, such as the Straw Hats, face them against overwhelming odds, that they can be defeated, countered by the small group which is propelled by the same revolutionary (or reactionary) spirit.

The ludic adventures of pirates in *One Piece*, usually centering around fights between equally-skilled opponents with the aim of establishing the supreme fighter (play as *agon*), have serious, world-changing consequences. The pirates in *One Piece* have tremendous power which affects everyone around them, and it is worthwhile to consider how the difference in the attitude toward play informs the perception of the pirates, as can be demonstrated by the example of contrasting attitudes of Luffy and Doflamingo. Each of the story arcs features the Straw Hat Pirates as the agents of social reform, attempting to defeat seemingly invincible tyrants and often trying to support deposed or betrayed kings or rulers. As such, they inadvertently become heroes who give hope to the oppressed. Such is the case in the sky island of Skypiea, where they defeat the man with the ambition to become a god (Episodes 153–195). Similarly, in Alabasta, they support Nefeltari Vivi, the princess of a desert country ruined by a secret organization which covertly controls the weather (Episodes 92–130). Another illuminating example of such a conflict can be observed in the Dressrosa Saga (Episodes 579–746). In its course, it is discovered that the seemingly idyllic kingdom of Dressrosa is just a façade for the rule of a psychopathic gangster and manipulator, Don Quixote Doflamingo. Having deposed and defamed the king and his family, Doflamingo has turned the former ruler literally into a puppet, a fate shared by a large number of other citizens. Through the magic of his subordinates, he rules the land for over ten years, not only changing the inconvenient subjects into toys, but also causing them to be forgotten by anyone who ever knew them. Should they form new attachments to humans as toys, or recover the memory of their past lives, they would be immediately discarded in a subterranean trash heap.

The same fate meets the gladiators who participate in the championship in the coliseum at the moment when they expect to have their wounds tended by doctors. One of the gladiators tells Luffy that in Dressrosa trash in society is hidden, which causes the country to "look good, but only on the surface" (Episode 657).[2] The hiding of inconvenient facts beneath the surface is most blatantly and ruthlessly portrayed in the transformation of humans into puppets and wiping of any memory of their existence, bringing to mind not only the practice of erasing the past in George Orwell's novel *1984*, but also real life totalitarian machinations of Stalin who erased people from photographs, or even the similar practice of *damnatio memoriae* in ancient Rome, as in the case of Emperor Geta. The last example especially seems to be relevant to the land of Dressrosa, resembling the Mediterranean, as its former king, Riku Doldo III, as well as his granddaughter, Rebecca, are forced to fight as gladiators in the coliseum, perhaps as a nod to Ridley Scott's *Gladiator* (2001) as well.

On the other hand, the villain, Doflamingo, is a degenerate gangster but also a pirate warlord (*Shichibukai*) himself who deals arms in the black market and fuels conflicts in neighboring countries. Moreover, he is a descendant of the Celestial Dragons, a privileged group who are regarded as the rulers of the world. Certain of his untouchable status, he exploits it to influence and control the media, convinced that he can stifle any attempts at an insurrection. His signature ability is the power to control other people with invisible strings. As a result, he is able to force them to commit suicide with their own weapon or attack other people against their will. As he sees that his rule might be in danger, he utilizes an ultimate weapon, which is a mass extermination program. Using his strings to trap the entire island of Dressrosa in a swiftly narrowing "birdcage," he puts everyone's lives in danger and causes them to attack one another. Unable to restrain his playful nature, he also announces a hunting challenge, which consists in killing the appointed twelve people for the exorbitant amounts of 100 to 500 million Berries (the *One Piece* currency). When, after a long struggle, Luffy finally delivers the final blow to Doflamingo, the hero shouts that he feels that, because of the latter, he is suffocating. While Doflamingo, who made himself known in the underworld as the "Joker," seems to treat the lives of people below his status as negligible objects of his play, Luffy sees it as immoral and stifling. Although they are both pirates and seem to be following their desire to play as examples of "homo ludens," their motivations are entirely different. While Luffy sees piracy as an occasion for playful, óneiric behavior detached from outward gains (other than filling his belly with exorbitant amounts of food), Doflamingo's playfulness is stigmatized by *pragma*. His play is based on the premise that everything is entirely conditioned by himself, with others being mere playthings, or puppets, which he can lead on a string. As such, all his actions follow the theme of the desire to exert total control over others, which the hero found so unbearably stifling.

Both Luffy and Doflamingo are pirates and revolutionaries, but above all they can be seen as examples of a *homo ludens*, governed by the principle of *óneiros* and *pragma* respectively. Their approach toward the play could not be more disparate. Luffy as a player consistently tries to keep the stakes low, despite constantly betting his life and ultimately fighting for the fate of royal families and entire countries. However, subsequently he does not care for rewards or recognition, remaining within the oneiric rather than pragmatic realm of play. Moreover, he refuses to acknowledge social constraints, seeing them as unnecessary complications. Such an attitude reinforces his revolutionary and socially subversive streak: he lacks any awareness of the public subtleties and constantly disrupts social relations (usually, although not exclusively with humorous outcomes). This is enabled by his status as an outlaw, the comic *homo ludens*, who can escape the consequences of his actions while exerting a crucial influence on the world around him.

One Piece is replete with examples of pirates showing playful attitudes and unwilling to obey laws or social conventions. Luffy and his companions constantly get into trouble because they see their pirate status as a justification to use force to avoid following laws meant for ordinary people, necessitating special treatment by those who witness their actions. The events at the end of Dressrosa arc can serve as a typical illustration of such a behavior. Once the adventure is over and the enemy is defeated, Luffy abducts princess Rebecca. Although he does so with her agreement, he once again assumes the role of a villain and a pirate. In the beginning his motivations are purposefully left unclear. When he asks the princess to come with him, it looks as if he wants to take her on his travels. It transpires, however, that Luffy wants her to reconnect with her father, Kyros, which was deemed improper by the latter due to his low social standing. Kyros, who married Rebecca's mother and caused her repulsion from the royal family, was unable to stop the onslaught of Doflamingo's pirates. Consequently, he was turned into a toy soldier, who nonetheless retained his memories and trained Rebecca from a very early age, to be able to fight and triumph as a gladiator without being able to tell her that he was her father. Even after he is returned to his human form and is once again remembered by everyone, Kyros believes himself to be of too humble origins to be considered part of the royal family—as a former criminal and gladiator, he thinks that he should not be associated with the princess. Rebecca too is trapped by conventions, surrounded by servants who make her don a new, beautiful dress instead of her old gladiator uniform. By breaking the conventions, Luffy once again frees her and he does so by tearing out the bars in her chamber window and physically dragging her outside. Once freed, she continues to run through the woods on her own, to stop her father from leaving. As she does so, she keeps falling, is scratched by branches, her new dress is torn and destroyed. Yet, when she arrives at her father's cabin, they both acknowledge each other and both cry profusely. It is one of the many sentimental scenes that occur frequently in the series, when the protagonists finally allow themselves to show their emotions. In such instances, Luffy and his crew are the catalysts for the revelations of their true feelings, which remain hidden until the official laws and regulations are broken.

A similar illustration of the young pirate's ability to break conventions and engender a change in people through his oneiric and seemingly illogical, ludic behavior occurs immediately afterwards. Despite having saved Dressrosa, Luffy and his crew are still wanted by the Navy. Due to his desire to assist Rebecca in her reunion with her father, Luffy gets carelessly embroiled in a fight with a powerful opponent, the blind Admiral Fujitora who can control the force of gravity. Despite facing the dangerous enemy, Luffy announces all his attacks before he performs them. This angers the admiral, who thinks that his young opponent is underestimating him. Yet Straw Hat explains during the fight that he does not want to take advantage of a blind man whom he likes. This takes the Admiral aback, who laughing states that they should both fight as is appropriate for their position and that Luffy should not announce his sympathies so openly in battle. Luffy does not mind losing his prestige or dignity, while the old admiral sticks to the propriety and acts against his own sentiments but as is expected of him (accordingly, the title of the episode 743 is "Men's Pride–Luffy vs. Fujitora, Head-to-Head").

Both situations at the end of Dressrosa arc allude to the propriety and flout conventions, instead suggesting that as a pirate the hero should follow one's own heart and stay true to one's dreams. What is impossible for a navy officer, who is bound by his duty and by what is considered appropriate for his status, does not restrict the pirate in any way. However, Luffy's oneiric playfulness is unreasonable and he is at last restrained by his fellow men to facilitate their escape. Finally, the situation is resolved in an unexpected manner. As Admiral Fujitara prepares to deal a deadly blow to the escaping criminals by unloading all the rubble from the obliterated city on them and their ships, thousands of inhabitants of Dressrosa run out after the pirates, shouting that they want their princess back. As the Admiral ascertains due to his keen sense of hearing, the inhabitants are actually cheerful and hold no resentment against Luffy (to whom they refer as Lucy, their hero from the coliseum). They are perfectly aware of what was being hidden from them—that Kyros is Rebecca's biological father and that the princess herself is secure. Their actions are only to safeguard the escape of the pirates, since they know that the admiral would not attack the pirates risking so many civilians as collateral causalities. They are playing a game of masquerade, laughing as they run towards East Port, thus showing their gratefulness and returning the favor. Their appropriation and employment of the ludic, pirate tactics is pragmatic in nature, as it has a well-defined purpose—returning the favor to the pirates who saved them. They put themselves in harm's way under the guise of trying to capture him as a criminal.[3] The admiral is left alone on shore, thinking about how foolish the young captain of the Straw Hats is in his honesty and how this causes people to want to help him. He wonders what Luffy looks like and, smiling for the first time, admits that he wished he had not blinded himself after seeing the horrors of war. He therefore acknowledges that there is still hope beyond the terrible events of the past and that the pirate has something that he lacked—the ability to retain his innocence through his playful attitude that overlooks social conventions and rational responses to life's challenges.

The final crucial event of the Dressrosa arc also stresses the oneiric attitude of the Straw Hats, which is at odds with the attitudes of other pirates. The small crew of the Straw Hats meets the other pirates, former prisoners of Doflamingo and participants in his coliseum fights, who are grateful for being freed from captivity and want to pledge allegiance to Luffy. Yet the latter once again surprises everyone, when he refuses to be called their superior and "father," hence rejecting the idea of forming a fleet 5600 people strong. Flatly declining their offer, he instead proposes that they should retain their "freedom," and should come to each other's aid when asked for. He further baffles them by saying that he wants to "become the king of pirates, and not someone important" (Episode 745). Unable to understand his stance of a carefree, oneiric *homo ludens*, the other pirates decide to take an oath themselves, thus exercising their own freedom, vowing to protect him and fight for him, hence forming the Straw Hat Fleet even against his wish.

As it was argued, the world of *One Piece* abounds in events which point to the totalitarian and criminal character of the authorities. People are thus enticed to join the ranks of the pirates and exercise their freedom through rebellion. The fact that their skirmishes with the Navy are often playful and the actions of the Straw Hats are done without their self-interest in mind only serves to highlight the difference between the authorities and the pirates. Accordingly, it should be stressed that despite the mostly lighthearted humor and swashbuckling adventures characterizing *One Piece*, the notion of killing innocents on a massive scale appears time and again. Although the Straw

Hat Pirates, following the example of Gol D. Roger, seem to stubbornly follow their dreams and ambitions the authorities are attempting to hide secrets which would threaten their position and consequently are trying to stop them at all costs. This desire to keep the truth secret led them to banish an entire century (called Void Century) from archaeological history and to destroy the entire island of Ohara, housing all the world's archaeologists capable of reading the ancient writing, with one attack of a fleet. The World Government feared the fame of Golden Roger to the point that they attempted to kill any of his known associates. One of the few survivors, Portgas D. Rouge, mother to Golden Roger's son, Portgas D. Ace, was constantly watched by the authorities that wanted to make sure he had no offspring. Desperate to save her child's life, she prolonged her pregnancy to twelve months and died after giving birth to a healthy son.

The desire to preserve the status quo on the part of the antagonists often has tragic circumstances. However, in accordance with the humorous character of the series, it is sometimes used for comic effect. For instance, one of Donquixote's officers, Senor Pink, seems to be a parody of exaggerated, assertive manliness. He is always surrounded by female fans, who adore him despite his obnoxious conduct, which is also at variance with his appearance—tall and overweight, he dresses like a baby, wearing a pink bib and swim trunks which resemble a diaper. Not ashamed of his looks, he treats women with contempt. Only later it is revealed that the reason for his behavior is the mourning of his late wife, whom he was trying to cheer up as she was lying comatose after the loss of their baby son. On the other extreme of this desire to preserve one's prestige and unwillingness to be seen as the losing party are the actions of a member of the New Fishmen Pirates, Zeo. He is so protective of his honor that he refuses to admit the fact that he has been defeated. While his opponent holds his foot on his face, he proudly announces to his followers that he is utilizing a new technique which allows him to attack his enemy's foot, announcing that "It's called Super Sole Head-Butt!" causing his subordinates to gasp in exasperation at his effort to name a new technique under such circumstances (Episode 561). This action, apart from its intended comical consequences, also serves to illustrate that the proud antagonist does not see the rivalry as playful competition (*agon*), because he does not allow himself to think that there is a possibility of his loss. It finds its correlation in the selfish and callous actions of the World Government, which sees the ludic actions of pirates as unwelcome bid for power.

The sprawling series of *One Piece* therefore belongs to an action-comedy genre and uses humor as much as brutal conflicts to convey the author's observations concerning social problems. During an interview, Eiichirō Oda admitted that when he set out to write *One Piece*, he wanted primarily to convey a world of manliness and a "man's world" (Oda "Monochrome Talk").

As this essay demonstrates, among the many notions that form the rich fabric of the series, man's honor is not the sole or even the most significant factor. Related to it is the characters' desire to preserve the social structure, despite the often-unbearable circumstances that plague entire nations. It is made apparent that the status quo cannot be preserved yet the members of societies encountered by the Straw Hat Pirates have no means of changing it without disrupting the stability of the social structures. Hence, the characters that are free from such restraints, the pirates, who do not compromise and do whatever they desire, are the only ones who can help the citizens of the various societies. In spite of being unwilling to profit from his actions, Straw Hat Luffy's oneiric attitude to play yields pragmatic benefits for others. As the future King of Pirates, Luffy is an example of a *homo ludens* who is depicted as someone who can fix the broken reality because he does not allow himself to come under its influence, as an outsider, untainted by its corruption.

Notes

1. Similarly to the real world, Olivier Levasseur, the famed pirate who threw a cryptogram to the crowds during his execution, inviting them to search for his immense treasure.
2. This sentiment of being in a country with an attractive front but a seedy underbelly resembling the place in which Luffy grew up is later repeated by his rediscovered brother, Sabo, in episode 667.
3. This is not unlike the behavior of the highly vocal and aggressive soldiers at the end of the Punk Hazard arc, who did not want to let their sympathy for the pirates show despite having survived only thanks to the help of the Straw Hats.

Works Cited

Caillois, Roger. *Man, Play and Games*. M. Barash (trans.). Urbana: University of Illinois Press, 2001.
Clarke, James. *Animated Films*. London: Virgin Books, 2004.
Huizinga, Johan. *Homo Ludens: A Study of the Play-Element in Culture*. London: Routledge & Kegan Paul, 1949.
Oda, Eiichiro. "A Manga to Connect People." *MEN'S NON-NO*. December 10, 2009. English translation available at http://www.thegrandline.com/odanon.htm. Accessed on 09/10/2017.
Oda, Eiichiro. "ONE WORLD." *Switch*, November 29, 2009. English translation available at http://www.thegrandline.com/odaswitchint.htm. Accessed on 09/10/2017.
Oda, Eiichiro. "Vicky the Pirate, The Origin of an Adventure Comic." *AERA*. December 21, 2009. English translation available at http://www.thegrandline.com/odaaeraint.htm. Accessed on 09/10/2017.
Oda, Eiichiro, and Akira Toriyama. "Monochrome Talk." *Color Walk*. July 24, 2001. English translation available at http://www.thegrandline.com/odainterview.html. Accessed on 09/10/2017.
One Piece, Episodes 1–802, Toei Animation, July 22, 1997–.
Skweres, Artur. *Homo Ludens as a Comic Character in Selected American Films*. Cham, Switzerland: Springer, 2017.
Taves, Brian. *The Romance of Adventure: The Genre of Historical Adventure Movies*. Jackson: University Press of Mississippi, 1993.

About the Contributors

Jayson **Althofer** works at the Toowoomba Regional Art Gallery in Australia where he provides public access to the Lionel Lindsay Gallery and Library Collection and curates exhibitions. He has published on Australian art and taught English literature and Australian history at the University of Southern Queensland.

Michael **Charlton** is an associate professor of English at Missouri Western State University where he teaches writing and rhetoric. His research includes visual rhetoric, popular culture, and writing with new technology. His work has appeared in several academic journals and in edited collections on *Game of Thrones* and *Doctor Who.*

Eurydice **Da Silva** is a Ph.D. candidate in Portuguese studies at Paris Nanterre University in France. She holds an MA in English literature from Sorbonne University and a certificate in screenwriting and producing from the University of California, Los Angeles. Her research includes art, film, Portuguese history and censorship.

Racheal **Harris** is completing an MA in studies of religion at the University of New England in Australia. Her research includes religion and popular culture. She has contributed an essay to an upcoming edited collection on The CW series *Supernatural.*

Clint **Jones** is a professor at the University of Kentucky. He has published on utopia including two books: *A Genealogy of Social Violence* and *The Individual and Utopia*, as well as an essay on pirates and social mythology. His research includes critical social theory, applied ethics, environmental philosophy and deconstruction.

Minke **Jonk** earned her Ph.D. from the University of Southampton in England and teaches at the University of Leiden. Her research interests include maritime literature and the maritime supernatural of the nineteenth century, representations of sailors, the seascape and the sublime, and Victorian maritime nostalgia.

Christopher **Ketcham** earned his Ph.D. at the University of Texas at Austin and teaches business and ethics at the University of Houston–Downtown. His research includes risk management, applied ethics, social justice and east-west comparative philosophy. He has written chapters in popular culture and philosophy texts.

About the Contributors

Alexandra V. **Leonzini** is a joint-masters' student at Free University of Berlin and Humboldt University of Berlin. She was the 2015/2016 Global Humanities Junior Fellow at the School for Advanced Studies in the Social Sciences in Paris.

Nick **Marsellas** is an English composition Ph.D. candidate at the University of Pittsburgh with interests in Caribbean gender and sexuality and the rhetoric of relationality and exchange. His work uses historical and literary representations of pirates to understand queer theory's relationship to antinormativity and the state.

Sue **Matheson** is an associate professor of English literature at University College of the North in Manitoba. She is the editor of *Love in Western Film and Television* and *A Fistful of Icons* and the author of *The Westerns and War Films of John Ford*.

Nicholas **Moll** is a researcher and lecturer at Federation University Australia, as well as a freelance tabletop game designer. He has published on popular culture, franchising, genre and gamification, and his primary research interests are the translation of genre form into function and narrative in gameplay.

Brian **Musgrove** has a Ph.D. from the University of Cambridge and has taught there and at the University of Southern Queensland. He is an independent writer and researcher and has published widely on drug literature, drug subcultures and political language.

William **Newton** earned his MA in medieval history from the University of East Anglia (UK) and is a curator at the Victoria and Albert Museum of Childhood. His research interests include toys, electronics products and plastics.

Jeff **Parish** is an English instructor with Angelina College in Texas. His research interests include film, television, graphic novels and video games. His essay on *The Last Unicorn* appeared in *Plaza*, and he has presented video games as interactive narrative and migration on the frontier in *Shadows West*.

Joan **Passey** is a Ph.D. researcher studying between the University of Exeter and the University of Bristol under the South West and Wales Doctoral Training Partnership. Her research focuses on identifying a nineteenth-century Cornish Gothic.

Antonio **Sanna** completed his Ph.D. at the University of Westminster in London. His research interests include English literature, horror and epic films and adaptation studies. He has published over 70 essays and reviews and contributed to five encyclopedias. He is the coeditor of *A Critical Companion to Tim Burton* and is also coediting volumes on James Cameron and *Twin Peaks*.

Tiago A.M. **Sarmento** is a training psychoanalyst and Ph.D. student in the psychoanalytic theory department at the Federal University of Rio de Janeiro (UFRJ). His research interests include Freudian theory, fantasy and the relationship of the contemporary individual with superheroes.

Artur **Skweres** earned his Ph.D. in literary studies from Adam Mickiewicz University in Poland where he is also an assistant professor of English. His research interests include English and American literature, media ecology, film adaptations and popular culture.

Jessica **Walker** is an assistant professor of English at Alabama A&M University, where she teaches courses in medieval and Renaissance literature, literature on film, and the history of the English language. Her publications include essays on *Good Omens*, *A Song of Ice and Fire*, and Richard Loncraine's *Richard III*.

Susanne **Zhanial** studied English literature and theatre, film, and media studies at the University of Vienna and Aberdeen. Her research interests include romantic and Victorian literature, film, gender studies and postmodernism. Her Ph.D. work analyzes Disney's *Pirates of the Caribbean*.

Index

Across a Moonlit Sea (novel by Marsha Canham, 1996) 111, 113–114
The Adventures of Tintin (film, 1991–92) 4, 133–142
The Adventures of Tintin: The Secret of the Unicorn (film, 2011) 4, 133–142
Ahab 23, 231
Algiers 16, 190, 191
Anne of the Indies (film, 1951) 19, 23, 126
Antarctica 17, 88–96
Aristotle 29, 36n2, 207
Avery, Henry 13, 14, 58, 65

Ballantyne, Robert Michael 16, 98, 99, 171, 175n2
Ballou, Maturin Murray 16
Baring-Gould, Sabine 77–84
Barrie, James Matthew 3, 17, 22, 98–108, 155, 157, 159, 163, 171, 214, 215, 218, 219, 233
The Black Pirate (film, 1926) 19, 173
Black Sails (TV series, 2014–17) 4, 24, 54, 59n4, 145, 178–186
The Black Swan (film, 1932) 17; (film, 1942) 20, 126, 176n3
Blackbeard (fictional) 18, 19, 104, 127, 223n2, 238; *Blackbeard* (TV miniseries, 2006) 19; *Blackbeard: Terror at Sea* (film, 2006) 19; Blackbeard the Pirate (character in *Pan*) 158–164; *Blackbeard the Pirate* (film, 1952) 19, 127
Blackbeard (historical figure) 11, 21, 24n1, 58, 178, 202, 214, 215
Blow Me Down (novel by Katie MacAlister, 2005) 113, 116, 117
Bones, Billy 96, 105, 124, 125, 128, 129, 149, 178, 184
Bonny, Anne 13, 14, 18, 23, 32, 134, 138, 178–180, 222
The Book of Pirates (novel by Howard Pyle, 1921) 124
buccaneer (definition) 8
The Buccaneer (film, 1938) 20
The Buccaneer (film, 1958) 19
Burg, Barry 50–53, 57–58, 122–123

buried treasure 17, 35n1, 94, 146, 205
business organization 3, 37–49
Byron 15, 98, 167–174, 194–197

Captain Blood (film, 1935) 126, 173
Captain Cruel Coppinger 75–87
Captain Finn 12
Captain Hook 23, 98, 102, 106–107, 159–165, 165n8, 171, 203, 214
Captain Kidd 16, 202
Captain Kidd (film, 1945) 19
Captain Misson 32–36
The Captain of All Pleasures (novel by Kesley Cole, 2003) 114
Captain Singleton (novel by Daniel Defoe, 1720) 14, 58, 95, 137
Captain Tew 32–36
Captain Vane 12, 43, 65
The Charm School (novel by Susan Wiggs, 1999) 112
clothing 214–218, 230
code of conduct 10, 15, 23, 30–32, 36n3, 41–45, 49n13, 65, 71, 122, 162, 216, 219, 222
compensation for losses 10, 37, 41, 45, 47, 48n4
Conan Doyle, Arthur 18, 75
Cooper, James Fenimore 15
Coral Island (novel by Robert Michael Ballantyne, 1858) 16, 98–99, 175n2
Cordingly, David 1, 2, 8, 9, 10, 12, 17, 20, 23, 30, 102, 103, 123, 170
Cornwall 18, 75–86
corsair (definition) 8
The Corsair (poem by Lord Byron, 1814) 15, 98, 168, 194–195
Il Corsaro (opera by Giuseppe Verdi, 1848) 188–191, 197
Cuba 16, 130n2
Cutthroat Island (film, 1996) 23, 167

Dampier, William 9
Defoe, Daniel 9, 14, 32–36, 36n4, 51, 58, 95, 98, 99, 134, 137
democratic lifestyle 3, 9, 28–35, 37–39, 44, 46, 51, 61, 65, 67, 72, 180, 181, 197

251

Depp, Johnny 23, 30, 50, 59n1, 59n2, 127, 167, 169, 174, 203
Drake, Francis 8, 10, 48n7
drinking habits 9, 22, 30, 63, 65, 70, 120–130, 135, 138, 140–142, 149, 169, 204 211
Du Maurier, Daphne 18, 109

Elizabeth: The Golden Age (film, 2007) 19
England, Edward 14, 214, 224n8
Esquemelin, John 13, 64, 68, 122, 123
executions 11–12, 14, 27, 42, 178, 183, 237, 246n1

Falkner, J.M. 3, 99, 104
Fanny Campbell (novel by Maturin Murray Ballou, 1844) 16
flag 19, 38, 152, 217, 222, 223; *see also* Jolly Roger
Flynn, Errol 20, 140, 172, 173
Frenchmen's Creek (novel by Daphne Du Maurier, 1941) 18
Freud, Sigmund 4, 17, 102, 103, 107, 155–163, 165n 2, 165n3, 165n5; Oedipal Complex 156, 159–160; *unheimlich* 4, 156–160, 165n2, 165n6
The Frozen Pirate (novel by William Clarke Russell, 1887) 3, 16, 88–96, 124

A General History 13–14, 32, 122, 215
The Ghost Pirates (novel by William Hodgson, 1909) 17
"The Gold Bug" (short story by Edgar Allan Poe, 1853) 16
golden age piracy 3, 8, 10, 12, 23, 24, 26, 28–35, 37–40, 47–48, 48n6, 53, 54, 65, 89, 95, 99, 134, 141, 152, 178, 183, 185, 204, 213, 217, 230, 233
Gospel of the Flying Spaghetti Monster (Pastafarian text, 2005) 200–204
Gothic fiction 15, 17, 75–76, 79, 80, 82, 84, 85, 86, 117, 192
Gow, John 14, 15

Hawker, Robert Stephen 77–86
Hawkins, Jim 71, 72, 99, 101, 105, 145–147, 152
A High Wind in Jamaica (novel by Richard Hughes, 1929) 18
Hispaniola 8
Hodgson, William 17
Hook (film, 1991) 22–23, 155–164, 165n8
Hughes, Richard 18

In the Roar of the Sea (novel by Sabine Baring-Gould, 1891) 79–80, 82
Island Flame (novel by Karen Robards, 1981) 112, 115–116
L'italiana in Algeri (opera by Giacomo Rossini, 1813) 188–191, 197

Jack, Calico 12, 13, 32
James, William 26–28

Johnson, Charles 13–14, 19, 32, 43, 122–123, 214–218
Jolly Roger 10, 19, 27, 61, 136, 186, 207, 208, 216, 217
Julius Caesar 28

King Charles II 135, 214
King George I 12
King George II 122
The King of Pirates (novel by Daniel Defoe, 1720) 14
Kingsley, Charles 98

Libertalia/Libertatia 30–35, 36n4, 52
Lindsay, Lionel, Sr. 3, 61–72
The Loose Canon: A Really Important Collection of Words (Pastafarian text, 2010) 200, 204–210
Lowe, Ned 11, 58

Madagascar 10, 11, 14, 32, 38
manliness 16, 64, 65, 144–153, 199, 245
Marryat, Frederick 15–16, 98, 123
Moonfleet (novel by J.M. Falkner, 1898) 3, 99, 102–106
More, Thomas, Sr. 26, 29, 36n2
Morgan, Henry 9, 18, 20, 32, 36n3, 48n7, 65, 121, 124
Muppet Treasure Island (film, 1996) 22, 145–146

Navy 10, 11, 14, 15, 25, 38, 47, 97n2, 99, 121, 127, 170, 174, 180, 217, 219, 232, 243, 244
Nietzsche 3, 61, 64, 70

On Stranger Tides (novel by Tim Power, 1987) 18–19, 123–125
One Piece (anime by Eiichiro Oda, 1997-) 4, 24, 236–246
orphans 3, 22, 79, 98–108, 158–159, 163

Pan (film, 2015) 22, 155–163
Panama 9, 32, 36n3, 48n1
Pastafarianism 4, 200–211
Peter Pan: film, 1953 22; film, 2003 22, 159; play and novelization by J.M. Barrie 17, 22, 98–108
Il Pirata (opera by Vincenzo Bellini, 1827) 188–197
The Pirate (novel by Frederick Marryat, 1836) 15, 98, 123
The Pirate (novel by Walter Scott, 1822) 15, 124, 170
The Pirate City (novel by Robert Michael Ballantyne, 1874) 16
Pirate Latitudes (novel by Michael Crichton, 2009) 18–19, 125–126
The Pirate Lord (novel by Sabrina Jeffries, 1975) 114–115
Pirates (film, 1986) 21, 126, 167, 240
Pirates of the Caribbean franchise 1, 4, 23, 24, 50, 127–128, 137, 167–175, 200, 202–203,

220, 231, 240; *At World's End* (2009) 170–173; *Curse of the Black Pearl* (2003) 127, 169–174, 231; *Dead Man's Chest* (2006) 128, 169–174; *Dead Men Tell No Tales* (2017) 127, 169, 172; *On Stranger Tides* (2011) 172
Pleasures of a Tempted Lady (novel by Jennifer Haymore, 2012) 113
Poe, Edgar Allan 14, 16, 98, 108n1
Port Royal 19, 31, 89, 123–126, 173
Power, Tim 18, 123, 125
privateer (definition) 8
Pyle, Howard 18, 124, 144, 145, 153, 216–218

queer pirates 2, 3, 4, 50–59, 172, 178–186, 186n2

Rabelais 3, 61–64, 69
rape 23, 50–59, 59n8, 59n10, 112, 115–116, 203
Read, Mary 13, 23, 32, 138, 178, 180, 185
The Red Rover (novel by James Fenimore Cooper, 1827) 15
Rediker, Marcus 1, 31, 35, 52, 58, 70, 72, 89, 93, 97n2, 180, 184, 185, 213, 216, 219
Roberts, Bartholomew 10, 12, 31, 122, 214, 216, 218
Robinson Crusoe (novel by Daniel Defoe, 1919) 14, 99, 134, 139, 218
romance novels 18, 109–118
romanticized pirates 1, 3, 14, 24, 25, 28, 30, 35, 53, 61, 63, 64, 72, 78, 83, 92, 98, 107, 109–118, 134, 135, 139, 141–142, 146, 194 200
rum 4, 27, 28, 64, 65, 66, 120–130, 130n1, 130n2, 137, 138, 169, 171, 204, 209, 210, 232
Rum & Bones (board game, 2015) 4, 225–234
Russell, William Clarke 16, 88–96, 97n3, 124

Sabatini, Rafael 17
Salgari, Emilio 17, 21
Scott, Walter 14, 15, 124, 170
Sea Change (novel by Darlene Marshall, 2011) 117
The Sea Hawk (film, 1940) 17, 19, 20

The Secret of Monkey Island (videogame, 1990) 220
Silver, Long John 17, 22, 71, 102, 105, 106, 128, 134, 144–153, 170–174, 178, 184–185, 202–203, 214, 215, 218, 219, 231
slavery 19, 23, 29, 36n2, 39, 46, 55, 126, 163, 196
Somali pirates 12–13
Sparrow, Jack 4, 23, 30, 50, 59n1, 127–128, 137, 167–175, 203, 211, 222
split of the booty 37–48, 48n3, 49n16, 72, 95, 96, 123, 136
Stevenson, Robert Louis 3, 4, 14, 17, 21, 22, 24, 59, 61, 64, 71, 72, 96, 99–105, 123–126, 128, 134, 142, 146, 149, 153, 170–172, 178, 184, 214, 215, 220
Swift, Jonathan 9, 14

Teach, Edward *see* Blackbeard (historical)
Thief of Hearts (novel by Teresa Madeiros, 2007) 112
Tortuga 8, 31, 50, 54, 89, 94, 95, 169, 172, 206
Treasure Island: (film, 1934) 22, 128, 130; (film, 1950) 22, 128, 130, 145, 219; (film, 1990) 22, 129, 130; (film, 1999) 22, 129, 130; (film, 2012) 22, 129, 130, 145; (film, 2015) 22, 130; (novel, 1883) 3, 4, 17, 22, 24, 61, 66, 71, 72, 96, 99–108, 123, 126, 145, 147, 153, 170, 171, 178, 179, 185, 200, 214, 215, 217, 218, 221, 231
Treasure Planet (film, 2002) 21, 144–154, 154n2, 200
Turley, Hans 2, 53–54, 58, 59n4, 89, 95, 96, 137

utopianism 3, 25–35, 36n2, 54, 57, 58, 70, 72

Vikings 7, 56, 78

walking the plank 19, 25, 35, 146, 158
Worley, Richard 14

www.ingramcontent.com/pod-product-compliance
Lightning Source LLC
Chambersburg PA
CBHW051216300426
44116CB00006B/598